STRATEGIC OPERATIONS MANAGEMENT

A VALUE CHAIN APPROACH

D0141254

Strategic Operations Management

A Value Chain Approach

David Walters
&
Mark Rainbird

© David Walters 2007

All rights reserved. No reproduction, copy or transmission of this publication
may be made without written permission.

No paragraph of this publication may be reproduced, copied or transmitted save
with written permission or in accordance with the provisions of the Copyright,
Designs and Patents Act 1988, or under the terms of any licence permitting
limited copying issued by the Copyright Licensing Agency, 90 Tottenham Court
Road, London W1T 4LP.

Any person who does any unauthorised act in relation to this publication may
be liable to criminal prosecution and civil claims for damages.

The authors have asserted their right to be identified as the authors of this work
in accordance with the Copyright, Designs and Patents Act 1988.

First published 2007 by
PALGRAVE MACMILLAN
Houndmills, Basingstoke, Hampshire RG21 6XS and
175 Fifth Avenue, New York, N. Y. 10010
Companies and representatives throughout the world

PALGRAVE MACMILLAN is the global academic imprint of the Palgrave
Macmillan division of St. Martin's Press, LLC and of Palgrave Macmillan Ltd.
Macmillan® is a registered trademark in the United States, United Kingdom and
other countries. Palgrave is a registered trademark in the European Union and
other countries.

ISBN-13: 978–0–230–50765–4
ISBN-10:   0–230–50765–4

This book is printed on paper suitable for recycling and made from fully
managed and sustained forest sources.

A catalogue record for this book is available from the British Library.

A catalog record for this book is available from the Library of Congress

10 9   8   7   6   5   4   3   2   1
16 15 14 13 12 11 10 09 08 07

Transferred to Digital Printing in 2011

In memory of

F J Rainbird

1928–2004

Brief contents

Detailed contents

Case Studies, Figures and Tables

Case studies

Figures

Tables

Foreword

What originally started out as a simple rewrite of the original *Strategic Operations: a Value Chain Approach* has resulted in an entirely new book. This came about by a chance reunion meeting with co-author Mark Rainbird and from the comments and contributions of many students over the past three years, during which the topic has been taught as a subject in the MBA programme at the Sydney Graduate School of Management within the University of Western Sydney.

Mark Rainbird brought a large element of pragmatism into the project. He is a practitioner who uses many of the disciplines we introduce in this text. He also crystallised our thinking on the important role of demand chain analysis, essential if supply chain design and management is to be more than just a cost-efficient response to customer logistics within the value chain. As a result of Mark's efforts the resulting book reflects concepts and approaches that we know do work from practical experience.

The contributions of the 600 or so students that have used the original text have resulted in a number of changes to the original book. Their constant challenge to the logic of the various concepts that it espoused and their application of the value chain model in assignments have resulted in making its successor much richer in its message and in the examples and case studies that are included. Their contribution is acknowledged here. It is hoped that future groups of students will be as helpful.

Introduction

If you ask a manager what their ultimate goal is in running a company, the answer to be hoped for has something to do with increasing the value of the business. Certainly if you ask a shareholder what they are looking for in their investment, the answer will very likely be: an increase in its value. If you ask a consumer what they are looking for when they buy the company's products again the answer is likely to include some concepts of value, perhaps expressed in terms of price or quality.

Value seems a simple notion to express the ultimate goal of most if not all economic exchanges, but is it an oversimplification? One of the goals of this text is to explore the various perspectives which are encompassed in the notion of value.

This also raises the question, how do you increase value? The traditional answer for most companies was to own as much of the means of production as possible and create bastions where competitive forces could be harnessed if not tamed. It is often supposed that mass capitalism had as its role model the great oil companies of the early twentieth century who owned everything from the oil well, to the ships that carried the petroleum, to the refineries, to the distribution network and finally to the retail or commercial outlet, and ran the lot as very profitable cartels.

Very quickly that role model has been replaced by that of companies like Dell, who seem in fact to do very little, outsourcing what would have traditionally been thought of as core processes such as manufacturing its own products and instead focusing on a few key activities. This has produced very high returns on investment in a very competitive market.

This change has profound implications for the structure of markets and how firms should behave to best create their own version of value. These changes have been labeled by some the 'new economy' and this is a term we use in this text. At this point a sizeable number of readers will be tempted to close this book and proceed no further, as the term 'new economy' still conjures up images of the excesses of the dot.com era when large amounts of money were raised and ultimately destroyed on the promise of companies who indeed did very little and trumpeted it as a virtue.

What this text attempts to do is to lay out is a map to explore the issues impacting the changes occurring within this broader notion of the 'new economy'. It uses the analogy of the *value chain* to underlie this map.

This notion of 'value chain' is a concise way of expressing the central themes we are exploring. First, as already noted, it is important to understand what the desired outcomes of any strategy are – what is the value that is being aspired to?

Second, what are the market structures that are beginning to predominate and how does a firm respond to them?

Describing markets as a 'chain' is not new and is a neat way of understanding how for example the oil majors operated – dominating the chain from oil well to forecourt. Other analogies like value nets, value networks and clusters all look to do the same – drawing out the concept of organisational networks and the importance of positioning the firm in the right place – traditionally by owning the lot and more recently by forming partnerships with others who do some things more effectively than they can be done internally. This usually goes by the sometimes maligned term of 'outsourcing'.

In this sense the value chain operates at three levels of analysis. First, it is a landscape map of the industry or the market, identifying all the links in the chain between the oil well and the petrol pump. Second, it is a topographic map of the individual firm – what or where is my territory? – where should I pitch my tent and how do I fit into the overall landscape? Finally, it is the architects' plans of what my tent should be like to make the most of my position.

This text tries to identify the building blocks of the value chain – what it is that needs to be understood to map the industry, to identify the best positioning and to execute a strategy. It looks at notions of assets and in particular the increasing importance of the intangible as opposed to bricks and mortar. It looks at the importance of seeing things in terms of processes rather than functions and it looks at the various overlapping ideas surrounding competencies and capabilities.

It is interesting that if you do a 'Google' search of the words 'value chain' you will end up with a lot of information that relates to supply chain management. This is perhaps not a surprise as supply chain managers seem to have supplanted the marketers as the new corporate heroes. However it also shows the confusion in terminology that dogs this subject.

In fact the supply chain can be seen as just part of the overall value chain equation, and – with a nod to Adam Smith – it also warrants a detailed look at its counterbalance: the demand chain. This is a relatively new concept, but one that perhaps restores some perspective to exactly what happens in markets and in individual firms every day – the battle to supply the customer with what they want, but still at a profit.

In this sense the notion of the 'chain' can give the wrong impression – of immutable and solid links tying together market participants – that is, until the rust sets in and the chain breaks. No doubt in some instances and in some industries this is exactly what happened and the term 'rust belt' is quite graphic.

Instead the value chain we are trying to portray is flexible and the links are easily interchangeable. Some chains will be more mature than others and this may have implications for how they operate. Not every link in the chain has an equal role holding it together, either. Clearly there are value chain builders and coordinators as well as simple participants of varying importance to the whole.

Finally, we look at what all this means in terms of planning and control and how it might be applied. We also venture into the emerging debate over what the key success factors are that help in building and successfully operating in a value chain context and explore notions around knowledge, technology, relationship and process management.

This text has researched both the theoretical and the practical aspects of the concept. It is based on a valuable and increasing body of work in this area, illuminated by case studies and relevant vignettes. It also reflects the backgrounds of the authors – academic and industry. Just as one of the underlying tenets of the value chain model we propose is the tension between supply and demand chain drivers as a key catalyst in driving value, so too the tension between theory and practice in writing this book has, we hope, enlivened the outcomes.

CHAPTER 1

'New Economy' – New Business Models – New Approaches

LEARNING TOPICS

On completing your study of this chapter you will have been introduced to and considered the following topics:

- The 'new economy'; a new business environment
- The changing attitudes towards the ownership and management of assets in the 'new economy'
- The importance of network design and management in the 'new economy'
- Clusters, value nets, value streams and value chains as new business models
- Why business structures are seen as processes rather than functions
- The new concepts and a new vocabulary in the 'new economy'
- Value led management
- A model for value chain analysis, planning and control

Introduction

Business operates everywhere in an environment that is increasingly dynamic and challenging. Markets have globalised, technology has become all embracing, and relationships with suppliers, customers and competitors are undergoing constant change. *New business models* are emerging, ones in which competitive advantage is based upon *managing processes* that facilitate rapid and flexible responses to 'market' change, and ones in which new *capabilities* are based upon developing unique relationships with partners (suppliers, customers, employees, shareholders, government and, often, with competitors). The business model has often taken second place to strategy in management thinking and focus. Normann (2001) discusses 'a new strategic logic'. He suggests that: '... managers need to be good at *mobilizing, managing,* and *using* resources rather than at formally *acquiring* and necessarily *owning* resources. The ability to reconfigure, to use resources inside and particularly outside the boundaries of the traditional corporation more effectively becomes a mandatory skill for managements.'

Drucker (2001) noted that while the traditional response to market pressures was vertical integration on a large scale, citing Standard Oil and Ford as leading examples, today even the large corporations are leading the changes in strategic posture. General Motors, for example, are creating a business for the ultimate car consumer – they aim to make available what car and model most closely fit that consumer's preferences. As Drucker noted, the changes to facilitate this are not just sales and marketing driven, but encompass design and development, and production responses. Products and services now have multiple applications and business organisations are redefining their core capabilities and processes. In other words, 'value chains' are competing with 'value chains'. At this macro, industry level, value chains can be seen as business network structures, or confederations, that are developing from traditional corporations.

Magretta (2002) suggests, using the example of American Express in the nineteenth century, that: 'a successful business model represents a better way than the existing alternatives. It may offer more value to a discrete group of customers. Or it may completely replace the old way of doing things and become the standard for the next generation of entrepreneurs to beat.' Magretta adds substance:

> ... all new business models are variations on the generic value chain underlying all businesses. Broadly speaking, this chain has two parts. Part one includes all the activities associated with making something: designing it, purchasing raw materials, manufacturing and so on. Part two includes all the activities associated with selling something: finding and reaching customers, transacting a sale, distributing the product or delivering the service. A new business model's plot may turn on designing a new product for an unmet need ... Or it may turn on a process innovation, a better way of making or selling or distributing an already proven product or service.

Magretta cites Dell as a company that has created a powerful business model by identifying value chain processes that it will engage in, and seeking partners, complementors, to undertake those it will not. In this way Dell, by selling directly to end-users, has the vital information necessary to manage inventory better than its competitors *and* avoids the high costs of holding inventory and the very high cost of obsolescence due to the rapid application of technology. A question that must be asked is, is there a generic approach or model that may be used to understand the successes of Dell, Wal-Mart and others?

Processes designed around value creating networks

The holonic, or virtual, organisation structure is one model that is finding favour. According to McHugh et al. (1995), the holonic organisation or network is:

... a set of companies that acts integratedly and organically; it is constantly re-configured to manage each business opportunity a customer presents. Each company in the network provides a different process capability and is called a holon.

Holonic networks are not hierarchical structures – rather, each business within the structure is equal to each of the others. The network is in dynamic equilibrium and it is self-regulating. Access to, and exchange of, information throughout the network is open, as is access to and exchange of information across the network boundaries. The network is evolutionary and is constantly interacting with its environment. It is a knowledge network, a learning organisation. McHugh et al. suggest a number of advantages accrue to holonic networks:

- Asset leverage; increased utilisation from distributed operations through synergy
- Speed; specialist inputs enhance time-to-market
- Flexibility and agility; the ability to meet requests for changes in order size and delivery pattern as well as for product and service changes within existing response times
- Faster growth and increased profitability; through improved response (time) rates
- Increased customer loyalty; longer and more profitable customer relationships
- Shared assets and lower total capital investment; investment by partner organisations is limited to its core processes and working capital requirements are influenced by a 'just-in-time' approach
- Shared risk at reduced levels; risk is reduced by being dispersed among network members *and* because of the high aggregate level of expertise that is deployed

It follows that a 'network' or value chain design should reflect these advantages. To do so will result in:

- Lower investment in fixed costs and working capital
- Lower operating costs due to optimal economies of production and increased customer response (reducing customer acquisition costs and increased transaction values)
- Reduced business risk (defined here as fluctuations in planned market volume (and market share(s))
- Reduced financial risk (defined as the probability of failure to achieve a target return on net assets)
- Decreased response times (both time-to-market, a strategic consideration, and operationally, the order cycle time)

There are four roles within such a network. First, operational roles are occupied by specialists, each of whom bring a core capability that combines with others to produce or to deliver the product that the end-user buys. Examples include manufacturing and logistics. The second role is to supply a support process, such as procurement or customer service management and/or facilities; McHugh and his co-authors suggest this is a functionally oriented role and that typically there is only one member supporting the value chain. Emerging examples of this can be seen in the large B2B buying exchanges appearing in industries such as the automotive industry. The third role is that of resource provider to the operational role members. Resources include skilled labour (such as designers), information/data management services and, increasingly important, customised facilities (such as those required for computer chip manufacturing). Fourth, an 'integrator' role completes the structure. The integrator has one of two functions (and may well perform both): one is to provide the initial 'strategic vision' around which the virtual organisation is structured. The other is a coordinating role within the value chain, identifying, matching and directing resources. Piore and Sabel (1984) provide an example of the integrator roles taking place in the Italian textile-apparel industry located around Prato. Small specialist companies have developed long-term relationships with one another along the value chain. An 'impannatore' undertakes a strategic visionary role, together with an organising and coordinating role. The result is a very competitive value chain that offers currency and competitive prices in a fashion led industry.

Clusters, value nets, value streams and value chains

More recently the concepts of *clusters, value nets, value streams* and *value chains* have focused interest due to the increasing influence of *virtual integration* as an alternative to *vertical integration*.

Clusters

Value creation through clusters has been well documented in the applied economics literature. Porter (1990) defined clusters as:

> ... a geographically proximate group of interconnected companies and associated institutions in a particular field linked by commonalities and complementarities.

Porter identified the components as: end-product or service companies; suppliers of specialist inputs; financial institutions; firms in related industries; firms in downstream industries; producers of complementary products; specialised infrastructure providers; governmental and other organisations providing dedicated education and information inputs, and trade associations.

Porter explored a number of examples using a basic model comprising four interrelated components to explain international successes. First, *factor conditions* (that is, basic factors of production that are necessary to compete successfully and to create competitive advantage). Second, *firm strategy, structure and rivalry* (the goals, strategies and organisation structures that when managed creatively result in international competitive advantage). Third, *related and supporting industries* (the presence of national supplier or related industries that are internationally competitive). Fourth, *demand conditions* (the quality and quantity of home demand has an impact on economies of scale and upon innovation, both important influences on competitive advantage). While these remain important, the developments in information communications technology have reduced their impact. The costs of *interconnectivity* have modified their importance. The use of EDI and net and web based communications has reduced the time as well as costs of transactions management, thereby making it possible to expand supply and manufacturing bases across international boundaries. Porter revisited clusters (1998), talking of:

> [connections] broader than industries, capture important linkages, complementarities, and slipovers of technology, skills, information, marketing and customer needs that cut across firms and industries ... Such connections are fundamental to competition, to productivity, and especially to the direction and pace of new business formation and innovation.

In a broader context it can be argued that clusters comprise an effective combination of knowledge, technology, relationship and process management, that together, in a particular combination, provide an 'organisation' with the means of developing competitive advantage. The important issue is that success is driven by entrepreneurial vision, a vision that identifies not only the opportunities but the unique (or exclusive) alternatives for combining 'cluster capabilities', assets and resources that achieve both customer and corporate satisfaction.

Value nets

Parolini (1999) argues that the changes in the business environment require a new or different approach to strategic analysis, suggesting that models developed in the 1970s and 1980s are limited to a fundamentally different economic paradigm. Parolini comments (as does Dunning 1997) on the changes in 'strategic boundaries', suggesting that the 'new business model' is characterised by an emphasis on specialisation *and* a capacity to identify and participate in alliance networks. For Parolini a shift in emphasis has occurred (at least amongst the successful organisations) in which the focus has shifted from the inward, enterprise focused perspective to an outward, customer focus that considers how additional value (relative to that offered by competitors) can be delivered to customers via *value creating systems.*

Value creating systems were identified by Normann and Ramirez (1994) who argued that successful companies focus their strategic analysis and decisions on the value creating system (VCS) – the suppliers, business partners and customers – and how they can work together to *co-produce* value. Parolini proposes a basic difference between Porter's original value chain and the approach taken by Normann and Ramirez (and indeed subsequent approaches), suggesting:

... the former [Porter] takes the company value chain as his starting point, whereas the latter (Normann and Ramirez) underline the greater importance of the value creating system.

This comment does not identify the fundamental difference: *value creating systems (VCS) first consider customer expectations then consider the capabilities, assets and other resources required to meet customer value drivers – or exceed them!* Of course there are constraints: from a corporate viewpoint customer expectations typically represent an ideal that may be unrealistic, so they need to be viewed within the context of corporate value drivers.

Parolini (1999) summarises the main characteristics of the value creation system thus:

- A set of activities creates value for its end-user customers
- Activities use tangible and intangible resources that are linked by information flows
- End-user value is influenced by the way in which the end-user uses the delivered value
- End-users can (and often do) participate in value creating activities
- Value creation is successful only when a coordinating activity (or process) is present and links customer expectations to the economic activity of the VCS
- VCS partners may participate in more than one value creation system

Bovet and Martha (2000) use the term *value nets* in an argument suggesting them to be '... a business design that uses advanced supply chain concepts to achieve both superior customer satisfaction and company profitability'. And: '... a value net begins with customers, allows them to self-design products, and builds to satisfy actual demand'. The customer (business unit) is central to the decision process, is surrounded by the company (or business unit), which in turn is surrounded by a constellation of providers that perform some or all of the sourcing, assembly and delivery activities. The authors offer five characteristics that distinguish a value net business from the traditional business model:

- *Customer aligned* Customer expectations initiate sourcing, building and delivery activities in the net. 'The customer commands the value net.'
- *Collaborative and systemic* Companies engage suppliers, customers and possibly competitors in a unique network of value creating relationships. 'Each activity is assigned to the partner best able to perform it.'
- *Agile and scalable* Flexible manufacturing and distribution enhanced by information flow design facilitates responsiveness. 'Everything in the value net, physical or virtual, is scalable.'
- *Fast flow* Lead times are rapid and compressed. 'Rapid delivery goes hand in hand with reliable and convenient delivery.'
- *Digital* E-commerce is a key enabler. However, it is the flow of information and its 'intelligent use' that drives the value net. 'Rule based, event driven

tools take over many operational decisions. Distilled real-time analysis enables rapid executive decision making.'

Value net advocates argue that identifying the *activities* involved in end-user satisfaction does have problems. One problem concerns the extent of the analysis; the VCS activity system could become too large to be analysed effectively, resulting in a waste of management time on activities that the individual company cannot influence in any way. Parolini suggests:

> ... it is important to have an overall reference model but, within the framework of this model, the magnifying glass needs to be used to scrutinise only those parts of the system that the company under investigation can influence in some way.

Sawhney and Parikh (2001) ask questions concerning value trends in the network age. They contend that value in a networked world behaves very differently than it does in the traditional, bounded world. They suggest the elements of infrastructure that were once distributed among different machines, organisational units and companies will be brought together. Shared infrastructure (*value in common infrastructure*) will include not only basic information storage and dissemination but common functions such as order management, and '... even manufacturing and customer service'. This is a similar view to that proposed by Hagel and Singer (1999).

They also suggest *value in modularity* as a trend. Here their concern is with the entire range of 'devices, software, organisational capabilities and business processes'. These will be 'restructured as well-defined, self-contained modules', and 'value will lie in creating modules that can be plugged into as many different value chains as possible'. Examples of modularisation can found in automobile production. And they conclude: 'value in orchestration' will become '... the most valuable business skill'. Modularisation will require an organisational ability, so the authors suggest: 'Much of the competition in the business world will centre on gaining and maintaining the orchestration role for a value chain or an industry.'

A fundamental difference between the value net model and Porter's value chain model is that the VCS is considered to be a set of value creating activities (rather than companies), and these activities are defined from the final customer's point of view. Parolini argues that:

> Taking the VCS as the focal point of strategic analysis is of utmost importance for those companies who want to avoid being trapped in outdated perspectives as to how to compete in their particular industry, and which understand that there is little sense in enjoying a strong competitive position and having a high bargaining power in relation to their direct customers, if they (and their customers) form part of a losing system.

This assumes that all organisations are primarily customer focused. Value net analysts assume that if customer satisfaction is maximised then so too is shareholder value, or perhaps (as the arguments of many suggest) shareholder interests may be ignored!! This approach clearly has problems. Understanding customer expectations is essential, but the claim that meeting them precisely guarantees shareholder satisfaction does not follow. Many practitioners would argue that corporate expectations are the overriding consideration and that provided these are met the parameters of shareholder value are satisfied. This may imply that often customer value expectations are optimised within constraints set by corporate value drivers and that marketing objectives such as market share may be revised, but, they argue, the business will remain viable.

Value streams

Hines et al. (2000) offer an operations led 'lean management' perspective to value creation. They argue that:

> This focus on value is therefore translated across functional and company boundaries in both design and delivery of the appropriate product-service bundle ... the lean message suggests that the focus of attention should not be on the company or functional department but instead on the complete value stream. The value stream is the set of tasks and activities required to design and make a family of products or services that are undertaken with a group of linked functions or companies from the point of customer specification right back to the raw material source.

And:

> Value stream thinking goes beyond simplistic academic models of single buyer/single supplier relationships or even supply chains involving one customer, a local firm and its single supplier. Instead, a more realistic approach is adopted involving a complete network of companies arrayed in each tier of supply ... the lean approach seeks to go beyond partnership rhetoric and seeks solutions at the value stream level that will benefit all the organisations involved.

The value stream concept uses 'value stream mapping' to identify and differentiate between processes that create value *and* waste. Hines et al. refer to their own research in which waste and value generating processes are identified; the waste producing processes are eliminated while opportunities to enhance the value generating processes are sought. They argue that the value adding processes make the final product/service more valuable to the end-consumer than it otherwise would have been.

Value stream mapping is in effect the identification of seven 'commonly accepted' areas of waste (based upon practices in Toyota): overproduction, waiting, transportation, inappropriate processing, unnecessary inventory, unnecessary motion (an ergonomics consideration), and defects. There is an array of 'mapping tools', each being used where it brings focus to a specific area of waste.

The authors suggest a fundamental difference between value stream and value chain thinking. Their classification of these differences suggests an operations management focus to the value stream concept:

> The difference between the traditional supply or value chain and the value stream is that the former includes the complete activities of all the companies involved, whereas the latter refers only to the specific parts of the firms that actually add value to the product or service under consideration. The value stream is, therefore, a far more focused and contingent view of the value adding process.

As we will demonstrate, this is clearly not the case. The supply chain and the value chain are two very different and quite distinct concepts. Furthermore neither includes *all* of the activities of the companies involved. It is arguable that specialist supply chain companies may be engaged in all of the activities involved, but increasingly they work with partner organisations who offer cost efficiencies or processes they themselves do not have. The whole concept of the value chain is one of cooperation and collaboration. Organisations such as Dell identify specialist process owners and work with them within an exclusive business model that integrates and coordinates the owners of relevant and efficiently managed assets, processes and capabilities that create added value via innovative products or innovative processes. The value chain approach is driven by the notion of delivering end-user satisfaction through a low capital intensity (high 'return') business model.

Value chains

The value chain approach offers a model that includes both customer and corporate expectations. It offers a means to undertake strategic and operational analysis of an opportunity at a macro (process) level and at a micro (activity) level. As with the value net approach it starts with an assumption that there are no constraints on *how* customers' value expectations may be met. But it then adds the constraint that unless the innovator/visionary, with its partner organisations, meet specific financial objectives the VCS (the value chain system) cannot survive. Needed are both *feasibility* (customer perceptions are equal to or exceed their expectations) and *viability* (stakeholder partner perceptions are equal to or exceed their expectations). Furthermore it is argued that free cash flow is the primary requirement for success. *This view is based on the simple premise that profit (in all its variants) is opinion: cash flow is fact*!! (Ellis 1999).

The value chain: integrated demand and supply chains

Supply chain management supporters have argued that that the supply chain has attempted to meet all the changes identified within the 'new economy'. Yet supply chain management has focused on moving products and services *downstream* towards the customer. Typically the supply chain is coordinated by manufacturing companies or dominant resellers who use in-house manufacturing and distribution facilities to achieve market based objectives such as market share volumes and customer penetration. Meanwhile, demand chain management changes the emphasis towards 'customisation', *responding* to product and service opportunities offered by specific customers or customer groups sharing particular characteristics. The preference is to outsource rather than own the functions and processes that facilitate and deliver value. The focus is on asset leverage and communication through distributed assets and outsourcing. There is thus a large incentive to integrate supply and demand chains – it provides new opportunities for creating (or adding extra) market value. Working both together results in more specific and manageable value propositions and increases the returns to value chain participants. There is an interdependent relationship between supply and demand: companies need to understand customer demand before they can manage it, create future demand and, of course, meet the level of desired customer satisfaction. Demand defines the supply chain target, while supply-side capabilities support, shape and sustain demand.

Processes not functions

More recent views of the value chain model suggest the importance of taking a *process* based perspective of the organisation, and extend this with the idea that processes are not simply *intra-organisational* but have become *inter-organisational* and often *intercontinental*!! Value chain analysis identifies the core processes and core capabilities involved in meeting the essential corporate and customer value drivers. Thus, according to Johansson et al. (1993), 'A core business process "creates" value by the capabilities it gives the company for competitiveness.'

Core business processes are the processes identified by the organisation as being central to its strategy for competitive advantage. Normann (2001) suggests that the core business process of a company in the long term is to form new 'dominating' ideas. There is a similarity here with Porter's argument for what constitutes long-term success. Long term the company requires a strategy for value delivery that not only offers competitive advantage through differentiation but is built around a core process to renew (or perhaps form new) 'dominating' ideas – the drivers of long-term competitive advantage. Normann contends:

> No other process in any organisation is more fundamental in the long term than this renewal of the dominating ideas, this re-appreciation of an organisation's identity and the way of manifesting it, in the face of environmental change.

Hammer (2001) argues that as businesses become accustomed to the *customer economy*, 'process thinking' becomes essential. 'In order to achieve the performance levels that customers now demand, businesses must organise and manage themselves around the axis of process; moreover, they must apply the discipline of process even to the most creative and heretofore most chaotic aspects of their operations.' And: '... processes are what create the results that a company delivers to its customers'. Hammer continues by offering a *customer economy* definition of a process:

> ... an organized group of related activities that together create a result of value to customers.

Hammer's discussion of this definition suggests increasing opportunities for the virtual organisation. He establishes a process as a *group* of related activities that work *together*, pointing to the fact that value is created by the entire process. It is the result of 'value production and coordination'. Activities are *related* and *organised*, with none of them irrelevant, and performed sequentially, giving some structure to the process and requiring process management. Effective process management is *result* oriented.

A strategic perspective is taken by Armistead et al. (1999). The authors identify themes 'associated' with business process management. Strategic choice and direction suggest that because an organisation cannot pursue every opportunity it makes choices or trade-offs; these determine the resource patterns of the organisation and, eventually the development of core competencies. These, in turn, lead to competencies that influence subsequent strategy. Strategic business process management forces companies to 'examine their form and structure' as having an influence on boundaries, structure and power within organisational design. An important component of the authors' model is the market value chain, which 'links the stages which add value along a supply chain'. They suggest that *within* an organisation the market value chain can be taken to be a conceptualisation of the core processes and activities which represent the organisation in process terms: 'They capture the activities which start and end in the organisation and link with other organisations in the chain.' They further suggest that the market value chain reinforces the resource based view of the organisation because it forces the identification of core processes from which core competencies and competitive advantage emerge. Performance management is another perspective of strategic business process management which 'relies on the management of resources and on a series of measurement systems', without which progress towards goals and any necessary corrective action are not possible. Organisational coordination occurs internally and externally (that is, with both suppliers and customers). This is particularly 'pertinent as the boundaries of internal processes become more ill-defined'; it could be argued that it is even more important for the boundaries between value chain organisations (such as in the 'prosumer' relationship between customer and supplier, which we will introduce shortly). This perspective adds emphasis to the importance of relationship management. The authors also identify knowledge management as a component of their model. Business process management enhances organisational learning and knowledge management. It 'provides a framework for organisational learning and can incorporate the management of knowledge'. Clearly these are determined by the specific application but suffice it to say they are essentiam to the successful performance of the value chain.

New concepts and a new vocabulary

Accompanying these new approaches is a new vocabulary. Terms such as *prosumerism* – the involvement of consumers in the design of products (a creative role that results in products that meet *specific needs* of customers). *Co-productivity* is a more operational role on the part of suppliers, distributors and customers in which they undertake tasks that hitherto were the role of other channel/chain participants. *Co-opetition* (often also known as *co-ompetition*) describes the situation in which competitors work together to meet individual objectives using mutual facilities. *Co-destiny* is used to ascertain the extent to which members of a business coalition share the same objectives, strategies and values. Examples of how these concepts are being introduced into new business models will appear in subsequent chapters.

Another important concept is that of *value migration*. Value migration occurs as both economic and shareholder value flows away from obsolescent (and obsolete) business models. Slywotzky (1996) argues that new models offer the same benefits to customers but at lower cost by changing the model structure. This change often results in a restructuring of profit sharing throughout the business model. Uren (2001) quotes Schremp (CEO, DaimlerChrysler) who expresses the view that '... within 10 years the price of a car will represent only a quarter of the total value provided to a customer with the balance consumed in maintenance, finance and other services'.

Value migration is the shift of business designs away from outmoded designs toward others that are better designed to maximise utility (value) for customers and profit for the company. Slywotzky contends that business designs (in a similar way to products) also have cycles and reach economic obsolescence. Customer expectations have a tendency to change over time but business model designs tend to stay fixed. By combining both, alternative added value structures may be evaluated.

Slywotzky measures the power of business design by using market value relative to the size of the company (the latter measured as revenue). Thus we have:

$$\text{Power of business design} = \frac{\text{Market value}}{\text{Revenue}}$$

where market value is defined as the capitalisation of a company (shares outstanding multiplied by current share price plus long-term debt).

Uren also identifies differences between Qantas and Ansett, suggesting that Qantas, with its international networks and travel agency links, together with an investment in services, is building a strong advantage. Similarly in the B2B sector Amcor and Visy (both in packaging) are using IT based e-commerce systems to increase customer service. In each of these examples, four basic issues emerge. First, that of the 'value' of the brand as being enhanced by service extensions or additions to the basic product. Second, that of the increased importance of intangible assets and the shift in investment patterns. Third, that of the importance of partnerships/alliances in the containment of fixed asset investment, and therefore increased utilisation, albeit the assets are shared. Fourth, that of the way business organisation or 'models' have changed; virtual enterprises have expanded, as has the principle of outsourcing, such that the maxim 'Why own it when you can rent it?' has resulted in many businesses opting for a new model.

The basis for adopting the alternative (or new) model rests on a simple thesis. Some competencies or capabilities are 'distinctive' and as such offer possibilities of sustainable competitive advantage; others, the 'reproducible' competencies/capabilities, offer no such benefits and in fact are readily available in supply markets. Uren's observations suggest that typically distinctive competencies/capabilities are 'intangibles'. They also substantiate the inference to be drawn from Brookings Institution findings concerning the fixed asset ownership of large manufacturing and mining companies in the US: fixed tangible assets as a proportion of total assets fell from 67 per cent in 1982 to 38 per cent by 1992. By 2000 this was reported to be less than 30 per cent. These topics will be discussed in detail in subsequent chapters.

A question arising from the Brookings Institution research concerns the reasons for this continuous trend. Two possibilities appear likely. One is that businesses are investing less in fixed tangible assets because they are increasingly benefiting from the 'asset leverage' resulting from partnership arrangements. The other is that more investment is occurring in brands, research and development, knowledge based intellectual property, patents and franchise building. Clearly we need to know if overall total assets are increasing or whether there is a shift in investment. Perhaps both are occurring. The important point would appear to be the strategic implications of such decisions.

Investment by high-tech companies in fixed assets may not be the wisest use of opportunities. Technology life cycles are shortening, making profit *and* capital recovery difficult. The investment in intangible assets such as R and D strengthens the organisation, as does the investment in brands and corporate reputation. Clearly both are important but both have risk issues to be concerned about. The risk with R and D investment concerns time-to-market and eventual success. The risk with building strong brands and a reputation is more difficult to deal with as many of the activities may not be within the direct control of the brand owner. Problems can occur, and are occurring, for many of the international brand owners as their partners come under question concerning ethics and conformity to social responsibility demands.

Value migration is a significant factor in a number of industries. Industries undergo structural changes as end-user customer expectations change. For example, numbers of industries have become more service oriented in recent years, reflecting supplier efforts to differentiate their value offer between target customer groups. Another example concerns the application of new technology to both product and production processes. In both these examples we see changing patterns of value production, suggesting that the structure of the added value contributions from value production processes results in a shift (or 'migration') of value in the industry value chain. The significance this has for organisations that work in partnership networks is that due to changing patterns of value migration some firms may find it necessary to reposition themselves within the value chain, leave the network, or perhaps develop more relevant processes and capabilities.

Gadiesh and Gilbert (1998) offer a similar model based upon the notion that 'Successful companies understand that profit share is more important than market share.' A 'profit pool' is defined as the total profits earned in an industry at all points along the industry's value chain. The pool may be 'deeper' in some segments of the value chain than in others and variations may be due to customer, product and distribution channel differences, or perhaps there may be geographical reasons. Often the pattern of profit concentration differs markedly from revenue concentration. Gadiesh and Gilbert use the US automotive industry to demonstrate the variations of revenue and profit distribution and to provide an approach to mapping profit pools:

- *Define the pool*: determine which value chain activities influence the organisation's ability to generate profits, now and in the future.
- *Determine the size of the pool*: develop a baseline estimate of the cumulative profits generated by all profit pool activities.
- *Reconcile the estimates*: compare the outputs of steps two and three and reconcile where necessary.

The authors recommend that the model be used to identify profit trends and to create an awareness of the implications of future structural shifts. The profit pool approach does explain why a number of the large automotive manufacturers are questioning their long-term viability as just manufacturers and are researching the feasibility of involvement elsewhere in the value production system. However, in the virtual organisation the strategic implications are more significant. Profit pools can be used to identify structural options and to question them in terms of optimal stakeholder value delivery. Additionally we can identify trends, establish scenarios and identify not only where relationship strategies and structures need to be changed but also the financial implications of each of the options.

Gadiesh and Gilbert argue that many companies '... chart strategy without a full understanding of the sources and distribution of profits in their industry'. Plotting the revenue, profits (and therefore cost profiles), productivity and cash flow characteristics of alternative value chains enables options to be identified in the knowledge and understanding of critical financial performance parameters.

Value led management

The argument developing here is that corporate structures (as well as decision making processes) are changing. The point may be made a little stronger: it is becoming very clear that 'value' is migrating in many industries. For example, the automotive industry is experiencing a shift in value profile. Hitherto, value was maximised in the production process; current indications and expectations for the future are that it will migrate towards the marketing and service processes.

Three major changes are suggested. The first concerns the emphasis on performance. Currently many organisations emphasise cost led efficiency as a primary objective. Not only is this constraining, but it has been shown not to be in the shareholders' interests: cost reductions typically have a negative impact on customer service and this, in turn, has the same impact on revenues. The second change involves a switch from an internal focus in which assets and resources *must be owned* to one of cooperation and collaboration in which assets and resources are *managed*. The third change is one in which the organisation becomes *proactive* in its operations and this obtains for both customer and supply markets. *Market responsive* organisations tend to be inflexible and typically have very slow 'time-to-market' responses. In other words they are imitators rather than innovators!!

This notion can be expanded upon. The role of the entrepreneur is to balance the allocation of resources between *transformation inputs* and *interaction inputs*. Central to the decision is not who owns the inputs but rather how they may be incorporated into the business organisation and how this then is structured to ensure that customer and stakeholder expectations may be met. There are three important decision areas. First, there are decisions that influence physical products; quality and production costs are important and the resource allocation decision can be influenced by production alternatives that offer an organisation the opportunity to utilise the production facilities of partner organisations that have production expertise or cost advantages. Here, the management of 'intangible assets' can add differentiation to the physical product and improve the customer appeal by a 'brand promise' that in some way increases customer perceptions of the benefits received. Second, there are decisions concerning innovative product and/or service design; designs that increase, or extend, 'value-in-use' for customers also differentiate both the organisation and its products. Third, there are decisions concerning where, how much, and by whom investment should be made in both tangible and intangible assets, and how these should be integrated and coordinated. The 'virtual community' approach that value nets and chains propose offers to increase an organisations' abilities for focused response, flexibility of response and an ability to organise a 'timely' response.

Tapscott and Caston (1993) proposed a 'generic' model of the value chain/virtual organisation. By modifying their model and using it to contrast the traditional and emerging organisation, the structural *and* resource inputs requirements of the new model become apparent. The significant, and perhaps fundamental, difference is its interrelationship focus. The emphasis shifts from ownership and intrafunctional capabilities towards those based upon cooperation and collaboration, and towards managing inputs without necessarily owning them. This in turn suggests that profitability becomes less significant. Rather the value delivered to the shareholders is oriented towards free cash flow discounted to give a net present value.

A model for value chain analysis, planning and control

A number of approaches have been proposed for implementing the value chain model. Many have been somewhat conservative in their approach and are essentially modified supply chain models. Typically the reasons given for these are that the marketing concept now fundamental to most organisational philosophy ensures that any decisions made at strategic or operational levels of a business are customer based. Our research suggests this not to be a safe assumption. The notion that an effective supply chain alone will ensure adequate customer satisfaction through reducing costs and therefore prices is not necessarily an adequate model by itself. Sainsbury's (the UK former market leader in food retailing) noted in the late 1990s in an annual report the positive impact on overall profitability of its increased logistics productivity, and saw this as a key corporate strategy. This reflected a business model dominated by a downstream oriented supply chain, assuming a relatively 'steady state' amongst its customers. The problems that Marks & Spencer, and to a degree Sainsbury's, experienced during the 1990s and again in 2004 were not because they mismanaged the operational efficiency of the business, but rather because they missed the shift in customer expectations and did not appear to respond to those expectations.

It can be argued that the future cannot hold much that is different for either company (or for that matter any company that shares this philosophy) if the current attempts to apply stringent cost control on operational activities continue, rather than the strategic issues of making the organisation effective in the marketplace being tackled. This suggests that a purely mechanistic supply chain approach entirely driven by *cost efficiency* needs to be replaced with a broader view of overall *effectiveness*. It is interesting to recall a comment by Porter (1996) concerning the mistakes that can be made by confusing *operational efficiency* with *strategic effectiveness*. Porter is suggesting that the attraction of the cost efficiency offered by the increasing range of production techniques has directed management towards short-term profitability at the expense of increased strategic advantage gained from understanding customer value expectations. Clearly both Sainsbury's and Marks & Spencer would appear to have been doing just this!!

Figure 1.1 outlines the approach that will be taken by this text. It is based upon a substantial period of researching and teaching value chain analysis and management. The model proposes a number of simple philosophies. The first concerns the approach taken by an increasing number of organisations which appear to assume that simply by being efficient they will succeed. There is ample evidence to conclude that while a certain amount of 'leanness' is essential, continuous cost reduction very soon has an impact on response to the customer and by the customer! This suggests a second philosophy; by developing a clear understanding of the *demand chain processes* that are involved in customer satisfaction and of the strategy decisions based upon this analysis, an optimal approach to both customer and shareholder expectations can result. A third philosophy is the acceptance that increasingly market opportunities are often more successfully pursued by collaborating with other organisations. Quite frequently this can include not simply closer liaison with suppliers and distributors, and possibly customers but also with competitors!!!

Figure 1.1 is proposing that the value chain is an integrated management activity that first explores and understands markets that appear attractive;

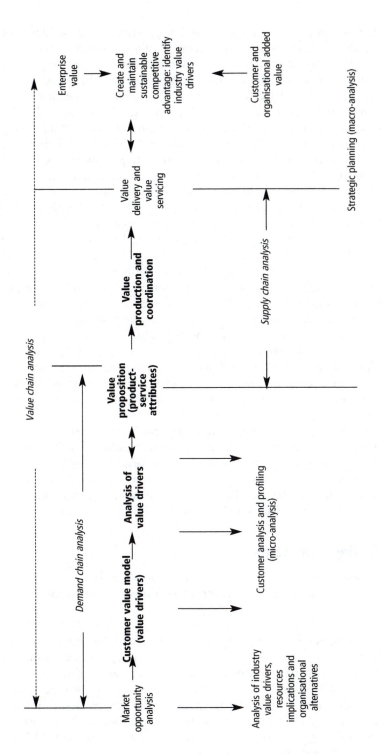

Figure 1.1 Strategic operations planning: an overall industry perspective of value chain analysis

Enterprise value

Create and maintain sustainable competitive advantage: identify industry value drivers

Customer and organisational added value

Value delivery and value servicing

Strategic planning (macro-analysis)

Value production and coordination

Supply chain analysis

Value proposition (product-service attributes)

Analysis of value drivers

Customer analysis and profiling (micro-analysis)

Customer value model (value drivers)

Demand chain analysis

Market opportunity analysis

Analysis of industry value drivers, resources implications and organisational alternatives

Value chain analysis

second, through processes such as *market opportunity analysis* identifies the industry drivers and resource requirements; third, considers the potential organisational alternatives that are available and that are likely to prove to be successful in achieving realistic marketing and financial objectives. An important outcome is a model of customer value expectations, the *customer value model*, and from this a very clear understanding of *customer value drivers*. Together these provide a thorough understanding of customer demographics and socio-economics, and these in turn provide the basis for planning an effective product-market strategy from which a *value proposition* may be developed. The value proposition is important from two aspects: it identifies for the customer what it is the organisation is offering in response to customer expectations, *and* it identifies for the external and internal stakeholders what their roles and tasks comprise if those expectations are to be met.

It is at this point that supply chain decisions can begin to be considered. In all the models currently emerging is a shared view that unless a demand chain profile is established it is unlikely that a cost-efficient supply chain can be devised. Within this decision-set it is not unusual to find product and process design processes, procurement decisions, as well as an integrated inventory management/manufacturing process. Hence *value production and coordination* decisions now closely reflect customer product and purchasing behaviour preferences, and furthermore, extend well beyond the single organisation, becoming inter-organisational and often intercontinental in their nature. The continued advances being made in information communications technology, making information transfer more accurate and rapid at decreasing costs, are largely responsible for these developments.

For ongoing success the organisation must ensure that it establishes a strong market position by creating *sustainable competitive advantage* that insulates it from the obvious competitive activities of other organisations.

This model forms the structure for the remainder of this text. Subsequent chapters explore both the model and the developing management philosophies, processes and activities that underlie its successful implementation.

Concluding comments

Some lessons have been there to be learnt and issues for consideration have been identified. Boulton et al. (2000) make a useful contribution when they contend:

> The encompassing challenge that companies face in this new environment is how to identify and leverage all sources of value, not just the assets that appear on the traditional balance sheet. These important assets including customers, brands, suppliers, employees, patents, and ideas – are at the core of creating a successful business now and in the future ... But what assets are most important in the New Economy? How do we leverage these assets to create value for our own organisations in a changing business environment? What new strategies are required for us to create value?

The authors continue by making the point that the new business models comprise asset portfolios whose success is influenced by the interaction of the assets. Furthermore, in the 'new economy' business model, asset portfolios are far more diversified than those of traditional organisations and include intangible assets such as relationships, intellectual property and leadership. They suggest that new business models are becoming commonplace in 'every industry' in the new economy:

> In these emerging models intangible assets such as relationships, knowledge, people, brands and systems are taking center stage. The companies that successfully combine and leverage these intangible assets in the creation of their business models are the same companies that are creating the most value for their stakeholders.

For Boulton et al. it is clear that 'the ultimate success of each of these companies depends not on its ability to make the most of just one or two assets, but on its skill in optimising all assets that make up the business model'. They broaden the definition of an asset by way of the following considerations:

- Assets are tangible and intangible and extend beyond the balance sheet. They should be located where they will be strategically effective.
- Assets are, therefore, both owned and leased, controlled and uncontrolled. They offer sources of value that are within an organisation's control and outwith it.
- Assets are sources of both financial and non-financial benefits. Intangible assets such as customers provide information as well as cash from sales revenues. Employees provide skills and ideas and, over a period of time, knowledge and learning. organisations provide processes and systems
- Assets have distinct lifecycles.
- Assets include internal and external sources of value. The asset base of the virtual organisation includes numerous external relationships.

Pebler (2000) summarises the development of virtual organisation structures and offers a prescription for the future virtual organisation:

> The virtual enterprise of the future will be much more dynamic and sensitive to the need for tuning operational parameters of the enterprise as a whole, including capital spending for both producers and service companies, optimising the whole chain of value creation. The future world will be characterised by knowledge management and collaborative decision-making by way of virtual teams. Virtual enterprises will be empowered by a willingness to do business in more productive ways and by information technologies that eliminate barriers between stakeholders and radically improve work processes.

CASE STUDY 1.1

Value chain integration: the 'new economy' business model vs the traditional approach

(Based upon 'United States vs. China: value chain integration – the China Vision: opportunities and challenges for US manufacturers, a White Paper – Grant Thornton LLP', Anonymous contribution, *Industry Week*, October 2005)

A US management services company, Grant Thornton, issued the results of a study suggesting that Chinese manufacturing plants show greater tendency towards value chain integration than their US counterparts. Their white paper compares and reports upon 'extensive integration' between manufacturers' suppliers and their customers. The report suggests that integration with suppliers for Chinese manufacturers is 29 per cent as against 11 per cent for US manufacturers, and with customers 33 per cent as against 16 per cent for the US sample.

Grant Thornton draw some interesting conclusions. They suggest that many manufacturers operate in markets that are becoming viewed as commodities, and that being tightly integrated with customers creates an opportunity more readily to provide 'total solutions' that extend well beyond mere products. They find that the high-performing plants in China were joint ventures involving foreign enterprises, while state owned and private plants were based upon the more traditional vertically integrated model. They continue by suggesting that the joint ventures are more integrated because of the 'Western' management approaches but also because they (the joint venture models) are provided with the opportunity to apply new and proven business models. Grant Thornton also suggest another reason, namely that the joint ventures are also more integrated because 'their customer is often their parent or partner firm'. The report also suggests cost advantages to this kind of integration.

Discussion topics

Does the Grant Thornton report imply a greater sophistication as regards organisational structures and business relationships in the emerging economies in respect of the view they are developing?

Are there problems confronting organisations who adhere to the traditional business models?

REFERENCES

Armistead C, J-P Pritchard and S Machin (1999) 'Strategic business process management for organisational effectiveness', *Long Range Planning*, 32(1)

Boulton R E S, B D Libert and S M Samek (2000) 'A business model for the new economy', *Journal of Business Strategy*, July/August

Bovet D and J Martha (2000) *Value Nets: Breaking the Supply Chain to Unlock Hidden Profits*, Wiley, New York

Drucker P (2001) 'Will the corporation survive?', *The Economist*, 1 November

Dunning J (1997) 'Governments and the macro-organisation of economic activity: a historical and spatial perspective in Dunning (ed.) *Governments, Globalisation and International Business*, Oxford University Press, Oxford

Ellis J (1999) Doing Business in the Knowledge Based Economy, Pearson Education, Harlow

Gadiesh O and J L Gilbert (1998) 'How to map your industry's profit pool', *Harvard Business Review*, May/June

Hagel J III and M Singer (1999) 'Unbundling the corporation', *Harvard Business Review*, March

Hammer M (2001) *The Agenda*, Crown, New York

Hines P, R Lamming, D Jones, P Cousins and N Rich (2000) *Value Stream Management: Strategy and Excellence in the Supply Chain*, Financial Times/Prentice-Hall (Pearson Education), Harlow

Johansson H J, P McHugh, A J Pendlebury and W Wheeler III (1993) *Business Process Reengineering*, Wiley, Chichester

Magretta J (2002) 'Why business models matter', *Harvard Business Review*, May

McHugh, P, G Merli and G Wheeler III (1995) *Beyond Business Process Reengineering*, Wiley, Chichester

Normann R (2001) *Reframing Business*, Wiley, Chichester

Normann R and R Ramirez (1994) *Designing Interactive Strategy: From Value Chain to Value Constellation*, Wiley, New York

Parolini C (1999) *The Value Net*, Wiley, Chichester

Pebler R P (2000) 'The virtual oil company: capstone of integration', *Oil & Gas Journal*, 6 March

Piore M and C F Sabel (1984) *The Second Industrial Divide: Possibilities for Prosperity*, Basic Books, New York

Porter M (1990) *The Competitive Advantage of Nations*, Free Press, New York

Porter M (1996) 'What is strategy?', *Harvard Business Review*, December

Porter M (1998) 'On competition', *Harvard Business Review*, December

Sawhney M and D Parikh (2001) 'Where value lives in a networked world', *Harvard Business Review*, January

Slywotzky A J (1996) *Value Migration*, Free Press, New York

Tapscott D and A Caston (1993) *Paradigm shift*, McGraw-Hill, New York

Uren D (2001) 'To winners go more spoils in rivalry tango', *Australian*, 10 March

CHAPTER 2

The Consumer as the Principal Driver of Value

LEARNING TOPICS

On completing your study of this chapter you will have been introduced to and considered the following topics:

■ The concept of value as one that can be useful in business planning

■ Utility and value: economists' views and those of business – consumer and producer surplus, exchange value

■ Customer value criteria; value-in-use

■ The consumption chain

■ Customer value drivers

■ The concepts of prosumerism and co-productivity

■ Building a customer value model

■ Application: setting value not price

■ Customer value builders

■ Value delivery

Introduction

'Value' is a term frequently used but infrequently understood and of which numerous interpretations exist. Value is not a new concept. It will be recalled that Adam Smith introduced the notion of 'value-in-use' in 1776. He argued for two aspects of value. He was of the view that value was determined by labour costs (subsequently modified to 'production costs'). Smith also argued that 'value-in-use' from a user's point of view is important. It is only when it is used that the full costs and benefits of a product-service may be identified.

In a business context, value implies stakeholder satisfaction, which is a broader consideration than simply that of customer satisfaction. Stakeholder satisfaction ensures that not only are customers' expectations met, but also those of employees, suppliers, shareholders, and the investment market influencers, the community and government. It follows that stakeholder satisfaction presents the business with a broader range of decisions and, typically, a larger number of ways in which satisfaction can be delivered. This is explored in more detail in the next chapter.

Since the marketing concept emerged in the 1980s, supposedly replacing production driven management philosophies, the customer has been seen as at the core of business processes and customer satisfaction as the key objective. The creation of value has then taken on strongly customer-centric perspectives. It is those perspectives that are explored in this chapter.

Understanding value

Value is an interesting concept. The underlying motivation for changes in customer expectations is a shift in the consumer perspective of value, which has moved away from a combination of benefits dominated by price towards a range of benefits in which price, for some customer segments, has very little impact. Value is assumed to be the benefits received from a product choice less their costs of acquisition.

Senior academics have commented on the role of value creation and delivery in strategic management. For example Porter (1996) suggests:

> A company can outperform rivals only if it can establish a difference that it can preserve. It must deliver greater value to customers or create comparable value at lower cost or do both. The arithmetic of superior profitability then follows: delivering greater value allows a company to charge higher average unit prices; greater efficiency results in lower average costs.

Payne and Holt (2001) offer an extensive review of the literature addressing 'customer value'. They identify customer value in a number of contexts. Their contribution considers both the economists' approach (presented by Bowman and Ambrosini (2000) and discussed in detail below) as well as the more pragmatic approaches offered by management academics. The authors identify four streams: customer values and consumer value, the augmented product concept, customer satisfaction and service quality, and the value chain. We now expand upon each of these in turn.

Customer values and consumer value as a theme is of interest in the context of this book as it reflects the view that the 'deeply held and enduring beliefs' of consumers influence purchasing behaviour. They refer to the 'values and lifestyles' (VALS) methodology of Mitchell (1983) and the 'list of values' (LOV) developed by Kahle (1963). Of particular interest to us is the concept of 'value-in-use', which considers value in an extended context. This suggests that consumers' view or assessment of value should extend beyond the time of purchase and should include such elements as installation of the product, staff training, maintenance, operating and even disposal costs. This concept is discussed in detail later in this chapter.

The augmented product concept develops a view of value that is based more on the way in which a product is differentiated by service, packaging, distribution characteristics and other features that people value and defined by Levitt (1981) as:

> ... a promise, a cluster of value expectations of which its tangible parts are as integral as its intangible parts.

Levitt's approach focuses on the inputs and processes needed to produce the 'promise' and consumers' perceptions of the offer as solutions and benefits. As Payne and Holt suggest, this approach is helpful because it recognises that customer preferences may be influenced by product-service characteristics, thereby opening new areas for competitive advantage to be established.

Customer satisfaction and service quality research is helpful inasmuch as it involves tracking customer perceptions which, when compared with their expectations, provide a measure of customer satisfaction. Given the possibility of making relative perceptions across a range of similar product-service offers, competitive positioning may ascertained. Payne and Holt identify the work of Parasuraman, Zeithaml and Berry (1985, 1988, 1991) as significant here in that their model SERVQUAL offers a five-dimensional measure of service quality. The PIMS research (Profit Impact of Market Strategy) by Buzzell and Gale (1987) is also cited for its important contribution to identifying the high correlation between quality and profitability. The authors also cite concerns that the approach is limiting, suggesting that other consumer issues such as values and desires may be important in the choice process.

The value chain perspective is based upon Porter's (1985) model. Payne and Holt remind us that this in turn was based upon earlier work of McKinsey & Co (the 'business system') that was described by Bauron (1981) and Gluck (1980). Porter claimed that his approach to competitive advantage was based upon the management of internal activities, linked with those of suppliers and customers rather than the functional approach taken by McKinsey and Bauron and Gluck. Subsequently McKinsey revised their approach. Their subsequent model was based upon the view that the business is a 'value delivery system'.

Interestingly, this concept has been referred to as an approach in known as the 'value proposition', emphasising the need for companies to shift from the traditional functional view of an organisation (typically internally focused and often suboptimal) to an externally oriented view that is process based.

A very relevant point is made by Payne and Holt: 'The value delivery sequence, in contrast to the value chain, depicts the business as viewed from the customer's perspective rather than a set of internally- oriented functions' (2001). This is also an important point because it represents the direction that is essential in the business environment currently prescribed by the 'new economy'. Payne and Holt introduce the 'value constellation' (Normann and Ramirez 1993, 1994) that opposes Porter's value chain approach. They argue that the focus of strategic analysis is not the organisation but the value creating system itself, within which a series of partnerships/alliances work together to 'co-produce' value. The essence of this argument is that unless stakeholder value *as well as* customer value is produced, the system lacks stability and is suboptimal. Discussion of this approach will be developed in later chapters.

Slywotzky and Morrison (1997) introduced the term 'customer-centric thinking'. They consider as redundant the traditional value chain, which begins with the company's core competencies and its assets and then moves to consider other inputs and materials, to a product offering through marketing channels and then finally to the end-user. In customer-centric thinking the modern value chain reverses the approach. The customer becomes the first link and everything follows. This approach changes the traditional chain such that it takes on a customer driven perspective. They suggest:

> In the old economic order, the focus was on the immediate customer. Today business no longer has the luxury of thinking about just the immediate customer. To find and keep customers our perspective has to be radically expanded. In a value migration world, our vision must include two, three, or even four customers along the value chain. So, for example, a component supplier must understand the economic motivations of the manufacturer who buys the components, the distributor who takes the manufacturers products to sell and the end-user consumer.

The authors also comment upon three more recent perspectives on value. They identify a number of contributions that make 'calls for organisations to become more market and customer-focused':

Creating and delivering superior customer value, the essential thrust of this approach being for organisations to create and/or strengthen the linkages between customer value (expectations and delivered value) and organisational financial performance and competitive advantage. The argument made is that a company's success is dependent upon the extent to which it delivers relevant value to its customers.. Slywotzky and Morrison in their 'customer-centric' approach to the value chain (discussed below) develop a commercial perspective on this.

The customer's value to the firm focuses on the value outcome to the organisation that can be derived from providing competitively superior customer value. Hence the research orientation is based upon the cost–benefit relationship of customer retention. Both quantitative and qualitative approaches are reported. Quantitative approaches are essentially based upon net present value measures of future profit flows over an estimated customer lifetime period. Qualitative models consider the relationships between marketing programmes, and others consider the linkages between customer responses to service and quality aspects of the value offer.

Customer value and shareholder value has become a significant research area following the emphasis placed on value based management (VBM) in the late1990s. By and large the VBM models failed. They did so for two primary reasons: first, due to their requirements for very detailed information and the cost in time and managerial effort needed to produce the data; second, because most of the models ignored the need for customer interests to be considered. Interestingly, the emphasis is now on the argument that customer value drives shareholder value. Payne and Holt cite Cleland and Bruno (1996) who suggest that an organisation should ensure that its customer value strategies are successful in generating revenues that deliver levels of profitability (margins) which exceed its cost of capital sufficiently such that the organisation consistently builds wealth for the shareholders. Doyle (2000) was more succinct in emphasising that shareholder value maximisation requires a focus on delivered customer value and proposes this as a primary objective for marketing.

Utility and value

Traditionally we have considered the utilities of form, possession, and time and place as drivers of consumer utility satisfaction. *Form utility* has been provided by a company's production function, which was centralised. Finished product reaches the market through a distribution process which provides *possession utility* created by marketing activities, creating awareness of a product or service and facilitating transactions. Logistics create *time and place utilities*.

However, as Rayport and Sviokla (1995) suggest, the move towards digital products changes the entire value creation, production, communication, and delivery and service process. Furthermore, customer expectations themselves have created new aspects of utility such as *convenience, choice, information, communication and 'experience'*. In a comment on the *Tomorrow Project*, a view of the future of relationships in the UK, Worsley (2000) identifies another dimension of value, that of *fit*. Worsley argues that if the consumer can now purchase clothes to meet an individual specification, can buy CDs with 'individualised' tracks, there is good reason to believe that the view 'It must fit me exactly' will become the defining outlook and expectation of the next few decades.

Evidence already exists to this effect. Toffler (1980) coined the term *prosumer* to identify consumer involvement in product design and manufacture and, if we consider the IKEA approach, we can include logistics. Nike offers customers the facility to design their own shoes using the Nike website. Customers in the US can choose between a cross trainer or a runner, select their shoe size, desired colour combinations and add personalised identification. The customer can view their 'creation' in three dimensions and when satisfied consummate the transaction by providing credit card details. A fee of US$10 is charged for this customised service, together with a delivery charge, both of which are added to the retail price. Delivery takes two to three weeks and if the shoes are not satisfactory can be returned to a Nike store. Levi-Strauss (Day 1999) offers a similar service. *Personal Pair* is a service in which jeans for women are made to their exact specifications. Day also cites *Custom Foot*, which offers to make shoes to order from a choice of 10,000 variations for women and 7,800 for men. Dell Computers' build-to-order approach is well documented and requires no detailed comment but offers a customised product with short delivery time.

The utility, or value characteristics, of the *experience economy* are of interest. Pine and Gilmore (1998) extend the difference between service products and 'experiences'. They argue that as goods and services become 'commoditised' experiences will become a distinct (differentiated) offering. In the *experience economy* the value delivered is a structured combination of memorable sensations that are *staged* rather than simply manufactured or sold. The value (or utility) is a memorable event individual to the person who is 'engaged on an emotional, physical, intellectual or even spiritual level'.

Pine and Gilmore suggest that 'outsourced' children's' birthday parties are an example of this type of value. Theme based restaurants such as the Hard Rock Café are another example of *experience based value*. In other situations experience can be used to add 'live' explanation to an event. For example, the museum Stirling Jail (Stirling, Scotland) uses actors who play roles in order to add reality for visitors. The authors forecast developments such that a company may be able to charge admission to what is essentially a merchandise based offer. They suggest that experience based value has two dimensions. The first is *customer participation* that may involve passive participation in which the customer has no part to play, through to active participation in which customers assume key roles. The second dimension is *connection*, or environmental relationships in which the involvement varies from absorption to immersion. The attempts by Asda, the UK superstore multiple, to introduce 'singles nights' into regular shopping visits is an example of connection. Customers seeking partners were expected to get involved (immersed) in the activity.

Four experience value products emerge from the authors' discussion: entertainment, education, aesthetics and escapism. They argue that experience value offers opportunity for premium pricing through distinctive differentiation. It follows that during any purchasing situation certain attributes of a product or service will represent utility or value to the purchaser. Furthermore, it is likely that one particular combination of attributes will represent more value to a customer than does another. A customer value criterion may be defined as:

An attribute (or characteristic) of a product or service considered by a purchaser to be a primary reason for selecting a specific product (or service) because it enhances the value of the purchaser's output (business to business customers) or improves their lifestyle (consumer product-service customers).

Customer value criteria

Customer value criteria, therefore, represent extensions of the basic economic utility characteristics of form, ownership, time, convenience, and so on. Such features may be expressed as generic customer value criteria:

- Asset management – issues of capital intensity, utilisation and productivity of significance to industrial (B2B) customers
- Time management – relating to: time-to-market (NPD), production cycle time, order cycle time
- Cost management – purchase price plus; *fixed costs concerns* (supply sourcing and evaluation, transaction and negotiation, installation), and *variable costs concerns* (operating costs, maintenance, and product disposal)

- Performance management – 'customisation', quality, reliability, unit cost of output, warranties and service support, flexibility, choice options and aesthetics
- Information management – shared, relevant, timely and accurate information is essential for organisations that operate in the 'new economy'. Typically organisations now see benefits from exchanging information with partners rather than assuming it to be confidential competitive advantage.
- Risk management – *financial risk* ('market'/investor response, shareholder 'value' management), *marketing risk* (customer response and 'stakeholder' response), *personal and social risk* to B2B and B2C customers (prestige, commitment and other relationship based problem outcomes)

Figure 2.1 is a hypothetical view of these together with an organisational response.

It follows that value is determined by the utility combination of benefits delivered to the customer; but there is a cost to the customer of acquiring such benefits: *value then from the consumer's perspective is a preferred combination of benefits compared with acquisition costs.*

From an organisation's perspective, the response to customer expectations is a *value proposition*, which is a statement of what value is to be delivered to the customer. Externally, the value statement is the means by which the organisation 'positions' the offer to the target customer. Internally, the value statement identifies how the value is to be produced, communicated, delivered and maintained. The internal statement specifies processes, responsibilities, volumes and costs to be achieved if the customer and each of the other stakeholders is to receive satisfaction. Webster (1994) suggests that 'the value proposition should be the firm's single most important organising principle', and implies that the traditional perspective of marketing with its transaction based approach has shifted. According to Webster:

> Our definition of marketing is built around the concept of the value chain. Marketing is the process of defining, developing and delivering value.

Value-in-use: a closer look

A number of companies use the 'value-in-use' concept to arrive at pricing decisions. The notion that an end-user should consider all aspects of a product-service purchase, not simply the price to be paid, enables both vendors and purchasers to identify all of the elements of the 'procurement – installation – operation – maintenance – replacement' continuum. The process encourages both parties to look for trade-off situations such as high acquisition costs with low operating and maintenance costs, together with relevant supplier services packages. This approach introduces the possibility of integrated activities in which the supplier–customer relationship expands from a one-to-one relationship into a fragmented, but economically viable, value delivery system.

It follows that the supplier of industrial products who considers the total cost of ownership incurred by customers is able to price a product competitively if the post-purchase costs of a product are considered during the design and development process. By simplifying equipment installation and operations and by designing simple maintenance procedures the total cost of ownership becomes lower. Within the context of value chain partnership structures it is not unusual to find some of the post-purchase activities, such as routine servicing, undertaken by specialist organisations. Roadside services offered by automobile manufacturers are but one example.

This situation is currently more the exception than the rule. Value creation (for that is what stakeholder value actually is about) has a history of development. Band (1991) traces the history of value creation, comparing North American interpretations with those of Japanese management philosophies which, ultimately, defines what it is the customer is offered and how this is accomplished, by whom, how, when and, of course why (which is usually the reference to corporate/stakeholder objectives). Band suggests that during a whole range of changes occurring in the 1980s, 'Executives who got the quality and service "religion" ... failed to remember that quality and service are the means, but *value for the customer* is the end.' Band interprets this simply and succinctly: 'The idea of creating value may, indeed, be reduced to a concept as simple as striving to become ever more "useful" to customers'. And:

> But of course good intentions must be transformed into practical reality. The businesses that will succeed in the decades ahead are not those with advantages defined in terms of internal functions, but those that can become truly market focused – that is, able to profitably deliver sustainable superior value to their customers. This means being able to do the following:
>
> ■ Choose the target customer and combination of benefits and price that to the customer would constitute superior value, and
> ■ Manage all functions rigorously to reflect this choice of benefits and prices so that the business actually provides and communicates this chosen value, and does so at a cost allowing adequate returns.

It follows that it is management's responsibility to identify what is valued by the end-user and indeed other 'customer groups' and to create, monitor and modify organisational systems that add value to the product-service. Thus, for Band, the assertion is that creating and delivering value is much more than a 'passing business fad'. Rather it is an approach to strategic management that can be used to ensure that organisations respond to customer expectations, doing so with organisational structures that are flexible. Value creation, he suggests, is *strategic* (because it entails both organisational and behavioural change), and it is *continuous* (because the challenge of delivering customer satisfaction in a dynamic marketplace requires unrelenting attention to achieving higher and higher levels of performance).

Customer 'value' expectations

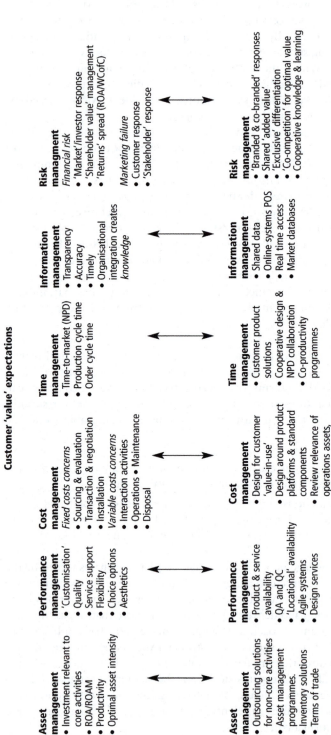

Asset management
- Investment relevant to core activities
- ROA/ROAM
- Productivity
- Optimal asset intensity

Performance management
- 'Customisation'
- Quality
- Service support
- Flexibility
- Choice options
- Aesthetics

Cost management
Fixed costs concerns
- Sourcing & evaluation
- Transaction & negotiation
- Installation

Variable costs concerns
- Interaction activities
- Operations • Maintenance
- Disposal

Time management
- Time-to-market (NPD)
- Production cycle time
- Order cycle time

Information management
- Transparency
- Accuracy
- Timely
- Organisational integration creates *knowledge*

Risk management
Financial risk
- 'Market'/investor response
- 'Shareholder value' management
- 'Returns' spread (ROA/WCofC)

Marketing failure
- Customer response
- 'Stakeholder' response

Asset management
- Outsourcing solutions for non-core activities
- Asset management programmes.
- Inventory solutions
- Terms of trade

Performance management
- Product & service availability
- QA and QC
- 'Locational' availability
- Agile systems
- Design services

Cost management
- Design for customer 'value-in-use'
- Design around product platforms & standard components
- Review relevance of operations assets, capabilities & processes

Time management
- Customer product solutions
- Cooperative design & NPD collaboration
- Co-productivity programmes

Information management
- Shared data
- Online systems POS
- Real time access
- Market databases

Risk management
- 'Branded & co-branded' responses
- Shared 'added value'
- 'Exclusive' differentiation
- 'Co-opetition' for optimal value
- Cooperative knowledge & learning

'Corporate' responses

Figure 2.1 A typical 'organisation' response to customer value drivers

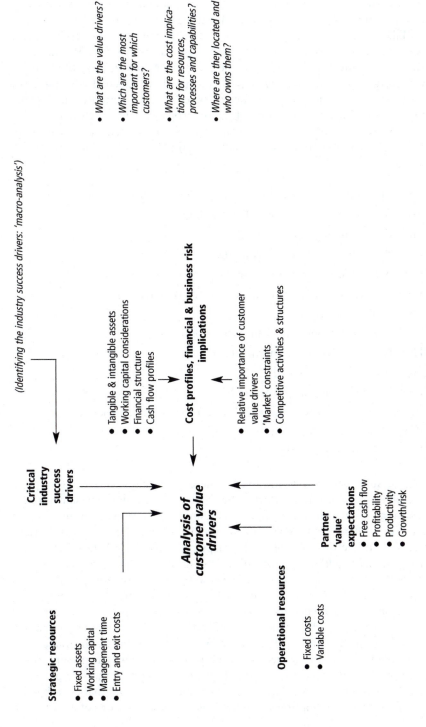

(Identifying the industry success drivers: 'macro-analysis')

Strategic resources

- Fixed assets
- Working capital
- Management time
- Entry and exit costs

**Critical
industry
success
drivers**

- Tangible & intangible assets
- Working capital considerations
- Financial structure
- Cash flow profiles

**Cost profiles, financial & business risk
implications**

- Relative importance of customer value drivers
- 'Market' constraints
- Competitive activities & structures

*Analysis of
customer value
drivers*

**Partner
'value'
expectations**

- Free cash flow
- Profitability
- Productivity
- Growth/risk

Operational resources

- Fixed costs
- Variable costs

- *What are the value drivers?*
- *Which are the most important for which customers?*
- *What are the cost implications for resources, processes and capabilities?*
- *Where are they located and who owns them?*

Figure 2.2 Value driver analysis

The consumption chain

Differentiation has been an acknowledged component of competitive advantage for some time. While many companies focus on products or services, MacMillan and McGrath (1997) argue that the customer life cycle, or the consumption chain, is a means by which 'they can uncover opportunities to position their offerings in ways that they, and their competitors, would never have thought possible'. Using a process they have labelled 'mapping the consumption chain', they capture the customer's total experience with a product or service. Such a process identifies numerous ways in which value can be added to a product or service. The mapping process to identify the consumption chain comprises a series of questions aimed at establishing aspects of behaviour:

- How do people become aware of their need for a product or service?
- How do consumers find a specific offering?
- How do consumers make final selections?
- How do customers order and purchase a product or service?
- How is the selected product or service delivered?
- What happens when the product or service is delivered?
- How is the product installed?
- What is the customer really using the product for?
- How is the product or service paid for?
- How is the product stored?
- How is the product moved around?
- What do customers need help with when they select a product?
- What about returns or exchanges?
- How is the product serviced?

It is suggested that there is an omission here: a question concerning disposal or recycling of the product, which is becoming an important consideration.

Essentially the authors are applying Kipling's 'six loyal serving men' to an audit of customer product selection and use behaviour. Their argument is reinforced with numerous examples. The mapping process is an ideal method for identifying 'value adding' opportunities, but another benefit, not identified as such, is the opportunity it offers to review the value creation processes and consider alternative delivery methods. Clearly these may not be 'in-house', and the analysis therefore encourages the use of external suppliers who may add even greater value to the product-service, either through extended differentiation or by cost reductions. This is the very essence of value chain strategy and management. While it is argued that each process or activity is present in the consumption chain for all purchasing decisions, it is certain that the processes are likely to differ in importance. It is also of interest to note that prior knowledge of specific consumption chain profiles will lead to more effective value delivery and pricing decisions. It will be seen in Chapter 10 that it also provides valuable input for understanding the demand chain.

Another important element is an understanding of the purchasers' use of the product – the value realised – and MacMillan and McGrath suggest that competitive advantage may be realised if the *consumption chain* is identified. The authors claim that:

> ... a company has the opportunity to differentiate itself at every point where it comes into contact with its customers – from the moment customers realise they need a product or service to the time when they no longer want it and decide to dispose of it.

MacMillan and McGrath's consumption chain has an interesting and worthwhile application for strategic value chain decisions, particularly their implementation through the value chain. The technique identified – 'all the steps through which customers pass from the time they first become aware of your product to the time when they finally have to dispose of it or discontinue using it' – describes the customer life cycle typically used in life cycle costing. The process considers a number of questions: awareness, availability, choice, purchasing procedures followed, product-delivery installation, financing payment, storage, mobility, end-user uses, applications service, returns or exchanges, maintenance and disposal issues. Each of these activities creates cost for customers and, as such, needs to be considered when the customer is making a purchase decision. Customer acquisition and life cycle costs must be deducted from the benefits delivered by the product or service to derive a measure of total delivered value.

The information provided by consumption chain mapping can be directly applied to value chain decisions. Two examples will illustrate the benefit of such an analysis. First, ordering procedures are being revolutionised with internet technology and, in the future, these may be automated as wireless technology is applied to both B2B and B2C markets, making reordering an automatic response to levels of use and inventory holding. The American Hospital Supply application of customer installations of computers to inventory management has been widely adopted over the years. The recent wireless technology developments are forecast to replace this technology with even more intelligent replenishment systems. Value chain intermediaries are currently developing intelligent technology (using 'smart' technology) that will link consumers' refrigerators with home delivery services.

Second, remote diagnostics are used by Tandem Computers and Caterpillar Construction equipment for identifying product component malfunctioning. This advance notice of failure allows early dispatch of replacement parts, thereby reducing field inventories and the alerting of technical staff (increased utilisation of human resources), both of which reduce costs for customers and the value chain.

The authors explore 'customer's experience' as a means to gaining insight into the customer by 'appreciating the context within which each step of the consumption chain unfolds'. A series of simple questions – What? Where?

Who? When? How? – are used to identify opportunities for additional directions in which the product-service may be offered. The question 'Why?' (omitted by MacMillan and McGrath) should be included as this may identify two important strategic questions: Why this product-service? And why this particular value delivery alternative and not another? Not only can 'Kipling's six serving men' identify additional options for differentiation; they can also be used to reinforce the existing value offer.

Both the consumption chain and an analysis of customer experience are useful approaches when using the *customer value model* and they can also be helpful in exploring value chain configuration options. The knowledge that specific expectations are critical in a customer's choice set may require particular competencies that are not available 'in-house' and therefore must be coopted.

Customer value drivers

Creating value incurs cost and for many organisations there is a decision to be made concerning the precise relationship between the *value delivered* to the customer (and the value generated for the organisation and other stakeholders) and the *cost of creating, producing, communicating, delivering and servicing the value*. The value chain has a strategic principle: the notion that to optimise value and cost it establishes partnerships (or alliances) with other organisations who offer competencies and/or assets not otherwise available.

Typically value drivers are not exclusive to a specific core competence nor to key success factors. It is more likely they influence one or some of these. If an organisation is to develop a strong competitive position it clearly needs to identify the value drivers that are important to the end-user customer and to structure a value delivery system that reflects these *and* the objectives of the other value chain participants. Slywotzky and Morrison (1997), in their 'customer-centric' approach to the value chain, suggest:

> The value of any product is the result of its ability to meet a customer's priorities. Customer priorities are simply the things that are so important to customers that they will pay a premium for them or, when they can't get them, they will switch supplier.

The 'things that are so important to customers' are the value drivers, and the important value drivers are those adding *significant* value to customers. Within the context of the value chain, value drivers assume a twofold significance: that of adding value for customers, and that of being able to differentiate the value offer such that it creates competitive advantage. Four questions emerge:

- What is the combination of value drivers required by the target customer group? What is the customer group's order of priority?
- What are the implications for differentiation decisions? Are there opportunities for long-term competitive advantage?

- What are the implications for cost structures?
- Are there opportunities for trade-offs to occur between value chain partners that may result in *increased* customer value (and stakeholder value) or *decreased* value system costs or the costs of the target customer group?

It follows that the relationship between value drivers and cost drivers is important. Scott (1998) comments:

> Since time immemorial there have been two sorts of activities in companies; those that drive value creation and those that drive unproductive cost ... .

Scott suggests that the harsh reality of globalisation and the accompanying increase in competition has forced most companies into making efficiency gains. However, the persistence of competitive pressures means that the speed of efficiency gains in production, and the speed of market responsiveness necessary to compete, are increasing. And:

> Cost structures are shifting dramatically year by year as new producers come on line and new technologies propel shifts in business processes. Everything is moving faster and will continue to accelerate. Today's competitive 'paradigms' will be tomorrow's old hat.

There are a number of implications for value chain structures arising from Scott's comments. Value chain structures are essentially virtual organisations and as such have the flexibility to meet changes either in customer value expectations or in the way in which value is delivered. Meeting value expectations and creating differentiation around important value drivers requires close and careful monitoring of the consumption cycle *and* of the ways and means by which value can be created, produced, communicated and delivered. The application of technology developments (process and product technology as well as information communications technology) is an important aspect of *how, by and to whom, when* and *where* value is delivered. Figure 2.2 explores the complex process that identifying and 'organising' value delivery entails.

There are a number of considerations involved. Clearly the first of these is to identify the value drivers and their *relative importance* to the target customer group. If there are any major discrepancies (difficulties in reaching consensus on value driver rank ordering) it would suggest there is more than one target group involved in the analysis. Supposing that this is not so, we can continue to identify competitive offers and structures – what the offer comprises in terms of value content, who are the major competitors and the value delivery structure(s).

At this point of the analysis it is useful to begin to identify the risk accompanying the current and available delivery organisation structures. The details of the risk associated with alternative organisational structures will be dealt with in a subsequent chapter. However, there are aspects of risk that impact on consumer purchasing decisions. Purchasing activities often are required to overcome *barriers* and these may be practically based or influenced, or be psychological in their nature. For example, a *value barrier* is a product's lack of performance relative to price when compared with substitute products.

Assael (1995) suggests manufacturers can overcome the value barrier in two ways. The first is to use technology to reduce the price. The second is to communicate value attributes (to potential consumers) that they have not been made aware of or have not identified for themselves. Assael is suggesting the use of process technology to reduce costs and then price, but product technology may have the effect of reducing in-use costs.

This leads to the notion of *usage barriers*. Usage barriers occur when a product or service is not compatible with consumers' current practices. This may be due to system incompatibility, such as computer systems being unable to 'connect', or it may be caused by user doubt concerning the efficacy, quality or security of the 'innovation'. Problems concerning credit and security have inhibited internet sales in consumer markets. Assael advocates the use of change agents as opinion leaders who use their credibility to convince potential users that their concerns are unnecessary.

According to Assael, *risk barriers* represent 'consumers' physical, economic performance or social risk of adopting a social innovation'. Assael identifies consumer product risk barriers but business-to-business risk barriers can be financially catastrophic. The risk in this context concerns such considerations as capital equipment investment, new product introduction timing and product modification programs. Risk barriers can be financial – the business to business consideration – or 'social/psychological', typical in fashion apparel markets. Solutions to risk barrier problems are often similar to those to usage barrier problems, in other words, the use of opinion leadership to introduce the product (or concept) so as to establish credibility.

Strategic and operational resource requirements will impose conditions for the production and delivery of customer expectations. As Figure 2.2 suggests, there are a number of investment and ongoing cost decisions to be examined, which will have implications for *partner 'value' expectations* and which are typically based upon financial performance measures. There may well also be 'market' issues; for example, the supplier of a 'branded' component (such as Intel in computer manufacturing) is undoubtedly concerned about the use of the brand in any marketing activities and will have conditions that are to be met. 'Positioning' in a marketing context is important. Within the value chain it assumes even more importance as the decisions made concerning the role of the value chain partners are crucial to the success of the value creation system.

It follows that value expectations will not necessarily change, but the way in which value is created and delivered almost certainly will do so. Consequently to remain both competitive and cost-effective/efficient, an ongoing surveillance of value expectations, value drivers (and cost drivers) becomes essential. And, equally importantly, the search for more effective value chain structures is an ongoing task. We will consider this topic in more detail in subsequent chapters.

Consumer surplus

Bowman and Ambrosini (2000) offer a theoretical approach to value, from a business strategy perspective. They address value creation and value capture and the role of value in strategy. They suggest two aspects to value: use value and exchange value. *Use value* is subjectively assessed by customers, who base their evaluation of value on their perceptions of the usefulness of the product. Hence the total monetary value is the amount the customer is *prepared* to pay for the product. *Exchange value* is realised when the product is sold; it is the amount paid by the buyer to the producer for the perceived use value. Figure 2.3 illustrates the consumer surplus concept.

The authors use the economists' concept of *consumer surplus* to explain the consumer/customer view of value. The price the customer is prepared to pay is 'price + consumer surplus'. Consumer surplus in a business context is equivalent to the benefits the product or service delivers. Exchange value, the price realised, and costs of producing the product or service determine the profit made. Clearly profit is only made if the exchange value exceeds the costs of the input resources.

The authors assume that 'Profit can only be attributed to the actions of organisational members as their labour is the only input into the production process

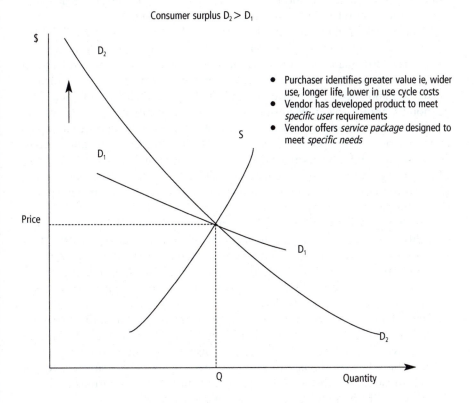

Figure 2.3 Identifying the consumer surplus

that has the capacity to create new use values, which are the source of the realised exchange value. So ... labour performed by organisational members is the source of the firm's profit.' This assumption is arguable and, despite the definition of categories of labour and acknowledgment of entrepreneurial skill, requires debate.

Bowman and Ambrosini contend that profitability is determined by comparisons customers make between the firm's product, their needs and feasible competitive offers, and the comparisons resource suppliers make of the opportunity costs occurring among alternative customers. Hence the authors conclude that the extent of value capture and the realisation of the exchange value is determined by the bargaining relationships between buyers and sellers, the availability of substitutes, the bargaining power between suppliers and customers, and the costs to be borne.

The arguments presented and conclusions reached by the authors have a certain logic but may need closer scrutiny when applied to industrial situations. The authors have, however, identified a conceptual basis against which other contributions to the debate can be considered. Of particular importance is the role of the consumer surplus (or its marketing context, value-in-use). The introduction of the notion that *use value* is 'the specific qualities of the product perceived by customers in relation to their needs' identifies the strategic implications of value creation. Thus the styling of products, their safety, performance and reliability are characteristics of use value.

Bowman and Ambrosini quote Bach et al. (1987) and Whitehead (1996) as using 'price + consumer surplus' to more formally express the colloquial 'value for money'. Bowman and Ambrosini do not pursue the argument to suggest that use value or value-in-use (the marketing application) may be expanded by persuasion and the use of past experience with this and similar products. The economist argues that the consumer surplus is equivalent to the difference between a *reservation price* (the highest price the consumer is prepared to pay) and the actual market price. Johansson (1991) suggests that consumer surplus 'expresses in observable monetary units an observable gain in utility'. The role of marketing therefore is to identify the value-in-use utility gains and present these to the customer, thereby using persuasion to reinforce the perceptions the consumer may already hold.

Returning to Figure 2.3, it follows that value-in-use characteristics may well differ among customers. Furthermore once these are known they may well form the basis of differentiation by which, through a process of 'customisation', a supplier is able to develop an exclusive arrangement with a customer (or group of customers) that results in the customers' acceptance of a product-service/price trade-off.

This is based upon the increased level of satisfaction (that is, the consumer surplus) available from the selected product. The notion of consumer surplus explains why in, for example, the OTC (over the counter) pharmaceutical market, branded products can compete with 'generic' versions, often at significant price differences. The strength of the consumer surplus is closely associated with the previous topic, that of value drivers.

As we saw, value drivers are in fact 'the things that are so important to customers that they will pay a premium for them or, when they can't get them, they will switch supplier'. The features and importance of the consumer surplus can be researched. In Figure 2.4 an example is given of a hypothetical pharmaceutical product. In this example it can be seen that five characteristics are deemed important and these are 'rank ordered' to give a level of importance. Product offers are assessed against theses criteria and the comparative strength of each identified. Where the 'company' has a perceived lead (or consumer preference) over a competitive product a consumer surplus can be said to exist. It is important to remember that this analysis extends across *all competitive product-solutions*, therefore the physical product characteristics may be entirely different. The value chain approach offers an opportunity to expand the consumer surplus. By identifying the all of the features comprising the specific customer consumer surplus it is possible also to consider alternative delivery methods using a partnership network. This may result in an increase in customer satisfaction, margins and customer loyalty without additional investment in facilities.

Exchange value

Exchange value is defined by Bowman and Ambrosini (2000) as: 'the amount paid by the buyer to the producer for the perceived use value'. Exchange value is realised when a sale is made and this occurs when there is a 'customers' view that a product confers more consumer surplus than other feasible alternatives'. Thus the authors argue that firms create exchange value and that through the sale of products exchange value is realised. It follows that the production process creates use value and subsequently realises exchange value. The amount of exchange value is known only at the time of sale. In other words the authors are suggesting that the organisation 'will not know what the newly created use value is worth until it is exchanged'. This presents problems for any organisation, and clearly a counterargument is that within acceptable ranges of probability the exchange value realised *will* be that forecast by customer research and through

	Company	Customer perceptions (+5 – -5) Nearest competitor	Consumer surplus
• Safety (1)	+4	-1	+++
• Performance (1)	+4	+1	++
• Convenience (3)	+3	0	++
• Economy (4)	+2	0	+
• Reliability (2)	+2	+2	--0

Figure 2.4 Exploring the characteristics and strengths of a consumer surplus situation

negotiation with resource providers. The basis of Bowman and Ambrosini's argument concerning the creation of the value and then exchange value is that resources such as raw materials are homogenous, and 'new use value creation derives from the actions of people in the organisation working on and with procured use values'.

Profit is made if the amount of exchange value realised on sale exceeds the sum of the prices of the inputted resources. The authors then argue that profit can only be attributed to the actions of organisational members, as it is their labour *alone* which has the capacity to create new use values, which are the source of the realised exchange value. It is, the authors argue, the inputs of heterogeneous and entrepreneurial labour that are ultimately responsible for performance differences between organisations, not material or capital inputs. Hence we might conclude that it is *managerial expertise* in identifying, producing, communicating, delivering and maintaining value that creates competitive advantage by expanding the perception of the customers' consumer surplus. It follows that managerial expertise may be more concerned with *value delivery* than perhaps with *value creation*. This suggests that competitive advantage may be developed and enhanced by focusing on *process innovation* rather than *product innovation*. The entry of Dell into the PC market is an example of process innovation, not product innovation. The managerial expertise in this case concerns the development of supplier relationships that maintain current and low levels of inventory, and of customer relationship management systems that offer customers a degree of involvement in the specification of the product.

Prosumerism and co-productivity

Toffler's (1980) term *prosumer* (used to identify consumer involvement in product design and manufacture) was discussed earlier. Essentially this term identifies the consumers' *creative role* in product design and development.

Hobsbawm (2000) also comments on the increasing trend towards prosumerism by extending the concept into the future. He suggests that eventually end-user involvement will go beyond the current situations in which they play an active role in manufacturers' production processes, helping reduce the costs of manufacturing staff and costs by specifying design features online and building their own bespoke product. Hobsbawm further suggests that the current relationship between consumers and manufacturers in which the consumer is designing the next generation of products and services will continue to expand. He gives the example of Netscape which has released its browser source code on the net, inviting users to collaborate in virtual product development teams. The rise in employee share ownership and the explosion of online investing will create a new wave of owner-worker-consumers which, suggests Hobsbawm, will blur the distinction between companies, customers and employees still further.

Hobsbawm has clearly identified an important technology/relationship management interface, one that is likely to increase in significance very rapidly.

Prosumerism is becoming increasingly important. The involvement of the end-user in the design and development process is another feature that differentiates collaboration in the value chain from collaboration in both strategic alliances and joint ventures.

Co-productivity is a similar concept but is more operational. Co-productivity, it will be recalled, is the concept according to which the production process is distributed within the value chain and is conducted by members with specific skills (such as initial component manufacture), followed by assembly later in the process chain because of cost advantages that can be realised. It differs from prosumerism in that whereas the latter suggests involvement in the design and production of product or service, co-productivity is the involvement of suppliers, reseller/distributors and customers in the process that adds value to the end product. Therefore it is more expansive in terms of its consideration of the activities involved and in terms of the participants.

The IKEA philosophy is an example of a series of external alliances established to achieve an increase in stakeholder value. IKEA offers its customers an opportunity to 'trade off' price for their involvement in manufacturing (self-assembly from 'flat packs') and logistics (the customer bears the cost of transporting the flat pack from the store to their home). Similarly agreements between company, management and employees, whereby 'multi-skilling' is adopted into work practices, are internal alliances. These can be seen in the 'discount' airline operators such as Southwest, easyJet, Ryanair and Jetstar.

Co-productivity can only be developed if *co-destiny* is strong. Co-destiny is a shared perspective of (and of the means for achieving) growth. It follows an agreed strategy and agreed implementation roles, which should be reinforced if co-destiny is to be sustained.

Building a customer value model; qualitative and quantitative factors

Customer value models are benefit *and* cost based

Anderson and Narus (1998) argue that very few suppliers in business markets are able to answer questions concerning what value actually is, how it may be measured and what the suppliers' products (or services) are actually worth to customers. They comment:

> Customers – especially those whose costs are driven by what they purchase – increasingly look to purchasing as a way to increase profits and therefore pressure suppliers to reduce prices. To persuade customers to focus on total costs rather than simply on acquisition price, a supplier must have an accurate understanding of what it is customers value, and would value.

The authors suggest that the successful suppliers in business markets are successful because they have developed *customer value models*, which are data driven representations of the worth, in monetary terms, of what the supplier is doing, or could do, for its customers. Customer value models are based on assessments of the costs and benefits of a given market offering in a particular customer application. Value is defined by Anderson and Narus thus:

> Value in business markets is the worth in monetary terms of the technical, economic, service, and social benefits a customer company receives in exchange for the price it pays for a market offering.

Value is expressed in monetary terms. Benefits are net benefits: any costs incurred by the customer in obtaining the desired benefits, except for the purchase price, are included. Value is what the customer gets in exchange for the price they pay. Anderson and Narus add an important perspective concerning a market offer. A market offer has two 'elemental characteristics: its value and its price. Thus raising or lowering the price of a market offering does not change the value such an offering provides to a customer.' And finally, value takes place within a competitive environment; even if no competitive alternative exists the customer always has the option of 'making' the product rather than 'buying' it. This proposition can be summarised as an equation:

$$(\text{Value}_s \ less \ \text{Price}_s) > (\text{Value}_a \ less \ \text{Price}_a)$$

Value_s and Price_s are the value and price of the supplier's market offer and Value_a and Price_a are the value and price of the next best alternative. The difference between value and price equals the customer's incentive to purchase. In other words, the equation conveys the idea that the customer's incentive to purchase a supplier's offer must exceed their incentive to pursue the next best alternative. This is, in effect, a practical application of the consumer surplus discussed by Bowman and Ambrosini. We shall return to this topic in the next chapter and consider its relevance in a strategy context.

Anderson and Narus are offering a structured approach to 'value-in-use' pricing, or life cycle costing. They consider the activities involved in generating a comprehensive list of value elements to be 'anything that affects the costs and benefits of the offering in the customer's business. These elements may be technical, economic, service or social in nature and will vary in their tangibility.' The authors consider both tangible and intangible aspects of value, commenting on the difficulties that exist in ascertaining the value impact of benefits such as design services. They also discuss the problems associated with establishing monetary values for many of the elements, such as social factors like 'peace of mind'. Depending upon the nature of 'peace of mind', it is possible to consider the monetary outcome if it does not exist. For example, peace of mind may be available from an alternative because it eliminates pollution or some other problem. Not to choose that particular alternative may result in prosecution for pollution offences – the legal costs and potential fine indeed have monetary values!

Anderson and Narus are aware of the need to match value delivered with costs. They identify what they label as *value drains*, services that cost the supplier more to provide than they are worth to the customers receiving them and that offer no competitive advantage.

They also identify two important advantages of the approach. Given the understanding of its customers' businesses, customer value models enable an organisation to be specific concerning its value proposition, and from this position of advantage another follows: customer relationships are strengthened. Possibly the most important benefit comes from the fact that understanding value in business markets, and translating this into delivered value, gives suppliers the means to receive an equitable return on their efforts and resources.

Figure 2.5 simplifies the Anderson and Narus model. The model here identifies the *benefits* sought and acquired by the customer and acknowledges the fact that customers are confronted with *acquisition costs*. The customer will reach a purchase decision based upon *net benefits*, that is, the optimal result (for them) of the benefits they receive less the costs involved in their acquisition. Clearly this varies by customer, or perhaps market segment, and the role of service support becomes important. While some customers may rely heavily on service support such as installation, staff training and maintenance, others may prefer to be able to purchase only the product because they have an adequate internal service infrastructure. This is often referred to as 'bundling' and 'unbundling' – both product and support services are made available as a product-service package or simply as a 'product only' option.

The notion of a customer value model is not new. Heskett et al. (1997) propose a *customer value equation* which, in addition to customer benefits and acquisition costs, also includes process quality and price. The model is described by:

$$\text{Value} = \text{Results produced} \quad + \quad \text{Process quality}$$
$$\text{for the customer}$$

less

$$\text{Price to the customer} \quad + \quad \text{Costs of acquiring}$$
$$\text{the product}$$

In their model *results produced for the customer* are based upon results, not products or services that produce results. *Process quality* has been described by Parasuraman et al. (1985) as:

■ Dependability – did value provider do what was promised?
■ Responsiveness – was value provided in a 'timely' manner?
■ Authority – did the provider elicit feeling of confidence during the delivery process?
■ Empathy – was a customer view taken?
■ Tangible evidence – was evidence left that the value was delivered?

Price, observe Heskett and his co-authors, is often used by both the customer and the supplier, but clearly acquisition costs may be high and possibly exceed price. The authors suggest that suppliers who can lower customer acquisition costs may be able to charge premium prices. This relationship has been used in value based pricing where the life cycle costs of products are considered as an

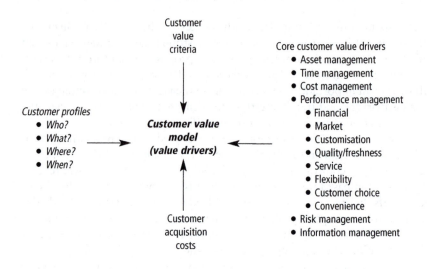

Figure 2.5 Building a customer value model

aspect of the total purchase (that is, acquisition costs) and these, with price, are the value actually delivered. This argument was presented earlier in the discussion of consumer surplus. It will be recalled that 'Value-in-use = Consumer surplus + price'. Thus the above idea can also be expressed as:

$$\left(\begin{array}{c} \text{Positive benefits} \\ + \\ \text{Reductions in} \\ \text{acquisition costs} \end{array} \right)$$

Reductions in acquisition costs may be realised by considering how design and development can be directed towards technical concerns (improved quality, reduced maintenance costs), economic aspects (such as volume discounts through scale operations), service (such as free installation, staff training) and social factors (such as pollution reduction). Some or all of these features may have such a large impact on customers' costs that, as Slywotsky and Morrison (1997) suggest, they will be prepared to pay an extra premium to obtain them or to switch suppliers. While marketing principles suggest that costs should not be used to determine prices, cost efficiencies may be used to influence prices. Thus the producer surplus may be used (together with the consumer surplus) to increase value-in-use.

Using the consumption chain to build a customer value model

The *consumption chain* is useful for application to both value chain design and as an influence on customer purchasing decision making. A detailed analysis of the consumption chain will also identify *rigidities* in the consumer decision process, and an in-depth analysis of these will reveal reasons and potential optional solutions. An example of a *rigidity* is given in MacMillan and McGrath's (1997) hypothetical example of petrol (gas) purchasing, in which, in a business-to-consumer context, personal security is identified as a possible influence in the choice between a remote and poorly illuminated outlet and one offering the assurance of safety. Similarly, in a business-to-business context, security may again be considered an important issue, so that 24-hour service availability may be a significant factor in the selection process. MacMillan and McGrath's example 'solves' the problem in the B2C context by offering pump attendants a mobile phone service (made available through a partnership arrangement) as well as the adoption of additional lighting. In the B2B context, the security may be added by a partner organisation specialising in a quick-response service on a 24-hour basis with a regional/national network.

Current purchasing and product-use experiences facilitate value delivery system design

The *customer experience* concept can be applied both to purchasing and to prod-uct-service usage experiences. Both are particularly useful in designing value delivery systems. Product-service use may require (for some customers) an instal-lation or assembly service. IKEA promotes an assembly service in its stores, which is offered by a partner organisation. Similar but often more specialised services are offered in home improvement or DIY outlets, where plumbing, electrical and joinery services are available. Experiences vary during the specifi-cation, search and evaluation stages of a purchase decision. For large capital equipment purchases, suppliers typically work alongside customers to 'design and develop' a product-service that is capable of delivering specific value. Pine (1993) discusses the development of 'mass customisation', the use of technol-ogy to offer customers 'exactly what they want – when, where and how they want it'. Customisation (and mass customisation) are both candidates for partnership arrangements. Increasingly the application of knowledge management to supplier/customer situations provides an opportunity for an organisation to identify differentiation attributes that partner organisations can contribute (through well managed relationships) and to use partners' assets (an aspect of technology management). This is the value chain approach.

The role of supplier influence

The *strength and influence of suppliers* can also be responsible for directing purchasing decision making. Three 'influences' are present. First, clearly brand strength is important, but recent developments in communication and distribu-tion processes through net technology have raised the issue: whose brand? It is likely that brand leverage will be increasingly influenced by service response and service flexibility; thus internet intermediaries' brands can be expected to be as strong as the producer brands. The second influence, service, follows. Manufac-turing technology is now following the trend set by information technology: it is becoming less expensive but at the same time offering greater capability to control quality of output, variety and customisation. Therefore, the service augmentation around conventional product offers becomes increasingly important. Moreover, in terms of costs of response, it is usually 'less' expensive to use service features to augment or differentiate the value offer. Third, loyalty is also a strong influence and loyalty programs are becoming essential features in marketing activities. The adage of 'it costs much less to keep a customer than it does to attract a new customer' is well ingrained in corporate philosophy. Not only do financial incentives promote and influence loyalty but 'convenience' in ordering and transaction processes, together with information technology based linkages, are commonplace in business-to-business transactions.

Understanding customer 'buying organisations'

The structure of the customer's *buying organisation* and its decision making process is an important factor to consider. It is usual to consider organisational issues in business-to-business markets, where typically a purchasing decision may require agreement across a number of relevant interests. The more complex the purchase, the more expensive in terms of a capital budget or perhaps as a proportion of input costs, the more involved the organisation members become. In these situations, it becomes essential to identify both the 'customers' and their value criteria, together with their perspectives of customer acquisition (or life cycle costs). Clearly in a B2B transaction the customer value model becomes complex. Value criteria may be extensive, ranging from the convenience of ordering the product, quality consistency, to availability of parts. Acquisition costs may comprise technical support (during specification and installation), operating and maintenance costs, and so on. Not only may these be extensive, but they may well be expressed across an organisation – even across a number of organisations as internet based buying exchanges expand. However, a moment's reflection will identify many similar consumer product purchasing decisions. These may extend well beyond durable products to encompass also consumable products, particularly when differing lifestyles have to be considered.

Lifestyle: activities, interests and opinions

Lifestyle characteristics are clearly important. We saw that MacMillan and McGrath's hypothetical example of petrol (gas) purchasing identified one aspect of lifestyle, security, that has an important influence on purchasing decisions. Yet what may appear to be uncomplicated decisions concerning, for example, breakfast cereals, are influenced by attitudes towards health, by time availability and often fashion or fad.

The lifestyle inventory variables first proposed by Plummer (1974) remain valid. A number of approaches to identifying and measuring lifestyle variables have appeared since Plummer's original contribution. An issue for the value chain approach is to identify how value may be enhanced by an inter-organisational approach through value adding partnerships. Partnership contributions will include both product and service infrastructure contributions. The lifestyle concept is also applicable to business-to business-markets where activities, interests and opinions are equally relevant.

For example, under *activities* Plummer listed 'community', and many B2B companies make explicit their activities within the community to express social responsibility. Retailers offer 'computers for schools' programs and many manufacturers offer educational scholarships. Both are approaches that can and do influence customer purchasing decisions. *Interests* for B2B firms have similar application. For example under this heading 'achievements' are applicable to both B2B and B2C market situations: the B2B organisation publishes awards from government given for 'excellence' (services to export), industry (quality and service) and from influential customers. These are clearly used by the organisation's customers in reaching purchasing decisions. Finally, commercial organisations can, and do, express *opinions* on social issues, the future and often on business itself. Once again these expressions of opinions are important for customers who may express similar views or who may share those views, even if they do not make them explicit.

Expenditure size and importance as a significant influence

The *significance of expenditure* is an important influence for B2B and B2C customers alike. Capital equipment procurement decisions may take considerable time, not only because of the dollar value of the purchase but also because of interrelated functions and activities as well as the life cycle span of the purchase. This factor brings similar concerns in relation to consumables. An input that accounts for a significant proportion of total input costs will be constantly reviewed in terms of cost, quality and supplier service to ensure that all aspects of value are met. One consideration often overlooked by suppliers is the level of use of its products within an organisation; thus, for instance, the fact that some equipment (and perhaps some components) has complexities not fully understood by the customer's workforce is often overlooked and the need to provide training, advice or at least detailed information is neglected. Again this can have important implications for the purchasing company, for whom a training package will recover costs and may improve workplace safety. The value chain approach offers a means by which specialist partners may be cost-efficient contributors.

Customer purchasing influences are summarised in Figure 2.6. They have an important role in customers' development of a value model and should result in the customer both identifying benefits that are expected and eventually taking a view on the extent to which they have (or have not) been delivered. It also results in the customer identifying the costs, that is the total costs, of alternative sources of supply or solutions to specific problems. As with the *consumption cycle*, the organisation should take steps to understand the structure of customer buying models. Knowledge of both will greatly improve the value that is delivered to customers and strengthen the relationship between the organisation and its source of income.

Application: setting value not price

Leszinski and Marn (1997) offer a model which, although it may not result in setting a precise value related price, raises a number of concerns which management should address. Their model identifies an important and fundamental factor: 'Customers do not buy solely on low price. They buy according to *customer value*, that is, the difference between the benefits a company gives customers and the price it charges. More precisely, customer value equals *customer-perceived* benefits minus *customer-perceived* price.' Within this equation the costs involved in obtaining and owning the product-service may be seen as 'negative' benefits or a component of the price. See Figure 2.7(a).

The authors propose a 'value map' to explore customer value and price/benefit trade relationships. They suggest that with constant market shares the market's offers will align themselves along a *value equivalence line* (VEL) identifying the range of choice available to customers. Any changes in market share will be indicated by horizontal movement (leftwards suggesting share loss as the customers perceive less value, rightwards suggesting an increase in relative value).

As the authors contend, the value equivalence line may shift downwards and/or towards the right, reflecting either a decrease in market prices or perhaps an increase in the benefits that are available. This may occur because of production efficiencies developed by one or more competitors, or due to design or technology advances that individual R&D processes have developed. See Figure 2.7(b). A number of other features are discussed by the authors.

Customer value builders

Just as customer value drivers identify the features or characteristics of a value proposition that meet the customer's existing expectations, value builders reflect the features that will be necessary if the customer organisation is to meet its growth expectations. Value builders have a long-term impact on the future value of a customer organisation. We will consider the measurement of value in a subsequent chapter, but for our purposes here we will consider what the influencers of growth are.

Ansoff (1968) presented a simple but effective model describing strategic pathway alternatives for organisations based upon the pursuit of opportunities in existing and new product-markets. Value builders act as facilitators in this pursuit and may reflect the necessity for the organisation to reposition itself within an existing or adjacent product-market or perhaps reposition itself within the existing relationship structure that it enjoys with suppliers and customers.

Chapter 1 discussed value migration as a significant factor in a number of industries. It will be recalled that industries undergo structural changes as end-user customer expectations change. For example, numbers of industries have become more service oriented in recent years, reflecting supplier efforts to differentiate their value offer to target customer groups. Another example concerns the application of new technology to both product and production processes. In both these examples we see changing patterns of value production, suggesting that the structure of the added value contributions from value

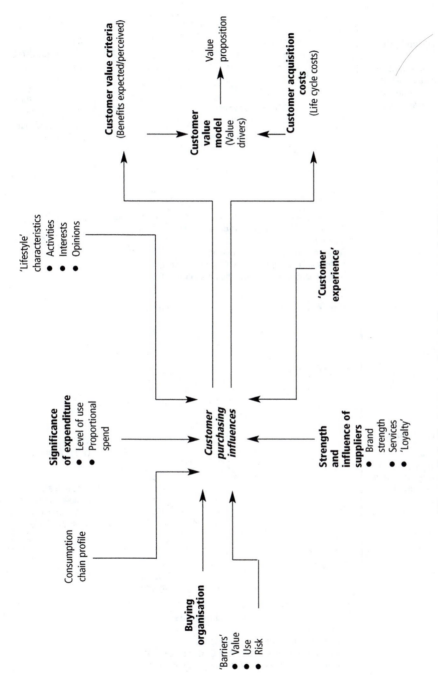

Figure 2.6 Customer value: influences and delivered value

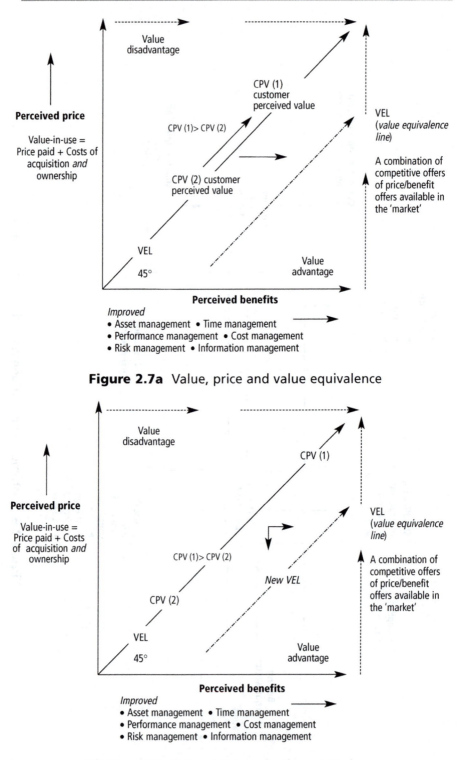

Figure 2.7a Value, price and value equivalence

Figure 2.7b Value, price and value equivalence

production processes results in a shift (or 'migration') of value in the industry value chain. The significance this has for organisations that work in partnership networks is that due to changing patterns of value migration some firms may find it necessary to reposition themselves within the value chain, leave the network, or perhaps develop more relevant processes and capabilities.

The implications of growth for most organisations concern shareholder value management. It follows that to ensure the ongoing prosperity of a firm its management's decisions should reflect the 'ownership expectations' for growth. Typically these are reflected in financial terms. Chapter 3 explores this issue in depth but essentially we are considering the reinforcement of strategies that enhance profitability, productivity and cash flow. Therefore any help that suppliers give to customer organisations that impact positively on these factors will be construed as a move towards reinforcing the customers' value building activities.

Phelps (2004) suggests value builders give an organisation the ability to take advantage of future opportunities and risks. He is arguing that to do so require processes and capabilities that are future oriented. The intelligent partner is one that identifies how this may be achieved, what the fundamental value builder component is, and works with the customer to achieve this.

Value delivery: a series of processes

The value delivery models that are now becoming familiar with the 'new economy' are becoming focused around an alliance or partnership based consortium. As Figure 2.8 suggests, value creation and delivery is becoming complex as an overall process. Increasingly it is likely that the process will be centred on an innovative organisation that identifies a market opportunity, explores the tangible and intangible aspects of customer expectations, and develops a value chain structure that is both most suitable to meet customer expectations *and* is capable of developing a strong competitive positioning within the market or market segment. It follows then that the overall value delivery process can involve a number of organisations. For example, both Ford and General Motors have moved towards value chain structures that identify their specialist skills, which then become core processes and capabilities, while those they regard as widely available, such as manufacturing, are increasingly becoming outsourced. Similarly in the pharmaceutical and computer industries the value delivery tasks are being focused on areas of expertise essential to the overall value package which are *competitive necessities*, as distinct from aspects of the overall value process that contribute to creating *competitive advantage*.

Concluding comments

Understanding value presents a problem for many organisations. In this chapter we have explored some of the important issues and have considered the economic concepts underlying that of value. Customer value builders were introduced as being important in influencing the future growth of a customer organisation. The following chapter takes the discussion further by reviewing value from an organisational perspective.

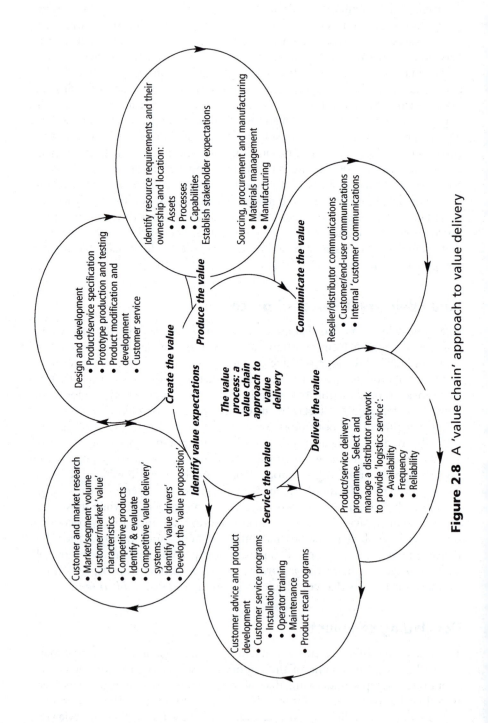

Figure 2.8 A 'value chain' approach to value delivery

CASE STUDY 2.1

Some of the unwelcome costs of 'fast fashion'

(Based upon 'The world pays a heavy price for our cheap Christmas miracles', Madeleine Bunting, *Guardian*, 19 December 2005)

Clothing items feature on as much as 74 per cent of 'wish lists' at Christmas in the UK. And when this is considered in the context of an average spend of £366 per person, it amounts to a large spend. Much of the clothing spend will be directed towards the 'fast fashion' segment. Madeleine Bunting argues that this segment has both social and environmental costs. Typically the low-cost, 'fashion-of-the-day' garment will have served its purpose before the seams unravel and it joins other similar garments that are no longer required or beyond 'repair'. She contends that the British dispose of 'about a million tonnes of clothing straight into the dustbin every year, and only 10% of our discarded clothing is reused here. Some will go into car-seat filling, but it is more likely to be shipped by the tonne to developing countries, many in Africa, as part of a huge global trade in second-hand clothes.' She describes the markets in the shanty towns of countries such as Mozambique: 'Large quantities of every kind of textile and footwear [are] on sale here.'

Madeleine Bunting argues that we may choose to ignore any qualms we may have over much of Africa dressing itself in Western cast-offs and consider the positive side. A very large number of Asian workers are employed making clothes from which Westerners receive pleasure for a few months, or even a year while the style is fashionable, and then pass them on; a Mozambican then receives a 'still-decent' item of clothing at an affordable cost. According to US economist Juliet Schor, there is a problem. Madeleine Bunting quotes Schor's research in which she identifies the 'imperial consumer'. She contends that rising living standards in the West are increasingly dependent upon cheap goods that do not meet their ecological and social costs. She argues that because the goods are so cheap, consumers purchase more of them, which drives up the ecological costs. She gives as an example the decrease in the cost of clothing in the US in the 1990s as huge quantities of low cost goods were imported – usually from the PRC. As a result, hyperconsumption boomed, so that by 2002 the US was importing 48.3 pieces of clothing per person per year. A similar trend had occurred in children's' toys: every child had 69 new toys each year by 2001. Concurrently, the 'bottom fell out' of the US secondhand clothing market as the volume of dumped US clothes soared.

The ecological costs are high for this accelerating global cycle of new and cast-off clothes. The cultivation of cotton involves high concentrations of fertiliser, herbicide and pesticide. While cotton accounts for only 2.5 per cent of all agricultural land use, it accounts for 22.5 per cent of all insecticides applied in agricultural production. Processing requires more chemicals to be used in bleaching and dyeing. Finally every stage of cotton agriculture and processing is water-intensive – often taking place in areas where the water is not in plentiful supply. Thus, argues Madeleine Bunting, 'If the T-shirt is going to end up in a landfill after a couple of outings, it represents a spectacular waste of environmental resources of soil and water.'

Madeleine Bunting continues by suggesting that this rate of wear is not far off that of disposable clothing, and suggests that as prices continue to decline the retailers are visited more and more frequently. The driver here is the recently coined 'fast fashion'; where there were two to four fashion seasons a year, the norm has become six to eight each year – the purpose being to increase purchasing frequency.

The high social costs have been identified on numerous occasions. Low wages, long hours in poor working environments with poor safety records are commonplace. Madeleine Bunting suggests they are probably becoming higher as the 'wish list-must have items' are rushed into retail outlets. Some of the lading retailers in this sector are claiming a three week time cycle 'from catwalk to retail store'. Such short lead times typically require long working hours (70 hours a week being not unusual) to meet the time-to-market. And to maintain competitive prices, suppliers 'scour the globe for the cheapest, most flexible labour and force down prices with the threat of moving business elsewhere'.

This market also presents longer-term problems. Schor argues that the second-hand clothes markets in countries such as Maputo in Mozambique prevent the development of a local indigenous textile industry in Mozambique's post-civil war economic rehabilitation. It will be recalled that during the Industrial Revolution in the eighteenth and nineteenth centuries in the UK, textile production was a major industry because of its low-skill and capital investment requirements. However, because of the size of the secondhand clothes trade it is very unlikely that such production is an option for Mozambique. Schor argues that there is no room for manoeuvre in an industry that operates on such small margins in the production stages.

Schor contends that the 'imperial consumer' consumes two-thirds of the annual $US1 trillion clothing production. According to her, the market is only maintained by the exercise of political and economic power, citing the recent WTO summit in Hong Kong at which both the US and the EU offered little to benefit African cotton producers. US cotton farmers receive more than $US4 billion in subsidies. African representatives at the WTO were disappointed at the empty gestures; one described the Western response as: 'like putting a Band-Aid on a wooden leg'.

Discussion topics

While political solutions to the problem underlying this case are beyond the scope of this text, it raises important issues concerning the definition of the 'end-user customer'. Does the value chain end with the 'first end-user'? Are there logistics solutions that can be used to improve both the economic resources problem and particularly the social costs?

Millions of tonnes of waste plastic, paper and board are shipped from the UK through Hong Kong into PRC each year. China is now finding resources are expensive and that recycling waste (albeit someone else's waste) is becoming a cost-effective resource strategy. As an example, 24 'dead' plastic bottles are recycled into a jacket at a total cost of one US dollar. A vital input into the decision is the fact that a few million containers of product are shipped out of Hong Kong each year and were returning empty!! Now they have two-way utilisation and the PRC's resources problem is being assisted (bbcnews.com, 15 March 2005). Is this a solution? If so how can it be incorporated into the value chain?

CASE STUDY 2.2

The growth of 'e-retailing'

(Based upon 'Clicks, bricks and bargains', *The Economist*, 1 December 2005)

Post the Thanksgiving holiday in the US is the traditional start of the Christmas shopping period. This year [2005] was marked by a significant increase in activity. Visits to some websites more than doubled and Visa reported a 26 per cent increase in purchases compared with the same day in 2004. Despite what appears to be a decline in consumer expenditure as evidenced by year-on-year decreases in conventional retail outlets, online purchasing is increasing rapidly in many countries. And increasingly the websites of conventional retailers are growing fastest. *The Economist* article reports that Wal-Mart's site visits exceeded those of Amazon.

In the US online sales [in 2005] were expected to exceed $US19 billion in November and December – an increase of 24 per cent on the same period in 2004. A research organisation (comScore Networks) reported online sales of toys, computer games, clothing and jewellery as being 'more than 30% higher' compared with 2004. As the 'high spend time of year' approaches retailers are gaining in optimism. Tesco, with its 30 per cent of UK grocery sales, must have been content with the Nielsen//NetRatings forecast that said almost 70 per cent of online purchasers planned to purchase groceries from tesco.com that Christmas.

An interesting change is occurring in the product-mix of the major internet operators. Both Amazon and eBay have expanded their merchandise offers, and they now resemble online versions of vast department stores. In the Thanksgiving period [2004] Amazon sold more consumer electronics than it did books. These changes are reflected in the rapid growth rates of Wal-Mart and Target (USA), Argos and Tesco (UK), Tchibo (a diversified multiple chain) and OTTO (a mail order specialist) (both Germany), and Fnac (audio/visual, books, etc.) (France).

Shopping comparison sites appear to be enhancing web sales. Shopzilla (US) and Ciao (a European site) are among the fastest growing web destinations. Funded by direct and indirect advertising, they offer the large retailers cost-efficient access to additional customers and the opportunity to increase the advantage of their huge economies of scale. The article also makes the very important point that 'cyberspace expansion' avoids the problems associated with planning regulations and, increasingly, the protests from environmental groups. Another important point made here is that the conventional retailers view online services as complementary to those of their stores.

Increasingly we see variations of the online retail model appear. The article reports on Circuit City, a consumer electronics retailer and a pioneer of the 'pick-up in-store' option. It is reported that around half the customers purchasing online from Circuit City collect their purchases from a shop. During the Thanksgiving period Circuit City offered a '24/24 Pick-up Guarantee' – if the merchandise ordered is not available for collection within 24 hours of being ordered, the customer is entitled to a $24 gift voucher. It is suggested that the 'pick-up' option offers a number of benefits to customers: they can examine the purchase before accepting the merchandise, they can save on delivery costs, and there is the security of the known brand and a physical contact where goods can be returned conveniently if there is a problem.

Large retailers already perceive other benefits. Both Tesco and Wal-Mart are expanding their sales of 'digital products' (audio, video and digital photography prints). *The Economist* article suggests that competition is increasing. While Wal-Mart's sales are five times the annual sales of Target, Target's website is growing faster and the average online sale at Target is approximately three times the size of that at Wal-Mart. Wal-Mart is expanding its online product range to include diamond rings!

One other development in the expansion of online facilities is the move by Amazon to run the websites of large, traditional retailers such as Target (US) and Marks & Spencer (UK).

Discussion topics

What does this suggest about consumer 'value' expectations?
What will be the impact on traditional manufacturers of branded products who have sold through conventional retailers: will they enter the online arena or will they support retailer web based ctivities? What are their options? What are the implications?
Will brands retain their attraction or will other features replace their traditional benefits?
What can be deduced about the future of consumer purchasing behaviour?

REFERENCES

Anderson J C and A Narus (1998) 'Business marketing: understand what customers value', *Harvard Business Review*, November–December
Ansoff H I (1968) *Corporate Strategy*, McGraw-Hill, New York
Assael H (1995) *Consumer Behaviour and Marketing Action*, South-Western, Cincinnati, OH.
Bach C, R Flanagan, J Howels, F Levy and A Lima (1987) *Microeconomics*, 11th edition, Prentice-Hall, Upper Saddle River, New Jersey.
Band W A (1991) *Creating Value for Customers*, Wiley, New York
Bauron R (1981) 'New-game strategies', *McKinsey Quarterly*, Spring
Bowman C and V Ambrosini (2000) 'Value creation versus value capture: towards a coherent definition of value in strategy', *British Journal of Management*, 11, March
Buzzell R D and B Gale (1987) *The PIMS Principles: Linking Strategy to Performance*, Free Press, New York
Cleland A and A V Bruno (1996) 'Building customer and shareholder value', *Strategy and Leadership*, 25(3)
Day G (1999) *The Market Driven Organisation*, Free Press, New York
Doyle P (2000) 'How shareholder value analysis re-defines marketing', *Market Leader*, Spring
Gluck F (1980) 'Strategic choice and resource allocation', *McKinsey Quarterly*, Winter
Heskett J L, W E Sasser Jr and L A Schlesinger (1997) *The Service Profit Chain*, Free Press, New York
Hobsbawm A (2000) 'We're all prosumers now', *Financial Times*, 26/27 February

Johansson P O (1991) *An Introduction to Modern Welfare Economics*, Cambridge University Press, Cambridge.

Kahle L R (ed.) (1983) *Social Values and Social Change: Adaptation to Life in America*, Praeger, New York

Leszinski R and M Marn (1997)) 'Setting value, not price', *McKinsey Quarterly*, 1

Levitt T (1981) 'Marketing intangible products and product intangibles', *Harvard Business Review*, May/June

MacMillan I C and R G McGrath (1997) 'Discovering new points of differentiation', *Harvard Business Review*, July/August

Mitchell A (1983) *The Nine American Lifestyles*, Warner, New York

Normann R and R. Ramirez (1993) 'From value chain to value constellation: designing interactive strategy', *Harvard Business Review*, July/August

Normann R and R Ramirez (1994) *Designing Interactive Strategy: From Value Chain to Value Constellation*, Wiley, New York

Parasuraman A, V A Zeithaml and L L Berry (1985) 'A conceptual model of service quality and its implications for future research', *Journal of Marketing*, 49(4)

Parasuraman A, V A Zeithaml and L L Berry (1988) 'SERVQUAL: a multiple-item scale for measuring consumer perceptions of quality', *Journal of Retailing*, 64(1)

Parasuraman A, V A Zeithaml and L L Berry (1991) 'Refinement and reassessment of the SERVQUAL scale', *Journal of Retailing*, 67(4)

Payne A and S Holt (2001) 'Diagnosing customer value: integrating the value process and relationship marketing', *British Journal of Management*, 12(2)

Phelps R (2004) *Smart Business Metrics*, Pearson Education, Harlow

Pine B J III (1993) *Mass Customisation*, Harvard Business School Press, Boston, MA.

Pine B J III and J H Gilmore (1998) 'Welcome to the experience economy', *Harvard Business Review*, July/August

Plummer J T (1974) 'The concept and application of life style segmentation', *Journal of Marketing*, 38, January

Porter M (1985) *Competitive Strategy*, Free Press, New York

Porter M (1996) 'What is strategy?', *Harvard Business Review*, December

Rayport J F and I T Sviokla (1995) 'Managing the marketspace', *Harvard Business Review*, November/December

Scott M (1998) *Value Drivers*, Wiley, Chichester

Slywotzky A J and D J Morrison (1997) *The Profit Zone*, Wiley, New York

Toffler A (1980) *The Third Wave*, Morrow, New York

Webster F E (1994) *Market Driven Management,* Wiley, New York

Whitehead G (1996) *Economics*, 15th edition, Butterworth-Heinemann, Oxford

Worsley R (2000) 'Our society is geared to the search for pleasure', 'Podium', *Independent*, 10 March

CHAPTER 3

Value in the Context of the Firm

LEARNING TOPICS

On completing your study of this chapter you will have been introduced to and considered the following topics:

- Traditional measures of organisational value – their limitations
- Cash flow as the firm's primary objective, and why
- Enterprise value – a cash flow based measure of a firm's value
- The influence of shareholder value management
- Future value
- A review of how firms express value
- Value propositions – customer and supplier perspectives
- Added value – the central purpose of a firm being in business
- Added value and the producer surplus

Introduction

In the previous chapter we explored the concept of value in its broadest sense and in particular the relationship between customer-centric perspectives and the maximisation of value across industries and markets. However when the term 'value' is used in the context of an individual business or firm, it is unlikely to be expressed in terms of simple customer satisfaction.

Few would argue with the proposition that on a day-to-day basis managers should be principally concerned with creating value. The problem, however, is what exactly the term 'value' really means. It seems the word is often used on the presumption that there is some single objective standard or measure of value that everyone understands and which all companies should strive for. But is this true?

This chapter explores the notion of 'value' in the context of the firm and in particular asks what appropriate measures of that value are. It suggests that a broader perspective is needed than that of historical accounting measures, and looks at the importance of free cash flow, notions of enterprise value, future value and the balanced scorecard, finally examining what role firms have in setting their own goals.

Traditional organisational measures of value

Key to understanding notions of value in the context of the firm is an appreciation of what the firm is and why it exists at all. At its simplest a business is operated by a sole trader. As groups of people come together to pursue common business objectives the law has over time accommodated more complex forms of organisations to facilitate this – agencies, partnerships, trusts and now most commonly the limited liability company. As a generalisation the principal objective of these organisations has been to build the wealth of its owners. It is true that business organisations have other legitimate objectives which are discussed further below, but generally for the purposes of this discussion it will be assumed that the 'profit motive' is paramount.

Wealth creation has then traditionally been reduced to money terms and measured by accounting practices and standards. As firms have grown larger owners have become increasingly simple passive providers of capital, indeed to the point where that capital is freely traded via share markets. That capital is increasingly deployed not by the owners themselves but by a class of professional managers. To protect owners and allow them to understand what is happening to their capital these accounting measures have grown more complex, as has the legal framework surrounding the operation of the firm.

While no doubt some mastery of accounting measures is a necessary prerequisite to understanding notions of value in the context of the firm, this chapter explores whether they are adequate alone. Certainly there have recently been some spectacular failures of accountancy as a reflection of underlying value – Enron, Worldcom, Tyco and others have been glaring examples where the accounting value of the company presented to its owners through audited accounts was clearly misleading. These may of course be examples of blatant manipulation and inadequate policing and accountants at least may argue that they are not due to inherent shortcomings in methodology.

The question remains, however, whether even a properly prepared and audited set of accounts tells you all you need to know about the creation of value in a company. It is suggested that other perspectives are required. As Ballow et al. (2004) point out of accountancy: 'Its world view was formed during a time when businesses created value through tangible resources, such as buildings, equipment, or the transformation of raw materials into intermediate and finished products. In today's knowledge-based economy, companies are much more likely to create value by using intangibles and intellectual capital resources such as proprietary processes, brands, relationships and knowledge' – none of which are adequately accommodated by traditional accounting measures.

Cash flow is the firm's primary objective

Even within the confines of traditional accountancy it is clear that the notion of 'profit' is quite an artificial one, being derived from the application of various rules, and having potentially different meanings in different contexts. In this text it is generally proposed that to the extent that 'value' is measured in purely monetary terms then, as has often been quoted, 'profit is a matter of opinion, cash is a matter of fact' (Ellis 1999).

Simple cash measures have, however, often failed to take into account the fact that cash is generated in different manners over different timeframes. This has particular implications when considering what a firm's key success factors are and how these should be managed, a topic explored further in a later chapter.

For current purposes it is proposed that in quantitative terms value in a firm is best measured in terms of anticipated free cash flow (AFCF). This is illustrated in Figure 3.1 and incorporates three elements:

- *Operating cash flow*, which is the traditional measure of cash flow starting with the firm's earnings, from which direct and indirect costs associated with performing its activities are deducted.
- *Cash flow from assets*, which takes into account the short-term working capital and capital structuring or investment costs, required to perform the firm's activities.
- *Strategic cash flow*, encompassing the cost of fixed assets, long-term working capital requirements and entry and exit costs associated with performing the process.

One important qualification needs to be added to any formulation of a firm's anticipated free cash flow and that is taxation, which is not a constant and which varies from jurisdiction to jurisdiction not only in quantum, but also structurally in how it is levied.

Enterprise value

In a discussion on 'the philosophies of risk, shareholder value and the CEO', Knight and Pretty (2000) offer another interesting model of the business. They note that:

> The core value of a quoted company has three components: tangible value, premium value, and latent value. Tangible value reflects the bedrock of the real and tangible assets which will sustain the company's value in times of crisis. It is usually measured as book value ... Premium value represents the value in excess of book value at which the company trades in the open market. This element is the source of a company's competitive advantage ... Latent value represents the potential value within a company. Sources of hidden value might include operating efficiencies yet to be realised ...

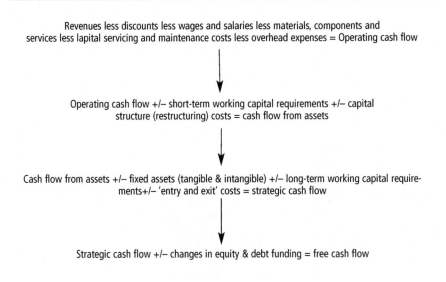

Revenues less discounts less wages and salaries less materials, components and services less lapital servicing and maintenance costs less overhead expenses = Operating cash flow

Operating cash flow +/– short-term working capital requirements +/– capital structure (restructuring) costs = cash flow from assets

Cash flow from assets +/– fixed assets (tangible & intangible) +/– long-term working capital requirements+/– 'entry and exit' costs = strategic cash flow

Strategic cash flow +/– changes in equity & debt funding = free cash flow

N.b.: Tax payments have been omitted. These may occur at operating, asset management and strategic cash flow management levels depending upon tax regulations. Other charges may also be relevant.

Figure 3.1 The determinants of free cash flow: the primary value chain objective

The authors argue that tangible value has been downgraded as the market valuation of internet based companies, which 'with a little or no book value but promises of great wealth outshone their traditional competitors.' The events since June 2000 (when it will be recalled that a number of 'dot.com' internet companies failed due to their failure to generate positive cash flows) suggest this not to be the case, but it is interesting to note that the emphasis on intangible assets persists and is a major contribution to the growth of virtual enterprises. The *enterprise value model* described by the authors has a simple structure, as shown in Figure 3.2.

Knight and Pretty discuss enterprise value from a risk management perspective. They argue that it is the role of the chief executive to identify the risk confronting the organisation and to make decisions 'first to develop a clear philosophy of risk and then to formulate clear corporate policies to guide the management of risk'. Their thesis is that it is the role of the chief executive to identify and realise sources of value and the risk each presents to the organisation; by doing so an *optimal* growth strategy will be evolved in which returns will be achieved at acceptable levels of risk.

An important observation made by Uren (2001) concerns a comment originating from McKinsey and Co. They suggest there have always been markets in which a small difference in performance makes a huge difference in rewards. Uren comments to the effect that this offers a large opportunity to the business than can identify the important *customer value drivers* and match them with cost-effective delivery strategies. Given the evidence that partnerships and outsourcing are favoured methods of either reinforcing or adding service based

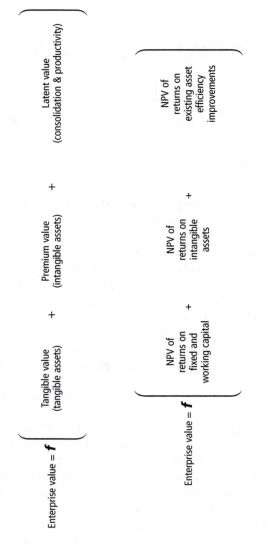

Figure 3.2 The enterprise value model described by Knight and Pretty has a simple structure

differentiation, value chain analysis becomes increasingly important, as does a model for measuring the value of the inter-organisational enterprise.

The Knight and Pretty model addresses both of these issues. Clearly no approach to valuing the enterprise (be it one single organisation or the partnership based inter-organisational value chain structures that are becoming commonplace) can avoid the issues of quantifying the components.

The enterprise value model has obvious attraction. It offers not only the facility to consider the enterprise as a number of individual (but related) components but also the facility to explore strategic growth alternatives. Figure 3.3 identifies the three components and the methods for quantifying the value for each.

The investment market view, suggested by Rappaport (1983), Reimann (1985) and Copeland et al. (1994) considers that what a business is worth (that is, the enterprise value) is the net present value of its future cash flows discounted at an appropriate cost of capital. This approach avoids the inadequacies of traditional financial measurements and recognises the time preference for money and the risk of an investment. This is suggested by Knight and Pretty as a means for measuring tangible value where future cash flows are discounted at a relevant cost of capital. No proposals were made for either premium or latent value. Given the Brookings Institution findings we presented in Chapter 1, this is an important consideration, one requiring attention due to either the increasing leverage of partners' fixed assets (the Dell approach) or the increasing importance of intangible assets (such as brand values and innovative R&D) or, clearly, the two together.

It follows that given three growth options the innovative organisation will identify an option (or perhaps a combination of options) that offers the highest net present value (NPV). Further, the options may require searching for suitable partners to contribute to the required competencies/capabilities. The major benefit of the model is that it encourages the search for strategic alternatives that may create significantly larger opportunities for competitive advantage.

The following is an attempt to provide a template for this. It is framed in the context of a listed company operating in a market economy, but the framework should be equally applicable to other circumstances. There are three core premises. First, a firm's target or individual *value objectives* should be clearly defined. These value objectives must be capable of *defined outcomes*. This is based on the simple idea that if an objective cannot be tracked and measured it is of little worth. Second, to the extent value objectives contradict each other, which is indeed likely, the *trade-offs* should be made explicit. It is a simple equation that the lowest price to the customer, and the highest wages to the employee are unlikely to produce the largest profit for the owner. Third, if a firm declines to pursue certain potential markets for political or ethical reasons, this should also be explicitly measured so that it is not just the managers of the enterprise, but its owners and other audiences that appreciate the cost of that trade-off and can form their own views. In a practical sense this is where the notion of *ranking* of objectives is important. As noted above, in all too many of the companies surveyed above there is simply a 'laundry list' of customers, employees and

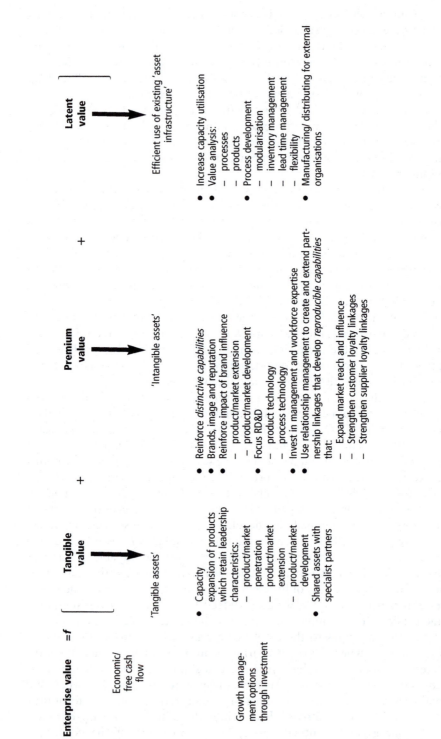

Figure 3.3 Managing the growth of enterprise value: virtual structures expand alternatives

other stakeholders all of whom seem to rank equally, when in fact this is probably impossible.

How then to apply these premises? At least in the common-law world there seems little doubt that the principal legal duty of those who control and manage a commercial enterprise is to act in the best interests of the *shareholders* of that firm. In a market economy the expectations of the owners of the business are principally thought of in terms of *financial targets*. However, even these financial targets are not necessarily complementary. In the case of a company listed on a stock exchange, there may well be a tension between targets that maximise the short-term share price and those which drive long-term cash flows. Particularly in their infancy, firms may well focus largely on sales growth, while more mature companies may well be orientated to working-capital management. As a generalisation these financial targets, however expressed, will be the *primary value objectives*. This is reflected in the fact that regardless of the rhetoric of their mission statements, Fortune 500 companies are ultimately judged largely on their financial results.

It is interesting to note that fund managers are questioning the traditional measures. For example, the assumptions underlying price/earnings (P/E) ratios are suggested as being 'a misleading simplification of a company's value and one that is too focused on short-term performance' (Eyers 2004). Eyers cites Macquarie Bank equity strategist Tim Rocks, who argues that 'Some of the changes in the Australian corporate landscape have driven a wedge between P/Es and other valuation of stocks.' Rocks suggests these include structural forces, which include cash flows that are growing faster than earnings in many companies, and reductions in capital expenditure that also result in increasing cash returns. Another influence is the decrease in debt. It is argued that most of the assumptions made when assessing P/E ratios are very likely to change in the future. An interesting suggestion made by Rocks is to use a ratio of enterprise value to free cash flow as a measurement. For Rocks, enterprise value is calculated by adding debt to the market value of equity, while free cash flow is defined as operating cash flow less investing cash flow. The model of enterprise value described earlier is not dissimilar to this. It has a different emphasis in that it encourages a firm to consider and evaluate all of the organisational alternatives available to it.

It is probable that a firm's shareholders will also have value objectives other than purely financial ones. The shareholders or owners may well, for example, have *legitimate, non-financial, qualitative objectives*. The rise of 'ethical' and 'green' investment funds is a recent and clear manifestation of this. It is also reflected in shareholder support of firms for regional or nationalistic reasons or other social criteria. It is suggested that these are likely, though not always, to be *secondary value objectives*. Often these play an important role in the selection of partners. The exploitation of third-world workers has led a large number of organisations to set 'conformity' criteria for their partners. These determine rates of pay and working conditions that must be adhered to if partnership arrangements are to be agreed.

The influence of shareholder value management

Shareholder value management, then, is the identification and ranking of *shareholder value objectives* and the management of value delivery processes and activities that maximise those objectives.

There are also legitimate notions of value that an enterprise should consider other than those directly related to shareholders. It has become generally accepted that business organisations have other, multiple stakeholders and that the interests of these stakeholders will in certain circumstances outweigh those of the owners of the enterprise. This is legally sanctioned in things like employment and environmental laws, under which a firm is obliged to act in a manner which is not necessarily in the best interests of the financial returns to shareholders.

This outweighing is not necessarily limited to legal obligations. For example, many gambling companies, including a lot of casinos in the more conscientious jurisdictions, have voluntarily adopted responsible gambling charters, which amongst other things allow customers to limit their wagering by self-exclusion as a means of addressing 'problem' or habitual gambling. In terms of maximising revenue and cash flow this seems odd – deliberately and voluntarily refusing to sell the firm's product to a seemingly willing customer. This is however a valid response to the various ethical and social dilemmas presented by the very nature of the operation and reflects the demands of various other stakeholders including licensing authorities and the customers themselves. That is not to say that a firm adopts and recognises such other *stakeholder value objectives* for altruistic reasons alone, but nevertheless they are real and tangible and have a cost.

This notion of a range of stakeholders other than purely the owners of the business has a longer tradition in European thinking than in the common-law world but is rapidly gaining currency. It remains likely however that such stakeholder targets in this context will also be secondary value objectives.

Stakeholder value management, then, becomes the task of identifying, ranking and realising partner objectives other than that of maximising financial returns.

It is likely that there will be tension between shareholder value objectives and stakeholder value objectives and even within each of these sets. The challenge then is to balance these differing expectations and to arrive at some overall desired *value outcome* for the firm. The primary criticism that can be levelled at most publicly listed firms is not necessarily that they do not acknowledge these varying interests, but that they avoid establishing any explicit primacy of values, let alone attempting to identify the trade-offs this necessarily implies. A firm's 'mission statement' should be a vehicle for defining desired value outcomes, but it is a question whether hard decisions are often replaced by platitudes.

In the context of public companies this is a challenge for the board of directors. It is suggested that failure to do so leads to *value confusion*, with no clear roadmap to resolve the various tensions between and within shareholder and other stakeholder expectations.

No doubt value objectives will change over time and need to respond to differing circumstances. It is hard not to conclude however that many firms are quite vague about what 'value' means to them and what their objectives are, simply because either they do not know, or cannot form a consensus, or are not brave enough to articulate what they really think. Is it really surprising that it is only perhaps one of the most visible global faces of the market economy – Coca-Cola – that lays down its value objectives in the equivalent of its mission statement in such explicit terms: 'our ultimate obligation – to provide consistently attractive returns to the owners of our business'.

Future value

Of course the simplest perspective on 'value' is that it is what the business is worth to an independent third party on a freely traded basis. In the context of a public company this is its share price.

Ballow et al. (2004) point out that a company's share price is not a simple reflection of 'the resources (assets) that traditional accounting practice handles well – monetary and physical assets– but (also) on the resources it hardly handles at all – intangible and intellectual capital', or what they term 'future value' or the expectations of future growth. They go on to suggest that 'many of the most successful companies in the US and world economy are more dependent on intangibles and intellectual capital for creating shareholder value than the old mainstays of monetary and physical resources'.

Pointing out that the notion of 'future value' can be traced to the work of Miller and Modigliani (1961), namely that expectations about the future are a component of share prices, Ballow et al. suggest that at May 2003 future value accounted for 77 per cent of market capitalisation and 59 per cent of the enterprise value of the companies on the Russell 3000, an index that covers 98 per cent of all listed US equities. Looking at market-to-book ratios, that is, how much of a company's market value can be accounted for by the traditional accounting assets on its balance sheet, Ballow et al. suggest that while these traditional accounting assets made up 80 per cent of market value 20 years ago, today they explain only 25 per cent. What is the gap? The authors suggest that it is 'intangible assets, especially those that fall under the rubric of intellectual capital', that explain much of the premium between market value and book value. This has important implications for management, the authors suggesting that:

> ... future value has never received the equal billing with current value it deserves from executives, analysts or shareholders in general. So while executives typically know everything there is to know about how the market evaluates their company's current operations, they lack an equivalent framework for assessing how the market is assessing their company's future value. And then because they tend to follow the reliable maxim of sticking to what they know, they tend to ignore what often is the most significant component of their company's value. The competency they have, managing current operations, is often not the competency they urgently need, getting a handle on future value.

The authors identify different types of resources that need to be managed. There is what are called traditional accounting measures – both monetary and physical; and there are intellectual property resources – relational, organisational and human, with all five resource types having both tangible and intangible components. Apart from purely monetary resources it is suggested that all the other resources are principally determinants of future value.

This is an interesting perspective, suggesting that while traditional accounting measures focus on today's resources, the greatest generators of value are in fact intellectual property driven generators of future value.

How do firms express value?

Finally another useful perspective may be that of how firms define 'value' themselves. In 2003 a group of MBA students at the Sydney Graduate School of Management undertook a study of a random selection of Fortune 500 companies to understand how those firms defined and measured value (Salvo et al. 2003). The study focused in particular on companies' 'mission statements' or their equivalents, on the basis that these general statements should give some indications of how a particular firm defined 'value' and what its objectives were in terms of creating that value. These 'mission statements' usually appear prominently at the front of a firm's annual report and often on its website. At least superficially, they appear to be clear statements to anyone who is interested about the firm and what it is trying to achieve.

From this study it appeared that firms tended to define their missions against four broad and somewhat overlapping categories:

Customer focus – those who defined themselves in terms of their customers or customer satisfaction:

> The Coca-Cola Company exists to benefit and refresh everyone it touches. (Coca-Cola)

> Harley Davidson's mission is to fulfil dreams through the experiences of motorcycling, by providing to motorcyclists and to the general public an expanding line of motorcycles, branded products and services in selected market segments. (Harley Davidson)

Product or market focus – those who principally defined their mission in terms of their products and the market they operate in:

> Establish Starbucks as the premier purveyor of the finest coffee in the world while maintaining our uncompromising principles while we grow. (Starbucks)

> To be the world's best quick service restaurant experience. (McDonald's)

To become the world's leading consumer company for automotive products and services. (Ford)

To bring innovation and quality to every home ... everywhere. (Whirlpool)

Company focus – more rarely, some firms defined their goals in terms of how the company itself is perceived:

To be the global energy company most admired for its people, partnerships and performance. (Chevron)

Changing themes – finally, one company at least adopted a series of themes that seemed to change year on year and were perhaps more akin to mottos:

Growth through leadership (2000)

Giving our best (2001)

Convenience, quality, service, value (2002) (Safeway)

It is interesting that nearly all the companies surveyed did recognise in some form or another some plurality of interests in their understanding of 'value'. This was usually as an addendum or qualification to their primary 'mission'. This also usually involved the explicit recognition of the interests of a series of 'stakeholders'. A good example is:

Harley Davidson is an action oriented, international company, a leader in its commitment to continuously improve its mutually beneficial relationship with stakeholders (customers, suppliers, employees, shareholders, government, and society). Harley Davidson believes that the key to success is to balance stakeholders' interests through the empowerment of all employees to focus on value-added activities. (Harley Davidson)

As noted above, the study however found very few examples where there was an explicit attempt to prioritise these interests and clearly state who came first and why. The most striking was that of Coca-Cola:

That is the key to fulfilling our ultimate obligation – to provide consistently attractive returns to the owners of our business. (Coca-Cola)

This seems curious. If the 'mission statement' is meant as a true statement of the firm's objectives some ranking or prioritisation of stakeholder interests appears hard to avoid. The reality is that the interests of different stakeholders will conflict and the firm is forced to make decisions about whose interests prevail, probably on a daily basis. It also seem curious that in the ranks of the Fortune 500 there seems, at least superficially, to be some reluctance to articulate that the primary reason that the firm exists is to generate profits for its shareholders.

It is also interesting that a significant proportion of the companies reviewed went on to qualify their 'mission statements' by elucidating what are variously called 'corporate values' or principles. These are usually far more detailed and lengthy than the actual 'mission statements'. A good example is Chevron:

> Our Company's foundation is built on our Values, which distinguish us and guide our actions. We conduct our business in a socially responsible and ethical manner. We respect the law, support universal human rights, protect the environment, and benefit the communities where we work. (Chevron)

This raises some interesting questions. It is not at all clear whether these ethical statements are indeed value objectives in their own right or simply platitudes. If they truly were part of the firm's 'mission' one would have thought that the company should quite rightly report and measure itself against them. None of the firms surveyed did so in their annual reports in any systematic manner, though no doubt many would argue it was implicit in their performance.

Indeed, the firms surveyed generally limited systematic quantitative measurement and reporting of 'value' in whatever form to the traditional reporting of financial gain encapsulated in the profit and loss statement, balance sheet and cash flow. Of course this is no doubt driven largely by legal requirements. This in itself however says something about the economic and social framework that these firms are operating in, with the primary objective of statutory reporting being the protection of those who have risked their capital in the enterprise. However, with the singular exception of Coca-Cola noted above, no one else seemed to explicitly recognise this in their 'mission statements' or equivalents.

Finally, it is evident from even a cursory examination of the 'mission statements' of the various companies studied that there is no uniformity in the terminology. For example, Ford uses the terms 'mission statement' and 'vision' as the obverse of what might be expected. Indeed, across the firms surveyed the terms 'mission statement', 'values', 'mission' and 'vision' are sometimes used interchangeably and often with shades of variation in meaning that are at best specific to their context and often not explicit at all.

Indeed, even discerning what a company's core 'mission statement' is often requires some interpretative judgement, as there are often a number of statements that potentially fill that role. Surprisingly few companies lay out things as clearly as 'The Chevron Texaco Way', with a pyramid showing 'Vision' at the top, flowing down through 'Performance', and 'People' to 'Values'.

Are these observations so surprising? The answer should be 'probably not'. The notion that there is some synthesis or holistic definition of 'value' that can be universally applied is probably wrong. The reality is that rather than defining itself in terms of some single concept of 'value', an organisation is more likely to be striving to achieve multiple outcomes, not all of which are necessarily complementary. This is reflected in the observations made in the study explored above – multiple perspectives, definitions and objectives with little comparative coherence.

The other important point is that 'value' is not a constant across organisations. For example, the value expectations in a large listed company are likely to be very different to those in a publicly owned enterprise or government department, even though in terms of some measures, such as cost budgets or number of employees, they might be of comparable size. Similarly the value expectations of a charitable organisation are likely to be very different from those of a bank.

Value propositions

Despite this inability to frame some universal concept of 'value', it remains only fair and reasonable that participants and other stakeholder audiences in an organisation have some explicit understanding of the objectives of that enterprise. No doubt this is what fostered the original attempts at framing 'mission statements'. It seems clear however that what is missing is some readily understandable template by which a firm can clearly set out its value objectives.

Clearly the *value proposition* must identify for the target customer how *customer expectations* are to be met. It should be an explicit statement of customer value attributes (both value criteria, and how acquisition costs are minimised for the customer). This will include both product or service characteristics *and* service support features. Customer expectations typically reflect availability concerns. These are not only concerns for service levels but include location and the range of intermediary or value adding resellers (VARs) that offer the product-service. The information needed has two aspects: one concerns the scope of availability and includes pricing and other product-service features, the other concerns product-service application and end-user details regarding optimal use of the product-service and the available support infrastructure.

Webster (1994) contends that positioning and the development of the value proposition must be based on an assessment of the product offering and of the firm's distinctive competencies *relative to competitors*. Hence the value proposition should make clear its *relative competitive positioning*. In doing so it should communicate to the target customer the distinctive competence portfolio of the value chain participants, demonstrating that it extends its collective skills and resources beyond the current dimensions of competitive necessity into creating competitive advantage that, in turn, offers customers an opportunity to do likewise.

A vital component of the value proposition is the part it plays in identifying the *roles and tasks of partner organisations*. Here the issue is one of communication to both partners and customers. If these roles and tasks are made explicit it serves to create credibility for the value chain in the eyes of the customers, and increases their confidence in dealing with the organisation. Various aspects should be considered. Cooperation implies an agreement within the value chain structure that an ongoing commitment to improving product-service offer and value production and delivery processes exists, and that this is prosecuted for the benefits of both customers and partners. Co-production seeks to identify where the 'production' process is most effectively conducted. The IKEA example used by Normann and Ramirez (1994) is widely published and is an excellent example of dispersed production across distributed assets to the benefit of all stakeholders. Figure 3.4 identifies the components, influences and interests of a value proposition.

Added value: the central purpose of business activity

It will be recalled from Chapter 2 that Kay (1993) introduced the concept of added value as 'the key measure of corporate success'. He defines it thus:

> Added value is the difference between the (comprehensively accounted) value of a firm's output and the (comprehensively accounted) cost of the firm's inputs. In this specific sense, adding value is both proper motivation of corporate activity and the measure of its achievement.

Kay calculates added value by subtracting from the market value of an organisation's output the cost of its inputs:

Revenues – (wages and salaries, materials, capital costs) = Added value

Added value in this context includes depreciation of capital assets and also provides for a 'reasonable' return on invested capital. Calculated this way added value is *less than* operating profit: the difference between the value of the output and the value of materials and labour inputs and capital costs. It also differs from the net output of the firm: the difference between the value of its sales and material costs (not labour or capital costs). Kay's measure of competitive advantage is the ratio of added value to the organisation's gross or net output:

Competitive advantage =
$$\frac{\text{Revenues} - (\text{Wages} + \text{Salaries} + \text{Materials} + \text{Capital costs})}{\text{Wages} + \text{Salaries} + \text{Materials} + \text{Capital costs}}$$

Such calculations are viewed as comparisons of added value to either gross or net output. Kay's added value is similar to the concept of a producer's surplus and has the additional benefit of being able to be calculated from accounting data. However, it should be said that inaccuracies are very likely if direct comparisons between organisations are made on a one-off basis. Local accounting practices differ and accounting statements therefore are not strictly comparable due to differing procedures and practices. But longitudinal comparisons are worthwhile, particularly over periods of three to five years when input/output and added value/output ratios may be compared.

Kay's model may be illustrated. Figure 3.5 depicts two possible outcomes: one, Figure 3.5a, shows a successful organisation making a positive added value (in Kay's terms, it must be remembered that added value < operating profit because the former includes a return on capital, therefore it *may not* be profitable). In Figure 3.5b the organisation represented has difficulties; wages,

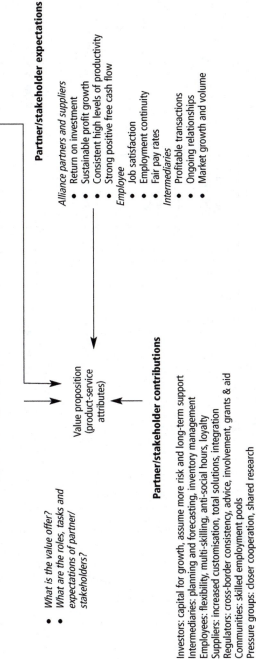

Customer contributions

- Profitable and frequent transactions
- Long-term loyalty
- Feedback – product-service delivery
  – competitive activities
  – product-service opportunities

Partner/stakeholder expectations

Alliance partners and suppliers
- Return on investment
- Sustainable profit growth
- Consistent high levels of productivity
- Strong positive free cash flow

Employee
- Job satisfaction
- Employment continuity
- Fair pay rates

Intermediaries
- Profitable transactions
- Ongoing relationships
- Market growth and volume

Customer/market offer

- Warranty & service
- Specification 'fit'
- 'Style' & appearance
- Time & location availability
- Life cycle cost/performance/price
- Maintenance period downtime –
- Replacement of major component

Value proposition (product-service attributes)

- *What is the value offer?*
- *What are the roles, tasks and expectations of partner/stakeholders?*

Partner/stakeholder contributions

- Investors: capital for growth, assume more risk and long-term support
- Intermediaries: planning and forecasting, inventory management
- Employees: flexibility, multi-skilling, anti-social hours, loyalty
- Suppliers: increased customisation, total solutions, integration
- Regulators: cross-border consistency, advice, involvement, grants & aid
- Communities: skilled employment pools
- Pressure groups: closer cooperation, shared research
- Alliance partners: co-development, co-productivity, shared information and shared costs

Figure 3.4 Developing a value proposition

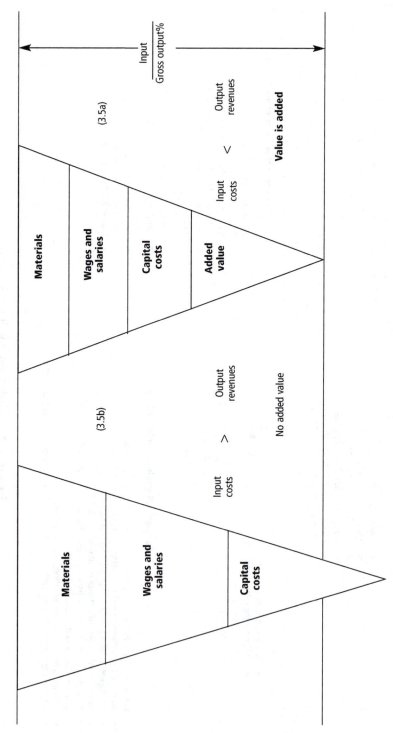

Figure 3.5 Kay's added value perspective
Source: adapted from Kay (1993).

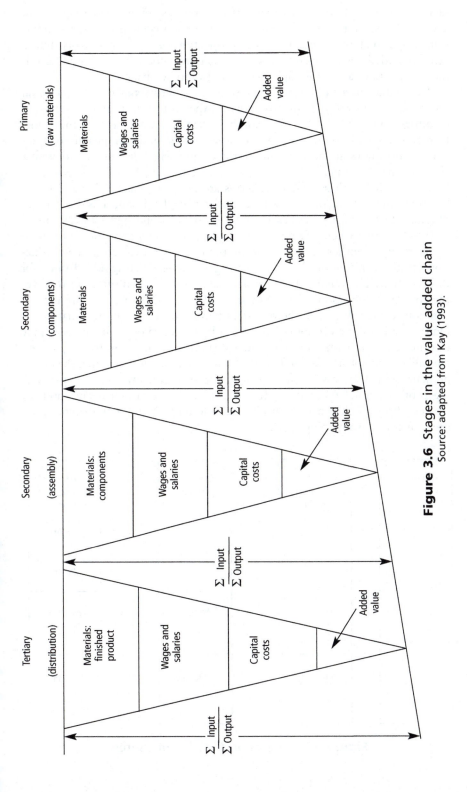

Figure 3.6 Stages in the value added chain
Source: adapted from Kay (1993).

salaries and capital costs are greater than revenues. Figure 3.6 suggests the added value structure of a value chain. At the raw materials (primary production) stage, materials costs are a low proportion of total input costs, but as value is added by successive processes, materials costs become significantly more important, as do the capital costs of inventory financing.

A potential source of error is confusion of the terms *added value* and *value added*. Value added is the principal basis of expenditure taxation in a number of countries. Value added is therefore not the same thing as added value, the former being the difference between the value of the material and semi-produced inputs which a firm buys in and the value of the output which it sells. It is therefore equal to the firm's net output. Added value is only a part of value added, as Figure 3.7 makes clear. Often the terms are used interchangeably and this is incorrect. In this book our interest is exclusively in added value: it is this concept of value which the firm searches for and tries to create and appropriate for itself.

It follows that when a firm is generating *economic profit* (considered here to be operating profit less a charge for the use of capital involved in the production of the operating profit), it is creating and appropriating added value for this coalition. The value of the sales generated is more than sufficient to cover the cost of all the resources used by the collective. This surplus represents an addition to the value of all the resources tied up in the coalition. What determines whether these economic profits can be sustained over time is the supply of other entrepreneurs that, spotting the success of an innovator or pioneer, are willing and able to cooperate with them. To put it another way, if the entrepreneur's initial success is easy for others to reproduce, any success in generating profit cannot be sustained. To the extent that a particular entrepreneur creates a firm which generates profits over a longish period then the enterprise itself must have something special.

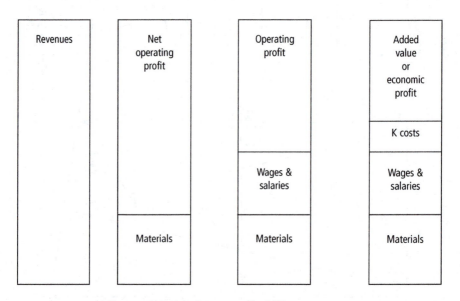

Figure 3.7 Various profitability measures

Added value and the producer surplus

However, this does not satisfactorily explain the organisation's perspective of value. The economist offers us the *producer surplus* to explain profitability. Johansson (1991) uses the welfare economics concept of the excess of revenue over total variable cost (quasi-rent) to identify short-term profit. It is agreed that quasi-rent is a 'rent' on fixed factors of production that may not persist over a long period of time since all factors are variable in the long run. The producer surplus may be increased by reducing costs in the short run or increasing the perceived consumer surplus (through marketing activities), both resulting in increased profitability either by increasing operating margin or by expanding volume and market share. An alternative is to increase the price of the product to identifiable customers who are prepared to accept a higher price for additional benefits. The welfare economists' argument is essentially an aggregate view and does not extend comfortably into segmented markets. Furthermore, if value is to be defined in a strategic context it should be capable of measurement and comparison; these issues are considered subsequently.

In Figure 3.8 it is assumed that customer satisfaction is maximised and consumer value is being delivered. The vendor organisation, if it is to meet its stakeholders' objectives, should now focus on increasing productivity. In Figure 3.8 the increase in producer surplus is illustrated by lowering the costs of supply (the total variable costs) from S1 to S2. This may be achieved a number of ways, none of which are exclusive. For example, specialist partners may be used; the automotive manufacturing industry is an example. A larger plant may have been designed and built because superior market knowledge suggested large growth potential, or again, using foresight, technology management configured a combination of capital equipment to meet both scale and scope economies. Another strategy to enhance productivity is through integrated operations such as co-productivity, defined as a 'producer' strategy trade-off that negotiates supplier and customer involvement in the 'production and distribution processes; in this instance, the materials or component supplier and/or the customer undertake to complete these processes 'at a price or cost' concession. The strategy of IKEA, whereby the IKEA supplier, IKEA itself, and the IKEA customer are all involved in manufacturing and logistics activities is an example of a co-productivity strategy.

Alternatively, packaging design may consider downstream activities within the distribution network, such as the innovation shown by Marks & Spencer's floral packaging that ensures flowers remain fresh throughout distribution and is only removed at the 'point of consumption'. Fast-food retailers have developed packaging systems that retain the heat of their contents during delivery. In markets that are dominated by resellers, for instance the fast moving consumer goods (FMCG) market in Australia, the economies of location are important contributors to the producer surplus. An example of this is the location of retail outlets by socio-demographic economics (identifying not only the volume/age-significant segments but also those based on disposable income and expenditure patterns). The other

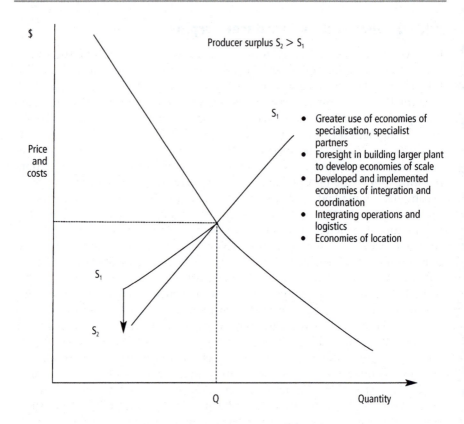

Figure 3.8 Identifying the producer surplus

aspect of the economies of location is the extent to which strong retailers 'influence' suppliers' facilities location strategies, often insisting they are within a specified distance of the retailers' regional distribution centres.

Both concepts can be used. The consumer surplus, together with price, combines to deliver customer value-in-use. The strategy implications here are for an organisation to develop strong customer links and to work with customers in developing products that are 'customised' to meet customer needs more specifically than those of competitors, using communications programs that identify benefits available rather than non-specific claims. Specific life cycle productivity performance and service support packages are also relevant. The vendor organisation should aim to ensure that his target market is satisfied with the use value delivered and structure the production, logistics and service organisation to meet the price acceptable to the customer and ensure an adequate return to the stakeholders, that is, the employees, suppliers, shareholders and distributor organisations. See Figure 3.9.

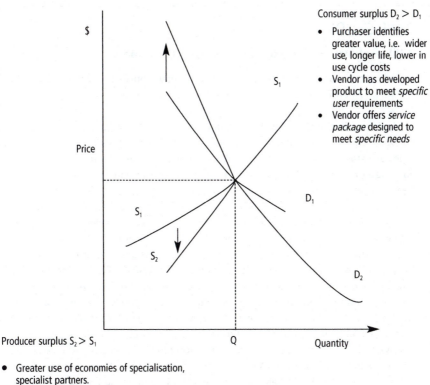

Consumer surplus $D_2 > D_1$

- Purchaser identifies greater value, i.e. wider use, longer life, lower in use cycle costs
- Vendor has developed product to meet *specific user* requirements
- Vendor offers *service package* designed to meet *specific needs*

Producer surplus $S_2 > S_1$

- Greater use of economies of specialisation, specialist partners.
- Foresight in building larger plant to develop economies of scale
- Developed and implemented economies of integration and coordination
- Integrating operations and logistics
- Economies of location

Figure 3.9 Integrating the consumer and producer surplus to realise customer added value *and* stakeholder value expectations

Concluding comments

This chapter has considered the changing view that business organisations have taken of the concept of value. Of particular importance is the view that the value of the business should be based upon the NPV of its free cash flow, in other words an objective assessment of its forecast revenues and costs discounted at a rate that reflects its realistic cost of capital. Knight and Pretty's (2000) contribution is useful because it can be used to explore alternative organisational structures that may introduce 'optimal structures' which move towards maximum cash flow at minimum weighted average costs of capital.

The introduction of the economic concepts of consumer and producer surpluses explores the organisational options open to the firm if it considers moving towards the multi-enterprise 'new economy' business models.

CASE STUDY 3.1

'Stakeholders' = Shareholders + Staff + Customers

(Based upon 'Banks need to keep the customer satisfied', Andrew Cornell, *Australian Financial Review*, 12 December 2005)

'Financial institutions, particularly the big banks, have belatedly begun to pay a lot of attention to the feelings of "stakeholders" – not just shareholders but especially staff and customers.' Cornell makes this comment after a recent strategy presentation by a major Australian bank concerning the neglecting of customers and business segments.

The major banks boast of a high level of staff satisfaction (employee engagement); some are better at it than others. Cornell quotes a comment by Macquarie Research that 'although often considered a "pink and fluffy" topic, employee engagement scores correlate highly with total shareholder returns'. He adds: 'Despite 1½ years of cultural change, NAB's (National Australia Bank) scores remain seriously low [NAB's 39 per cent score is well behind the ANZ (Australia New Zealand) consumer bank's high-performing 64 per cent]. Back of the envelope, the employee engagement differential against ANZ is costing NAB Australia additional profits of $A28.5 million per year.' Cornell further suggests that despite the not inconsiderable expenditures on customer relationship management (CRM) technology using tools such as CommSee, the banks remain 'unable to understand their customers' psychology'. Cornell makes an important point by suggesting that 'after a period of improvement, customer satisfaction is turning back down in the industry', and that this should cause concern as the new, non-bank competition continues to grow. He points to the rapid growth of mortgage lending 'by a new breed of mortgage originators' whose offer was a simplistic 'we'll save you from the banks'. His point here is that while the new competition offered a price advantage, the consumer picked up on being saved from the banks!

Cornell considers comments by David McKinna, a marketing and strategy consultant, who argues that many of Australia's large 'service' companies 'have a very sizeable rump of disgruntled customers who in the right circumstances would leave'. He labels this group the '*grudge customer* – someone who begrudgingly stays with a company or service even though they are demonstrably dissatisfied with the offering'. McKinna suggests that grudge customers occur in markets where there are two or three major providers dominating market share such as banks, the two big supermarket operators, airlines, telecommunications and others. McKinna estimates that in a number of industries grudge customers can represent up to 30 per cent of the customer base and most would change if they could be sure of a better alternative. He suggests that many stay 'because the cost and degree of difficulty in switching is too high ... they believe that there is no real alternative and that they risk being no better off after all the bother'. Cornell suggests the banks are not aware of this, pointing towards a half hearted attempt by ANZ to make it easier to switch banks. He also suggests that the Macquarie research shows customers are persuaded more by service and convenience than by price, a view confirmed by ANZ who suggest that only 20 to 30 per cent of customers are price driven. Cornell concludes: 'So price might not be enough to budge grudge customers, nor, indeed, perceptions of service ... But it would be a brave bank that continued to let customer satisfaction and staff engagement slide – with the lesson of how quickly great slabs of the customer base can disappear given the right conflation of circumstances.'

Discussion topics

What are the important aspects of any model that attempts to profile or map customers' decision making processes?

There is an implicit argument made here for the application of a customer value model that incorporates those aspects of an organisation's operations that can show an impact on cash flow or profitability. Identify a model (or models) from this part of the text that could prove to be helpful in this task.

REFERENCES

Ballow J, R Burgman, G Roos and M Molnar (2004) *A New Paradigm for Managing Shareholder Value*, Accenture Institute for Higher Performance Business, Wellesley, MA.

Copeland, T, T Koller and J Murrin (1994) *Valuation: Measuring and Managing the Value of Companies*, 2nd edition, Wiley, New York

Ellis J (1999) *Doing Business in the Knowledge Based Economy*, Pearson Education, Harlow

Eyers J (2004) 'P/E tool not sharp enough, say experts', *Australian Financial Review*, 18 September

Johansson P O (1991) *An Introduction to Modern Welfare Economics*, Cambridge University Press, Cambridge

Kay J (1993) *Foundation of Corporate Success*, Oxford University Press, Oxford

Knight R and D Pretty (2000) 'Philosophies of risk, shareholder value and the CEO', *Financial Times*, 27 June

Miller M and F Modigliani (1961) 'Dividend policy, growth and the valuation of shares', *Journal of Business*, 34

Normann R and R Ramirez (1994) *Designing Interactive Strategy: From Value Chain to Value Constellation*, Wiley, New York

Rappaport A (1983) 'Corporate performance standards and shareholder value', *Journal of Business Strategy*, Spring

Reimann M (1989) *Managing for Value: A New Standard for Business Performance*, Free Press, New York

Salvo L, E Vinod, S Chauhari, S Jovic and J Canoquena (2003) 'Analysis of value interpretations at the top', unpublished research report, Sydney Graduate School of Management, June

Uren D (2001) 'To winners go more spoils in rivalry tango', *Australian*, 10 March

Webster F E (1994) *Market Driven Management*, Wiley, New York

CHAPTER 4

Practical Issues and Applications

LEARNING TOPICS

On completing your study of this chapter you will have been introduced to and considered the following topics:

■ Value drivers and value builders; practical issues
■ Effectiveness and efficiency issues in value delivery
■ Mass customisation and product platforms; 'new economy' methods of increasing added value

Introduction

The preceding chapters introduced the concept of value and considered both customer and organisational perspectives of value. It is important now to address questions concerning how value can be created and delivered. The topic has two aspects. One concerns the individual organisation, and the other, as the following quotation from AeIGT (2003) suggests, concerns the industry structure that will be marshalled to implement value delivery:

> The nature of UK Aerospace Industry 2022 will have changed considerably, driven primarily by globalisation. The business model of the future will be value chain competing against value chain, not just single company versus single company as we witness predominantly today. Supply chains will have evolved to include the end-user or consumer in value creation and through this will have become known as value chains.

For this reason we must concern ourselves with the topics of value drivers and value builders from customer and 'supplier' perspectives. This chapter considers these issues and continues by reviewing contemporary value delivery systems.

Value drivers and value builders

Phelps (2004) considers value drivers and builders from the perspective of the organisation. Under the topic of identifying value drivers, he begins by asking, 'What drives value in your business? Who are the competitors? What are the characteristics of the market?' He suggests there are no generic answers or prescriptions; one company may derive the greatest value from improving brand image while another may do so by improving its recruitment policies.

According to Phelps, identifying value builders 'gives the ability to take advantage of risks and opportunities as they arise'. The author suggests organisations take a strategic perspective by identifying potential market developments and then addressing the scenarios with 'positioning decisions' (in other words, they develop ownership or access to processes and capabilities) that will enable the organisation to move rapidly into an opportunity.

Phelps' suggestions are in fact, equally applicable to the value producer and the value consumer. Examples of Phelps' value drivers and builders are:

- *Value drivers* include things like asset utilisation, bad debt ratio, supplier costs, market share, employee motivation levels, staffing flexibility, location of business units, market communications effectiveness, and brand equity. Value drivers are measured by EVA (economic value added), return on investment (ROI) and profit.

- *Value builders* are based upon *positional characteristics* (strategy, investment levels, and partnerships) and on *capabilities* (management quality, understanding customer trends, ability to make changes, key staff attraction and retention, organisational culture and the level of innovation within the organisation). Value builders are measured by future growth value (the NPV of free cash flow), survivability, opportunities and risk.

Phelps contends there is a structure of linkages between value drivers and value builders and between present value being generated and future value being built.

Customer-centricity and the increasing attractiveness of a virtual organisation approach accompanying the 'new economy' suggest a broader approach to both value drivers and value builders. Clearly both are important to the individual firm in evaluating its strategic opportunities. However, as Figure 4.1 suggests, an introspective view alone is not sufficient; account needs to be taken of a partnership structure of collaborating firms. The linkages suggested by Phelps are retained but the notion of a series of *value processes* is included and these are not necessarily 'owned' by just one organisation but rather evolve from an evaluation of the current and future opportunities and risks identified in the market. To this extent the appropriate value drivers and value builders need to be evaluated not just in the context of a single organisation, but in the context of the whole value chain.

Figure 4.1 then suggests a broader approach than that taken by Phelps. The organisational value builders are expanded to include partners and the emphasis on value drivers and builders is *customer led*. This has important implications. We

Planned growth

- Enterprise value ● Returns spread
- Share of market added value

Organisational value drivers

- Free cash flow
- Asset utilisation
- Share of market added value
- ROCE/ROAM spread
- Asset intensity

- Value chain positioning
- Market positioning
- Alliance(s) 'fit'
- Customer response loyalty

'Organisational' value builders

- Free cash flow
- Development of capabilities
- Development of processes
- Develop relevant and productive asset portfolio
- Targeted asset intensity
- Target operating cycle
- Target cash/cash cycle time
- Customer QC performance expectations

- Value chain positioning
- Market positioning
- Adaptive organisational architecture
- Strategic alliance(s) 'fit'
- Continued (extended) customer response loyalty

Customer value builders

- Meet changing requirements for customer 'positioning' enhancement
- Develop value chain loyalty relationships that encourage increased comprehensive cooperation & commitment
- Enhance customers' 'shareholder value' management
- Monitor 'value migration' & explore partner/ customer opportunities to increase share of market added value

Customer value delivery facilitators

Value chain positioning based upon:

- Co-destiny
- Co-specialisation
- Co- productivity
- Co-ompetition
- Collaboration

Value processes

- Identify the value
- Create the value
- Produce the value
- Communicate the value
- Deliver the value
- Service the value

Customer value drivers

Customer-centricity based upon:

- Asset productivity management
- Time management
- Performance management
- Cost management
- Information management
- Risk management

Figure 4.1 Adding delivery and organisational value builders for growth

would argue that these value drivers and value builders need to be initially understood and evaluated from two important perspectives. First, from a *feasibility perspective* (customer acceptance – the value proposed meets customers' expectations); second, from a *viability perspective* (the outcome is acceptable to the shareholders/stakeholders – it is 'deliverable' and their value expectations can be met). Unless both can be satisfied then there is little to be gained.

Another difference that can be seen is the inclusion of *customer value delivery facilitators*. These are alternative value delivery system structures. They determine the structure of the value chain or virtual organisation that results. This also implies that organisational value drivers and builders are derived from customer research and an agreement – explicit or implicit – reached within the partnership structure that develops.

Effectiveness and efficiency issues in value delivery

As disposable income increases, there tends to be an increased spectrum of choice available to the consumer so that expectations also change to include variety and immediacy in demand satisfaction. Simply put, the greater the ability to choose, the greater variety of choices the consumer is likely to demand.

A partial response to customer expectations for 'individualised/customised' product-services has been *mass customisation*. Through the application of 'new technology' (computer based design and manufacturing) together with new approaches to management, an alternative paradigm is emerging. Here the objective is to 'deliver' affordable products and services with sufficient variety and customisation such that nearly everyone finds exactly what they want. This differs markedly from the proposition offered by *mass production*, with its slogan, 'nearly everyone can afford them', best exemplified by the classic Model T Ford being available in every colour as long as it was black.

Pine (1993) offers a logic for mass customisation. Unstable demand for specific products results in market fragmentation; product variety becomes an essential feature of customer satisfaction. Homogeneous markets become heterogeneous. Niches become important. Manufacturers move into specific niches with a view to meeting specified and feasible customer requirements, typically through post-production methods. This is not profitable, and production systems change. Initially the requirements were for shorter production runs accompanied by expensive loss of production time and 'set-ups'. However, niche customers accept premium prices that compensate manufacturers. Experience eventually enables production costs to be reduced and product variety is achieved at the same, or even lower, costs. Varying consumer demand requires a rapid time-to-market response with shorter product development cycles, which in turn result in shorter product life cycles. Demand fragments but individual producers find stability in their operations with selected niche segments. Porter (1996) comments:

A company can outperform rivals only if it can establish a difference that it can preserve. It must deliver greater value to customers or create comparable value at lower cost or do both. The arithmetic of superior profitability then follows: delivering greater value allows a company to charge higher average unit prices; greater efficiency results in lower average costs.

These comments can be represented diagrammatically, see Figure 4.2. Porter added, following a lead by Skinner (1986) that:

> [competitive strategy] ... is about being different ... the essence of strategy is in the activities – choosing to perform activities differently or to perform different activities to rivals.

Porter was arguing that for too many organisations the temptation simply to pursue cost reduction strategies was an easier option than making an effort to understand customer expectations, research their value drivers and to offer a range of products or services that they respond to. Figure 4.1 suggests there is an endless range of options.

However, the reality of production economics is that an infinite choice of product characteristics and price combinations is not only unrealistic, but economically impossible to deliver. It follows that some segmentation of the available market is required. Figure 4.3 offers a range of alternative 'value positions' and emphasises the need to be precise concerning customer segments and the specific value response that eventuates. Mathur and Kenyon's (1997) research suggests that care should be taken in deciding upon a specific position

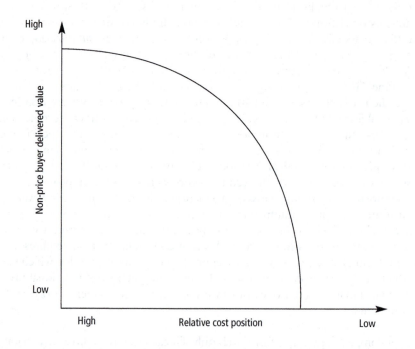

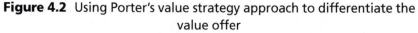

Figure 4.2 Using Porter's value strategy approach to differentiate the value offer

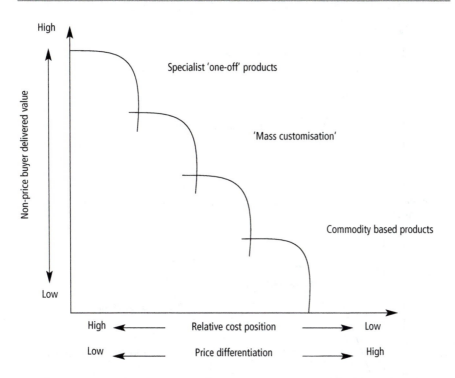

Figure 4.3 Using Porter's value strategy approach to identify value strategy options

by offering evidence of overdifferentiation and differentiation directed towards competitive response rather than as a specific customer response.

A 'new economy' solution: mass customisation and product platforms

An effective *mass customisation strategy* is indicated by Figure 4.4. It suggests that an attempt be made to identify a segment of the market where many of the non-price product characteristics are acceptable to a large proportion of the target customer base and the price selected presents few if any obstacles. Research for a durables manufacturer, by one of the authors, established that for products that offered a wide range of features, typically the range actually used was remarkably narrow. It follows that user research can identify these and the designer should focus on them as a means of effective differentiation.

The benefits of adopting a mass customisation strategy can be seen in Figure 4.5. The diagram suggests that operational costs are reduced and the value delivered is focused, because mass customisation encourages the application of *relevant operational processes and technology*, thereby containing costs.

A response to mass customisation has been found in the concept of *product platforms*. Product platforms are well known and the application of the concept first introduced by Black and Decker has expanded across a number of industries.

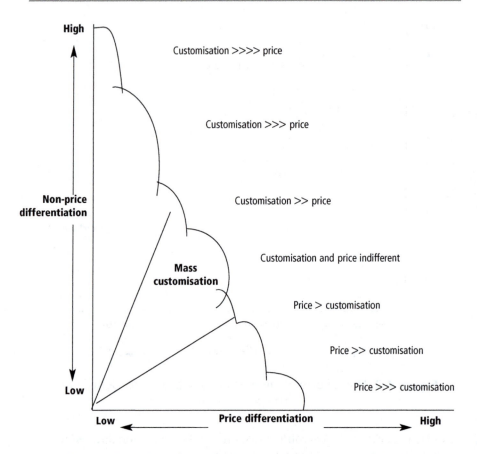

Figure 4.4 Identifying the options for mass customisation

A skilful approach to the concept can reap benefits of economies of scale, economies of differentiation and economies of integration. Meyer and Lehnerd (1997) describe the role and the importance of product platforms in the strategic planning of an organisation:

> They know they must generate a continuous stream of value-rich products that target growth markets. Such products form the product family, individual products that share common technology and address related market applications. It is those families that account for the long-term success of corporations.
>
> Product families do not have to emerge one product at a time. In fact, they are planned so that so that a number of derivative products can be efficiently created from the foundation of common core technology. We call this foundation of core technology the 'product platform', which is a set of subsystems and interfaces that form a common structure from which a stream of derivative products can be efficiently developed and produced.

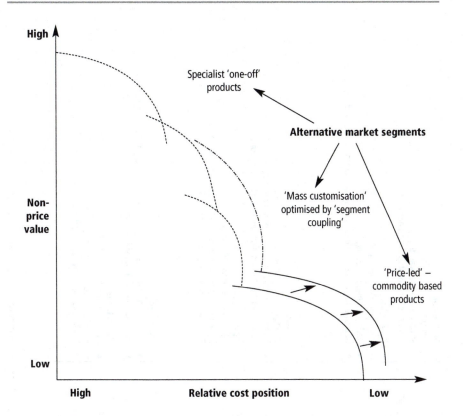

Figure 4.5 Operational costs are reduced as the value delivered remains is focused with mass customisation

The authors argue that the approach dramatically reduces costs in procurement and manufacturing, because so many costs are amortised across the product range. Furthermore, the 'building blocks' of product platforms can be integrated with *new* components to address new market opportunities rapidly. Hence, *time-to-market*, an important value driver and competitive advantage feature, can also be developed. Product platforms must be managed. Failure to monitor the development of customer expectations *and* to use developments in related technology implies that such derivatives as do emerge will fail 'customers in terms of function and value'.

Grant and Schlesinger (1995) suggest the need for the organisation to review and, if necessary, modify its processes (and structures) to meet a changing market place. In doing so the organisation acknowledges that customer expectations differ (and also that competitors may be active within specific value based segments of interest to the company). As a result both marketing and operations structures will differ depending upon which segment is targeted. Figure 4.6 illustrates possible differences that may be encountered. It identifies the necessity to consider addressing opportunities from a partnership base, because some of the organisational requirements do not exist within the

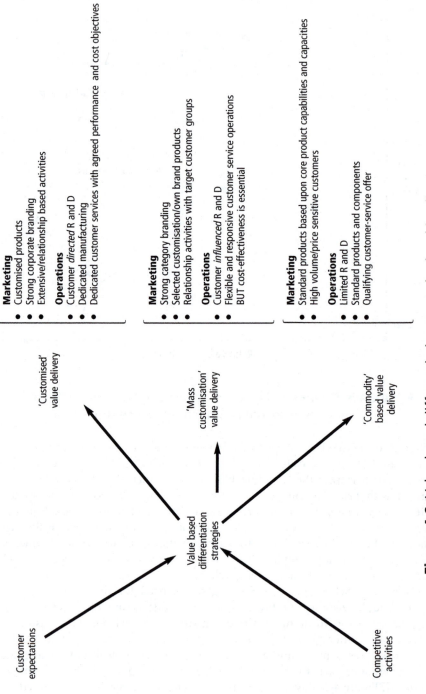

Marketing
- Customised products
- Strong corporate branding
- Extensive/relationship based activities

Operations
- Customer *directed* R and D
- Dedicated manufacturing
- Dedicated customer services with agreed performance and cost objectives

Marketing
- Strong category branding
- Selected customisation/own brand products
- Relationship activities with target customer groups

Operations
- Customer *influenced* R and D
- Flexible and responsive customer service operations
- BUT cost-effectiveness is essential

Marketing
- Standard products based upon core product capabilities and capacities
- High volume/price sensitive customers

Operations
- Limited R and D
- Standard products and components
- Qualifying customer-service offer

'Customised' value delivery

'Mass customisation' value delivery

'Commodity' based value delivery

Value based differentiation strategies

Customer expectations

Competitive activities

Figure 4.6 Value based differentiation: organisational implications

organisation. Furthermore, as markets become integrated, it is the view of Slywotzky and Morrison (1997) that value activities are sequential and that many structural elements have significance throughout the value chain process. Consequently organisation structure issues should be considered from both upstream and downstream perspectives.

Market applications identify the range of market segments and price points that define the scope of market opportunity. The concept of the product platform suggests that while it may not be economically feasible to pursue each cell in the market segment matrix at one time, by using an incremental and integrative approach it may become possible. *Product platforms*, as already established, are the set of subsystems and interfaces that form a common structure for the cost-effective development of a stream of derivative products. For Meyer and Lehnerd the *common building blocks* comprise consumer insights, product technologies, manufacturing processes and organisational capabilities.

Product platforms offer a solution to the problems posed by mass customisation. Figure 4.7 identifies notable differences across market segments, and provided these can be identified in such a way that the important features that appeal to customers can be used for product differentiation (competitive advantage), it is possible to consider the 'necessities' as base product platforms. For example, in the automotive industry the 'customisation' features may include interior finish, in-car entertainment and optional accessories such as ground position indicator (GPI) equipment. The necessities are the engine,

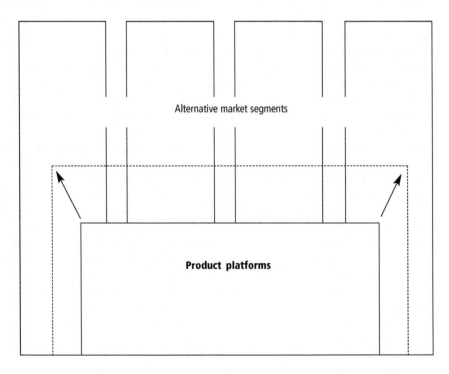

Figure 4.7 Using product platforms to contain the costs of customer choice

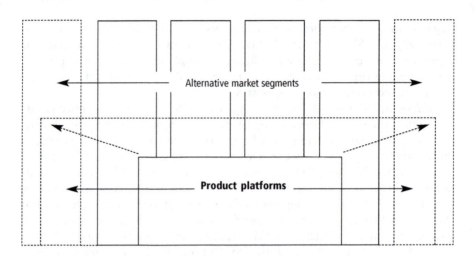

Figure 4.8 Using product platforms to expand the product range

transmission, braking system and features not typically 'seen' by the purchaser – they are assumed to be there but are not critical in the purchase decision. This also suggests that costs can be reduced by effective research into customers' preferences and their 'indifferences'. Figure 4.8 indicates another benefit. Here the concept offers an opportunity to expand the product range. Black and Decker (see Meyer and Lehnerd 1997) added a range of product applications to their product range simply by thinking through the range of applications that their end-user customers were likely to undertake. As a result the base platforms were designed with product range development as a long-term objective.

Clearly markets differ, and the range of differentiation (and hence the opportunities for mass customisation) also differs. In Figure 4.9 this situation is explored. It is an important issue to be considered when planning market entries and highlights the benefits that may be obtainable by considering the value chain (virtual organisation) alternatives. The example offered by Figure 4.9a suggests a much differentiated market, one in which the opportunity to apply the platform concept is limited if it is assumed that it can be implemented using *only the design and production facilities of the one organisation*. In Figure 4.9b the market is very different. It offers less differentiation, and although competition may be fiercely price-competitive the platform concept does offer the opportunity to identify areas of 'cost-sensitivity' that may be reduced in importance by applying the platform concept to the problem.

Product platforms may also be considered to be 'value platforms'. Figure 4.10 indicates how an automobile manufacturer may regard the automobile market. The initial design and development task is to identify the critical value drivers for each segment (the competitive advantage features) and ensure these are explicit in the value proposition that eventuates. The second task is to design the 'competitive necessities' such that they have *applicability* across the entire product range. By pursuing such a design and development strategy the organisation

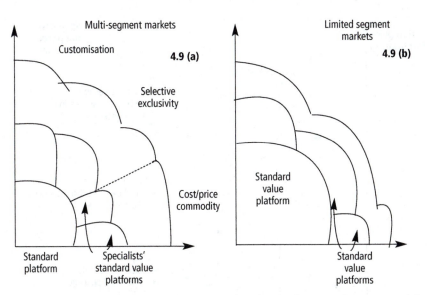

Ideally an organisation will prefer to pursue a limited number of product platforms. In this way cost economies will be maximised. But if they are pursued beyond a point at which any further exploitation is likely to meet with customer resistance because of the lack of customer expected differentiation the organisation must adopt an alternative strategy. The solution is to identify the limit to which a 'standard' production platform may be used and then seek partners with specialist expertise. The automotive industry is an example. Ford Motor Company has a number of major brands Jaguar, Land Rover, Volvo, Aston Martin as well as the existing Ford groups. It operates a platform strategy up to a point where customers begin to perceive value similarities. At this point they are no longer able to extend the application of the platforms and seek to add partners to add the differentiation important to customers.

With markets that demonstrate few segment variations the opportunity to expand the application of a standard value production platform is possible. The use of specific partners who can contribute expertise adds the necessary differentiation but the costs are contained at competitive levels due to the effects of the economies achieved with the initial design of the business model. This structure is typical of 'generic' product-markets, such as food and drink, in which segment volumes vary. The difficulty is to maintain productivity in the filling processes. Often the solution is resolved by using a specialist partner. In this instance the platforms are process based, having cost (and therefore price and competitiveness) implications.

Figure 4.9 Strategic market differentiation and value platforms – developing the economics of integration

can offer a product range that has *both* differentiation *and* price appeal. Figure 4.10 identifies the primary customer expectations of time, performance, and cost and risk management and interprets these as vendor responses.

A broader view of the product platform concept, one less focused on the existing business sector, would consider the relevant developments in knowledge, technology, relationship and process management. The growth of partnership and alliance agreements (as well as technology) is making collaboration between the most unlikely partners an everyday occurrence. An additional feature has been included: that of the *value proposition*. It is very clear from the preceding

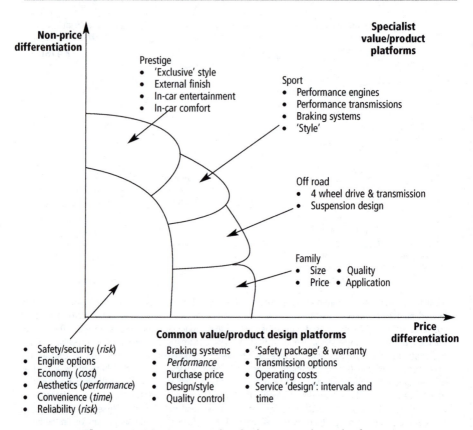

Figure 4.10 Automotive industry 'value platforms'

section that the customer is playing an important role in product specification and development (Toffler's *prosumer* in his 1980). Accordingly it is suggested that customer involvement in the overall process is becoming the norm, rather than an exception. Furthermore, not only does the value proposition reflect the nature of the overall response to the customer, but it also serves the purpose of communicating the roles and tasks agreed by the 'organisation'.

Kim and Mauborgne (1997) offer help here. The authors are offering a value based perspective for planning strategic growth. The process involves identifying customer expectations *and* perceptions, in other words, the consumer surplus. They contend:

> Companies that follow the logic of value innovation free up their resources to identify and deliver completely new sources of value. Ironically, value innovators do not set out to build advantages over the competition, but they end up achieving the greatest competitive advantages.

Kim and Mauborgne identify a *value innovation* logic which is focused on a target customer group, 'in terms of the total solution customers seek, even if that takes the company beyond its industry's traditional offerings'. In a very detailed case history based upon the French hotel group, Accor, they describe the *value innovation process*. Central to this process is a *value curve* that is derived from answers to four questions:

- Which of the value factors that our industry takes for granted should be eliminated, or does the industry actually deliver value to its customers?
- Which value factors should be reduced well below the industry's standard? Are there features offered which aim to be competitive as far as the competitors are concerned rather than arising from customer concern?
- Which value factors should be raised well above the industry's standard? Are there compromises forced upon the customers, some of which they may not wish to make?
- Which value factors should be created that have never been offered by the industry? What are the new sources of value that the changing customer dynamics are identifying?

In their case study Kim and Mauborgne describe the research undertaken by Accor to identify customer perceptions of the relative importance of features, or elements of service, of a hotel. The result is a 'plot' of the features ranked by the target customers to identify what they need most and what they can do without. Thus the result is that at a specific price the customer is given much more of what they need and much less of what they are willing to do without. It follows that Accor are qualifying the features of the consumer surplus and ensuring that for a specific target customer group the 'price plus consumer value' is maximising value-in-use for the customer. We shall return to this model later in the book.

Grant and Schlesinger (1995) discuss the concept of *value exchange* in which:

> ... companies can now optimise what we call the value exchange: the relationship between the financial investment a company makes in particular customer relationships and the return that customers generate by the specific way they choose to respond to the company's offering.

The authors are describing the successful customer loyalty programs operated by Tesco and Sainsbury's (in the UK) that are now widespread. The authors suggest that value exchange programs are not based upon last year's figures or market share. Rather they ask three very important questions:

- What percentage of target customers is currently sold to? What percentage could this be?
- What is the 'current customer' purchasing pattern? What would be the impact on revenues if their average expenditures were across the entire range or increased by a specific percentage?
- What is the average life span of an 'average' customer? What would be the financial implications for the company if the life span could be extended?

The *value exchange* approach suggested by Grant and Schlesinger offers an opportunity to develop a model in which both customers' value-in-use interests and the development of 'exchange value' may be considered and, where necessary, explored for trade-off potential among customers, suppliers and (if appropriate) a distributor network. The value exchange model identifies use value (or value-in-use) components as product value delivered, product support services value, the product transaction/ownership process, and price. The exchange value components are positioning, investment management, operational processes and organisational alignment.

In Figure 4.11 these components are expanded and value strategy responses are added. Each of these will be dealt with in detail in subsequent chapters; at this juncture it is important to identify the basic components and the basis of the response. It will be noticed that Figure 4.11 suggests that a trade-off of one or more components may occur. This is possible in the structure of new business-to-business, business-to-consumer organisational relationships. We also have the 'prosumer' concept (customer involvement in design and production) and that of 'co-productivity', whereby production and distribution processes can occur downstream (by customers rather than suppliers) in exchange for price or other benefit considerations. IKEA is an example of how this concept can be made to work successfully. Essentially the value strategy response comprises identifying value expectations (within the target customer group); identifying the competences and resources required, the alternative delivery processes, structures and capital considerations; creating the value; delivering the value, and servicing the value.

Concluding comments

This chapter has considered the need for organisations to be progressive in their approach to identifying customers' current and future expectations. As an example of how diverging customer expectations are being addressed by 'new economy' businesses, we have explored the strategic issues, and the operational implications of product platforms, and pointed to their application in both the automotive industry and in a similar way in the hospitality industry. Product platforms are becoming increasingly common in relation to service products. Financial services companies are creating product differentiation by using their basic products as core products to which additional features can be added – often these are provided by partner companies.

CASE STUDY 4.1

Product platforms and mass customisation: a platform too far?

(Based upon Robert Wilson, 'VW bones under Audi skin', *Australian*, 20 April 2005, and Chris Wright, 'The parts add up to more than the car', *Weekend Australian Financial Review*, 22–25 April 2005)

Developments in manufacturing have resulted in improving the ability of automobile manufacturers to offer selective differentiation to car purchasers. 'Mass customisation'

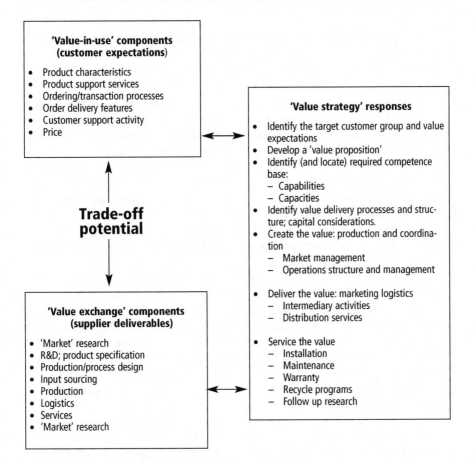

Figure 4.11 The value exchange process

replaced mass production in both a manufacturing operations context and marketing as a value proposition. Customer expectations have been influenced by increasing disposable incomes and the ability to reduce response time when meeting customer orders. As a result 'choice' and 'immediacy' are dominant characteristics as customer value drivers and as responses in the vendor's value proposition. Hence we can define mass customisation as 'a customer based process that offers *most customers most of the product-service features they seek at a competitive price* and doing so within acceptable cost limitations for the vendor'. Product platform design techniques and platform sharing have become commonplace and are practised with varying capability (and creativity) by competing organisations.

The concentration of ownership of marques and brands in the automotive industry, reinforced by strategic and operational alliances and partnerships, has facilitated the application of platform sharing, as a review of ownership patterns among some of the major global companies illustrates. For example, Ford owns Jaguar, Volvo, Aston Martin, and Land Rover, together with the Ford branded range of products. The company also has financial/investment interests in Mazda, which provides Ford with influence and control in design and development and in procurement and production. The General Motors group of companies and brands comprises Holden, Vauxhall, Opel, Buick, and Chevrolet together with parts of Suzuki, and, until recently a very large share in Fiat. VW owns Audi and Skoda and Lamborghini. Add to these a number of development, procurement and manufacturing alliances and it is not difficult to understand how both cost sharing and platform sharing can be used to meet both customer and shareholder performance expectations.

A recent road test report by Robert Wilson argues that VW/Audi have taken platform sharing too far with the comment: 'Platform sharing ... is the house speciality at VW, Audi's parent company. Its motto seems to be 'never waste a good design by marketing under only one badge'. Wilson then makes comparisons between the Audi A3 and the VW Golf, arguing or asking, '... does this commonality make the Audi A3 Sportback an overpriced VW Golf or is the Golf a bargain Audi? That's the $A9000 (or thereabouts, depending on the model, question.'

Wilson then identifies both similarities and differences. For example, the vehicles have a range of six engine options, with two exclusive to the Audi A3 and two exclusive to the Golf, while they share the two smaller petrol/diesel options. Both vehicles have the same internal security design, having the same number of airbags. Wilson asks questions concerning build locations, commenting that the Audi is built in Germany while the Golf is assembled in South Africa; he claims that the build quality of the Audi is superior and questions whether this is part of the differentiation package. But he also asks why this should be so, considering the developments in production technology!

Internally the cars are 'unmistakingly similar'; however, while both cars pay the same attention to materials quality and feel, 'it all seems to work better in the Audi'. Comments are also made concerning the accessibility and convenience of use of cruise control and air conditioning selectors.

A differentiating feature between the Audi A3 and the VW Golf is the Audi's electronic stability control (ESC), standard on the Audi, unavailable on the Golf. Wilson argues that as the safety reputation of ESC grows it may be a compulsory feature on all vehicles, 'but for now it is the best reason for paying a premium of up to $A9000 for an Audi badge over a similar Volkswagen'. And, 'Looking at the Australian dollar's relationship to the Euro, the A3 Sportback is priced at more or less what a German made Golf would cost. Fair enough – what you get is little more than a German made Golf ... So the premium paid by A3 Sportback buyers goes toward things that should be standard on a Golf – ESC and decent build quality. It's hardly news that either marque wants to hear, but hey that's journalism.'

Discussion topics

Robert Wilson's comments may be taken (at least in part) as being 'tongue in cheek' but nevertheless they have some foundation and there is a message here for automobile manufacturing and marketing management. It could be argued that Wilson has identified a situation whereby the economies of scale of production are so seductive that the cost profiles overcome any argument that marketing managers can use to maintain distance between the two marques. Conversely it could be argued that marketing management has been overwhelmingly persuasive and has attempted to use the differentiation features to make the Golf (in this instance) very competitive in comparison to its nearest competitors. Either way, the case raises an interesting topic concerning mass customisation and product differentiation and whether or not large organisations have (or should have) policy directives. And if so, what should they seek to clarify?

REFERENCES

AeIGT (2003) *An Independent Report on the Future of the UK Aerospace Industry*, Department of Trade and Industry, London

Grant A W H and L A Schlesinger (1995) 'Realise your customers' full potential', *Harvard Business Review*, September/October

Kim W C and R Mauborgne (1997), 'Value innovation: the strategic logic of high growth', *Harvard Business Review*, January/February

Mathur S and A Kenyon (1997) *Creating Value: Shaping Tomorrow's Business*, Butterworth-Heinemann, Oxford

Meyer H and A Lehnerd (1997) *The Power of Product Platforms*, Free Press, New York

Phelps R (2004) *Smart Business Metrics*, Pearson Education, Harlow

Pine B J III (1993), *Mass Customisation*, Harvard Business School Press, Boston, MA

Porter M (1990) *The Competitive Advantage of Nations*, The Free Press, New York

Porter M (1996) 'What is strategy?', *Harvard Business Review*, December

Skinner W (1986) 'The productivity paradox', *Harvard Business Review*, July/August

Slywotzky A J and D J Morrison (1997) *The Profit Zone*, Wiley, New York

Toffler A (1980) *The Third Wave*, Morrow, New York

CHAPTER 5

Perspectives on Resource Allocation in the 'New Economy'

<hr>

LEARNING TOPICS

On completing your study of this chapter you will have been introduced to and considered the following topics:

- Customer added value as an objective
- Added value; concept revisited and its measurement
- Sources of effectiveness in creating added value: industry, organisational and customer value drivers
- Assets, capabilities and processes
- The value chain establishes the concept and the means by which industry and organisational value delivery drivers
- A balance sheet approach to capability acquisition
- Process management rather than management functions
- Knowledge management, learning organisations and innovation
- Relationship management; supplier and customer considerations
- Technology management; an integrating and coordinating perspective that extends beyond information communications technology
- 'New economy' business models; components and planning and performance criteria

<hr>

Introduction

Much has been written concerning the evolution of the 'new economy' marketplace, and what is driving it. In most instances the suggested cause(s) are 'symptoms' or 'influences'. One of the key influences that is often referred to in this text has been technological. Bornheim (2001), for example, suggests that 'the emergent Digital Economy will cause profound social, technological, and economic changes', further suggesting that the 'fast-changing, intensely inter-linked environment of the digital age creates multiple challenges for corporations'.

A more general approach would be to suggest that the 'new economy' has evolved out of a number of interrelated influences, one of which undeniably, has been the digital economy. But at the end of the day the changes that have occurred have been the result of a number of interrelated and sequential influences that have been facilitated by changing attitudes within markets, their suppliers and their customers.

For example, the work by Coase (1937) on transaction economics was, at that time, largely hypothetical. Coase argued that commercial transactions take place where the cost of transaction is the lowest. It has been the impact of information and communication technologies (ICT) that has led to Coase's theory becoming practical reality. Bornheim cites Woodall (2000) who claimed that the transaction costs of purchasing products and services are being reduced by up to 60 per cent through e-procurement technologies. Bornheim also cites 'Metcalfe's law', which argues that the value of a network increases as the square of the number of users. Thus, additional users are attracted to connect to the network, resulting in 'a virtuous cycle of positive feedback'. There are obvious implications for competitive commercial networks.

Other influences are also responsible. For example, changes in attitudes towards suppliers, customers and competitors have accounted for other Coase-like changes. The notion of working with a competitor in any way, shape or form was anathema some 20 years ago but now we have the automotive manufacturers sharing R&D, sharing basic vehicle platforms, and working together in buying exchanges to reduce costs. Pharmaceutical companies share production, and sales and distribution facilities. There are numerous other examples.

A number of changes are occurring in the 'new' business environment and as a consequence organisations wishing to remain at the forefront of competition are reviewing and revising approaches to business planning. The author's research among a sample of companies suggests the following changes are of importance to their planning processes:

- The growth of customer-centricity, customisation and mass customisation
- The notion of 'value' and its application to both customers and 'organisations'
- An emphasis on cash flow performance rather than just profitability
- The decline of the vertically integrated organisation and the growing importance of virtual structures
- Asset 'leverage' rather than ownership
- The growth of the importance of intangible assets and the decline of tangible assets
- Processes and capabilities as resources and a move away from functional, 'silo' thinking
- Value migration

A comment by Lester (1998) summarises the consequences of these changes very well:

During periods of rapid change, investment in intangible assets – knowledge, ideas, skills, organisational capabilities – takes on special importance. The results of these investments – ideas for new products and processes, knowledge of new market possibilities, more competent employees, nimbler organisations – give the economy the flexibility to keep adapting and reconfiguring itself to new supply and demand conditions. They are the lubricants of the economic machinery.

Chapter 12 proposes a review of the industry value drivers (critical success factors) that were, and in many industries remain, key to the success of an organisation or networked organisation (which is the focus of this text). The discussion is introduced in this chapter and establishes a connection with resource allocation decisions through the 'added value' objective of customer satisfaction. In this chapter we add asset management and capability management to the discussion

Customer added value as an objective

A customer perspective

Band (1991) suggests that during a whole range of changes occurring in the 1980s 'Executives who got the quality and service "religion" ... failed to remember that quality and service are the means, but *value for the customer* is the end.' Band interprets this simply and succinctly:

> The idea of creating value may, indeed, be reduced to a concept as simple as striving to become ever more 'useful' to customers.

And:

> But of course good intentions must be transformed into practical reality. The businesses that will succeed in the decades ahead are not those with advantages defined in terms of internal functions, but those that can become truly market focussed – that is, able to profitably deliver sustainable superior value to their customers.

For this reason the following *value drivers* are considered as important in the overall decision making process:

- *Asset management*: understanding and responding to customers' requirements for productivity from their 'means of production' by offering warranty services, staff training, product installation, and maintenance services
- *Performance*: products and services that fulfil more of a customers expectations than those of customers will achieve
- *Enhanced 'returns'* for customers, that as a result will increase customer loyalty, evidenced by increased transactions

■ *Time management*: an ability to 'commercialise' innovations that provide customer-effective solutions is one aspect of time as a value driver. The other is the ability to provide 'quick response' solutions to routine customer order management

■ *Cost management*: the effective use of relevant aspects of 'value production economics' such as integration, coordination, specialisation, location (clusters), experience, as well as scale and scope

■ *Information management*: an effective infrastructure that avoids delays, is focused and accurate, credible and comprehensive, and accessible (transparent); 'cooperative' relationships between and among suppliers and distributors to share end-user information increases the success of interdependence

■ *Risk management*: financial risk ('market'/investor response, shareholder 'value' management, inventory obsolescence and excesses); marketing risk (reading market signals and customer and 'stakeholder' response, demand patterns and forecasting errors); personal and social risk for B2B and B2C customers (prestige, commitment and other relationship based problem outcomes)

Furthermore there is also the consideration of *downstream* competitive advantage; B2B customers seek to put themselves in strong market positions and can do so when suppliers offer the added opportunity of strong brands, R&D and other features.

A customer and stakeholder partner perspective

In what has become known as the 'new economy', the generation of revenues and the view of cost and generally resource input management have developed interesting perspectives. Expanding on the discussion in Chapters 2 and 4, we can see that:

■ *Revenues* may be enhanced by partnerships that result in more effective responses to key customer value drivers (such as time-to-market, quick logistics responses, flexibility, and customized service packages). Revenues may also be improved by such initiatives as cooperative R&D and product-market development with complementary and competitive organisations.

■ *Labour cost* profiles are influenced by outsourcing to obtain specialist skills or preferential labour rates. 'Capitalising' production processes is also a well used alternative. Becoming more important is the use of design (for example by designing around 'platforms') to reduce intra- and inter-organisational costs and in some circumstances eliminate duplications of process activities and therefore costs.

■ *Materials and services* are also influenced by inter-organisational cooperation. The automotive, pharmaceutical and chemicals industries have pioneered web based supply chain partnerships. Elemica is a global electronic network comprising 22 of the largest international chemical corporations. By forming a negotiations/transactions hub, interactions and transactions costs are significantly reduced and asset productivity throughout the 'organisation' improved by the elimination of unnecessary inventories, automated transaction systems, reduced transportation costs (not to mention a vast improvement in 'mode' utilisation) and storage costs.

■ *Capital costs* are optimized or reduced by improving the productivity of tangible assets such as manufacturing facilities and distribution systems. Partnerships in product-market development or with the application of product innovations (as in the biotech industry) increase overall productivity and decrease unnecessary investment. Working capital productivity may be improved by optimising inventory allocation and location supported by applying electronic systems to intra- and inter-organisational interactions.

An effective value creating strategy, therefore, takes an organisation beyond its own boundaries. It involves identifying the core capabilities necessary to compete and to produce and deliver customer value expectations and to *coordinate* the value production process. The well known examples such as Dell and Nike have established models that are being implemented by a number of industries through a value chain approach. But less well known examples of value chain positioning exist.

Added value is also a competitive issue as far as customer satisfaction is concerned. And the issues here concern how a customer (or group of customers) can be made more profitable and/or productive. Profitability and productivity can be safely assumed to be primary value drivers for any organisation and are the underlying factors for a number of value drivers that customers rate as important and monitor for supplier delivery performance. Typically the added value concerns of customers are presented as derived demand considerations for upstream suppliers. Clearly the successful organisations are those that are able to add more value for their customers than that added by their competitors.

Both customers and stakeholder partners benefit from resource allocation programmes that identify opportunities to add value. Clearly these should follow on from a study of market needs. Some possible methods to add value for both include the following.

Revenues, influenced by:

■ marketing strategy (positioning and segmentation)
■ product/service differentiation
■ 'quality' throughout value performance delivery
■ product/service mix
■ market reach and control (brand strength and influence)

- pricing and volumes
- distribution channels (length, complexity, distributor power and control)
- substitute products and processes
- competitive structures and competitors
- capacity management

less
Operating costs, comprising:
Wages and salaries, influenced by:

- skills ('manufacturing' and logistics processes)
- supervision (manufacturing complexity and dispersion)
- unique or exclusive specialist skills

plus
Materials, components and services, influenced by:

- supply channels (length, complexity, supplier power and control)
- operations strategy (quality control, flexible responses)
- 'manufacturing' processes (batch, flow line, and so on)
- 'manufacturing' processes (component assembly, modularisation)
- product/service differentiation from suppliers
- customer service policy (response times, product and service availability, control)

plus
Capital costs, comprising servicing and investment costs, influenced by:

- investment and management of brands, reputation and image
- research, design and development; investment and management
- 'asset leverage', cooperation with value chain/network partners
- plant set-up times and plant and equipment maintenance
- plant improvements and modification
- management development and staff skills updating
- 'investor returns' (shareholders and long-term creditors)

equals
ADDED VALUE

Therefore by understanding the importance of each of the components to customers (and the implications for partners), and the potential for improving the added value contributions, a targeted resource allocation programme can become an effective method to enhance both customer and supplier relationships.

Quantifying added value

Of primary interest to both shareholders and partners is a quantitative measure of 'value' and of 'added value'. Kay (1993) suggests that the added value generated by an organisation could be measured simply and effectively by deducting operating expenses and a 'cost of capital' from revenues. If the result is positive the organisation is 'adding value', if not then it is 'destroying value'. There is a similarity here with the Stern Stewart economic value added (EVA) measure. Both approaches use a 'comprehensive' cost of capital that includes not just depreciation but interest and dividend payments, management and employee development, and investment in intangible assets. Kay extended this argument by using it to provide a relatively simple quantitative measure of added value. However, it may take some searching of the 'notes to the accounts' to identify some of the cost items.

Kay uses the quantitative measure of added value to indicate viability and competitive advantage. In a value chain context we require additional measures in order that we might evaluate alternative business models, their strategies and structures, and their operational delivery alternatives. To this end we explore additional uses of the added value measure. Before doing so we consider the argument for preferring to measure share of market added value to market share as a performance metric.

Share of market added value is preferred to market share for a number of reasons. While the original Profit Impact of Market Strategy (PIMS) study by Buzzell and Gale (1987) suggested that high market share and high profitability have strong positive correlation, it does not follow that a strategy to increase market share by reducing prices and operating costs, together with an increase in promotional activities (and therefore costs) will maintain that momentum. More than likely it will be met with competitive responses that result in a distribution of the available market volume rather than an expansion of the market. Share of market added value considers the shift of added value (value migration) that is a current and observable phenomenon in many markets. Measurement can be conceptualised thus:

Commencing with Kay's model:

$$\text{Added value} = \sum \$(\text{Outputs} - \text{Inputs})$$

where Outputs = Revenues
and
Inputs = Wages + Materials + Cost of capital*
*Cost of capital = Capital consumed in producing outputs and added value during the period

Sources of effectiveness in the added value task

Chapter 1 briefly proposed that the in the 'new economy' competitive advantage in the value chain can be derived from four principal areas (i.e. knowledge management, technology management, process management, and relationship management). We also consider two additional, important drivers, namely asset and capability management, as we revisit each of those four drivers here. These six drivers are in effect a focal point for resource allocation.

The changing role of asset management

The 'new economy' has ushered in to the world of business planning two important concepts or management perspectives. One concerns the notion that in order to be responsive to existing and potential market-customer opportunities the corporate need is to be able to access relevant assets, not necessarily own them. The organisational response has been to develop network partnerships in which assets and processes, and to some extent capabilities, are 'shared'. Boulton et al. (2000) expresses this need when they contend:

> The encompassing challenge that companies face in this new environment is how to identify and leverage all sources of value, not just the assets that appear on the traditional balance sheet. These important assets including customers, brands, suppliers, employees, patents, and ideas – are at the core of creating a successful business now and in the future ... But what assets are most important in the New Economy? How do we leverage these assets to create value for our own organisations in a changing business environment? What new strategies are required for us to create value?

And Normann (2001) offered 'a new strategic logic', suggesting that:

> ... managers need to be good at mobilizing, managing, and using resources rather than at formally acquiring and necessarily owning resources. The ability to reconfigure, to use resources inside and particularly outside the boundaries of the traditional corporation more effectively becomes a mandatory skill for managements.

The other concept concerns the increasing role in business models of intangible assets. The growing importance of intangible assets has been identified by research by the Brookings Institution. They have reported the following significant changes in the structure of large manufacturing and mining companies in the US over the years 1982–2000:

- Since 1982 fixed tangible assets as a proportion of total assets have declined steadily.
- In 1982 fixed tangible assets, as a proportion of total assets, were some 67 per cent.
- By 1992 this was 38 per cent and by 2000 the figure was reported to be less than 30 per cent.

The changes in the business environment landscape have had a major impact for organisations on what value is, how it is created, produced, delivered and serviced. An Accenture report (Harris and Burgman 2005) discusses some of the emerging issues from an organisational perspective and from an asset management perspective. Their report suggests that value creation differs between tangible-intensive companies and intangible-intensive companies. In an argument based upon Porter's (1985) value chain model, they adopt a view that suggests that tangible-intensive companies create value by operating 'a series of input-process-output activities' and seek to build sustainable competitive advantage primarily through their effective use of monetary and physical resources. By contrast the intangible-intensive companies follow a 'value logic' that creates value based upon brand strength and proprietary knowledge.

The Accenture group make clear distinctions between value chain businesses, value shops and value networks. *Value chain businesses* are typically manufacturing companies 'heavy on physical assets', where the primary output is a physical product, largely efficiency driven. *Value shops* 'produce solutions, using human capital to creatively solve unique problems'. Output is design oriented, aimed at enhancing customer 'experiences'; examples given include entertainment organisations and construction design service companies. *Value networks* 'bring individuals or organisations together and help them transact business with each other'; eBay is given as an example. The authors refer to 'Metcalfe's law' (see above) as the reason why value networks are successful. They also make the point that while physical (tangible) assets are a necessary part of the value production process the important asset feature is a successful brand.

A useful classification of assets is given. The authors confirm the Brookings findings with a qualitative assessment asserting that in traditional asset based companies 'both physical and monetary [assets] are of shrinking importance to business success. Replacing them in significance are assets such as customer relationships, intellectual property, and a pipeline of senior executives.'

Traditional accounting for assets

In traditional accounting, tangible assets include monetary assets, cash, investments, receivables and payables; tangible physical assets include property, plant, equipment, and inventory. Intangible assets include credit ratings, undrawn facilities, borrowing capacity, unused borrowing capacity, and certainty of receivables and accruals ('blue chip' customers, quality of earnings, balance sheet strength); intangible physical assets include plant flexibility, plant currency, plant infrastructure, tradability of facilities, access rights, and useable obsolete inventory.

Intellectual capital assets

Intellectual capital assets are described as relational, organisational and human. The authors differentiate between *value networks* and *value shops*. There are both tangible and intangible asset groups:

- The value network/value shop 'balance sheets' will show *relational* tangible assets that include customer contracts, formal alliances and partnership agreements. Intangible relational assets (value networks) are customer loyalty, behavioural attitudes, quality of supply contracts, rights to tender, to compete and to design, strength of stakeholder support, networks, and regulatory imposts.

- Tangible *organisational* assets are systems, formalised processes, codified knowledge, patents, brands, mastheads. Value shops share a number of organisational intangible assets: structural relevance, informal processes, organisational reputation, brand equity, R&D productivity, quality corporate governance, expertise, and tacit knowledge.

- Tangible *human* assets comprise acknowledged skill sets, experience, employee loyalty.

- Exclusive to value shops are a number of intangible human assets: top management quality, top management experience, ability to execute strategy, capabilities (discussed in detail later), employee loyalty (behavioural and attitudinal), and personal reputation.

The classification of these 'assets' may be arguable, but what is of more interest is the extent to which the intangible assets are increasing, and their importance in differentiating companies.

Resource management is a critical management task. Harris and Burgman suggest that *value chain* management is easier and more conventional. The physical and monetary assets have accounting protocols in place and typically decrease n value over time. However, the *value shop* and *value net* management concern intellectual assets that are difficult to measure, can be used by a number of people at the same time and are not depleted by use; in fact they should become *more* valuable the more they are used.

Harris and Burgman have made a valuable contribution in helping to categorise assets. However, implicit in their comments on value chains is the suggestion that they are limited in their scope. However, as Boulton et al. (2000) and Normann (2001) suggest, the skills required in the 'new economy' are concerned with managing assets, which they do not suggest is limited by the structure of the business organisation. Indeed they infer that the networking approach is widely used by manufacturing companies who have developed large operational networks to manage the operational features of their businesses and who have built strong, sustainable competitive advantage based upon intangible asset networks. Names such as Dell, Nike, Levi Strauss, automotive industry businesses and a number of wine industry examples come to mind.

Capabilities management

The literature in the area of core competencies has been dominated by Hamel and Prahalad (1994) whose contributions are constantly cited. The growth of inter-organisational business structures refocuses attention on core competencies.

Hamel and Prahalad's work provides a basis on which to develop a model linking core competencies, key success factors and value drivers with the central focal point – customer value expectations.

Hamel and Prahalad (1994) have defined a core competence as:

> ... a bundle of skills and technologies that enables a company to provide a particular benefit to customers.

They suggest that the most valuable competencies are those offering a gateway to a wide variety of potential product markets. This contention is argued by citing Sony (for whom miniaturisation has led to a wide range of personal electronic products), and 3M, whose core competencies in adhesives, substitutes and advanced materials have been the basis of numerous products.

An interesting perspective that may be derived from this definition is that it is an aggregate of 'skills and technologies' which, as Hamel and Prahalad contend, 'represents the sum of learning across individual skill sets and individual organisational units'. And they suggest that '... it is unlikely to reside in a single individual or within a small team'. This is a primary reason for an organisation to consider participating with other organisations, together with the fact that the dynamics of competition, technology and consumer value expectations make investment in core competencies unattractive. Hamel and Prahalad make their views very clear concerning this issue:

> In the concept of core competence there is no suggestion that a company must make everything it sells ... although Canon has a very clear sense of its core competencies, it buys more than 75% of components that go into its copiers. What a company should seek to control are those core competencies that make the biggest contribution to customer value.

This view also identifies the clear need for core competencies to be linked with customer value generation. It also identifies the trend towards *virtual integration* in which the core competencies required to complete are identified and, rather than being developed or acquired, they are leased and aggregated to create an entity which answers the question, 'What can we do that other organisations could not easily do as well?'.

This is also expressed by Rumelt (1994), who argues that:

■ Core competencies support several businesses and products.

■ Products and services are only a temporary manifestation of core competence – the latter develops more slowly and is more stable than products.

■ Competence is knowledge and therefore increases with use.

■ In the long run, competence, not products, will determine who succeeds in competition.

Gottfredson et al. (2005) discuss capabilities from a strategic sourcing perspective, arguing that:

Now globalisation, aided by rapid technology innovation, is changing the basis of competition. Its no longer a company's ownership of capabilities that matters but rather its ability to control and make the most of critical capabilities, whether or not they are on the company's balance sheet ... Outsourcing is becoming so sophisticated that even core functions ... can and often should be moved outside. And that, in turn, is changing the way firms think about their organisations, their value chains, and their competitive positions.

The authors suggest that 'forward thinking' organisations are using 'capability sourcing' to make their value chains more flexible. They also suggest that this approach questions whether all activities should be outsourced. They identify a number of companies who have focused on their brand strength as the basis on which to continue to build their businesses. Companies such as Virgin and Nike are offered as examples. Capability sourcing is based upon a rigorous assessment of an organisation's capabilities to determine which of these match the requirements of an identified opportunity and where there are 'capability gaps'. The authors argue that:

Greater focus on capability sourcing can improve a company's strategic position by reducing costs, streamlining the organisation and improving quality.

We would argue that there are other factors to consider. For example, a capability sourcing audit may reveal that access to a process may offer exclusive differentiation that in turn offers an opportunity to become a significant force in a growth market segment.

Gottfredson et al. provide ample evidence in support of their argument that by the 1980s the basis of competition had shifted from 'hard assets to intangible capabilities'. Wal-Mart is cited as moving away from traditional retailing capabilities towards a proprietary approach to relationship management within its supply chain. The US automotive industry responded to the growth of market share on the part of its Japanese competitors by moving design, engineering and manufacturing work to specialist partners. Strategic sourcing relationships were established for complex assemblies, with agreement to sharing cost accounting data *and* cost savings. American Express outsourced its transaction processing to First Data, a new organisation, in 1992. The authors make an interesting and very significant point with this example; American Express realised that while this process was core to their business it was becoming commoditised and therefore declining in importance as an element of competitive advantage. With the processing outsourced to a reliable partner they were then able to focus on the card issuing aspect of the business.

Processes, competencies and capabilities

McHugh et al. (1995) suggest a connection between processes and core competencies, indicating that:

Companies usually have about half dozen or so core business processes. They are the processes that the business's strategic thinking has identified as critical to excel at to meet or beat the competition. They make up part of the company's set of core competencies.

And

A core competence may be a business process, a management skill, a 'new' asset or an applied technology.

They continue by citing Hamel and Prahalad's test, which suggests that a capability is a core competence if it:

■ Makes a disproportionate contribution to customer value
■ Offers an opportunity to build competitive distinction
■ Is applicable to other businesses, locations or products

McHugh and his co-authors address the issue of confusion concerning 'capabilities' and 'core competencies', suggesting that while these terms have broadly the same meaning, we should interpret a core competence as one of the critical subset of capabilities that satisfies the above three tests. Furthermore, because core business processes satisfy Hamel and Prahalad's test, most of the few core competencies of a business will be its core business processes. In addition they contend that a company's core competencies will include applied technologies or management skills. To this we would add the organisation's business model. The examples of Dell, Millennium, Nike and others suggest that a 'different' business model may also be fundamental in the success of a business, a value chain or network system.

Baghai et al. (1999) discussed the role of capabilities from a growth perspective. They argued that simply to focus on operational skills or competencies is limiting and that a broader definition that includes all resources useful in developing competitive advantage is required. They suggest that in addition to operational skills, privileged assets, growth enabling skills and special relationships are equally important. *Privileged assets* are physical or intangible assets that are hard to replicate and confer competitive advantage on their owner. These are infrastructure, intellectual property, distribution networks, brands and reputations, and customer information. *Growth enabling skills* are considered to be acquisition management, deal structuring and negotiating, financing, risk management, and capital management. *Special relationships* include the linkages with customers and suppliers, government and 'regulators', the authors suggest.

Kay (2000), in a discussion that compares competitive advantage with economic rent (the latter being what companies earn over and above the cost of capital to the company), suggests that competitive advantage is determined by capabilities. He classifies capabilities as *distinctive* and *reproducible*. *Distinctive* capabilities are characteristics that cannot be replicated by competitors, or if they can, only at considerable expense and with a time lag. They include brands, supplier and customer relationships, and patents resulting from strong R&D; Kay also includes government licences and statutory monopolies. *Reproducible* capabilities can be purchased or created by an able company with management skills and financial resources. They include infrastructure systems such as distribution facilities (and increasingly manufacturing), administrative roles, sales and marketing, and 'communications'. Kay makes a point with the comment that:

> ... only distinctive capabilities can be the basis for competitive advantage. Collections of reproducible capabilities can and will be established by others and therefore cannot generate rents ...

The value chain enables capabilities to be shared

Quinn (1992) emphasises the need to cultivate a core competence and suggests that manufacturing companies are becoming more and more dependent within the value chain on links consisting of services or intellectual activities. Olve et al. (1997) suggest that the underlying driver of long-term strategic performance is intellectual capital, using Stewart's (1997) definition to give the term meaning, namely that it is 'packaged useful knowledge'. They contend that this approach can explain why a company may be valued at more than the sum of its 'hard' assets. Other approaches suggest the term 'intangible assets' which has the advantage of including or detailing specifics seen as brand values, R&D and management development. The concern is to understand the influence of intellectual capital on core competencies. Given Olve et al.'s perspective, it could be suggested that there is a relationship that can be derived: *intellectual capital*, as packaged useful knowledge, acts as a data bank of knowledge from which *competencies* emerge. The point is how competencies are identified ahead of their application. In other words the business environment is becoming dynamic to the point at which competencies that are recognised may be becoming *core rigidities* (Leonard-Barton 1992) and as seen, have limited life spans. This view introduces the notion of core competencies appearing as balance sheet items. Olve et al. reproduce an item from the Skandia annual report (a supplement titled 'On Processes Which Create Value') and subsequently introduce a 'competence balance sheet', an idea which we develop below.

The competence/capability 'balance sheet'

Hamel and Prahalad (1994) comment that:

> Pre-emptive investment in a core competence is not a leap into the dark ... it is the simple desire to build world leadership in the provision of a key customer benefit, and the imagination to envision the many ways in which that benefit can be delivered to customers, that drive the competence-building process.

As we saw, they suggest that the competencies that are most valuable are those representing a gateway to a wide range of potential product markets; in other words, a core competence leader possesses the option to be a major participant in a range of end-product markets. This is a particularly important issue for value chain management because the options become much wider when a value chain approach is considered. Implicit in Hamel and Prahalad's original model is the requirement that some forward thinking be undertaken to determine the direction of 'potential product markets' prior to investing in core competence leadership. Indeed the value chain approach offers an option to spread risk and this would be reflected in an even greater proportion of externally sourced temporary competencies.

The analogy for planning competence requirements uses the principles of financing for growth. The 'assets' required for success are identified as competencies and the 'liabilities' indicate how the competencies are to be financed – who is to provide them. Olve et al. continue with the notion that competencies have limited life expectancies and therefore suggest that the liabilities reflect a degree of competence leverage. Figure 5.1 illustrates the proposal. In this hypothetical example, the major assets are the distinctive capabilities, suggested as being the product/service development processes such as market entry networks, market management networks, specialist processes and capabilities. These capabilities are largely 'financed' by value chain partners. Reproducible capabilities are 'leveraged'. The contribution made by non-specialist partners is externally sourced temporary competencies, required to meet non-specialist needs.

Figure 5.1 also suggests the relationships of the capabilities to the industry drivers discussed in Chapter 1 and developed further in this context below.

Process management

Processes have defined business outcomes, of which there are recipients that may be either internal or external to the organisation. They also cross organisational boundaries; that is, they normally occur across or between intra- or inter-organisational boundaries and are independent of formal organisational structures. Effective organisations now view process management as a means by which they work together to identify core processes across the demand and supply chains. They explore the implications of locating these core processes within specialist, partnership organisations.

Effective organisations also now work together to identify core processes. The scope of process management is such that it may be applied to strategic and operational tasks and structures alike.

Business processes have a clear impact on business performance and structure options. It follows that in a dynamic business environment organisational flexibility is required. Hagel and Singer (1999) suggest carrying out frequent reviews of organisational capabilities and as and when necessary making relevant changes to ensure market relevance and optimal performance. There is evidence of this approach that reaches back in time. For example, the growth

'Assets'	'Liabilities'
Market entry network (Exclusive distinctive capabilities) • Customer databases (KM) (AM) • Coordinated customer based design and development (RM) • Market liaison (RM) • Brand and reputation equity (RM) • Patents and licences (KM) (AM) • Specialist processes and services, e.g. design and development (TM) **Market management networks** (Exclusive distinctive capabilities) • Market reach (RM) (CM) • Market influence (RM) (CM) • Loyal customer base(s) (RM) **Specialist processes & capabilities** (Partner owned: exclusive capabilities) • Patents and brands (g; Intel) (TM) (RM) (AM) • Specialist processes and services, e.g. design and development (RM) (TM) • 'Access' to specialist inputs (TM)(RM) (CM) • 'Access' to specialist facilities, equipment & processes (TM) (RM) (CM)) • Service management networks (RM) • Product/service performance delivery and maintenance (PM) (RM)	**Production facilities and networks** (Reproducible capabilities) • Buying exchange agreements (RM) • Inter-organisational process management (PM)(RM) • 'Access' to 'commodity' inputs (RM) • 'Access' to non-specialist facilities, equipment & processes (RM) • Capacity and quality management (PM) • Service management networks (RM) (AM) • Product/service performance delivery and maintenance (PM)(RM)

Note:

KM = Knowledge management focus	TM = Technology management focus
RM = Relationship management focus	PM = Process management focus
AM = Asset management focus	CM = Capabilities management focus

Based upon Olve N, J. Roy and M. Wetter (1997), *Performance Drivers*, Wiley, Chichester.

Figure 5.1 The virtual enterprise 'balance sheet'

of 'third-party distribution' services was one of the original steps whereby contracting out distribution was often seen as the only way in which small and medium-sized companies could benefit from the obvious economies of scale available to their large competitors.

Many businesses are too structured and need to review these structures against the changing business environment. Hagel and Singer argue that the traditional organisation comprises three basic types of business: a customer relationship business, a product innovation business and an infrastructure business. They suggest each of these differ on the economic, competitive and cultural dimensions. They argue that as the exchange of information and 'digitisation' increases through electronic networks, the traditional organisation structures will become 'unbundled' as the need for flexible structures becomes an imperative and 'specialists' offer cost-effective strategy options in each of these basic businesses. They also suggest this is leading to car manufacturers, for example, adopting outsourcing models for manufacturing operations (as is beginning to occur) and to enter the after-market through partial acquisitions or partnerships or even full acquisition of downstream companies.

The argument underlying Hagel and Singer's model concerns a conflict of production economics. They argue that the customer relationship business is essentially driven by the need to achieve economies of scope and do so by seeking to offer customers a wide range of products and services. By contrast the product innovation business is driven by speed: by minimising its time-to-market the company increases the likelihood of capturing a premium price and a strong market share. The infrastructure business is dominated by economies of scale. They are typically characterised by capital-intensive facilities that entail high fixed costs. Given the relationship between throughput and fixed cost it follows that large volumes of product throughput are essential.

Hagel and Singer argue that 'these three businesses ... rarely map neatly to the organisational structure of a corporation ... Rather than representing discrete organisational units, the three businesses correspond to what are popularly called "core processes" – the cross functional work flows that stretch from suppliers to customers and, in combination, define a company's identity.' The solution for Hagel and Singer is to 'unbundle the organisation' and to restructure based upon maximising the effect of the economic characteristics of each of the individual businesses.

The issue for the 'traditional' organisation is to consider what the authors define as *interaction costs*. Interaction costs include transaction costs (as described by Coase and others) but add the costs of exchanging ideas and information. They argue that the three businesses correspond to what are popularly called core processes. Virtual organisations (or value chains) form around core processes and these expand to meet the specific customer needs identified. Hagel and Singer's argument is that as the exchange of information and 'digestion' increases through electronic networks, then traditional organisation structures will become 'unbundled' as the need for flexible structures becomes an imperative and 'specialists' offer more cost-efficient strategy options in each of these basic businesses.

Hagel and Singer conclude with: 'The secret to success in fractured industries is not to unbundle, but to unbundle and rebundle, creating a new organisation with the capabilities and size required to win.' This requires identifying and understanding fully the economics of scale, scope, specialisation and integration. Figure 5.2 explores this proposition. In addition to the three 'business processes' suggested by the authors, a fourth, 'market visionary: innovation and implementation', has been included. This addition is justified by the increasingly important role that is now played by the 'virtual organisation'.

In an argument that concludes with a view that organisations are changing rapidly and dramatically, Drucker (2001) comments on recent events and trends in organisational development. He suggests these have changed many fundamental philosophies, views and practices. Such a view sponsored the development of vertical integration on a large scale – and did so for many years. Drucker cites Standard Oil and Ford as examples.

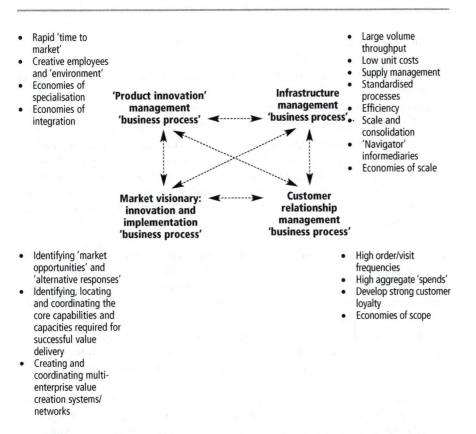

- Rapid 'time to market'
- Creative employees and 'environment'
- Economies of specialisation
- Economies of integration

- Large volume throughput
- Low unit costs
- Supply management
- Standardised processes
- Efficiency
- Scale and consolidation
- 'Navigator' informediaries
- Economies of scale

- Identifying 'market opportunities' and 'alternative responses'
- Identifying, locating and coordinating the core capabilities and capacities required for successful value delivery
- Creating and coordinating multi-enterprise value creation systems/ networks

- High order/visit frequencies
- High aggregate 'spends'
- Develop strong customer loyalty
- Economies of scope

Figure 5.2 Identifying business processes and their characteristics

It is noticeable that large corporations are leading the changes in strategic posture. General Motors, for example, have created a business that will buy for the ultimate car consumer – they will make available what car and model most closely fit the consumer's preferences. As Drucker notes, the changes go beyond this, into design and development, and production. Products and services now have multiple applications and business organisations are redefining their core capabilities and processes. In other words 'value creating systems' are competing with 'value creating systems'. Each of the systems are organisation structures, or confederations, that are developing from traditional corporations.

Campbell (1996) offers a typology of virtual organisational forms that helps identify the various alternative structures available:

■ *Internal virtual organisations*: autonomous business units are formed within a large organisation 'to provide operational synergies and tailor responses to specific customer demands'. Customer relationship management is a current response that targets selected customers with customised service packages.

■ *Stable virtual organisations*: these are conventionally structured organisations that outsource non-core activities to a small network of suppliers whose processes and activities become integrated with the initiator. Industrial designers are in this category.

- *Dynamic virtual organisations*: organisations that focus on core capabilities and introduce external partners in cooperative ventures. Dell Computers is an example of an organisation that has a core capability based upon integrating and coordinating component suppliers to meet specific customer orders.

- *Agile virtual organisations*: temporary networks that are rapidly formed 'to exploit new market opportunities through the mutual exchange of skills and resources'. The pharmaceutical companies are beginning to work with this model. They work with small R&D organisations and specialist manufacturers to meet very specialised market opportunities that may or may not prove to be highly profitable. This approach carries with it investment and risk.

It is interesting to note three points. First, the typology identifies a progressive move towards a structure built around 'intangibles'. Second, the typology reflects the growing confidence of these organisations in the continuous developments in process, knowledge, technology and relationship management applications. The third point concerns the ability to match structure with risk. For example, internal virtual organisations can manage low-risk situations such as brand leverage accompanying an extension of a product range. However, *product differentiation* required to meet the expectations of a small segment of a large market may be best resolved by working with an established partner – a stable virtual organisation. For unrelated product-market developments, developments requiring additional expertise to that available within the organisation, dynamic virtual organisations offer a suitable structure. To meet short life cycle opportunities, such as those often found in the 'fashion' segments of apparel markets, an agile virtual organisation may prove to be more suited. The issue here then is for the 'business organisation' to be responsive and flexible such that it can optimise financial and market success at an acceptable level of risk.

For an inter-organisational approach to process management to be successful it is first necessary to identify the customer expectations the value chain is to attempt to satisfy. From these the essential value drivers, the features that have significant impact on customer buying decisions and the continuity of the buyer/seller relationship, can be derived. Furthermore, detailed knowledge of these essential items is necessary if an effective process management structure is to be designed. Customer expectations initially identify the important value drivers and these are used to derive the process tasks that are to be undertaken. One further step is required, that is to determine from where the process inputs are to be sourced if customer expectations are to be maximised. Clearly any decision made within one process may have an impact on any of the others. For this reason the process decisions are 'overlapping'.

Knowledge management

Knowledge management is the organisational capability that identifies, locates (creates or acquires), transfers, converts and distributes knowledge into competitive advantage. Knowledge management influences R&D investment strategy and the application of experience based knowledge to emphasise commercial abilities. Knowledge is a resource, in the same context as financial, human and other resources.

Technology management is broader in scope than manufacturing/operations strategy; it is the integration of process and product technology to address the planning, development and implementation of technological capabilities and capacities to meet the strategic and operational objectives of an organisation or combination of organisations. Technology management can enhance the value delivered by planning manufacturing responses that deliver market volume and product and service delivery requirements. It develops an asset structure that meets cost and plant utilisation goals *and* customer value specifications. A technology strategy may be derived by deciding upon the *combined* manufacturing and logistics support needed to meet market demand.

Knowledge is a central defining characteristic of organisations and their ability to compete in respect of it is becoming increasingly important as capital- and labour-intensive organisations and routine work are replaced by knowledge-intensive firms and activity. This view is shared:

> knowledge has become perhaps the most important factor determining the standard of living – more than land, than tools, than labor. Today's most technologically advanced economies are truly knowledge-based. (World Bank 1998)

> ... is not only about new creative industries and high-tech business, it is relevant to traditional manufacturing and services, and to business ranging from construction and engineering to retailing and banking. (UK Department of Trade and Industry 1998)

> It is estimated that more than 50 percent of gross domestic product in major OECD economies is knowledge based. (Stevens 1998)

Drivers in the knowledge based economy include increasing knowledge intensity of the processes of generating, producing and commercialising new goods and services; exponential expansion of information and communications technologies to store, process and transfer 'vast amounts' of information; and the process of globalisation.

Knowledge is now accepted as being much more than just information. While information management techniques are required to access and disseminate knowledge, knowledge is structured experiences, and formal and informal responses to situations. But to be useful it has to be organised and structured. Knowledge management systems should reflect the use that is made of organisational knowledge. Codified knowledge can be 'written down' and stored for access by others. Non-codified (tacit) knowledge is 'accessible' only by observation and imitation. Tacit knowledge is typically based in the individual and skill is required to codify and structure such knowledge for broader access.

So knowledge is something that needs to be managed. The benefits are attractive. For example, such management fosters knowledge building activities like shared problem solving, involving experimentation, product and process prototyping; it encourages the importing and absorbing of technological market information, and the implementing and integrating of new technological processes and tools. These are crucial in defining technological capabilities, which in turn are integral elements in creating competitive advantage.

Knowledge intensity is growing. Useful indicators of this are the increasing expenditures on R&D, and on information and computer technologies; the increasing proportions of high-tech products in world trade, and the growth of intangible assets as a proportion of total corporate assets.

Innovation and knowledge

The link between knowledge management and innovation is accepted in the current literature. While it may seem obvious, it is worthwhile to explore precisely what we understand innovation to be and the link it has with knowledge management.

A feature of the dynamic business environment the 'new economy' has introduced is the response to rapidly changing consumer expectations for product-market differentiation. This has been manifested in a number of ways. Essentially we now see both *product and process innovation* in the marketplace. Examples of product innovation are the responses in *demand life cycles* that provide new solutions to very basic demand characteristics. Communication between businesses is an example. Not so long ago, facsimile communication was hailed as a breakthrough in reducing the time taken for interactions and transactions to be completed between suppliers and customers. Orders and order management details could be transmitted 'instantly and visibly' by telephone. Yet in no time at all, the internet replaced the fax with the facility to connect supplier and customer production schedules, providing real-time management.

Another aspect of product innovation concerns the continuous changes occurring in end-user expectations and the supplier response to expectations for 'performance' *and* competitive (typically low) prices.. Both the personal computer and the mobile telephone are examples of product innovations that have become commodity products. It is at this point in the demand life cycle that process innovation becomes more important. Within the market we observe segmentation occurring; the *innovators* remain focused on product features, while the *late adopters* and perhaps the *laggards* look for (and perhaps only need) the basic functions the product innovation offered on its introduction. The ability to manufacture and distribute the *basic* product cost-efficiently becomes a competitive necessity; clearly IBM saw this as a problem for themselves and as a result divested their PC manufacturing interests. The mobile telephone market has demonstrated similar characteristics. At this point it is process innovation that creates competitive advantage. Michael Dell is an example of how process innovation becomes important. Dell offers its customers convenience and time as major benefits and has constructed innovative processes around these benefits to ensure their delivery.

An important part played by the structure of knowledge management systems, capable of not simply tracking market trends but also of interpreting them and converting them into inputs requiring managerial action. At this point an organisation can claim to be a learning organisation.

Learning organisations

Learning organisations focus their efforts in order to transform themselves continually, with the aim of building and enhancing their capabilities. They learn *purposefully* and *productively*. Their learning occurs by means of investments in resources and staff development, stakeholders and other organisations with whom they have business relationships.

Learning is multi-faceted because it is long-term and is an integrated component of strategy; it is expensive, and it can be encouraged by a variety of external linkages. The organisational challenge is to transfer individual learning into group practices and corporate routines.

Housel and Bell (2001) approach learning from the point of view of 'monitoring and measuring'; they suggest that learning is accrued by monitoring the application of the organisation's core processes and its interactions with the marketplace. The interactions with customers, suppliers, and competitors identify successful (and unsuccessful) products and processes. They argue that the rate at which this knowledge can be transformed into core knowledge (and distributed to partner organisations) will determine how quickly value is created through the offering of new products and services. They suggest a *learning-knowledge-value cycle* approach, with four requirements that address the process of converting knowledge into realisable value:

- Accelerate the learning-knowledge-value cycle and the transferring of the knowledge output into core processes, thus not only reducing the time-to-market cycle but making it much more efficient.

- Identify existing and future knowledge gaps. Knowledge gap assessment identifies deficiencies in the knowledge necessary for current operations and identifies the knowledge assets that will be required to produce future value.

- Identify 'best practices' for embedding knowledge in people, processes and IT. Such a policy ensures the organisation is current in its thinking and practice.

- Measure the added value of knowledge to create an internal marketplace. This provides management with feedback on their ability to manage the learning-knowledge-value cycle efficiently. The authors suggest an accounting approach that allows managers to establish a price and cost per unit of knowledge. They also suggest linking this to organisational financial performance measures. While this is a useful control, it would also be helpful to measure the impact of having/not having the knowledge on the cash flow performance of the organisation.

McHugh et al. (1995) cite management consultants Pedler, Burgoyne and

Boydell, who have developed eleven practical insights into the characteristics of a learning organisation. Typically, such an organisation exhibits:

- A learning approach to strategy
- Encouragement of participation in policy making
- Supportive information systems
- Supportive accounting and control
- A climate that supports personal development
- Opportunities for learning at all levels
- Internal knowledge sharing
- Flexible rewards
- Enabling organisation structures
- Recognition of the 'front line'
- A policy of learning from competitors and customers

With some modification these criteria fit the needs of the value chain closely. An additional emphasis should be placed upon 'organisation' explicitly including stakeholder partners. This in turn identifies the need for total transparency to ensure the learning process is uniform.

Relationship management

Relationship management is the managerial activity which identifies, establishes, maintains and reinforces economic relationships with customers, suppliers and other partners which have complementary (and supplementary) capabilities and capacities, so that the objectives of the organisation and those of all other partners may be met by agreeing and implementing mutually acceptable strategies. Relationship management can influence positioning and strategy by identifying, developing and maintaining partnerships that achieve the product service objectives needed to meet customer expectations. Relationship management moves the organisation towards both cross-functional and inter-organisational decision making and control, and is clearly an important component in strategic operations management.

Relationship management prescribes the organisation structure within which the firm operates. Payne and Holt's (2001) description of the 'market' environment in which a firm operates determines a role for relationship management that extends the scope of relationship marketing into one in which a broad range of processes can be coordinated. Relationship management includes 'co-production' (the 'transfer' of production processes both upstream and downstream), in which 'managed' co-destiny becomes essential for success.

Luthans (2002), in a discussion of mergers and acquisitions, refers to the expanding phenomenon of 'relationship enterprises' (Mirman 1982). Luthans compares these with the virtual organisation model in which partners share costs, skills and access to markets. Each partner contributes to the virtual organisation 'what it is best at – its core capabilities'. Luthans lists the key attributes of the virtual organisation as *technology* (information and communications technology), *opportunism* (partnerships are opportunity-specific – they dissolve on completion of the role), *no borders* (cooperation, co-opetition have redefined corporate boundaries – many becoming seamless), *trust* (companies become interdependent and share a sense of co-destiny), and *excellence* (the notion of organisations contributing their core competences creates a 'unique' organisation. Luthans cites Boudreau et al. (1998):

> The alliances and partnerships with other organisations can extend world-wide, the spatial and temporal interdependence easily transcend boundaries, and the flexibility allows easy reassignment and reallocation to take quick advantage of shifting opportunities in global markets.

Luthans gives examples of relationship enterprises across a range of industries that includes aerospace, telecommunications, airlines, and the automotive industry. In recent years (2000–05) the attraction has expanded into computer hardware, pharmaceuticals, biotechnology and the fast moving consumer goods industry (food, personal care etc) and is also becoming prominent in healthcare.

Luthans suggests the reasons for the growing trend in relationship enterprises. Formal M&A structures present legal difficulties in many countries. but he considers political nationalism and organisational cultural values to be equally as important. Central to the success of these structures are issues such as trust, communication, and negotiation skills.

Zineldin (2000) offers a perspective – Total Relationship Management (TRM), which is concerned with:

■ External and competitive analysis
■ Internal analysis of all integrated activities within the organisation (internal relationships)
■ High quality customer satisfaction and in turn long-run profitability
■ Mutually beneficial relationships, communications and interactions outside the organisation with suppliers, dealers, distributors and other collaborators, such as bankers, trade unions, politicians or public bodies (external relationships)
■ Continuous improvement or these relationships, communication and interactions

He contends that TRM highlights the role of quality and customer service, the impact of the external environment on business rules, performance, relationships and networks, communications and interactions with suppliers, distributors, dealers, other collaborators and employees in different departments performing different functions, as well as customers (in consumer and industrial markets alike). The essence of any relationship is communication and interaction; communication links people or organisations together. In addition, everything that happens between two individuals (or organisations) can be seen as part of a continuous preparation for future interaction.

TRM is viewed by Zineldin as an integrated strategy and philosophy. It is *integrated*, because it considers and coordinates 'all' activities – internal and external relationships, networks, interactions and cooperation, as well as all activities involved in attracting, retaining, enhancing and satisfying customers through quality. It is a *strategy* because it emphasises maintaining high levels of quality of products/services, internal and external relationships, and retaining customers in the long run. It is a *philosophy* because it should be used to communicate the idea that a major goal of management is continuously to improve the integrated quality, and to plan and build appropriate, close and flexible long-term relationships with partner organisations who contribute to the organisation's success and long-term growth. It should also guide the overall strategic direction of the organisation, its decision making and the execution of predetermined plans. It follows that we can also call this approach an integrated strategic relationship management and philosophy.

Instead of the conventional marketing mix approach to customers, suppliers and partners, a total relationship approach or view is a more effective, serviceable and profitable way of addressing an effective relationship management and marketing strategy. The main role of the total relationship elements/mix is to turn existing and new customers or other parties into loyal clients or partners. A loyal client or partner can also be considered as a strong support and an effective marketer of the company and its products/services.

It is interesting to note the application of software packages to relationship management; 'solutions' are becoming available to manage both customer and supplier relationships. Solectron offers a package that has proven to be successful in this regard. Based upon three processes, the 'solution' offers:

- *Product design and launch support* Collaboration with customers to design and launch new products that emphasise customer added value expectations, and results in cost and time savings. Collaboration with a communications customer to design and launch an optical metro product led to a 50 per cent cost reduction over a period of 18 months.
- *Procurement and production operations planning* Manufacturing processes focus activities that add value. Supply chain design increases product availability, reduces inventory and response time. Supply chain design for a leading storage switch customer reduced the number of suppliers by 50 per cent and costs by more than 20 per cent – enabling the customer to gain market share.
- *Service support* Customer service times and support costs and inventory holding can be reduced. Repair processes add fault investigation activities to ensure changes may be incorporated to prevent future product failures. Implementing a rapid repair service improved a computing customer's end-user satisfaction rating from fifth to first in the industry – while lowering support costs by 60 per cent and inventory holding by more than $70 million.

Technology management

Technology management can enhance the value delivered by planning operating responses that deliver market volume and product and service delivery characteristics. It develops an asset structure that meets cost and plant utilisation goals and customer value specifications. A technology strategy may be derived by deciding upon the combined manufacturing and logistics support needed to meet market demand.

Technology management and innovation can improve the organisation's effectiveness (its strategic decisions) and its efficiency (its operational or productivity decisions). Management's task is to identify where investment will prove to be most effective.

A strategic perspective of technology requires an organisation to choose and develop the capabilities that shape the organisation's opportunities for innovation and continuing competitiveness. This requires that investment decisions are made with the intent of extending technological capabilities and organisational changes with the aim of linking product lines more closely with capabilities. Successful firms look beyond product lines and build a strategy around core knowledge and capabilities – these provide them with a sustainable and flexible strategic focus. Technology strategies involve identifying the key technologies that underpin the firm's present and future value creating activities and ensure they are improved, supplemented, effectively introduced and used.

Technology is a strategic issue because the development and application of technology is a key source of competitive advantage. It is required to ensure the development of a coherent and credible product/service range. The globalisation of technology and of supply and consumer markets now makes such a strategic approach essential. Technology strategy and corporate strategy should be integrated or at least compatible. Furthermore, a technology strategy must link technology with the firm's competitive strategies and integrate technology with the organisation's process and capability portfolios. It should also be developed jointly with marketing, operations and other functions because technology decisions can have a major impact on each area and vice versa. It should also be developed in conjunction with the organisation's business model and strategy because a correct choice of technology provides for the supplementation and the continuity of core/distinctive capabilities. Moreover it should provide support for any future revision of the firm's business model and strategy and its intentions to develop and/or change its competitive positioning.

Boisot (1998) suggests an interface role for technology management. Figure 5.3 illustrates the linkages among core processes, core capabilities and technology management. The interface is 'driven' by knowledge management to develop core products that in turn develop competitive advantage.

McHugh et al. (1995) have suggested that a number of industries now find themselves confronted with a major investment dilemma. Investment in core capabilities and the technologies to maintain them has become a strategic issue. Some technologies are changing so rapidly that it difficult to maintain technological currency. Companies must decide whether to continue investment in every 'core capability' or to become more selective with their investment and be content to maintain their support of their other capabilities. The authors report a comment that suggests that in future some 40 per cent of the cost of automobiles will comprise electronic components and assemblies. Kodama (1995) suggests that technologies are increasingly *fused* across industry boundaries.

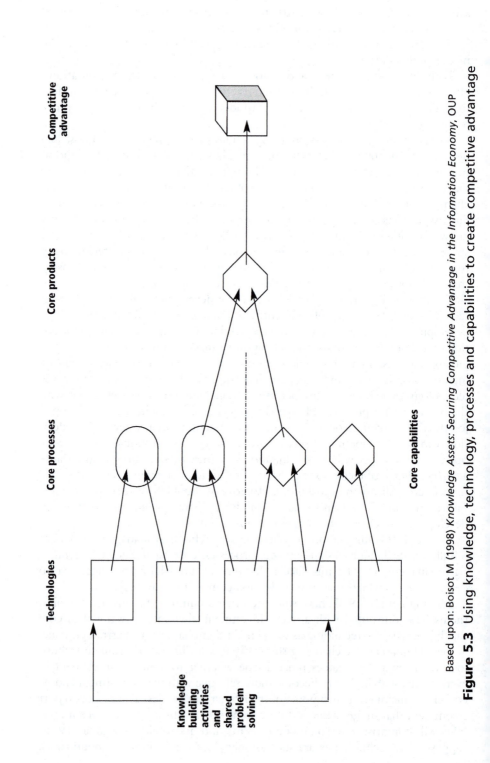

Technologies   **Core processes**   **Core products**   **Competitive advantage**

Core capabilities

Knowledge building activities and shared problem solving

Based upon: Boisot M (1998) *Knowledge Assets: Securing Competitive Advantage in the Information Economy*, OUP

Figure 5.3 Using knowledge, technology, processes and capabilities to create competitive advantage

Others such as Grupp (1998) add that technology developments are likely to involve *combinations* of technologies. The challenge for management will be to create the strategies and structures to encourage this cross-disciplinary and cross-technology synergy. Keeping pace requires a strategic decision. Alternatives include focusing on the process that uses a specific technology and thereby becoming a specialist supplier, following the lead suggested by Boisot (1998) that uses knowledge management to 'filter' trends and to invest selectively to maintain strategic direction.

Another option is to consider partnership arrangements that can lead to technological collaboration. The value chain/virtual organisation model suggests that such collaboration becomes an important aspect of technology management. This requires working with suppliers, distributors and customers to create technology/innovation alliances leading to the management of technological networks and to facilitating technology transfer across the value chain. McLoughlin (1999) suggests that the virtual organisation structure allows organisations to cope with the increasingly turbulent environments they face. ICT applications encourage the virtual organisation to be designed in ways which permit knowledge to be distributed throughout the organisation, thereby enhancing both strategic effectiveness and operational efficiency. Globalisation is an interrelated development. Internationalisation of procurement, production and service to secure competitive advantage, global corporations operating across international boundaries, the growth of free trade agreements (FTAs) and the resulting integration of world trade and the liaison between financial markets are all expanding the attraction of virtual approaches.

Service products raise particular issue; they become a *boundary problem*. A number of authors argue that a 'design company' in, say, the automotive industry may either be defined as a service company or be integrated into the base industry. Furthermore many services that were once personal services are now delivered mechanically or electronically. Probably more significantly, 'services' now differentiate physical products as they are bundled with products (mobile telephones) and service packages in B2B markets. And many organisations suggest their products are 'solutions'; IBM, having divested itself of much of its manufacturing, is now positioning itself as the provider of business solutions, 'business process transformation services – management consulting, business process outsourcing and engineering services' (London 2005).

An interesting aspect of value chain management is the importance of outsourced services. Many OEMs are finding warranty and after sales service an important aspect of customer relationships management, but are also finding the servicing of technological products expensive; consequently they are contracting this aspect of the product bundle to service specialists who can offer a cost-efficient solution.

'New economy' business models

Magretta (2002) points out the business model is the 'system, how the pieces of a business fit together', while a firm's strategy is the choices made about how to deploy that model in the marketplace. Using the example of American Express and the invention of the traveller's cheque in the nineteenth century, Magretta contends that 'a successful business model represents a better way than the existing alternatives. It may offer more value to a discrete group of customers. Or it may completely replace the old way of doing things and become the standard for the next generation of entrepreneurs to beat.' In particular:

> ... all new business models are variations on the generic value chain underlying all businesses. Broadly speaking, this chain has two parts. Part one includes all the activities associated with making something: designing it, purchasing raw materials, manufacturing and so on. Part two includes all the activities associated with selling something: finding and reaching customers, transacting a sale, distributing the product or delivering the service. A new business model's plot may turn on designing a new product for an unmet need ... Or it may turn on a process innovation, a better way of making or selling or distributing an already proven product or service.

However, this is often much easier said than done. Business model designs that succeed share common features:

- High customer relevance
- Internally consistent sets of decisions concerning scope (products offered and value chain processes performed)
- Value capture mechanisms or a profit model.
- A powerful source of differentiation and strategic control that gives investors greater confidence in future cash flows
- Organisational architecture that is designed to support and reinforce the company's business model design

An example of recent thinking is provided by Slywotzky and Morrison (1997) in Figure 5.4. The authors propose a shift towards a value emphasis to profitability rather than a market share approach. They claim that the notion that 'gain market share – profitability will follow' has been replaced by a 'logic' that proposes a 'customer-centric/profit-centric' approach. Their model suggests that customer focus is a key issue. However, recent views on the vulnerability of profit as a measure of performance compared with the more robust free cash flow approach suggest some changes to their proposal are applicable.

Developing a business model

A typical approach to the 'new economy' business completes the main part of this chapter. The purpose is to meet the objectives of both customers and stakeholders. There are six interrelated components: (1) *free cash flow* is the primary measure of success, realised by targeting (2) *a share of the market added value* of the industry or sector rather than just attempting to maximise market share. Both are supplemented by (3) *an ROI spread*, in which component organisations are attracted/recruited because they offer (4) *essential core*

Dimension	Key issue	Key questions
Customer selection	Which customers do I want to serve?	To which customers can I add real value? Which customers will allow me to make profits? Which customers do I *not want* to serve?
Value capture	How do we generate cash?	How do I capture a portion of the value I create for customers? What is my 'cash flow' model?
Differentiation	How do I protect my cash flow stream?	What do customers purchase? What differentiates my value proposition? What distinctive capabilities does the business have? What strategic controls can counterbalance customer or competitor power?
Scope	What processes do we perform? Are these the right processes? Are these processes that partner organisations should perform? Are there processes that customer could undertake more efficiently? What capabilities and assets are required to support the processes?	Which products, services and solutions do I want to sell? Which functions do I want to perform in house? Why? Which do I want to outsource? Why?

From Slywotsky A. J. and D. J. Morrison (1997), *The Profit Zone,* Time Books, NY

Figure 5.4 A customer-centric approach

resources that in turn enable the business model to develop and (5) *leverage its competitive advantage*. An essential feature is that the structure is designed to operate on the principle of (6) *low capital intensity*. The model appears as Figure 5.5, with each component itemised.

The purpose of the model is to act as a scoping medium. Given an assumption that most virtual organisations evolve around a 'visionary' or a 'coordinator', then it is also reasonable to assume that there some initial performance criteria will be determined.

Clearly there needs to be a 'primary' goal for the organisation; current thinking suggests free cash flow as bing the obvious choice. What follows is an iterative process that identifies alternative structures that will produce an optimal cash flow performance. It can only be an optimal level because the objectives (and possibly constraints) of the other participants will impact upon both the structure and the performance of the alliance. Issues such as the level of 'capital' investment (tangible assets) and its location(s), and the ownership of processes, capabilities and intangible assets are to be considered.

There are also 'qualitative' issues to be considered. These will include differences in organisation cultures and management styles, and the extent to which individual businesses are prepared to work as a cooperative and accept joint decision making. In addition there may be systems issues concerning the infrastructure the model requires if it is to be successful, such

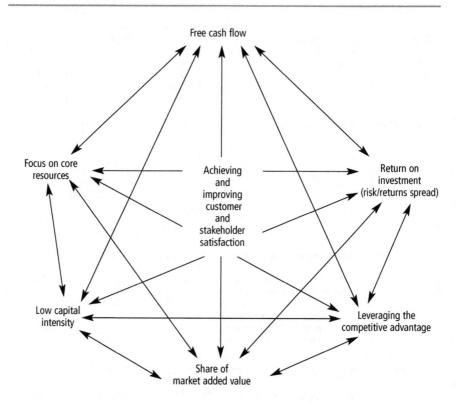

Figure 5.5 An example of a 'virtual business' model

as information management, attitudes towards conservation and the whole notion of 'value'.

Therefore to make the model active some ground rules should first be set:

■ Customers' expectations
■ Virtual enterprise stakeholders' expectations and trade-off flexibility
■ The ideal model performance and structure

From these the planning process should work towards a structure that 'fits' (as closely as possible) the stakeholder expectations given any flexibility in the expectations of the target customer group. For example, the possibility of a trade-off between variety, quality, service and price should be established at the initial stages of developing a 'virtual enterprise' so as to be able to pursue opportunities. The key elements are as follows:

■ Achieving and improving customer and stakeholder satisfaction
  – Assumes that customer satisfaction and stakeholder satisfaction are optimised in the long term
  – And that by maximising enterprise value (EV) this is achieved

- The weighted interest rate used to calculate EV represents the weighted cost of capital used to calculate the ROI spread

■ Free cash flow
  - Calculated from operating cash flow, cash flow from assets and strategic cash flow
  - The NPV discount rate is the same as that used to calculate EV and the ROI spread – a weighted average cost of capital

■ Measuring the risk profile
  - Risk and return are usually positively correlated. That is, projects offering high returns are typically accompanied by high levels of risk
  - Risk is often implied by the cost of borrowing (reflected in the cost of capital)
  - It follows that a measure of the return/risk profile is given by the returns spread – the difference between the returns on assets managed (ROAM) less the cost of capital

■ Low capital intensity
  - Low capital intensity represents an optimal position of asset ownership determined by performance measures (measured simply by total assets/total sales) which reflect specific customer based 'service achievements' that can be matched with customer value drivers (such as inventory availability and service response times) and that meet 'investment return criteria' set by stakeholder agreement and also reflect performance criteria (such as sales/assets and assets/sales)
  - Low capital intensity is an aggregate measure of partner capital deployments and is measured by comparing alternative virtual organisation structures using operational gearing (FC/(FC + VC)), net assets (tangible and intangible fixed and net current assets), and estimated aggregate overhead amounts for each alternative structure

Giving:
Relative
capital   =
intensity

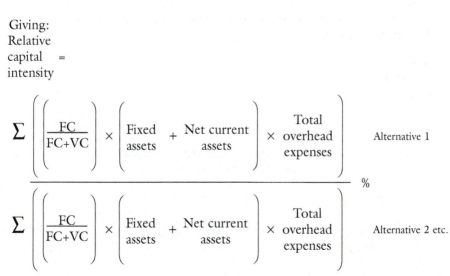

Measuring competitive advantage

Competitive advantage is derived by making comparisons with the corresponding performance of:

- the industry average (which may not be too helpful in an industry that is either fragmented in size or in the nature of its outputs)
- the 'worst' performer (again, problematic for reasons of processes and output focus)
- or perhaps the 'nearest benchmark' competitor

Whether the organisation is adding or destroying value can be measured in the following way:

$$\text{Competitive advantage} = \frac{\$(\text{Outputs} - \text{Inputs})}{\text{Inputs}} \qquad \text{(from Kay 1993)}$$

Therefore:

$$\text{Competitive advantage} = \frac{\$(\text{Outputs} - \text{Inputs})}{\$\text{Inputs}} = \frac{\$\text{Added value}}{\$\text{Inputs}}$$

Or:

$$\frac{\text{CA}_{\text{Organisation}}}{\text{CA}_{\text{Competitor (1...n)}}} > = <1$$

Similarly time comparisons are also helpful to determine the progress made by an organisation:

$$\frac{\text{CA}_{t+}}{\text{CA}_{t\,\text{Current}}} > = <1$$

If SCA >1 then the organisation is *adding value*
If SCA <1 then the organisation is *destroying value*

The following, derived using the Kay (1993) model, can show the leveraging of competitive advantage:

Relative
competitive   =
advantage

$$\frac{\left(\dfrac{\text{Revenues} - (\text{Wages} + \text{Salaries} + \text{Materials} + \text{Capital costs})}{(\text{Wages} + \text{Salaries} + \text{Materials} + \text{Capital costs})} \right) \text{‘Organisation’}}{\left(\dfrac{\text{Revenues} - (\text{Wages} + \text{Salaries} + \text{Materials} + \text{Capital costs})}{(\text{Wages} + \text{Salaries} + \text{Materials} + \text{Capital costs})} \right) \begin{array}{l}\text{Nearest}\\\text{competitive}\\\text{offer}\end{array}} \%$$

The objective would be to develop a significant lead over competitors. Share of market added value can be shown thus:

Per cent share of total available market added value $=$ $\dfrac{\text{Total organisational revenues less operating costs}}{\text{Total available market revenues less operating costs}}$ %

To deal with *value migration* other measures are required. Millennium Pharmaceuticals CEO, Mark Levin, has suggested that 'Value has started to migrate downstream, toward the more mechanical tasks of identifying, testing, and manufacturing molecules that will affect the proteins produced by the genes, and which become the pills and serums we sell.'

It follows that monitoring industry structural changes will identify just where the value is being added. Value chain systems and the value components can use the formula below to assess the share of market value they currently command. If the measurement is made over time any changes that occur should be investigated to determine whether they are due to aggressive competition or to value migration.

Share of total market added value (market effectiveness) $=$ $\dfrac{\sum\$(\text{Outputs - Inputs})}{\sum\sum\$(\text{Outputs - Inputs})}$

Where

$\sum\$(\text{Outputs} - \text{Inputs})$ = Organisation's added value
$\sum\sum\$(\text{Outputs} - \text{Inputs})$ = Total market added value

Another useful added value metric reveals the *efficiency resource* allocation. Efficiency measures compare the use of resources in a business model format. A comparable organisation may indicate a greater turnover:

Efficiency of resource utilisation = $\dfrac{\$\text{Outputs}(x)}{\$\text{Inputs}}$

As we saw earlier in this chapter, *share of market added value* is preferred to market share.

An estimate of the return on the investment to achieve an increase in added value is also a useful measure:

$\dfrac{\text{Incremental increase in organisational market added value}}{\text{Incremental investment for value creation and production}}$

The Australian wine industry: an example of a virtual approach

The 'new world' wine industry provides some interesting examples of a virtual approach. While contracted growing of grapes has been widespread for a long time, it was generally at the behest of the major producers as a supplement to their own capabilities. The major wine producers took a typical vertically integrated approach – from owning the vineyards through to their own distribution structures. Below this sat a raft of boutique producers who may not have been capable of replicating the whole value chain, and relied upon others for bottling and even wine making skills, but this was largely a function of size rather than capabilities.

More recently the 'virtual' wine producer has emerged, not competing in boutique markets, but in the large-volume, low-price segments. In a what might be called a 'low capital intensity' (virtual winery) model the investment/sales ratio is typically lower than that of traditional models by a significant amount – 30 per cent compared with often as much as 200 per cent, that is, an investment of 30 cents/dollar sales rather than $2.00.

Assuming similar costs and product quality, the required ratio of earnings before interest and tax (EBIT) to funds employed also becomes a much lower figure. For example, with a capital intensity ratio of, say, 40/50 per cent compared to the traditional level of 100 to 200 per cent, the required EBIT/funds employed figure can be as low as 10 per cent, considerably less than the 30 per cent required for viability by the traditional model.

It follows that target revenues are also lower, often by some 30 per cent – in retail terms this may be as much as 25 per cent less per bottle for the same quality wine! As a result the EBIT/funds employed ratio can show an impressive 75 per cent for the 'virtual' model versus approximately five percent for the traditional winery model. Comparative cost structures are shown in Table 5.1.

Cash flow improvements are equally significant. It can be calculated that, based on the assumption of same revenues, the cash generated can be shown to improve by a factor of between three and four times.

In reality, despite the attractiveness of the model the virtual winery has had its problems. To some extent while in an output sense the product is highly commoditised, the customer expectation is still for an individualised brand with regional characteristics. This suggests that market segmentation and therefore product-service 'customisation' is critical. Another concern for the 'virtual winery' is the need to identify core processes and to grasp the fact

Table 5.1 Comparison of capital structure models: traditional and virtual wineries

Capital element per $ revenue	Traditional wine organisation $	Virtual wine organisation: Cheviot Bridge $
Vineyards	0.35	0.00
Bottling	0.10	0.00
Inventory	1.00	0.10
Debtors	0.25	0.25
Creditors	0.10	0.10
Overhead	0.20	0.00/negligible
Total fixed and working capital	2.00	0.45

that while ownership is not critical, the ability to manage them is, ensuring consistent product quality.

This raises issues to be addressed concerning the impact of variable costs on total costs and therefore cash flows. It cannot be assumed that there is no cost penalty to having reduced fixed cost structures. For example, the transportation of low added value product inputs from one location to another can add significant variable costs to the operation. While it may be assumed that these are an acceptable trade-off for the 'perils' of servicing debt, the distance between process stages may involve excessive variable costs that inhibit strong cash flows.

The primary benefits of low capital intensity business models are the being able to operate at low break-even volumes, the problems of large amounts of fixed costs/overhead to be covered having been divested; and because of this, being able to use this flexibility in the marketplace through pricing policies. Such models also enable the virtual winery to use the free cash flow to invest in core processes and capabilities. But as we can see, there are dangers for the unwary.

Concluding comments

This chapter has approached the resource allocation task by considering emerging approaches to resource allocation in the 'new economy'. Added value creativity will be enhanced if management first identifies the linkages between industry and organisational drivers and the customers' value drivers. Figure 5.6 outlines the principle of this task. The skill is to align industry drivers with the value drivers in such away that can be strategically effective.

For example, in a knowledge led industry, knowledge management should be aligned with the customer value drivers that will produce the most synergy; these are likely to be information management, asset productivity management, and performance management. In a relationship led industry it is very probable that asset productivity management and performance management are the most essential value drivers that should be in alignment with the industry drivers.

With this realised, the next task is to identify the *customer facing processes* that will be successful in linking and aligning the industry drivers with the customer value drivers and achieving customer value expectations. This is suggested by Figure 5.7.

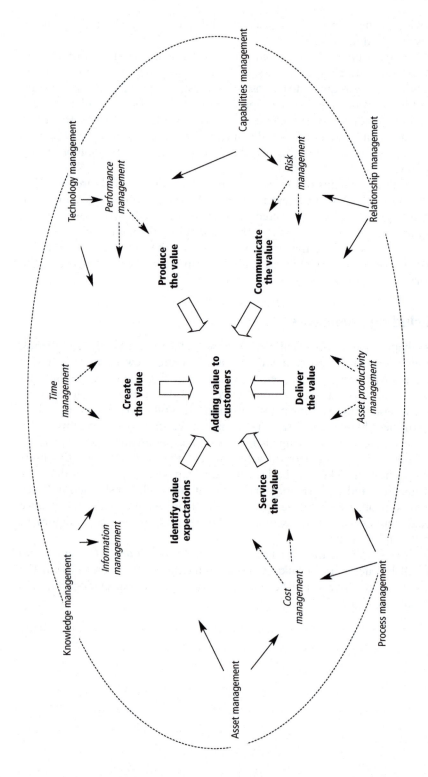

Figure 5.6 Linking industry value drivers to the value processes

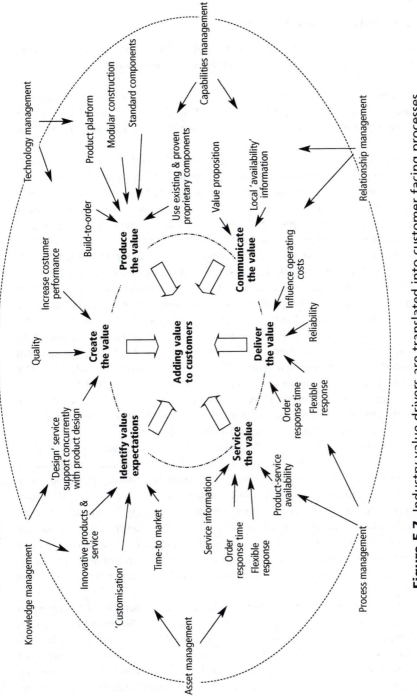

Figure 5.7 Industry value drivers are translated into customer facing processes

CASE STUDY 5.1

Capability sourcing: 7-Eleven

(Based upon Gottfredson M, R Puryear and S Phillips, 'Strategic sourcing from periphery to the core', *Harvard Business Review*, February 2005)

Gottfredson and his co-authors develop a convincing argument for taking a strategic approach to capability sourcing. They discuss the case of 7-Eleven, an organisation that has been the subject of a number of academic and practical business articles.

Gottfredson et al. pick up the discussion on 7-Eleven from 1991. The company was losing money and market share due to an aggressive strategy by the major oil companies to add convenience stores to their service station sites. The newly appointed CEO, Jim Keyes, saw some immediate ways of responding. More customer traffic was needed; and 7-Eleven needed to reduce operating costs, to expand the range of products and services and increase the freshness of food items.

An audit of 7-Eleven's activities identified the fact that there were too many of them, and that the organisation was not particularly good at any of them. 7-Eleven's core business skill was identified as being merchandising (positioning, pricing, and promotion of the product range to car bound consumers). They also identified the fact that 7-Eleven was vertically integrated, controlling all of the processes and activities in the value chain from milk production (they owned the cows!), making its own confectionary requirements and even ice. The company owned its own distribution system. Store managers were responsible for store administration and maintenance. Keyes' response was to pursue the Japanese *keiretsu* model. An extensive network of suppliers was established based upon Keyes' premise that 'to outsource everything not mission-critical' was probably the only way to restore the company to profitable operations.

A simple criterion was used: 'If a partner could provide a capability more effectively than 7-Eleven could itself, then that capability became a candidate for outsourcing.' Over time the company outsourced HR, finance, IT management, logistics and distribution, product development and packaging. 7-Eleven structured the partnerships to reflect their importance to the company's competitive differentiation. Routine capabilities such as ongoing accounting functions were outsourced to partners capable of consistently meeting cost and quality requirements. A more strategic activity such as petrol retailing (an important source of revenue) was not offered to a partner whereas the physical distribution of fuel was outsourced to a specialist company.

In an attempt to create synergy with some of its partners, 7-Eleven works closely with companies such as Frito-Lay. Frito-Lay is allowed to distribute its products directly to the stores – in this way 7-Eleven benefits from logistics economies of scale. However, Frito-Lay is not permitted to make decisions about shelf locations and quantities. 7-Eleven maintains extensive customer purchasing data on a store by store basis to make these decisions. Product range selection and management are critical to 7-Eleven's operational (and long-term) success.

Accordingly the company has a clear view concerning control over sensitive data; a data management company manages the collection and processing of customer data, but the interpretation and proprietary company implications are kept within the company. This ensures that 7-Eleven makes the critical product mix and product allocation decisions independently of the interests of its suppliers. This approach in turn enables 7-Eleven to structure supplier relationships in a way that accesses a capability 7-Eleven does not have but, at the same time, to maintain control over vital decisions.

An interesting development and diversion from this policy is reported by Gottfredson et al. The organisation became aware that it might be able to realise the benefits of leveraged creativity and production scale economies through sharing information with a select group of manufacturers by allowing them to manufacture customised products for 7-Eleven outlets. This has resulted in partnerships with Hershey and Coca-Cola. Typically 7-Eleven has an 'exclusive' with the new product for an agreed time period. For 7-Eleven this has proved to be an effective trade-off between the strategic risks of sharing confidential customer information and the benefit of receiving access to unique new products.

The 7-Eleven approach to capability sourcing has resulted in using partnerships to pioneer new capabilities. A consortium partnership with American Express, Western Union, CashWorks, and EDS resulted in an exclusive customer cash service facility, differentiating the company yet further from its competitors.

The organisation has adopted a particular approach to partner investment. Having made equity investment in a major IT partner, it is sharing productivity gains from a service agreement with Hewlett-Packard, and created a joint venture with a supplier of sandwiches and other fresh food items. The benefits have been twofold: distribution costs have been dramatically reduced (with the expectation that this will be repeated), but possibly more significantly, deliveries to 7-Eleven stores have been increased from twice weekly to daily, with a twice daily service soon to be introduced.

The 7-Eleven capability sourcing partnership strategy has produced outstanding results. The focus on a set of strategically important capabilities has reduced its tangible assets and streamlined the organisation. Staff numbers have been reduced by almost 30 per cent. Same-store annual sales growth reached 6.6 per cent (the industry figure being 3.5 per cent), inventory productivity 38.8 times (the industry figure being 22.2), and sales per employee $US239,000 (with the industry averaging $US98,000) for the period 2004/05.

Discussion topics

Collaboration and partnerships, and indeed outsourcing non-core capabilities, processes and even assets is not new in the retailing industry. In the mid-1980s the large retailers were involved in sale and leaseback arrangements with investment companies. While they were primarily interested in raising cash at relatively low cost to expand their businesses, they realised significant operational cost savings. Identify other organisations where similar results have been achieved.

CASE STUDY 5.2

Process and capability sourcing: Bendigo Bank

(Based upon Tracy Lee, 'Bendigo buys a financing firm', *Australian Financial Review*, 28 April 2005)

The formation of Bendigo Bank was a response to the major banks' withdrawal from rural locations in Australia. Initially it located its services in established retailing businesses in the population centres of rural Australia. Success influenced the Bank to establish locations in the central business district (CBD) areas of the larger cities and to expand the range of its services.

As we have seen with other organisations (for example 7-Eleven in Case Study 5.1), a number of options are available when considering an extension to the customer value proposition. In the example of 7-Eleven the company decided to maintain a very tight focus on what it considered to be its required core processes and capabilities – resulting in an extensive range (and types) of partnership arrangements. Often other factors dominate the choice. For example speed (time) and control of a process or capability require an alternative approach. Bendigo Bank saw a need to move into the small-business sector. It did not have the services offered by its competitors and to remedy this disadvantage it needed either to find a partner or to make an acquisition. Ashley Hood, head of business banking, said, '[the acquisition] was needed to plug product gaps and remove a competitive disadvantage'. Bendigo paid $A14.3 million for a cash flow financing business, Oxford Funding. Oxford buys commercial accounts receivables from businesses at a discount, thereby providing the customer organisation with immediate access to cash. The Bendigo managing director saw this as essential: 'Turnover for debtor financing and invoice discounting grew by almost 40 per cent last year, so this acquisition has the potential to add significantly to the profitability of Bendigo's business banking arm.' Market analysts met the news with positive comments, pointing to the rapid growth of the market sector and of Bendigo's competitors. Bendigo's major shareholder saw the acquisition as 'a solid move for the Victoria based bank. Oxford has had good profit growth for a few years. It's a profitable and expanding business with experienced staff and, together with the distribution channels of Bendigo, I think it's very positive.'

Discussion topics

This example contrasts with the strategy pursued by 7-Eleven. What issues arise out of this case for organisations seeking to expand their value proposition? Are there criteria that should be considered in order that an overall policy concerning 'make or buy' decisions can be made strategically?

CASE STUDY 5.3

Focusing on core assets: Seven Network

(Based upon Neil Shoebridge, 'Assets go as Seven puts focus on its key business', *Australian Financial Review*, 7 April 2005)

The Seven Network, one of Australia's large television companies, has been selling its non-core assets over the past few years. One sale, in April 2005, was of a 50 per cent stake in Ticketmaster7 to the US company Ticketmaster, raising a reported $A12–14 million in an ongoing strategy of focusing on its core media business (television and magazines). Neil Shoebridge reports that Seven has raised some $A250 million over the previous two years by selling investments in printing, telecommunications, an internet business and property in Sydney, Melbourne and Adelaide.

Seven's non-core assets now include holdings in a record company, a 50 per cent holding in a management and marketing consultancy, and a 25 per cent interest in a company that sells syndication rights to a defunct TV programme. The company continues to have property interests in land adjacent to its broadcast centre in Melbourne and in the Perth Entertainment Centre, which was closed after substantial losses were made. Negotiations for the site are ongoing. Other non-core media assets include the management, naming, marketing, signage, ticketing and seating rights to the Melbourne Telstra Dome.

Discussion topics

It is not suggested that Seven's investment strategy has been based upon serendipity but it raises an interesting point concerning investment portfolio policy in organisations that are essentially specialists. Does the move towards a virtual organisation strategy for specialist companies suggest they should invest in core assets, process and capabilities, or should their investment strategy be independent of the core business direction?

REFERENCES

Baghai M A, S C Coley and D White (1999) 'Turning capabilities into advantages', *McKinsey Quarterly*, 1

Band W A (1991) *Creating Value for Customers*, Wiley, New York

Boisot M (1998) *Knowledge Assets: Securing Competitive Advantage in the Information Economy*, Oxford University Press, Oxford

Bornheim S P with J Weppler and O Ohlen (2001) *e-roadmapping*, Palgrave Macmillan, Basingstoke

Boudreau M-C, K Loch, D Robey and D Straud (1998) 'Going global: using information technology to advance the competitiveness of virtual transnational organisation', *Academy of Management Executive*, 12(4)

Boulton R E S, B D Libert and S M Samek (2000) 'A business model for the new economy,' *Journal of Business Strategy*, July/August

Brookings Institution (1982–2000) www.brookings.edu.

Buzzel R D and B Gale (1987) *The PIMS Principles: Linking Strategy to Performance*, Free Press, New York

Campbell A (1996) 'Creating the virtual organisation and managing the distributed workforce', in Jackson P and J Van der Weilen (eds) *New Perspectives on Telework – From Telecommuting to the Virtual Organisation*, Report on workshop held at Brunel University, 31 July–2 August

Coase R H (1937) 'The nature of the firm', *Economica*, 4

Drucker P (2001)'Will the corporation survive?', *The Economist*, 1 November

Gottfredson M, R Puryear and S Phillips (2005) 'Strategic sourcing from periphery to the core', *Harvard Business Review*, February

Grupp H (1998) *Foundations of the Economics of Innovation: Theory, Measurement, and Practice*, Edward Elgar, Cheltenham

Hagel J III and M Singer (1999) 'Unbundling the corporation,' *Harvard Business Review*, March/April

Hamel G and C K Prahalad (1994) *The Core Competences of the Corporation*, Harvard Business School Press, Boston, MA

Harris J G and R J Burgman (2005) *Chains, Shops, and Networks: The Logic of Organisational Value*, Accenture Institute for Higher Performance Business, Wellesley, MA

Housel T and A H Bell (2001), *Measuring and Managing Knowledge*, McGraw-Hill, New York

Kay J (1993), *Foundation of Corporate Success*, Oxford University Press, Oxford

Kay J (2000) 'Strategy and the delusion of grand designs', in *Mastering Strategy*, Financial Times/Prentice-Hall, London

Kodama F (1995) *Emerging Patterns of Innovation*, Harvard Business School Press, Boston, MA

Leonard-Barton D (1992) 'Core capabilities and core rigidities: a paradox in managing new product development', *Strategic Management Journal*, 13

Lester R K (1998) *The Productive Edge: How US Industries Are Pointing the Way to a New Era of Economic Growth*, Norton, New York

London S (2005) 'IBM needs to press right buttons', *FT International in Australian*, 10 May

Luthans F (2002) *Organisational Behaviour*, McGraw-Hill, New York

Magretta J (2002) 'Why business models matter', *Harvard Business Review*, May

McHugh P, G Merli and G Wheeler III (1995) *Beyond Business Process Reengineering*, Wiley, Chichester

McLoughlin I (1999) *Creative Technological Change*, Routledge, London

Mirman R (1982) 'Performance management in sales organisations', in L Frederiksen (ed.) *Handbook of Organisational Behaviour Management*, Wiley, New York

Normann R (2001) *Reframing Business*, Wiley, Chichester

Olve N, J Roy and M Wetter (1997) *Performance Drivers*, Wiley, Chichester

Payne A and S Holt (2001) 'Diagnosing customer value: integrating the value process and relationship marketing', *British Journal of Management*, 12(2)

Porter M (1985) *Competitive Strategy*, Free Press, New York

Quinn J B (1992) *Intelligent Enterprise*, Free Press, New York

Rumelt R P (1994) 'Foreword', in Hamel G and A Heene (eds) *Competence Based Competition*, Wiley, Chichester

Slywotzky A J and D J Morrison (1997) *The Profit Zone*, Wiley, New York

Solectron, www.solectron.com/services/lean.html

Stevens C (1998) 'The knowledge-driven economy', in D Neef (ed.) *The Knowledge Economy*, Butterworth-Heinemann, Oxford

Stewart G B (1997) *Intellectual Capital: The New Wealth of Nations*, Currency Doubleday, New York

UK Department of Trade & Industry (1998) *Our Competitive Future: Building the Knowledge Driven Economy*, Stationery Office, London

Woodall P (2000) 'Untangling e-conomics', *The Economist*, 21 September

World Bank (1998) *World Development Report 1998*, World Bank, Washington, DC

Zineldin M (2000) *TRM: Total Relationship Management*, Studentlitteratur, Lund

CHAPTER 6

The Supply Chain and the Demand Chain

LEARNING TOPICS

On completing your study of this chapter you will have been introduced to and considered the following topics:

- The way supply chains focus too much on efficiency
- The demand chain as an emerging concept and a distinct entity
- The demand chain and the supply chain converge rather than conflict
- Using demand chain analysis to focus the supply chain

Introduction

The notion of the supply chain manager as the new corporate hero, championing reduced costs, improving efficiencies and rewarding customers with reduced prices, seems somewhat incongruous to those brought up on the notion that marketing was the dominant corporate philosophy. Indeed at least one generation of business students and practitioners were taught that it was marketing that was responsible for inculcating customer values into the organisation and that this was the ultimate means of fostering competitive advantage. Even a cursory glance at today's financial pages, however, suggests that instead it is firms that consistently and persistently manage their cost structures that are seen as the overachievers. In Australia two dominant retailing groups, Woolworths and Coles Myer, have made 'everyday low prices' their primary offer to customers, rooted in efficiency strategies. In the UK the efficacy of the supply chain was a prominent in the recent (and ongoing) battle for control of Marks & Spencer.

A number of potential dangers arise from this new supply chain dominance of corporate thinking. Not the least is that supply chain efficiency is mistaken for effectiveness, with undue short-term emphasis on cost reduction at the expense of contribution to broader goals. In particular customer needs may ultimately be seen in simplistic terms, revolving purely around reduced price as a major determinant of satisfaction.

This may, at least partially, reflect a failure by marketing as a discipline to provide the coherence to corporate organisation, operations and objectives that its proponents have claimed. In response this chapter proposes a broader perspective, based on the notion of the demand chain, which encompasses a more holistic view of all of those processes in the firm that do, or should, respond to the customer.

Supply chains: too much emphasis on efficiency?

The notion that organisations have supply chains that require active management to maximise efficiency is well recognised. Indeed across a number of industries, including the retail sector, supply chain efficiency has become a dominant corporate paradigm, driving firms' business models and at least in the short term delivering improved profitability.

Waller (1998) discusses 'customer driven' logistics as an increasingly accepted concept by suggesting that a customer approach will ensure supply chain efficiencies. He cites Marks & Spencer in the UK as having 'long been regarded as leaders in this'. Recent events would suggest this as a fraught strategy. As we saw in Chapter 1 with the examples of Sainsbury's and Marks & Spencer in the 1990s, the notion that an effective supply chain alone will ensure customer satisfaction through reducing costs and therefore prices is not necessarily an adequate model by itself. More recently, Sainsbury's admitted to not meeting customer expectations. CEO Justin King was told by a customer that due to poor ranging she used competitors' stores. King has commented: '... they [Sainsbury's] had built an unsustainable business model, [it had] become too driven by profit margins and was too heavily focused on short-term profits. Furthermore it had invested in infrastructure that had failed to deliver the intended benefits. The customer offering was neglected' (Gluyas 2004).

Industry analysts' comments in June 2004 also suggested Marks & Spencer continued to be supply chain driven, arguing that they had not responded to competitive threats to core merchandise groups by new entrants, and had certainly ignored customer expectations as regards quality. It is also suggested that their response to competition has been cost led – by is looking at ways to source products more cheaply, resulting in 'taking away from the quality of the product and that takes away the reason people used to buy from M&S'.

This suggests that a purely mechanistic supply chain approach, entirely driven by cost-efficiency, needs to be replaced with a broader view of overall *effectiveness*. It is interesting to recall a comment by Porter (1996) concerning the mistakes that can be made by confusing *operational efficiency* with *strategic effectiveness*. Porter is suggesting that the attraction of the cost-efficiency offered by the increasing range of production techniques has directed management towards short-term profitability at the expense of increased strategic advantage gained from understanding customer value expectations. Clearly both Sainsbury's and Marks & Spencer would appear to have been doing just this!!

Fisher (1997), for example, has suggested that the first step in devising a supply chain strategy is to consider the nature of the demand for an organisation's products, proposing that these are either *functional* or *innovative*. *Functional* products are typically staple fast moving consumer goods, widely available, which satisfy basic needs that do not change much over time. *Innovative* have short life cycles with volatile demand that is difficult to predict. Fisher argues that the supply chain has two distinct functions. First, a *physical* function, which 'includes the conversion of raw materials into parts, components, and eventually finished goods, and their transport between the various parts of the supply chain'. Second, the function of what is termed market *mediation*, which ensures 'that the mix of product variants which is brought to the market matches what customers want to buy'. Fisher then constructs a supply chain that links the nature of demand with the function of the supply chain. In Fisher's model functional products require an efficient supply chain in which the costs of production, transportation and inventory holding are minimised. The efficient supply chain is characterised by MRP/ERP software packages, driven by electronic data interchange (EDI) linkages between suppliers and customers. In this way the typical supply chain performance criteria of high availability, rapid replenishment and cost efficiency are achieved. Fisher also identifies the importance of effective enterprise-wide information management systems.

Towards an alternative model: the emergence of the demand chain as a concept

Fisher (1997) goes a long way to addressing the limitations of the uni-dimensional, cost focused supply chain. Some authors have taken the argument a step further, however, and suggested that the whole concept of the supply chain has changed through evolution so that 'It could be argued that it [supply chain management] should be termed "demand chain management" to reflect the fact that the chain should be driven by the market, not by suppliers ... ' (Christopher 1998). This is insufficient; simply changing the name is unlikely to change behaviour.

Tierney (2003) quotes H L Lee in saying that customers form a central part of the enterprise. He depicted a triangle with customer demand at the pinnacle and supply chain and demand chain management at the bases. He cites the success of 7-Eleven Japan, whose stock prices had kept rising despite Japan's recession for the previous ten years. The secret of its success is demand led management, which induced it to identify sales patterns and customer preferences and to match these by re-engineering its category management and store product layouts, resulting in increased sales and profitability.

Holmstrom et al. (2000) add emphasis to the argument that a pure supply chain focus is inadequate if we are seeking to add value for customers. They suggest the supply chain as a 'customer service led' process.

Langabeer and Rose (2001) take the argument a step further by looking at the demand chain as an entity in its own right, suggesting, first, a simultaneous standardisation and differentiation in consumer preferences for products (the demand chain), and, second, a continued emphasis on cost minimisation in manufacturing supply chains. Unfortunately, these two are often at odds with each other. This is an interesting differentiation between the supply chain and the demand chain and between demand management and demand chain management. They define the demand chain as 'the complex web of business processes and activities that help firms understand, manage, and ultimately create consumer demand'. They emphasise the point that demand chain management attempts to analyse and understand overall demand for markets within the firm's current and potential product range. Supply chains, by contrast, emphasise the efficiencies in the production and logistics processes, while the demand chain emphasises effectiveness in the business. A very useful point in their argument is that demand chain analysis and management help to improve an organisation's processes by aligning the organisation around a common plan, as well as its coordination within the supply chain by using forecasts and plans, and exploits the commercial processes both by understanding consumer demand and by selecting those markets that best meet an organisation's owned and/or 'leased' skills and resources.

This introduces the notion that an effective approach to demand chain management requires the organisation, first, to understand its current and potential markets, and second, to identify the essential (or core) processes and capabilities that are required for success. Table 6.1 offers a comparison of the two approaches.

Table 6.1 The supply chain and the demand chain

Supply chain	Demand chain
Efficiency focus: cost per item	Effectiveness focus: customer focused, product-market fit
Processes are focused on execution	Processes are focused more on planning and delivering value
Cost is the key driver	Cash flow and profitability are the key drivers
Short-term oriented, within the immediate and controllable future	Long term oriented, within the next planning cycles
Typically the domain of tactical manufacturing and logistics personnel	Typically the domain of marketing, sales and strategic operations managers
Focuses on immediate resource and capacity constraints	Focuses on long-term capabilities, not short-term constraints
Historical focus on operations planning and controls	Historical focus on demand management and supply chain alignment

Based on Langabeer and Rose (2001)

The authors go on to propose a demand strategy, comprising a supply chain strategy (focusing on manufacturing, distribution and network optimisation), a customer strategy (customers and markets), a product and brand strategy (focusing on key product requirements and customisation needs), and a sales and marketing strategy (creating awareness and demand). They suggest that these, when coordinated, create a demand strategy: 'the direction that a firm pursues to attract and retain desirable customers and improve its product positioning in profitable markets'.

The demand chain: processes rather than functions

Processes were defined in Chapter 5 as business outcomes of which there are recipients that may be either internal or external to the organisation. There, we saw that they also cross organisational boundaries, that is, they normally occur across or between either intra- or inter-organisational boundaries, and are independent of formal organisational structures. Effective organisations now work together to identify core processes. The scope of process management is such that it may be applied to strategic and operational tasks and structures alike. We also highlighted Hagel and Singer's (1999) view that the traditional organisation comprises three basic types of business: a customer relationship business, a product innovation business and an infrastructure business. They clearly identify the attitudinal and behavioural variations that occur between the three businesses, thereby adding emphasis to the difference between an efficiency driven supply chain orientation and an analytical and effectiveness driven demand chain orientation.

How then should we view this broader notion of the demand chain? Possibly the first step is to reinforce the point that both supply chain management and demand chain management are about *process management*. This has been defined in a number of ways. One relevant to this discussion is offered by Trinca (2003); it is particularly useful in that it addresses the need to consider both suppliers and customers: 'It's a systematic way of improving internal processes as well as the way you work with suppliers and customers ... '. Hammer (2001) agrees that as businesses become accustomed to the customer economy, 'process thinking' becomes essential – customer satisfaction is process led.

The second step is to revalidate the notion of the demand chain as a separate entity from the supply chain. To this end the following definition of demand management may add some direction: 'an understanding of current and future customer expectations, market characteristics, and of the available response alternatives to meet these through the deployment of operational processes'. This is not simply another restatement of the marketing concept. Marketing is a philosophy, stressing the customer-centric goals of an organisation. The demand chain is a practical description and analysis encompassing all those processes within the firm that adopt and apply that philosophy. Perhaps an example here will help. Dell Computers operate a demand led customer response supply chain. Their business model is an example of Bucklin's postponement (as opposed to speculation) channel model of some years ago.

There would seem to be little argument that the old downstream supply chain model is too limiting and that the customer needs to be brought into the equation. One approach has been to modify the scope of the supply chain, and another has been to develop the notion of the value net (Bovet and Martha 2000). These models are valuable to the extent that they explicitly recognise the role of the customer and their demands in maximising value for the firm. However, rather than assume some composite model, it should be explicitly recognised that there are in fact two different forces at work which are not necessarily complementary and indeed are often in conflict – the supply chain and the demand chain.

An interesting way of viewing this is to apply the model developed by MacMillan and McGrath (1997) who suggest that the customer life cycle, or the consumption chain, is a means by which firms '... can uncover opportunities to position their offerings in ways that they and their competitors would never have thought possible'. The idea of 'mapping the consumption chain' captures the customer's total experience with a product or service. Such a process identifies numerous ways in which value can be added to a product or service. The mapping process to identify the consumption chain comprises a series of questions aimed at establishing aspects of behaviour that occur. The answers to these questions identify opportunities to add value and determine the shape of both the demand chain and of the required supply chain responses. From an analysis of the answers it then becomes possible to identify the different process drivers, some of which can be categorised as demand driven and some as supply driven, which are all essential to motivate customer expectations and subsequently purchase decisions. An efficient supply chain alone provides only half the solution, as does an efficient demand chain.

The demand chain and the supply chain converge rather than conflict

Figure 6.1 illustrates the major differences between the supply chain and the demand chain. Because there is often a budget constraint in supply chain management (SCM) led structures, it follows that while the processes may share labels they invariably differ in the tasks they perform. For example in an SCM approach, design and development activities will be seeking to address broad appeal in an attempt to ensure financial viability. By contrast, demand chain management (DCM) led organisations empower R&D staff to work closely with customers to develop products and processes cooperatively.

In SCM focused organisations, procurement is typically an adversarial process. Suppliers are pressured by their customers so to produce high margins for the latter. This is often necessary to hedge against the risk of mark-downs should sales forecasts not be met. The DCM led organisation uses market knowledge to develop strong working relationships with suppliers. Given a precise understanding of customer needs (and market trends) it is possible for the procurement process to work with design and development to arrive at optimal solutions to product and process development options. As Figure 6.1 suggests, it is also very

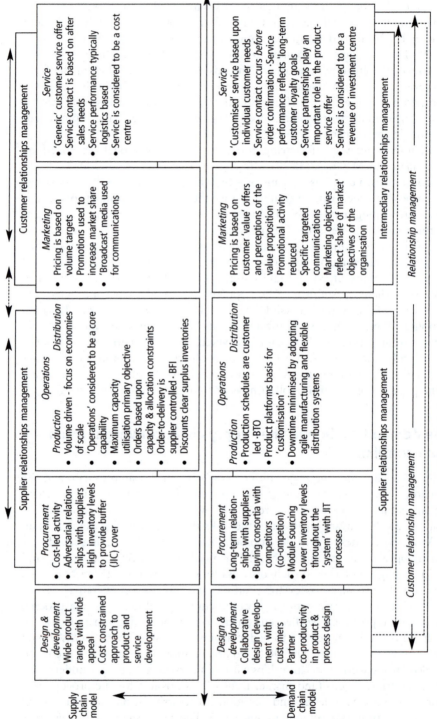

Figure 6.1 The processes differ

Supply chain model

Customer relationships management

Design & development
- Wide product range with wide appeal
- Cost constrained approach to product and service development

Procurement
- Cost-led activity
- Adversarial relationships with suppliers
- High inventory levels to provide buffer (JIC) cover

Operations

Production
- Volume driven - focus on economies of scale
- 'Operations' considered to be a core capability
- Maximum capacity utilisation primary objective
- Orders based upon capacity & allocation constraints

Distribution
- Order-to-delivery is supplier controlled - BFI
- Discounts clear surplus inventories

Marketing
- Pricing is based on volume targets
- Promotions used to increase market share
- 'Broadcast' media used for communications

Service
- 'Generic' customer service offer
- Service contact is based on after sales needs
- Service performance typically logistics based
- Service is considered to be a cost centre

Supplier relationships management

Demand chain model

Customer relationship management

Design & development
- Collaborative design development with customers
- Partner co-productivity in product & process design

Procurement
- Long-term relationships with suppliers
- Buying consortia with competitors (co-opetition)
- Module sourcing
- Lower inventory levels throughout the 'system' with JIT processes

Operations

Production
- Production schedules are customer led ·BTO
- Product platforms basis for 'customisation'
- Downtime minimised by adopting agile manufacturing and flexible distribution systems

Distribution

Marketing
- Pricing is based on customer 'value' offers and perceptions of the value proposition
- Promotional activity reduced
- Specific targeted communications
- Marketing objectives reflect 'share of market' objectives of the organisation

Service
- 'Customised' service based upon individual customer needs
- Service contact occurs *before* order confirmation ·Service performance reflects 'long-term customer loyalty goals
- Service partnerships play an important role in the product-service offer
- Service is considered to be a revenue or investment centre

Intermediary relationships management

Supplier relationships management

Relationship management

likely that web based 'buying exchanges' will be developed with competitors; these often result in joint activities that extend into shared components and manufacturing. The automotive industry offers examples of this.

Operations processes also differ. For both production and distribution the SCM led organisation favours a cost/volume driven approach. Given a product range, the optimum costs are realised when specific 'runs' can be made against sales forecasts and the finished product sold from inventory. Figure 6.1 also suggests there are problems with this approach, particularly if the forecasts lack accuracy or if some unforeseen event occurs. DCM led organisations adopt more flexible structures, typically minimising downtime by adopting agile manufacturing and QR (quick response) distribution systems. DCM companies often use a build-to-order (BTO) system (and usually not manufacturing unless all or part of the payment has been made), thereby removing the risk of discounted sales to clear inventory. Working closely with both customers and suppliers concurrently can also avoid the risk inherent in the build-for-inventory (BFI) systems.

Marketing as a process also differs between the two models. The volume bias of the SCM model will often favour price as a primary marketing tool. This is understandable in markets such as fast moving consumer goods (FMCG) where often there is very little scope for differentiation, and even where there is retailer dominance, may pressure suppliers for price led promotions. A demand chain led approach has more flexibility. Usually the decision has been made as to the extent to which price is part of an overall 'value package', and this is a result of a comparison of competitor value offers. Value-in-use plays an important role in setting price in DCM organisations because they involve partners in their value propositions.

The essential differences between service processes are that SCM organisations, being cost-efficiency focused, apply this same attitude to customer service, treating service as a necessity rather than as a feature that in itself may attract customers. Additionally, the SCM organisation tends to feature logistics service as the primary service focus. DCM organisations embrace all aspects of service in their view of customer service. Service propositions may be as important as product propositions, giving a richer emphasis to the overall value proposition. The interesting feature that often distinguishes DCM organisations is their response to *value migration*. Slywotzky (1996) suggests this to be a feature of the current business environment. It is the notion that the added value created in a demand chain/supply chain structure can be seen to move. For example, the added value within the automotive industry has shifted in two directions in recent years, leading to a move by the industry away from vertical integration towards virtual integration (Drucker 2001). Production was once seen as the focal point of added value creation, with attractive returns on investment from vertically integrated structures. The growth of product platforms built around buying exchanges, assemblies and modules has resulted in value migrating backwards in the supply chain towards the component manufacturers and forwards towards marketing and service processes. This is reflected in the Ford and GM structures that have emerged in recent years. This difference is suggested by Figure 6.1. The supply chain model shows linkages that are predominantly supplier and customer based. There are tentative linkages between the two. By contrast, in the demand chain led business there is an overall relationship management process that creates a flexible structure capable of responding to market shifts in added value opportunities. Champion (2001) gives an example of an organisation (Millennium Pharmaceuticals) that is planning its structure around integrating both the demand and supply chains.

Relationship management is an essential requirement for success. But differences are apparent between supply chain and demand chain led organisations. Essentially the DCM business structure is proactive, responding to changes in consumer and market expectations (Champion: 2001), possibly developing them. This will invariably involve working with customers as they identify and crystallise their product-service needs. It often requires coordinating both customers' needs with suppliers' capabilities to achieve a cohesive as well as an optimal solution to customer product-service needs.

Using demand chain analysis to focus the supply chain

A question remains: how does this all come together? Figure 6.2 suggests a model. Given an understanding of the *customer value drivers*, these may be used to identify the planning areas that need to be addressed when constructing the supply chain response. The response should be structured around the identified issues. For example, customer location and lead-time requirements should be used to establish an appropriate order administration process; 'offshore' customers operating JIT procurement and production systems have quite different needs to those who are within the same state and use a materials stock-pile approach to inventory management. The idea of evaluating the value delivery options suggests not only a review of the manufacturing and logistics issues, but also that relationships with customers are given priority. For example, a customer operating in a non-price-competitive market may see advantage from offering an established brand feature as a component of its own product-service offer and consequently demand some exclusivity and a guarantee of service if the arrangement is to be formalised. This is not unusual with relationships between large retailers and their suppliers. A well established and reported case study features the working arrangement between Wal-Mart and Proctor & Gamble.

The process of order assembly and inventory management may differ markedly between customers. In some industries we have seen specialist suppliers establish 'industries' around components manufacturing. Champion (2001) reports the view of Millennium CEO, Mark Levin. Levin is suggesting that the structure of the computer hardware industry success factors has changed. He argues that the value chain for other high-tech products has, after all, tended to break down into a few separate, largely independent markets (each majoring on specific value positioning characteristics). The computer industry is an example of this, with chip manufacturing; computer assembly and delivery, software and support services as now all quite independently distinguishable but interlinked markets. Where once IBM was dominant across the whole industry, Intel, Dell and Microsoft now co-exist as a value chain.

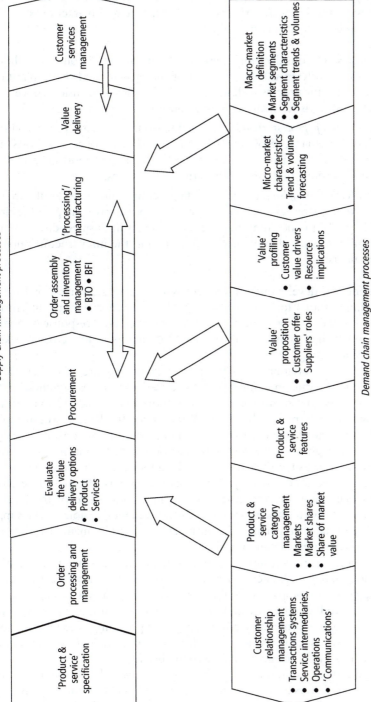

Supply chain management processes

Demand chain management processes

Figure 6.2 The demand chain and the supply chain; making effective strategy operationally efficient

Customer and market characteristics can influence the selection of a manufacturing process. Hill (2000) identifies some of the decisions to be made when considering the operations process appropriate to a market opportunity. Three broad considerations are suggested:

- *Type of process*: considerations here involve two 'dimensions', a technical dimension, involving the specification of the product and the implications this may have for process technology, and a business dimension concerning market characteristics such as volume and variety expectations.

- *Implications of process choice*: this is important because process choice accounts for a large proportion of the investment, operating costs and organisational infrastructure, and typically requires opportunity cost or trade-off decisions that, once committed, are binding.

- *Product/service profiling*: this is important because success will only occur if the marketing strategy is supported by the operations strategy. Questions should be asked concerning the effect of changes in business direction and the implications for alignment between this and the infrastructure support requirements.

In marketing, the development of concepts such as mass customisation have far reaching implications for product strategy, and therefore for manufacturing decisions. Product platforms have proven to be a successful response for industries within which incremental differentiation is an important factor in seeking competitive advantage.

An interesting development is the management of share of market value. The concept of value migration we introduced earlier has significance for supply chain design and management. The movement of added value in the automotive industry makes this point. Where once the largest proportion of total industry added value occurred in manufacturing the actions of the major manufacturers suggests some migration has occurred. Within manufacturing shifts have occurred such that modules and component manufacturing creates more added value than assembly, but processes such as design and development and marketing are responsible for an increasing share of total added value. Quite clearly this has implications for investment decisions in the supply chain, suggesting that partnership arrangements within manufacturing are becoming increasingly favoured options.

Customer service decisions are important for both customer relationship development and management. A recent study by McKinsey (Agarwal et al. 2004) suggests that companies should treat a customer relationship management solution as a product or service and its users as internal customers by making it valuable, pricing it appropriately, advertising it and providing after-sales support. They suggest success can only occur if such a solution has relevant structure, with specific managerial responsibility and accountability.

Figure 6.3 demonstrates the application of the principle. By identifying the customer value drivers a value proposition can be made to customers that will be implemented by a 'purpose built' supply chain. It will offer the levels of

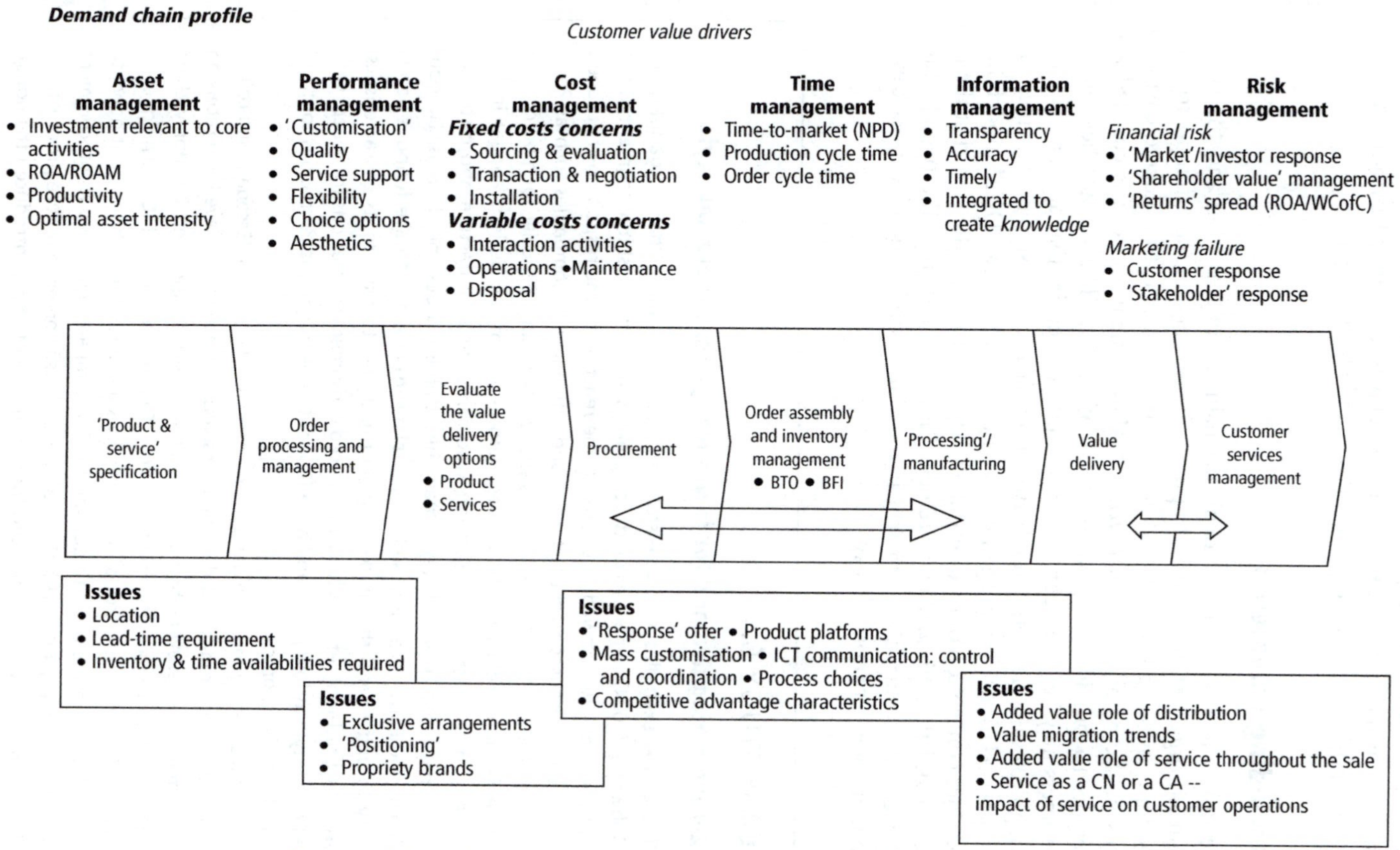

Demand chain profile

Customer value drivers

Asset management	Performance management	Cost management	Time management	Information management	Risk management
• Investment relevant to core activities	'Customisation'	*Fixed costs concerns*	• Time-to-market (NPD)	• Transparency	*Financial risk*
• ROA/ROAM	• Quality	• Sourcing & evaluation	• Production cycle time	• Accuracy	• 'Market'/investor response
• Productivity	• Service support	• Transaction & negotiation	• Order cycle time	• Timely	• 'Shareholder value' management
• Optimal asset intensity	• Flexibility	• Installation		• Integrated to create *knowledge*	• 'Returns' spread (ROA/WCofC)
	• Choice options	*Variable costs concerns*			
	• Aesthetics	• Interaction activities			*Marketing failure*
		• Operations • Maintenance			• Customer response
		• Disposal			• 'Stakeholder' response

'Product & service' specification

Order processing and management

Evaluate the value delivery options
• Product
• Services

Procurement

Order assembly and inventory management
• BTO • BFI

'Processing/ manufacturing'

Value delivery

Customer services management

Issues
• Location
• Lead-time requirement
• Inventory & time availabilities required

Issues
• Exclusive arrangements
• 'Positioning'
• Propriety brands

Issues
• 'Response' offer • Product platforms
• Mass customisation • ICT communication: control and coordination • Process choices
• Competitive advantage characteristics

Issues
• Added value role of distribution
• Value migration trends
• Added value role of service throughout the sale
• Service as a CN or a CA – impact of service on customer operations

Figure 6.3 Using demand chain analysis to focus the supply chain

product and service availability expected by the customer at the times and in the precise locations appropriate to them. Both product and service expectations will be met – just. Excesses of either will be avoided by adhering to a value proposition that emerges from demand chain analysis.

Concluding comments

The differences between the demand chain led organisation and the supply chain led organisation are based upon emphasis. Figure 6.3 attempts to make this point by suggesting that while the SCM model is to a degree customer focused, the emphasis is on *efficiency*. Management concern is cost led and attempts to provide an adequate level of service. The danger here is that customers may be 'aggregated' or fitted into categories that appear to be near enough relevant. Thus the link between supplier relationship management and customer relationship management is tenuous. By contrast, DCM model offers a broader conception of relationship management, taking the view that the two overlap and that *effective* management involves integrating the two. If this is achieved the result is one in which the often conflicting objectives can be brought together more closely.

CASE STUDY 6.1

Zara: meeting demand for low-price speed, variety and style

There are examples of successful demand chain/supply chain organisations. Rohweder (2004) comments on developments in the 'fast fashion' segment of the apparel industry. Rohweder reports on the reaction of the responses of Europe's elite fashion houses to the activities and influences of companies such as Zara, Hennes & Mauritz and large retailers such as Wal-Mart. Typically, long before the 'elite fashions' reach the boutiques, 'knock-offs' of the designs appear in the outlets of the fast fashion retailers who can copy, manufacture and distribute them much faster and cheaper than the established designer brands. London, Milan and Paris once dismissed Zara et al. as irrelevant but have found it necessary to understand this market segment and how to react to its characteristics. The 'fast fashion' retailers have influenced consumer expectations for speed, variety and style at low prices and have found it necessary to make changes to speed up the production cycle.

The marketing response has been to introduce 'hot fill-ins' (Escada), mini-collections reflecting trends that develop mid-season. Escada stores have been receiving new merchandise every two to three weeks. This is supported by supply chain processes that reduce both time and cost. Ferragamo has used ICT techniques to reduce the time-to-market of its designs by some 20 per cent, bringing it down to ten weeks from the usual three months. The company has linked its procurement and production systems with those of its suppliers in order to reduce process times for commissioning prototypes and for replenishment. It has introduced the notion of centralised inventory management, resulting in lower inventory holding and more rapid stock-turns. Etro SpA (Italy) divides its product line into theme and colour schemes from the moment of conception and changes the style and dominant colour monthly.

Birtwhistle et al. (2003) define and discuss the level of QR implementation by fashion retailers by exploring its impact on replenishment processes. They found that information technology is particularly important in driving supply chain responses. They comment that their results indicate that retailers have not fully understood the benefits of implementing a QR strategy, and suggest the retailers perceive it more as a strategy for internal supply chain management rather than one for the external supply chain. This may be a larger issue than they suggest; it means that the retailers have not explored their demand chains and identified a suitable supply chain structure to service their customer markets efficiently.

Zara is an interesting organisation, being part of the Inditex group. Customers of fast fashion expect to have a great variety and choice of up-to-date, well designed clothes. Quality of the garments and low prices are very important as well. Generally fast fashion products only cost 10 per cent of the price charged by elite fashion design houses. The value expectations of customers can be summarised as follows, in order of their importance to customers: current fashion designs; immediate availability of trends (garments from established high-end fashion European elite design houses (such as Gucci, Prada, Chanel, and so on); variety/choice; low price with commensurate quality, and service that includes attractive store design.

Zara also acquires fabrics in only four colours and postpones dyeing and printing until close to manufacture, thereby reducing waste and minimising the need to clear unsold inventories. Zara's production model includes a large outsourcing activity in which products are sewn by external workshops located close to Inditex factories (Heller 2001). Fabric is pre-cut into pieces and these delivered to the workshops where the worker stitches the fabrics according to easy-to-follow instructions into finished products. In their 350 workshops more than 11,000 workers are employed but none of the workshops is actually owned by Zara or Inditex. The network of workshops together with the modern distribution centres enables Zara to react quickly to market changes and new designs during a season. Zara is able to deliver the new design apparel from the drawing board to the stores in one or two weeks and therefore can respond very quickly to fast changing tastes of its young urban customers (Walker et al. 2000).

Figure 6.4 represents the Zara demand chain/supply chain decision structure. The demand chain profile identifies a demographic segment of 17 to 22 year olds that is fashion- but budget-conscious. Customer value drivers are clearly identified, suggesting the company has no doubt concerning the market segment within which it operates. The company's response to the value drivers is a value proposition that specifies merchandise characteristics, customer targeting and retail location strategy. The implications for Zara and its partner suppliers are clearly identified: rapid new product development and time-to-market are essential requirements for success in this segment, together with an ability to ensure the resulting product is manufactured and in distribution while the style remains fashionable.

Zara's supply chain responses are also shown in Figure 6.4. What is clear is the

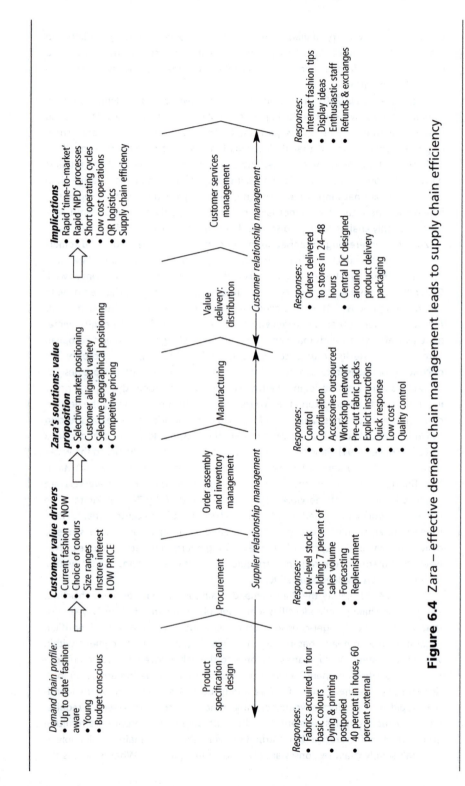

Figure 6.4 Zara – effective demand chain management leads to supply chain efficiency

use made of in-house skills (that is, the resources of Inditex), supplemented by selective outsourcing. Schedule and quality controls are essential features of the supply chain design; manufacturing is composed of a Zara managed process, garments are 'cut' by Zara staff and sent for completion by outsourced workshops that are given clear instructions for the work to be 'finished' with a low risk of the items being rejected. Zara checks each delivered item twice for quality. Physical distribution is a structured process within which product packaging needs play an important role. The distribution centre is built on two levels, one for folded apparel, boxed in cardboard cartons, the other for plastic covered garments on hangers. Tagliabue (2003) reports the system to be capable of handling 40,000 items an hour and of completing store deliveries within 24–48 hours by road and air.

Customer service is focused on developing both customer satisfaction *and* customer loyalty. A website provides customers with fashion hints and these are supported by in-store displays that offer 'ensemble' ideas. Staff identify with customers both demographically and in fashion preferences.

REFERENCES

Agarwal A, D P Harding and J R Schumacher (2004) 'Organising for CRM', *McKinsey Quarterly*, 3

Birtwhistle G, N Siddiqui and S Fiorito (2003) 'Quick response: perceptions of fashion retailers', *International Journal of Retail & Distribution Management*, 31(2)

BIS Shrapnel (2003) *Food Service and Eating Out*, BIS Shrapnel, Sydney

Bovet D and J Martha (2000) *Value Nets: Breaking the Supply Chain to Unlock Hidden Profits*, Wiley, New York

Champion D (2001) 'Mastering the value chain', *Harvard Business Review*, June

Christopher M (1998) *Logistics and Supply Chain Management*, Financial Times/Prentice-Hall, London

Drucker P (2001) 'Will the corporation survive?', *The Economist*, 1 November

Fisher M L (1997) 'What is the right supply chain for your product?', *Harvard Business Review*, March/April

Gluyas R (2004) article in *Australian*, 15 November

Hagel J III (2002) 'Leveraged growth: expanding sales without sacrificing profits', *Harvard Business Review*, October

Hagel J III and M Singer (1999) 'Unbundling the corporation', *Harvard Business Review*, March

Hammer M (2001) *The Agenda*, Crown, New York

Heller R (2001) 'Inside ZARA', *Forbes*, 28 May

Hill T (2000) *Operations Management: Strategic Context and Management Analysis*, Palgrave Macmillan, Basingstoke

Holmstrom J, W E Hoover Jr, P Louhiluoto and A Vasara (2000) 'The other end of the supply chain', *McKinsey Quarterly*, 1

Langabeer J and J Rose (2001) *Creating Demand Driven Supply Chains*, Chandos, Oxford

MacMillan I C and McGrath R G (1997) 'Discovering new points of differentiation', *Harvard Business Review*, July/August

Porter M (1996) 'What is strategy?', *Harvard Business Review*, November/December

Rohweder C (2004) 'Style & substance: making fashion faster; as knockoffs beat originals to market, designers speed the trip from sketch to store', *Wall Street Journal* (Eastern Edition), 24 February

Shoebridge N (2003) article in *Business Review Weekly*, 7 March

Slywotzky A J (1996) *Value Migration*, Free Press, New York

Tagliabue J (2003) 'Spanish fashion chain Zara rivals Gap by operating like Dell', *New York Times*, 9 June

Tierney S (2003) 'Tune up for a super-efficient supply chain with a Triangle', *Frontline Solutions* (Pan-European edition), Duluth, MN

Trinca H (2003) 'Reconstructing work', *Australian Financial Review: Boss*, 11 April

Walker B, D Bovet and J Martha (2000) 'Unlocking the supply chain to build competitive advantage', *Journal of Logistic Management*, 11(2)

Waller A (1998) 'The globalisation of business: the role of supply chain management', *Management Focus*, 11, Cranfield School of Management

CHAPTER 7

Demand Chain + Supply Chain = Value Chain

LEARNING TOPICS

On completing your study of this chapter you will have been introduced to and considered the following topics:

- Value optimisation rather than maximisation
- Value production feasibility and competitive possibility
- Value delivery viability as a competitive necessity
- The role and importance of organisational architecture in creating value
- The need to seek synergy with relevant partners
- The critical nature of fit and performance criteria
- Industry and organisational value chains
- Creating a value chain design
- Managing for equity in the value chain
- Value chain planning and control

Introduction

As we saw in Chapter 1, Drucker (2001) noted that the traditional response to market pressures was once met by vertical integration on a large scale, citing Ford, General Motors and Standard Oil as leading examples in the early twentieth century. In contrast the new successful corporations are adopting models based on virtual integration, where ownership of the means of production is not the critical factor; rather it is access to them via networks and partnerships that is important. As we also saw, the changes required to facilitate this approach are not just sales and marketing driven, but encompass design and development, and production. Products and services now have multiple applications and business organisations are redefining the critical success drivers together with their core capabilities and processes. In other words 'virtual

organisations' are competing with 'virtual organisations'. At this macro industry level, virtual organisations can be seen as business network structures, or
confederations, that are developing from traditional corporations.

Customer focused companies create additional value for their customers by
building *value chains* that identify, produce, deliver and service customer needs.
They create a multi-enterprise organisation that integrates supply chain efficiencies with demand chain management processes that anticipate customer expectations and ensure the availability of products and services in the right place, at the
right time, at the required level of service and at the lowest possible supply chain
cost. However, it would be somewhat trite to assume there to be no difficulties
here. According to AeIGT (2003), cited in Johns et al. (2005):

> In the business model of the future, value chains compete rather than
> individual companies, and the connectivity and process excellence are key
> challenges.

But there are other problems that are offering challenges, such as coordination, communication and overall control. These comments are not new; Johns
and his co-authors have identified 'coordinating management' as a common
theme in the literature. They suggest that organisational structures that are
functionally organised have difficulties in meeting the primary requirements
of value chain management – defining and meeting end-customer needs, and
ensuring these are transparent throughout the value chain organisation. Johns
et al. are suggesting that it is connectivity (and communication) that is the
problem; however, both connectivity and communication are based on value
optimisation and managed equity throughout the value chain.

One additional advantage of the value chain concept is that, by using added
value as a basis for assessing market opportunities and opportunity to increase
'value capture', it enables an organisation to monitor *value migration* and to
reassess its involvement and location within the demand chain/supply chain
(value chain) structure. Champion (2001) cites Mark Levin, CEO of Millennium
Pharmaceuticals, who, expanding a quotation we gave in Chapter 5, described
how perspectives of value have changed in the pharmaceutical industry:

> Value has started to migrate downstream, toward the more mechanical tasks
> of identifying, testing, and manufacturing molecules that will affect the
> proteins produced by the genes, and which become the pills and serums we
> sell. At Millennium, we've anticipated this shift by expanding into down-
> stream activities across several major product categories. Our ultimate goal is
> to develop capabilities and a strong presence in every stage of the industry's
> value chain –from gene to patient.

It follows that close monitoring of the value chain identifies significant
changes in value and value delivery opportunities. It also suggests that a
fixed view of an organisation's supply chain could result in significant
problems and financial difficulties.

Value optimisation rather than maximisation

The preceding chapters have considered the development of business models and the revised view of value from customer and from organisational perspectives. Of particular importance in the development of new business model alternatives is the potential for a clash of value interests – between customer expectations, partner expectations and those of shareholders. It follows that the new models should seek to *optimise value* rather than attempt to *maximise* the value delivered to any one set of interests. This is illustrated as Figure 7.1, suggesting that the value creation task is both short-term and medium-term. In the short term, basic value drivers (expectations) for customers and the remaining stakeholders are essential to ensure continuity, but any business structure should be considered to be an ongoing concern and therefore both customer and stakeholder *value builders* are a planning concern. Resolution of this issue is critical for the success of the value chain/virtual organisation. Unless each of the members receives a value response that is an improvement over and above that realised by its existing situation it is unlikely they will remain as members.

Customer expectations will vary by industry and by customer. Partner/stakeholder expectations are likely to be very similar across industry sectors, based upon financial viability. The task of management is to organise an effective response to customer expectations and, at the same time, one that involves its partners/stakeholders on satisfactory terms and returns. As suggested in Chapter 5, this is achieved by identifying the customer facing processes that create a total value package for customers. Being short-term focused, customer value drivers are concerned with enhancing customers' competitive position in existing markets. Value builders take a longer view. They take into account customers' strategic intentions and work with them to create a value base that will add value for both organisations. As discussed in Chapter 3, this is likely to involve considerations such as a repositioning strategy by the customer, and, possibly a review and restructuring of customers' operating infrastructure.

Value production feasibility and competitive possibility

Possibly the most significant task for value chain analysis and management is to identify customer value drivers in detail. Current thinking concerning the increasing importance of the demand and supply chains and their interaction and integration was dealt with in the previous two chapters. Here the concern is with the output from this activity. *Value production feasibility* occurs when there is a sufficient overlap of customer value expectations (customer value drivers) and customer satisfaction perceptions. As Figure 7.2 indicates, this is essentially a mapping process in which it is ascertained that not only does an opportunity exist but also there exist a number of delivery alternatives. In essence this becomes a *competitive possibility position*. It is identifying a value proposition that constitutes a starting point, one that meets a market/customer need and represents customers' minimum level of

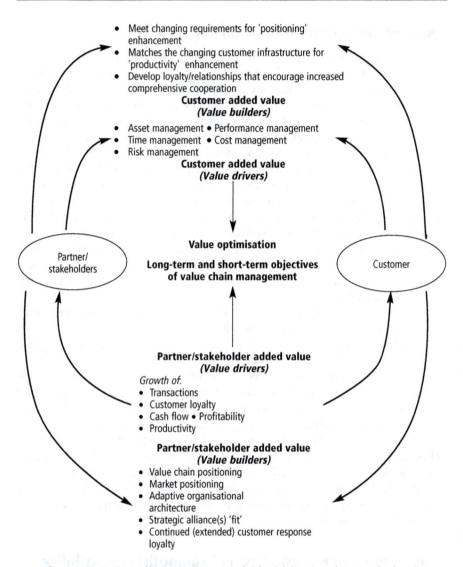

- Meet changing requirements for 'positioning' enhancement
- Matches the changing customer infrastructure for 'productivity' enhancement
- Develop loyalty/relationships that encourage increased comprehensive cooperation
  Customer added value
  (Value builders)

- Asset management • Performance management
- Time management • Cost management
- Risk management
  Customer added value
  (Value drivers)

Value optimisation

Long-term and short-term objectives of value chain management

Partner/ stakeholders

Customer

Partner/stakeholder added value
(Value drivers)
Growth of:
- Transactions
- Customer loyalty
- Cash flow • Profitability
- Productivity

Partner/stakeholder added value
(Value builders)
- Value chain positioning
- Market positioning
- Adaptive organisational architecture
- Strategic alliance(s) 'fit'
- Continued (extended) customer response loyalty

Figure 7.1 Supplier–customer relationships – value optimisation

satisfaction. No overlap implies that either no product-market exists or that (and this is most likely) the research misinterpreted the customer responses because of a research design fault. Clearly if a redesigned research project reaches the same conclusion it is safe to assume there is very little interest. However, as is often the problem with innovative designs, the issue is more one of understanding the additional benefits a 'new' product can deliver. The Sony Walkman is a classic case study. The success of the Walkman (and subsequent variants) has been based upon the mobility the product offers through miniaturising the delivery package.

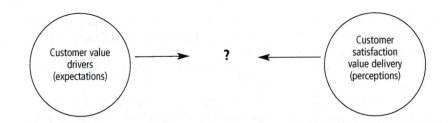

Value production feasibility: occurs when *demand chain analysis* identifies customer value drivers (asset management, performance management, cost management, time management, information management and risk management) are *'matched'* with the *supply chain processes* (such as, product-service specification, order management & fulfilment, order delivery management, customer relationship management and supplier relationship management) responsible for efficient value delivery. This can be described as a competitive possibility – unless the customer obtains some minimum level of their expectations. Clearly unless this occurs there is no possibility of creating the required value due to the fact that potential customers cannot identify the proposed benefits.

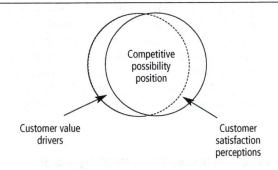

Figure 7.2 Matching customer expectations (value drivers) to achieve value production feasibility

Value delivery viability as a competitive necessity

The existence of a *competitive possibility* does not guarantee success; it is essential that there be *value delivery viability*. Customer value drivers are based upon an evaluation of the mix, or trade-off, of benefits and acquisition costs. It is in this evaluation process that price becomes important during customers' evaluation of 'value-in-use'. Value delivery viability exists when one or more of the value delivery options is acceptable to a group of partners/stakeholders. It is important to emphasise that such viability is not suggesting a cost led approach to pricing, but rather that viability can only exist provided that the partner/stakeholder value drivers (that is, growth of transactions, customer loyalty, cash flow and profitability) are met.

As for customers so too for partners/stakeholders, there is a clear requirement to 'enhance' their financial and market positioning if their participation within the value creation system is to be obtained. This is likely to comprise one of two options, either of which will result in an improvement in their cash flow, profitability and/or productivity. A volume increase or an opportunity to improve margin based upon operating efficiency is required. This can occur when an organisation becomes part of an integrated and larger organisation that is coordinated to identify opportunity and deliver 'value' using the collective expertise of the specialist expertise available through such collaboration. The primary issue is that unless this occurs partners will see no incentive for joining or remaining within an alliance.

Value delivery viability is an important and essential concept for value chain design. Its existence identifies the fact that a value chain structure is possible and the extent of the overlap identifies the number of potential configuration alternatives that may exist. As Figure 7.3 shows to be essential, the greater the overlap the more delivery alternatives are seen to be possible. Clearly a minimum overlap is required for a position in which competitive necessity can exist.

The insightful visionary is the entrepreneur/manager who combines assets, processes and capabilities into a combination resulting in meeting more closely the expectations of both customers and partners/stakeholders. Dell Computers is clearly an example of this phenomenon but many others exist. As we saw in Chapter 5, the Australian wine industry has a number of virtual wineries, small organisations which focus on niche segments by using their knowledge and intellectual property (intangible assets) and work with the owners of vineyards and processing plants to create value for their customers. Similarly in financial services, organisations such as Wizard Mortgages (Australia) generate very large cash flow and returns using the expertise of a very small number of experienced staff and their contacts.

Organisational architecture in creating value

The previous paragraph implies that organisation – organisational architecture – is an important consideration for the success of a value chain structure. Kay (1993) suggests that a firm is defined by its contracts and relationships and that added value is created by its success in putting these contracts and relationships together. He goes on to say that architecture adds value through the creation of organisational knowledge, through the establishment of a cooperative ethic and by the implementation of organisational routines. Brickley et al. (2004) offer an organisational architectural framework for 'addressing organisational problems and structuring more effective organisations'. They suggest three 'critical aspects of corporate organisation':

■ the assignment of decision rights within a company
■ the methods of rewarding individuals
■ the structure of systems to evaluate the performance of both individuals and business units

The authors explain their use of the term 'organisational architecture' to 'help focus specific attention on all three of these critical aspects of the organisation'. These are aspects of process within organisation structures and may differ in detail depending upon the nature of the organisation and its strategic direction. For any organisation to be successful, each should be present.

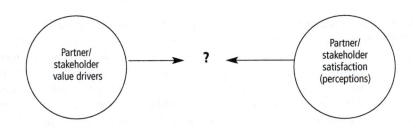

Value delivery viability: Unless potential partners realise their value expectations there will be no possibility of transactions occurring. It follows that these too must overlap to indicate that mutual benefit is being delivered. This is an essential condition for competitive necessity.

Figure 7.3 Unless partner stakeholders' expectations are met, an organisation cannot be successful

This moves us towards the question: what type of architecture is relevant within a value chain structure? Clearly this will be determined by a number of considerations. There are four basic issues of 'fit' that should be addressed prior to deciding upon the type of structure:

- *Strategic fit:* the extent to which all partners share the same view of the strategic direction – a sense of co-destiny
- *Relationship fit:* the cohesion that can be created despite differences in culture, management style and perhaps decision making processes
- The *business model profile:* this considers asset structures, postponement or speculation as value delivery options
- *Operational fit:* the 'methodology' of implementation

These features will be discussed in detail subsequently. Together with the 'three critical aspects of the organisation', they will be the basis around which the organisational architecture will develop. We can identify generic structures based upon observations of developing value chain structures. Kay (1993) suggests there are three types of architecture:

- *Internal:* the firm and its employees and among its employees
- *External:* between the firm and its suppliers and customers
- *Networks* between a group of collaborating firms

More recently the latter two have tended to merge as the extent of network collaboration has expanded. Campbell (1996) offers a useful typology of virtual organisation configuration, suggesting a basis for developing more workable forms of organisation. Figure 7.4 identifies a range of organisation models (based upon Campbell) that can be seen to exist within value chains.

Figure 7.4 suggests that there are a number of options, each offering specific advantages for particular situations. For example, *internal virtual organisations* are seen to occur within firms that have the need to add product or service characteristics to their offer but often cannot utilise all of the capacity. In these circumstances it is not unusual to find a separate strategic business unit (SBU) established to serve these needs *and* those of other organisations with similar problems. Examples can be seen in the wine industry, particularly in the capital-intensive processes. *Stable virtual organisations* exist in industries where there are *ongoing* requirements for specialist inputs. For example, in the automotive industry there exist complex components such as complete braking systems, automatic transmission and air conditioning; these are typically provided by external organisations that often are themselves a network of specialist producers. *Dynamic virtual organisations* are usually organisations that have appeal to larger 'generalists' who find it more cost-effective to outsource specialist roles and tasks that not only are capital-intensive but also offer competitive advantage. R&D in the pharmaceutical industry is an example; so too is the service offered by Real Brand Holdings, a Sydney based business (brand) development agency that accepts assignments from organisations to add value to their brand (*Australian Financial Review*, 12 April 2005). *Agile virtual organisations* have the clear core capability of being able to respond to complete product-service changes in very short amounts of time. Examples can be seen in the high fashion/low price segment of the garment industry. As we saw in case study 6.1 in Chapter 6, Zara, a European based company, has the capability of being able to convert a garment style into a product, in-store and available to customers, within two weeks. It can also replenish its inventories in 24–48 hours within Europe.

Competitive advantage is only likely to be achieved when feasibility and viability are integrated and coordinated by using an appropriate organisational architecture. Figure 7.5 suggests that it is the influence of this that moves an organisation from a position of competitive necessity towards one of competitive advantage. This is vital because it identifies the assets, processes and capabilities that are necessary for the transition, locates them, and configures the value chain into a strategically effective business model that will ensure operational efficiency.

Seeking synergy with relevant partners

A common characteristic of value chain structures is the decision 'to partner or not to partner'. There are a number of considerations, each of which comes with a trade-off or 'what if' concern. Typically these concerns are combinations of return/risk, control/opportunity cost, control/availability, and

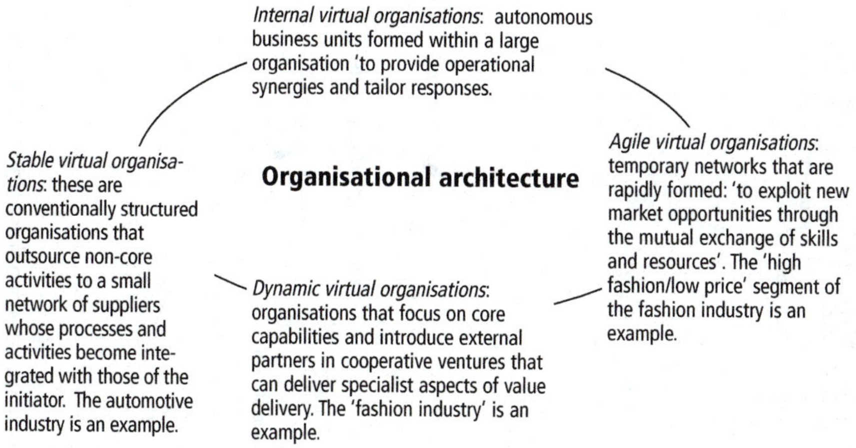

Internal virtual organisations: autonomous business units formed within a large organisation 'to provide operational synergies and tailor responses.

Stable virtual organisations: these are conventionally structured organisations that outsource non-core activities to a small network of suppliers whose processes and activities become integrated with those of the initiator. The automotive industry is an example.

Organisational architecture

Agile virtual organisations: temporary networks that are rapidly formed: 'to exploit new market opportunities through the mutual exchange of skills and resources'. The 'high fashion/low price' segment of the fashion industry is an example.

Dynamic virtual organisations: organisations that focus on core capabilities and introduce external partners in cooperative ventures that can deliver specialist aspects of value delivery. The 'fashion industry' is an example.

Figure 7.4 A distinctive collection of organisational relational contacts that develop organisational knowledge, flexibility in response and information exchange within or between organisations. This is achieved by establishing an ethic of cooperation and establishing organisational routines: • Internal • External • Networks

impact/urgency. Another interesting feature of the 'new economy' is the growth of specialist value chain roles taken by participants. Figure 7.6 identifies some of these, noting the industry sectors within which they are dominant. The dark shade identifies the area of expertise offered within the range of value chain processes. For example, in wine, computer manufacturing, travel, and financial services there are examples of organisations that operate across all of the value chain processes. In some instances they may have 'ownership' of a process, but more often it is their vision and organisational expertise that are the drivers. The 'brand manager' approach can be seen in the sports equipment and fashion sectors. Nike is a well known example of a marketing company that works with outsourced manufacturers and distributors that add value to Nike designs and brand management processes. Until very recently Haier, the People's Republic of China based white goods producer, was a 'contract manufacturer'. The company supplied a range of white goods products to North American department stores as store brand items. In recent years it began to market a Haier range of products within this range. Process or capability specialists offer product-service augmentation by adding specific value to customers' products. Intel is a well known example of processor supplier to major computer manufacturers, Amazon adds value by making its online ordering process available to an expanding range of consumer products.

Partnership and cooperation are cost-efficiency based. It has been well recognised that specialisation leads to expertise that expressed itself in both low cost and quality output. Chapter 5 described how process decisions have

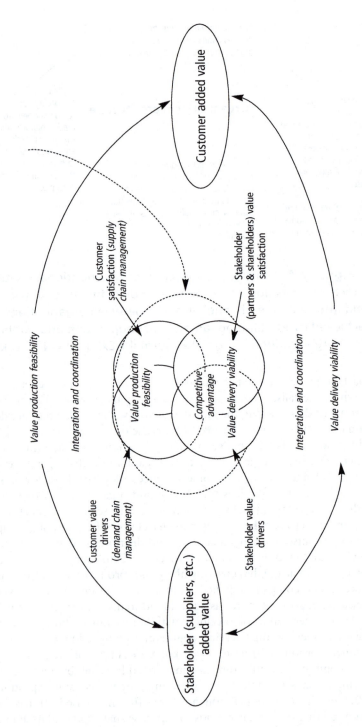

Organisational architecture: Selection of the most appropriate organisation structure will ensure that *competitive advantage at optimal costs can be* realised. The essential features of the decision concerns the optimisation of customer and stakeholder value expectations. Typically the successful structures are inter-organisational.

Customer added value

Customer satisfaction (*supply chain management*)

Stakeholder (partners & shareholders) value satisfaction

Value production feasibility

Integration and coordination

Value production feasibility

Competitive advantage

Value delivery viability

Integration and coordination

Value delivery viability

Customer value drivers (*demand chain management*)

Stakeholder value drivers

Stakeholder (suppliers, etc.) added value

Figure 7.5 Supplier and customer relationships – integrating processes into appropriate organisational structure

developed well beyond being seen to be low cost alternatives, and now consider the relationship of a process to the core business of an organisation.

Baglieri and Zamboni (2005) discuss the role of demand chain management in the decision to develop cooperation between customers and suppliers. They describe the collaboration between Amplifon and Siemens in the development of a new product. Their paper reviews the early work in the area (Chandler 1965; Coase 1991; Williamson 1985) and more recent contributions that distinguish outsourcing from collaboration suggesting that outsourcing was, and remains, a relationship based upon predefined service levels. They suggest that collaboration is more complex, taking into account the need to seek complementarities of skills and expertise that eventuate in a high level of interaction between the collaborating partners.

Baglieri and Zamboni discuss the nature of strategic relationships. Their research, conducted in Italy and therefore possibly reflecting some cultural bias, nevertheless identifies some interesting distinguishing features of long-term (strategic) relationships. Characteristics of strategic relationships, in order of 'frequency' of occurrence (very often 76–99 per cent) appeared as:

- An extensive exchange of operational information
- Extensive coordination in the planning phase
- Significant tuning of processes
- Sharing and developing business plans
- Information system integration
- Supplier involvement in each stage of process development, for example, new product development (NPD)

A case study based upon Amplifon and Siemens demonstrates the need for strategic assessment factors at the supplier selection phase, and the effectiveness of creating departments within each of the collaborating organisations charged with managing the collaboration between the companies. The research suggests that to be successful strategic relationships share three factors:

- Long-term relationships that reduce the probability of opportunistic behaviour and that reinforce mutual trust
- Significant specific investments by both organisations that indicate commitment to collaboration and a willingness to cooperate that result in an increase in switching costs
- Clear and unambiguous distinctiveness of partner competencies and a balanced integration of them

Butler et al.'s (2004) contribution to this topic is broader. They introduce the notion of 'interactions', suggesting they account for over a third of economic activity in the US. Interactions are broader than transactions:

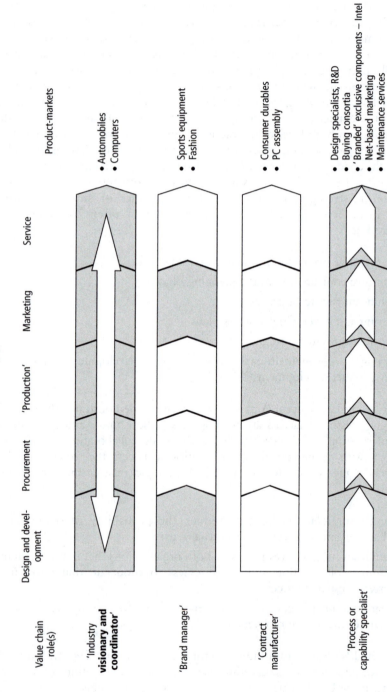

Figure 7.6 Strategic alternatives in the value chain

Individuals and organisations interact to find the right party with which to exchange; to arrange, manage, and integrate the activities associated with this exchange; and to monitor performance. These interactions occur within firms, between firms, and all the way through markets to the end consumer. They take many everyday forms – management meetings, conferences, phone conversations, sales calls, problem solving, reports, memos – but their underlying economic purpose is always to enable the exchange of goods, services, or ideas.

... the searching, coordinating, and monitoring that people and firms do when they exchange goods and services, or ideas – pervade all economies, particularly those of developed nations ... interactions exert a potent but little understood influence on how industries are structured, how firms are organised, and how customers behave.

The authors argue that any major change in the level or nature of these transactions would trigger a new dynamic in economic activity, suggesting that the current convergence of technologies is a catalyst that will increase the capacity for' interactive capacity'. The 'convergence of technologies' refers to the growth of networks. The improvement in connectivity with broadband is multiplying the interactive power of networks. The continued expansion of computer processing and power, accompanied by lower costs, and the acceptance of a new set of standards (HTTP and HTML, for example) are increasing the growth in internet, intranet and extranet usage. The continuous penetration of basic technologies such as telephone infrastructure and the number of PCs on a global basis will accelerate the growth rate of interaction capability.

The predicted impact of 'the age of interactions' proposed by Butler et al. is already visible. They are suggesting a number of new ways in which business may be structured.

The shift away from vertical organisation towards virtual organisation is clearly under way. The authors suggest that specialisation is fragmenting integrated business systems such as those of the textile and utilities industries. For example, the introduction of electronic data interchange (EDI) has resulted in the disaggregation of procurement, spinning, weaving, finishing, logistics and retailing in the apparel industry. They argue that horizontal integration and cooperation will become more economically attractive due to economies of scope. As interaction costs decline, companies are better able to coordinate marketing and distribution of an increasingly wide range of products and services. Amazon is an example of this. It has expanded the range of products available and manages the electronic offers of a number of traditional book retailers. The traditional production economies of scale are declining in importance and this is likely to continue. Where once scale was essential, falling interaction costs are now making smaller business sizes increasingly viable.

The increase in interaction efficiency will increase the number of businesses working together as networks and it will also increase the application of network applications within businesses. Butler and his colleagues provide examples of intra-organisational networks such as Caterpillar, which is now linking designers, distributors and technicians with customers as it builds a global parts service network. They also contend that as interaction costs decline so too will transaction costs, resulting in more market information transparency. An interesting aspect of all of this is the impact that it will have on traditional intermediaries, who exploited the lack of transparency. Their role as providers of market information is now being undertaken by 'informediaries', organisations that provide search facilities across markets.

Clearly such changes have implications for business organisation. Internet transactions will facilitate both customer and supplier relationship management. Product customisation will become easier, faster and less costly as interaction facilities increase, resulting in cost-efficiency, and communications which become more closely targeted, frequent and accurate.

Fit and performance criteria are critical

It is arguable then that as business models become moulded around a customer-centric structure, and that because customer expectations have become much more fluid in a dynamic and competitive business environment, the virtual structures we see currently may well become commonplace. The purpose of this proposal is to identify the important characteristics that determine the success of the 'fit' of business model alliances and to extend this into a discussion on the theoretical linkages between the strategy-structure-performance analogues. There are four 'fit' criteria: strategic fit, financial fit, operational fit, and relationship fit.

Clearly, while each of the above four criteria is important it is likely that *strategic fit* dominates the model. It gives *effective direction* by identifying opportunities for growth from strategic alliances that are unlikely to be available to non-aligned organisations. Given that the purpose of an alliance is to identify opportunities for growth that may not otherwise be accessible, and also given that these are sought on the basis of 'high' return/'minimal' risk, then it follows that strategic fit will have priority. Figure 7.7 identifies a number of planning issues, such as the need to identify an opportunity to maximise competitive advantage by focusing on core resources and/or developing a new business model. *Financial fit* is important here because not only is enhanced and improved financial performance a basic business motive. it is also essential that the business model that emerges be financially viable. Concerns here are the overall impact of decisions on not just revenues but also on investment and costs. Any alliance model that results must have *operational fit*. Simply put, the structures that emerge must ensure efficient implementation of the business model. Essentially we are concerned to be able to achieve key operational objectives cost-efficiently.

Relationship fit is also an important element of this model. Fundamental concerns here should consider the 'fit' of both corporate cultures and management styles into an alliance structure. Without compatibility across these two components it is unlikely that the remaining concerns will be viable.

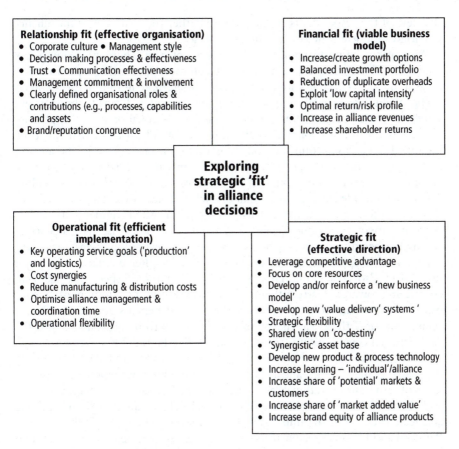

Figure 7.7 Exploring strategic 'fit' in alliance decisions

Measuring fit and performance

Bamford and Ernst (2004) report on research conducted for McKinsey investigating the extent to which corporations are able to measure the performance of their alliances. The authors questioned more than 500 companies around the world and despite the 'ubiquity of alliances' – most companies have at least 30 and many over 100 – and despite the considerable assets and revenues involved, there appears very little evidence of systematic tracking of their performance.

Not only was it found that performance was not measured in any meaningful way, but the implications of not agreeing mutual objectives leaves open the problem of whether the alliances are at all relevant. Another, related problem concerns the failure to recognise performance patterns across the range of alliances. These are important because a failure across an alliance portfolio may relate to the types of partners, the structure of the relationship or the tasks being performed. A third problem reported by Bamford and Ernst suggests that few of the respondents had any idea whether the structure of the alliance portfolio supported the organisational strategy.

Measuring the performance of alliances is not easy. There are a number of concerns. Clearly the first is to agree a common approach to performance measurement. As partners are likely to have different goals (and these are likely to be qualitative as well as quantitative) agreement is likely to be difficult. Furthermore as partnerships are concerned with collaboration the primary interest is the 'health' of the relationship. A second problem that has been identified concerns accounting policies within each organisation. The authors make the point that operations become entwined, further complicating accounting measurement. This can be made yet more complex by difficulties experienced in identifying the inputs of each partner. Measuring the benefits delivered is just as problematic. Alliances often generate revenues from related or complementary products, sales that would not otherwise have occurred. Intangible benefits accrue, such as access to new technologies and processes, together with opportunities to acquire knowledge. Being linked to a major brand will also create intangible benefits. All of these aspects are likely to contribute towards a strengthening the competitive positioning of one or other of the organisations. Somehow the accrued benefits and costs must be accounted for if the performance of the alliance is to be measured and if the value of each organisation is to be measured. See Figure 7.8.

A measurement of the free cash flow profiles appears to be a favoured approach to evaluating the potential and actual performance of partnerships. There are four levels of cash flow: operational cash flow, cash flow from assets, strategic cash flow, and the resulting free cash flow. This model permits an analysis of optional alliance structures at the important decision levels. The topics highlighted by Bamford and Ernst are readily incorporated. They suggest that any revenues that accrue to one or other of the partners be included. These are 'cash flow from earnings of joint venture', 'transfer pricing, royalties, fees and other cash flows', and 'value to parent not recognised in joint venture'. Costs that are to be included are 'parent management costs' and 'operating costs'.

Measurement of financial fit will indicate the viability of the business model. The important metric here is free cash flow. Operational fit metrics are clearly output and service based. Operational performance decisions can be evaluated and monitored against the cash flow model. The model offers a means of exploring the impact of delivering customer added value expectations. Dominant issues here would concern the use of working capital but clearly some thought should be given to the longer-term concerns of relationships that indicate signs of permanence.

Measuring relationship fit requires the introduction of some qualitative metrics. These will include measurement of the importance of the relationship to members and the degree of confidence and trust that exists in the alliance. Measurement of decision making effectiveness may also be attempted, as can the role performances and contributions of partner members. An important measure in this regard concerns stakeholder satisfaction. Customer satisfaction, in both the short and long term, is a concern of strategic fit and in many respects is the raison d'être of the alliance. However, an important relationship

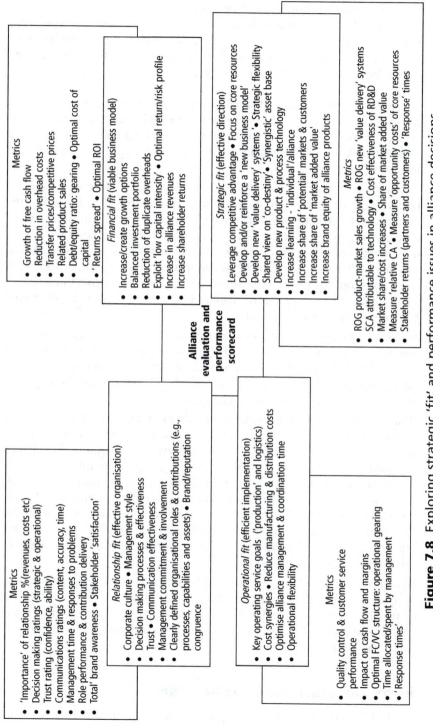

Metrics
- 'Importance' of relationship % (revenues, costs etc)
- Decision making ratings (strategic & operational)
- Trust rating (confidence, ability)
- Communications ratings (content, accuracy, time)
- Management time & responses to problems
- Role performance & contribution delivery
- Total' brand awareness • Stakeholder 'satisfaction'

Relationship fit (effective organisation)
- Corporate culture • Management style
- Decision making processes & effectiveness
- Trust • Communication effectiveness
- Management commitment & involvement
- Clearly defined organisational roles & contributions (e.g., processes, capabilities and assets) • Brand/reputation congruence

Operational fit (efficient implementation)
- Key operating service goals ('production' and logistics)
- Cost synergies • Reduce manufacturing & distribution costs
- Optimise alliance management & coordination time
- Operational flexibility

Metrics
- Quality control & customer service performance
- Impact on cash flow and margins
- Optimal FC/VC structure: operational gearing
- Time allocated/spent by management
- 'Response times'

Alliance evaluation and performance scorecard

Metrics
- Growth of free cash flow
- Reduction in overhead costs
- Transfer prices/competitive prices
- Related product sales
- Debt/equity ratio: gearing • Optimal cost of capital
- 'Returns spread' • Optimal ROI

Financial fit (viable business model)
- Increase/create growth options
- Balanced investment portfolio
- Reduction of duplicate overheads
- Exploit 'low capital intensity' • Optimal return/risk profile
- Increase in alliance revenues
- Increase shareholder returns

Strategic fit (effective direction)
- Leverage competitive advantage • Focus on core resources
- Develop and/or reinforce a 'new business model'
- Develop new 'value delivery' systems • Strategic flexibility
- Shared view on 'co-destiny' • 'Synergistic' asset base
- Develop new product & process technology
- Increase learning – 'individual'/alliance
- Increase share of 'potential' markets & customers
- Increase share of 'market added value'
- Increase brand equity of alliance products

Metrics
- ROG product-market sales growth • ROG new 'value delivery' systems
- SCA attributable to technology • Cost effectiveness of RD&D
- Market share/cost increases • Share of market added value
- Measure 'relative CA ' • Measure 'opportunity costs' of core resources
- Stakeholder returns (partners and customers) • 'Response' times

Figure 7.8 Exploring strategic 'fit' and performance issues in alliance decisions

measure may be that concerned with the reputation of the overall alliance and the impact this has on 'total' brand awareness.

However, while there are clearly benefits available from a business model that incorporates partners who bring expertise and economies to the alliance, there is also a degree of risk. *Structural risk* factors constitute a number of variables. These are best seen as operating at four levels:

- *Capability risk* is the moxst obvious and important measure of risk and is the actual ability to operationally perform the process in question – whether the alliance member can actually make the product or deliver the service. High capability risk should be a significant discount factor against any anticipated free cash flow benefits.

- *Business model risk* is a measure of the overall risk to its viability that an organisation attracts or avoids by owning or acquiring (or delegating the ownership and management of) a core process. It reflects either the avoidance of, or increase in, internal transaction costs and the impact on process integration within the firm's business model generally. For example, a firm may have what seems a relatively unimportant manufacturing process such as a paint shop that can be outsourced with low capability risk, but in doing so this may disrupt the entire manufacturing flow and incur substantial hidden internal transaction costs.

- *Strategic risk* reflects the importance of the process and the degree of direct control over it needed to impact the firm's overall strategic positioning in the market. For example, outsourcing a process that is driven by unique intellectual property that is key to the firm's market positioning and competitive advantage would entail a high strategic risk.

- *Alliance risk* reflects the introduction of virtual integration. It is more than simply the viability and dependability of particular partners, which are inherent in the notion of capability risk, but reflects the strength of the alliance (or holonic network) as a whole. Alliance risk may be influenced by a number of factors. For example, an established alliance undertaking a new or expanded venture will increase the risk previously identified. A new alliance will be 'riskier' than one built from known partners. Equally an alliance built around a new business model and one that has members from a diverse group of industries (that have yet to prove they can work together) also attracts high levels of risk.

- *Structural risk* is the aggregation of the previous three risk factors. The comparative weighting of the risk factors will obviously be driven by the particular circumstances and will be to some degree subjective. In this sense the purpose and usefulness of this model are as much to act as a checklist of critical factors as anything else.

Industry and organisation value chains

Scott (1998) takes a strategic management view. He uses the value chain concept to identify the tasks necessary to deliver a product or service to the market. His approach is to combine segmentation and value chain analysis and he suggests a number of questions:

- In which areas of the value chain does the firm have to be outstanding to succeed in each customer segment?
- What skills or competencies are necessary to deliver an outstanding result in those areas of the value chain?
- Are they the same for each segment or do they differ radically?

Scott argues:

> All firms, whether industrial or services have a value chain, each part requires a strategy to ensure that it drives value creation for the firm overall. For a piece of the value chain to have a strategy means that the individual managing is clear about what capabilities the firm requires to deliver effective market impact.

It follows that the firm may not have the relevant competencies to match opportunities. Two questions follow: (1) Is the structure of the organisation relevant and are its managers competent? (2) Can the firm compete effectively by forming a partnership/alliance with other firm(s)? Scott's value chain has seven core elements:

- Operations strategy
- Marketing, sales and service strategy
- Innovation strategy
- Financial strategy
- Human resource strategy
- Information technology strategy
- Lobbying position with government

Coordination across the value chain is essential and Scott identifies the fact that traditionally this did not occur. The relationship between a company's value chain and its SBUs is discussed. He suggests that certain parts of the value chain are likely to be common to all its SBUs. These include human resources, information technology and large parts of its financial and selling functions. It could be argued that the information requirements of individual SBUs might differ and require specific services. It could also be argued that in a market/customer focused business (and most make this claim) the core elements of the business should be capable of developing specific service inputs to ensure competitive advantage.

Contrary to what we saw in an earlier section of this chapter, it has been argued that value chain strategy and management has the *expansion* of customer satisfaction as its primary objective as opposed to the *optimisation* of supply chain costs while meeting specified customer objectives. Value chain management is a proactive approach to customer satisfaction while supply chain management is a cost-efficient response to existing customer objectives. Manufacturer Glynwed (see Burt 2000) identified the fact that their customers had many more 'product' aspirations other than their Aga and Rayburn ranges. Consequently Glynwed established a web based information resource that identifies 'product' ideas and sources. As a consequence, Glynwed plays an important role in the expansion of a response to the customer value satisfaction needs of an expanded customer base.

Brown (1996), using the newspaper, video entertainment and banking industries as examples, suggests:

The emerging value chains in these examples promise to restructure these industries and redistribute value among different components and players in the value chain.

Brown also suggests, using Porter's views on competitive advantage, that 'The way in which [a business] manages its value chain will affect its cost structure and the differential benefits offered to its customers, and thereby its competitive advantage.' This latter comment is of less interest than the first. The restructuring and redistribution of value issues are central to value chain analysis, strategy and management.

The value chain concept offers management a means by which it can evaluate both existing and new strategic opportunities. To some extent this requires a 'clean sheet', assuming no restrictions from existing processes, capabilities or assets, so that management can identify 'ideal' strategy and structure alternatives. In the real world there may be (indeed it is very likely there will be) constraints and reasons why the 'ideal' cannot be selected and implemented. However, the analysis will have provided an insight into how best the opportunity might be pursued and identify potential problems for successful implementation of the selected strategy. Industry level value chain analysis is an effective way to identify the interplay between different players in any specific industry. It helps identify the resources required to compete successfully in an industry and where individual organisations should locate within that industry to maximise their 'returns' and those of the value chain. It is also potentially a useful method for describing the processes and activities within and around an organisation and relating them to an analysis of the organisation's competitive strengths and weaknesses (Lindgren and Bandhold 2003). While the value chain is becoming more widely accepted as a planning and management model, much remains to be done concerning performance management and the issues this presents for inter-organisational relationships. If a value chain only operates based on altruistic cooperation between players, the model is clearly flawed. Rather it is suggested that value chain analysis not only charts optimum strategic options for a firm, but also highlights the perils of these.

Value chain analysis is as applicable to vertically integrated organisations as it is to virtual organisations. The whole point of the approach is to identify optimal solutions; solutions that are optimal are acceptable to all stakeholders – customers, suppliers and investors. Any organisation should be aware of the structure of the value adding processes within its industry and of its own location within this 'structure'. Value chain analysis identifies the flow of added value through the value creation processes within both the industry and the firm. It follows that regardless of its configuration it is the role of the firm's executive to be aware of where and how value is created and who benefits from the processes. Value chain analysis does not necessarily imply being restricted to the search for and evaluation of suitable partners. Time can be an important consideration, and if the acquisition of tangible or intangible assets rather than a partnership with the owner appears more suitable, then outright purchase or partial equity ownership may offer a more effective solution. This option may offer other solutions, such as more control of the required asset, process or capability. The move in July 2005 by Haier, the manufacturer we mentioned above, may be an example of such a development. Haier may well be seeking a number of benefits: a global brand, to extend its product range entry into the US, or, less likely, additional production capacity. If the value processes are monitored frequently, the flexible and aware organisation can configure itself (and its partners if these exist) and play an important role to capture a dominant share of the value created by these processes.

Creating a value chain design

In previous chapters we met the work of Hagel and Singer (1999), according to which the traditional organisation comprises three basic kinds of business: a customer relationship business, a product innovation business and an infrastructure business. These were augmented by a fourth 'business', one in which a 'visionary and integrator' coordinates each of the traditional businesses in order to create an exclusive business model that offers greater customer and stakeholder value. Product innovation will occur in the design and development process of the value chain, and is increasingly likely to be the province of small creative units often outwith the organisation, and if within it, free of the bureaucracy typical of large organisations. Customer relationship management responsibilities are shared by the marketing and service processes. Marketing identifies and communicates with intermediaries and end-user customers, providing an opportunity for economies of scope to operate efficiently. Service creates strong loyalties by offering product knowledge and post-sales service. This process may well be divested. Many durables manufacturers have outsourced service in order to provide a more responsive service to customers and to reduce the high fixed costs of facilities and inventories. Service companies, banks and other financial product providers use call centres to manage customer services with similar motives – to benefit from economies of scale.

Aspects of infrastructure businesses have been outsourced for some time. Third party distribution service companies have offered economies of scale through consolidation of inventories and deliveries. Manufacturing/production processes are increasingly becoming outsourced. The automotive industry is one in which an increasing proportion of the product is manufactured by outside suppliers while the manufacturers restructure their organisations around processes and activities offering greater added value return on investment.

Bornheim (2001) shares these views and proposes a customer-centric model for the automotive industry in which value creating activities are reorganised around customer needs. The elements of the model 'are highly specialised, intensely inter-linked, and aim at synchronisation of resources and information flows with true customer demand'. Bornheim predicts a future automotive business model similar to that of Dell's built-to-order model, 'in which customised demand nearly exactly matches supply and which revolves around a digital order processing, inventory management, and manufacturing system, that removes the assets from an asset-intensive process'.

Both Hagel and Singer and Bornheim take a similar perspective to that of Doz and Hamel (1998). They suggest gaining competitive strength through co-opetion (co-ompetition) and leveraging co-specialised resources, and gaining competence through internalised learning. Within value chain design and management, learning should be across processes and across organisations.

Managing for equity in the value chain

A major problem that occurs in value chain structures is the imbalance of 'power' and the implications this has for individual members' performances. The growth of large retailers with dominant market positions is a common global phenomenon. Reports of use (and abuse) of channel power are numerous. Typically these relate to pricing and service expectations but they also include payment schedules. The use of negative working capital by large retailers is well known, but the impact of this financial strategy can be dire, forcing many small suppliers into liquidation. For the value chain to be effective, the implications of 'stocks and flows' of product, cash and information must be understood by all members and optimal schedules derived.

A recent example of the far reaching implications of the problem was made by Younge (2005). The McDonald's repositioning strategy into the 'healthier eating' sector of the fast-food market has been accompanied by some serious implications for their new suppliers – apple growers. Younge describes the changes that are under way within the supply industry, comparing these with the structure of the McDonald's dairy suppliers, large vertically integrated businesses that are constantly under pressure to lower prices to McDonald's. A quote from a United Farm Workers Union regional director suggests that there is an inevitable increase in size and that the constant pressure on price (and therefore supplier margins) has an equally inevitable impact on the pay and conditions of the labour force. For more on McDonald's, see case study 7.1 at the end of this chapter.

There are also implications for inventory management. Each member of the value chain will seek to minimise inventory holding (for cost, storage and obsolescence motives); at the same time they will attempt to maximise cash flow. Clearly such individual (and selfish) actions can only result in problems. Not only will there be financial difficulties for many members, but it is very unlikely that inventory will be in appropriate places at appropriate times, and the end result will be failure because intermittent and erratic supply can only result in customer dissatisfaction and defection.

Cash cycles are also difficult to manage. By extending payables to suppliers, very large organisations are being subsidised by their smaller competitors. A 'white paper' from the Competitive Capital Management Group (2004) argues that suppliers faced with this situation recover the increase in their cost of working capital through their pricing policies. The paper is suggesting that the cost of funding the cash flow efficiencies of the supplier's large customers is met by it increasing its prices to *all* customers to cover the increased interest charges it encounters. The paper continues by suggesting that while the supplier funds the inventory on a short-term interest rate, the large customer is very likely investing the cash not paid to the supplier within the agreed terms of payment time and receiving a return (or increasing shareholder value). Supplier discounts clearly represent 'attractive' investment opportunities!!

It is suggested that there is no easy resolution, but it would appear that an obvious factor to include is customer expectations concerning availability, and purchasing frequencies (rate of sale), to provide input for estimating an overall optimal materials flow efficiency and to establish the maximum and minimum operating cycle times necessary to meet POS requirements. While it is unrealistic to expect that large organisations will take the 'road to Damascus' and experience a blinding light of reality and reason, it can be argued that as the costs of transactions and interactions and the interdependencies in the operating cycle become better understood, there is every possibility that optimal operating efficiencies and cash flow efficiencies will be achievable. This will be discussed in more detail in Chapter 12.

Value chain planning and control

The design, coordination and control of the value chain is a complex management task. Just how complex is described in Figure 7.9, in which the three levels of decision management activity are shown. At a strategic or industry level there are a number of decisions that are important. First, the customer and stakeholder (partner) expectations should be understood and the value drivers determined in order of priority. If there is a possibility of working with adjacent market segments some time should be spent establishing the extent to which some of the value drivers overlap. This component of the planning process is essentially strategic and is aimed at identifying customer and stakeholder expectations and the value creation and production alternatives that exist for their delivery. A critical part of the process is to identify an alternative that creates an optimal level of value for the customers and stakeholders, and at the same time creates competitive advantage for the value delivery system. In many respects this is a scoping exercise that identifies and evaluates alternatives.

Given a satisfactory outcome to the first part of the process, the next step is to consolidate the value delivery structure identified. This requires matching the processes, capabilities and capacities of potential partners that the optimal delivery system requires. The partnership management process is the

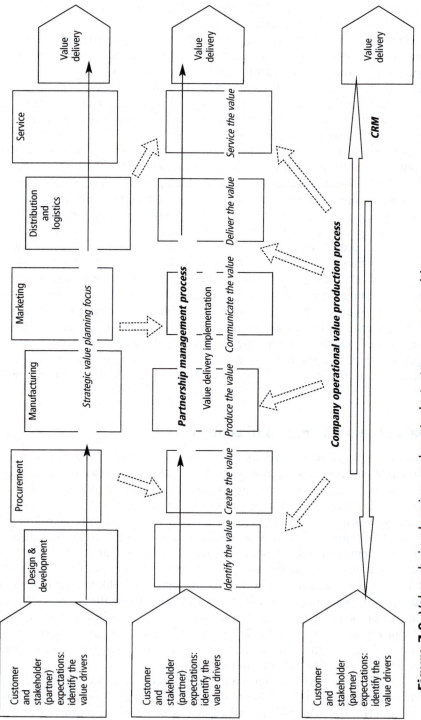

Figure 7.9 Value chain planning and control: strategy – partnership management – company operations

integration and coordination processes that will be responsible for the eventual success of the value creation/delivery system. It must identify the customer (and stakeholder/partner) sensitivities because failure to do so will result in likely failure because specific (individual) expectations fail to be met.

The third step involves the stakeholder/partner organisations. As individual organisations that are part of a larger value delivery system it is their role to contribute specific expertise. This is likely to involve working with both suppliers and customers (and these may be internal or external to the structure), but will require specific policies for the management of both supplier and distributor relationships. Each member company is therefore responsible for integrating its company operational production focus into the partnership management process. Processes to achieve this will be discussed in subsequent chapters.

Concluding comments

Value chain structures offer customer focused companies a facility to create additional value for their customers by understanding the simple fact that they themselves are unlikely to possess all the resources to service customer needs.

Such companies create a multi-enterprise organisation that integrates supply chain cost efficiencies which are a response to an understanding of the characteristics of the demand chain. Value chain management is an approach that synthesises the activities of all partner organisations in the value chain: cooperation is essential, not competition, and certainly not conflict. In the value chain, competitors can become partners.

CASE STUDY 7.1

McDonald's: using the demand chain to effect a recovery strategy

McDonald's 'traditional' approach in trouble

Leaving to one side whatever views one may have of the merits of its products, the growth of McDonald's Corporation over the last four decades from a hamburger stand to a major international corporation has been impressive. However, in 2003 McDonald's for the first time reported a quarterly loss amidst wide-scale discontent amongst franchisees, changes of CEOs, and a plunging share price at ten-year lows. What had gone wrong?

In many respects McDonald's was one of the pioneers of both efficient and effective supply chain management and of marrying these with traditional marketing techniques, fostering a whole new category of food retailing. McDonald's delivered new levels of product consistency through standardised menus and strict supplier controls. It maximised the impact of its delivery points by developing and applying demographic research to its store placement. It maximised throughput and asset and inventory utilisation by focusing on speed of production and delivery through new standards of staff training and process control. It deployed economies of scale and bargaining power to deliver affordable products. By fostering the concept of franchising McDonald's in effect not only outsourced the actual production and delivery of its products, but also outsourced operational risk by putting the onus to raise and manage working capital on the franchisee. In this sense McDonald's was a 'business orchestrator' (Hagel 2002) long before that term was coined.

Despite the historical excellence of its supply chain it would be misleading to see McDonald's as a purely supply driven operation. Again from an historical perspective the company has excelled in implementing classical marketing techniques, particularly the '4P's'. 'Price' competition has been a consistent theme with 'dollar deals' the latest attempt at retaining market share against direct competitors such as Burger King. 'Place' has been reflected both at the level of individual store placement and at a broader level in a still expanding campaign to open more stores in more locations in more countries. Indeed the company seems to measure its own performance by this as much as anything else. 'Promotion' has seen the Golden Arches, Ronald McDonald and a myriad of successful advertising and point of sale campaigns successfully targeting various market segments, including in particular that of children where again it was a pioneer, albeit it has been criticised for doing so. Finally McDonald's traditional 'Product' set, including the ubiquitous Big Mac, set new standards for consistency and reliability.

Overall this was a stunningly successful model in which the process fusion between the demands of the emerging fast-food market was skilfully combined with new supply chain capabilities to the extent that it is debatable whether McDonald's created fast food or the other way around. Most importantly, this model was not a creation of the emerging 'new economy' of the 21st century, but was a child of the 1970s.

However, in the face of falling profits and investor wariness, these are the strategies and themes the company was persisting with. One presentation was described as follows (*The Economist*, 12 April 2003):

> The top team's wooden presentation on April 7th [2003], liberally doused with marketing clichés and soundbites about the importance of 'people, product, place, price, promotion' and 'improving focus' only reinforced the impression ... [that management] lacks the vision or stomach to make the necessary changes.

The reality appears to be that the nature of the market McDonald's is operating in is changing, at least in its more mature geographic segments. For example, in Australia a BIS Shrapnel study (2003) suggests the average Australian is eating out less often, 83 times in 2002 compared with 94 in the year 2000. Furthermore the reasons have changed: whereas 'convenience' was the main determinant three years ago, the principal reasons now are 'special occasion', 'break in routine' and 'meeting friends'. The report also identifies changing tastes: consumption of hamburgers is down, consumption of takeaway Thai, Sushi, and Indian foods is increasing.

This was reflected in McDonald's stagnating growth and poor financial performance. The company is reluctant to reveal same-store sales growth but rivals estimate that in 2002 it was less than 1 per cent. Comments by Peter Bush, a senior executive, reported by Shoebridge (2003), suggested that the company was at least partially aware of its problems:

> Our rivals are not just other fast-food chains; they are any other informal eating-out occasion. For example, about 6500 new coffee shops have opened over the past four years, all competing for a share of the money people spend on eating away from home.

And:

> The real opportunity for McDonald's is to develop compelling reasons for people to visit us more often ... That means having more relevant menu variety, and offering menu solutions rather than promotional products. There are lots of promotional products on the menu at the moment, but they need to be under-pinned by changes to the core offering. [McDonald's is seeking to become] more relevant to contemporary consumer values.

In this changing environment, Bush also indicated that the rigidity of the McDonald's operating and supply chain systems was no longer a competitive advantage but a limiting factor in its response. It is admitted that the new-menu activity 'placed strains on McDonald's purchasing department, operating systems and restaurant staff'. McDonald's appears to be a good example of the limitations of simply pursuing supply chain efficiency and what might be termed classical marketing exploitation techniques in a rapidly changing environment. In effect McDonald's responded to new pressures in a traditional way – lower the price and use cost-efficiencies to wear out the competition.

What McDonald's seemed to have missed, or only partially realised, was that the market had been changing around them, and it is arguable that the firm's demand chain fundamentally failed to respond to this. Could the company now simply realign its supply chain to meet new demand requirements using its traditional techniques and expertise? This appeared to be the company's strategy. Some commentators thought the issue was a more fundamental one and questioned the ongoing viability of the company's business model, calling on it to 'manage for cash' rather than growth, liquidate some of its vast real estate holdings and return that cash by way of higher dividends. In effect they were casting doubt on the efficacy of McDonald's value chain and the business model supporting it, as the fundamental alignment between what McDonald's produces (its supply chain) and what the customer wants (its demand chain) seemed to have faltered.

McDonald's revival: a demand chain orientation

Clearly disturbed by both the poor results (and the press response), McDonald's reacted. The CEO, Jim Cantalupo, issued a 'McDonald's Revitalisation Plan' (McDonald's website). The company embarked upon a new strategic course, 'reflecting a fundamental change in our approach to growing the business.

Previously we emphasized adding new restaurants. Today, our emphasis is on building sales at existing restaurants.' 'System-wide sales growth' of 3 to 5 per cent per year was planned. Sales increases were planned to be between 1 and 3 per cent, 2 per cent growth resulting from new restaurants. Growth of operating income was planned to be between 6 and 7 per cent.

The 'Revitalisation Plan' is clearly based upon effective demand chain management, reinforced by supply chain changes to implement the demand led changes:

> We've introduced Premium Salads in the US ... Salads Plus Menu in Australia ... On a broader level, we are in the early stages of taking a global cross functional approach to menu management. We are creating 'menu management centers' around the world that will use a consistent consumer-driven process to develop world-class products that leverage our size and our scale.
>
> We have also become more disciplined in how we monitor and measure our restaurants.
>
> In addition we are differentiating McDonald's by creating a more relevant restaurant environment ... to create a more welcoming contemporary ambiance as well as testing new ideas – such as providing wireless internet access.

The plan is still designed around the traditional marketing mix, this time the '5P's' of people, products, place, price and promotion:

People – service, hospitality, pride

- Elements: service speed improvements; staff attitudes and behaviour; staff training
- Performance metrics: speed of service and friendliness scores; reduction in service related complaints

Products – quality, taste, choice

- Elements: premium products at affordable prices; more choice – healthy menus for children; lifestyle – healthy menus for adults; 'local menus'
- Performance metrics: improvements in hot and fresh food rating scores

Place – clean, relevant, modern

- Elements: restaurant cleanliness; internet 'hotspots'; McCafe; restaurant renovation programme (NZ and France)
- Performance metrics: cleanliness scores

Price – productivity, purchase value

- Elements: variety of product and price options; promoting brand and price together

■ Performance metrics: 'value for money scores'; restaurant margins

Promotion – marketing, leadership, trust

■ Elements: 'I'm Loving It', a brand promotion targeting children; an appeal to young adults with music performed by popular recording artists; building popularity with families (Premium Salads, McCafe, Happy Meal toys); protecting and monitoring bonds of trust (community involvement)

■ Performance metrics: brand awareness; customer responses

Improving profitability

■ Elements: working with suppliers to identify potential production and sourcing efficiencies worldwide; improving staff productivity by expanding the use of labour saving equipment such as automated dispensers, 'bulk oil' machines to filter and change cooking oil, 'self order' kiosks

■ Performance metrics: increase brand McDonald's company operated restaurant margins by 35 basis points per year from 2005

Controlling expenses

■ Elements: selling, general and administration (SG&A) expenses (costs associated with supporting restaurants)

■ Performance metrics: reduce SG&A expenses as a percentage of systemwide sales by one tenth of 1 per cent per year

Allocating capital more effectively

■ Elements: generate maximum long-term returns; generate cash flow ($US2.8 billion in past five years); capital expenditure to be less than $2.0 billion; decrease debt; return $500 million to $1 billion to shareholders through dividends and share repurchases

■ Performance metrics: increase returns; strengthen the balance sheet; decrease debt; funding capital expenditure from cash flows

Clearly McDonald's has taken positive steps to understand its demand chain. The McDonald's 'Revitalisation Plan' reflects process responses to the demand chain characteristics. Changing customer expectations have been identified and 'customer facing processes' put in place with relevant performance measurements to ensure that the plan is monitored. Financial results at February 2004 suggested that the plan was beginning to make an impact.

REFERENCES

AeIGT (2003) *An Independent Report on the Future of the UK Aerospace Industry*, Department of Trade and Industry, London

Baglieri E and S Zamboni (2005) 'Partnering along the demand chain: collaboration in the new product development process', paper delivered at the 2nd European Forum on Market-Driven Supply Chains, 'From Supply Chains to Demand Chains', European Institute for Advanced Studies in Management, Milan, 5/6 April

Bamford J and D Ernst (2004) 'Managing an alliance portfolio', *McKinsey Quarterly*, August

Bornheim S P with J Weppler and O Ohlen (2001) *e-roadmapping*, Palgrave Macmillan, Basingstoke

Brickley J, C Smith and J Zimmerman (2004) *Managerial Economics and Organisational Architecture*, 3rd edition, McGraw-Hill, New York

Brown S (1996) *Strategic Manufacturing for Competitive Advantage*, Prentice-Hall, London

Burt M, J Harvey, R Guthrie, A Voyle, R Islam and N Tait (2000) 'Carmakers take two routes to global growth', *Financial Times*, 26/27 February

Butler P, T W Hall, A M Hanna, L Mendonca, B Auguste, J Manyika and A Sahay (2004), 'A revolution in interaction', *McKinsey Quarterly*, August

Campbell A (1996) 'Creating the virtual organisation and managing the distributed workforce', in Jackson P and J Van der Weilen (eds) *New Perspectives on Telework – From Telecommuting to the Virtual Organisation*, Report on workshop held at Brunel University, 31 July–2 August

Champion D (2001) 'Mastering the value chain', *Harvard Business Review*, June

Chandler A (1965) *Strategy and Structure*, MIT Press, Cambridge, MA

Coase R H (1991) *The Nature of the Firm: Origins and Evolution*, Oxford University Press, Oxford

Competitive Capital Management Group (2004) 'White Paper', CCMG, Sydney

Doz Y L and G Hamel (1998) *Alliance Advantage: The Art of Creating Value through Partnering*, Harvard Business School Press, Boston, MA

Drucker P (2001) 'Will the corporation survive?', *The Economist*, 1 November

Hagel J III and M Singer (1999) 'Unbundling the corporation,' *Harvard Business Review*, March/April

Johns R, V Crute and A Craves (2005) 'Improving value delivery: challenges in establishing value chain delivery', paper delivered at the 2nd European Forum on Market-Driven Supply Chains, 'From Supply Chains to Demand Chains', European Institute for Advanced Studies in Management, Milan 5/6 April

Kay J (1993) *Foundation of Corporate Success*, Oxford University Press, Oxford.

Lindgren M and H Bandhold (2003) *Scenario Planning*, Palgrave Macmillan, Basingstoke

McDonald's, www.McDonald's.com, accessed 29 October 2003

Scott M (1998) *Value Drivers*, Wiley, Chichester

Williamson O E (1985) *The Economic Institutions of Capitalism: Firms, Markets, Relationship Contracting*, Free Press, New York

Younge R (2005) article in *Australian Financial Review*, 19 April

CHAPTER 8

The Value Chain: An Industry Perspective

LEARNING TOPICS

On completing your study of this chapter you will have been introduced to and considered the following topics:

- Integrating value strategy and value production; from strategy to operational implementation
- Using the value chain for strategic market opportunity analysis; vertical and horizontal perspectives
- Value chain context mapping; the components and their application
- Value chain partnerships: identifying and working with partners
- Mature and developing value chains

Introduction

This text has on several occasions touched on the distinction between a company's strategy – where it positions itself in the market – and its business model – the where and how of what it actually does. There has been a tendency to compartmentalise these two perspectives, so that 'strategy' becomes the domain of senior management, some of whom even describe themselves as 'strategists'. In contrast, business model planning and implementation are seen as being 'operational'.

If nothing else, value chain management illustrates that this distinction is largely illusory. Instead the reality is what might be termed 'strategic operations management', which extends beyond product and technology to consider the structure of organisations and entire industries. It is customer or market focused, rather than being product and/or process focused, and it is likely to extend across industries and certainly within them. Baldwin and Clark (1997) propose two strategy alternatives: an organisation 'can compete as an architect, creating the visible information or design rules for a product made up of modules, or it can compete as a designer of modules that conform to the architecture, interfaces and test protocols of others'.

Again the similarity is strong. Strategic operations management has both the integrator and value chain specialist roles. However, the integrator role is more strategic and assumes a market strategist role, identifying opportunities for expansive customer satisfaction and extending well beyond specific products.

Baldwin and Clark discuss *modularity* in the computer and automotive industries and append a direction for further reading which includes contributions commencing in 1989 and numerous applications cases from the early 1990s.

The authors define 'modularity' as 'building a complex product or process from smaller subsystems that can be designed independently yet function together as a whole'. They contend that 'Many industries have long had a degree of modularity in their production processes,' but suggest that 'a growing number of them are now poised to extend modularity to the design stage'. The authors also suggest that it is the computer industry that has both facilitated and benefited from modularity. They contend that modularity has enabled companies to restructure products into subsystems or modules, resulting in flexibility, and that this allows different companies to take responsibility for separate modules, 'confident that a reliable product will arise from their collective efforts'.

The essence of Baldwin and Clark's concept is in product development. Strategic operations management is much more 'macro' in its approach. Its concern is with organisational development. This difference notwithstanding, there are some strong similarities and conceptually the two approaches are close. Indeed, many of the comments made by the authors concerning benefits that have been identified are well noted. And their comments concerning the evolutionary stages of modularity compare with the views of McHugh et al. (1995) and their 'holonic' organisation, which we met in Chapter 1.

Management practices play a similar role in the two approaches. Baldwin and Clark suggest that 'managers will have to become much more attuned to all sorts of developments in the design of products, both inside and outside their own companies ... Success in the marketplace will depend upon mapping much larger competitive terrain and linking one's own capabilities and options with those emerging elsewhere, possibly in companies very different from one's own.' The 'skills' required of the integrator and modularity architect are also similar in the two approaches. Both need to be able to link technologies, financial resources and human resources. They are essentially entrepreneurial. The authors quote a comment by Howard Stevenson, who described entrepreneurship as 'the pursuit of opportunity beyond the resources currently controlled'. Perhaps the quotation should now be updated to read 'the pursuit of opportunity virtually'.

A framework for integrating value strategy and value production

It could be argued that strategic operations management owes much to the work of Coase (1937) who, it will be recalled, provided an initial perspective of the economics of alliances and partnerships through the concept of transaction costs. The issue Coase addressed is the relationship between the cost of producing goods or services internally and purchasing them from an external supplier. In addition to 'market prices' there are transaction costs generated by the search and negotiating processes involved in finding an appropriate partner organisation, negotiating a supply agreement, and associated time based costs. Tedeschi (2000) comments that at the time Coase proposed this theory, transaction costs were 'prohibitively high' due to the lack of timely and accurate information and cramped and slow supply chains that fostered the preference for ownership of resources through vertical integration. Some 60 years on, within the 'new economy', rapid moving, accurate and low cost information offers 'virtual – instant' information about potential suppliers and business partners, thereby facilitating the formation of alliances at a fraction of the costs of even five or ten years ago. Coase maintained that with diminished transaction costs, more alliances would be inevitable. More recently, he has commented (in Tedeschi 2000) that understanding transaction costs in the 'new economy' will result in a return to the theories of Adam Smith and specialisation:

> It enables you to have more specialisation and greater production because you're more efficient ... You'll get more small firms as a result, but large firms will also get larger, because they can concentrate on core activities and con contract out what they can't do well.

The integrating role of value chain management

Value chain management faces a number of tasks in the process of integrating value strategy and value delivery. Figure 8.1 illustrates the proposal that strategic operations management is a process in which customer value opportunity is identified, value production processes are coordinated and, provided that partners' objectives can be met, customer value is delivered. Figure 8.1 also identifies the conceptual management infrastructure necessary to implement the value strategy. The value chain is a structure of networks between value producers and customers; if it is to be successful, then an understanding and an acceptance of tasks, roles, responsibilities and accountabilities are necessary. It is the role of strategic operations management to coordinate the network between and among the value chain producers and the customer. In the context of the value chain, the networks are not simply information technology based, but are relationship, knowledge technology and process based. They develop from the experience of working with partner organisations, developing an understanding of the specific skills and resources each possesses and also developing trust and respect for the owners of those skills and resources. Typically, as experience and trust expand, confidence grows and with it the willingness to share knowledge, so that eventually the network develops a knowledge base that it can use to its competitive advantage. Similarly, technology management also expands and the trust enables partners to develop dependencies upon each other. Dell (1999) gives examples of how trust developed relationships in the computer industry to the point where 'asset leverage' has become commonplace.

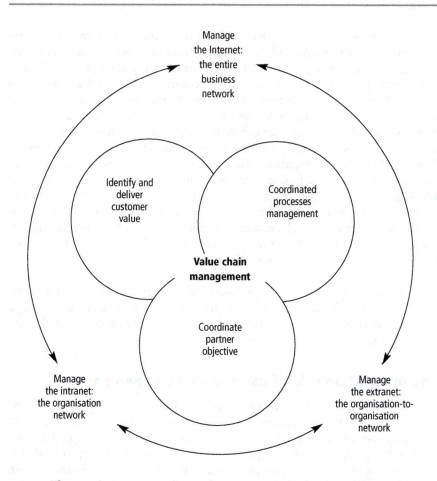

Figure 8.1 Integrating value strategy and value delivery

McHugh et al. (1995) identify 'the role of the virtual company integrator'. An integrator is 'often a visionary who sees how putting pieces together will create a better core business process'. The concern is to ensure the defined business moves along, arbitrates disputes, manages contracts with customers and monitors performance. Integrator roles differ and the authors identify two types. One concerns start-up situations, where the role is to identify participants and to define a structure which best meets the value expectations of the target customer group. The other role is one in which the complete network has been defined and the integrator is more involved with customer and contract relations. For both roles there is a communications management task; the integrator receives market feedback and communicates this feedback across the value chain structure. The integrator sets, monitors and evaluates performance measures. Performance measures concern 'not only the economic achievements ... but also the humanistic goals set (by the value chain)'. Thus the 'value chain integrator' has responsibility for:

- Creating and coordinating a multi-enterprise organisation
- Collecting, analysing, structuring and disseminating knowledge from and to stakeholders rapidly and efficiently
- Ensuring empowerment is effective at critical decision making points
- Developing and/or managing concurrent operations; simultaneous process management using a value chain approach
- Responding to the demands of customisation and mass customisation
- Creating and coordinating organisation structures that identify and respond to 'global' challenges and opportunities in a planned manner
- Maximising the value of the 'enterprise' by identifying, linking and coordinating core competencies from a range of value chain participants

This role predicates the requirements of a performance management system capable of reflecting composite performance across the value chain and which reflects the interests of the principal stakeholders. The structure of value chains implies that different approaches may be required and, therefore, that performance management becomes customised.

McHugh et al. discuss 'demand driven' logistics in much the same context as Beech (1998), commenting: 'It is the backbone of the actual day-to-day execution of a virtual company. By forming a virtual company among and integrating with a product's suppliers, the end customer can be more completely serviced.' The authors also introduce the term 'co-makership', which is used to suggest the integrated 'production and coordination' role in the organisation profile model discussed in the previous paragraphs. They suggest co-makership to be 'A partnering philosophy and technique that complements the process-oriented approaches'. They discuss the approach of manufacturing companies who now regard suppliers as partners, and comment on 'supplier equity' as a core competence. They differentiate between two quite different focuses: 'product-out', which is operations based, and 'market-in', which identifies business opportunities offered by the marketplace and translates them into products the company could make given its processes and capabilities. As this in itself is insufficient, they suggest that for success it is also increasingly necessary to 'have a culture that is group oriented'. They argue that the businesses that compete and win today, and will continue to do so during the rest of the twenty-first century, are those with what they describe as a venture/'market-in' approach. Put more pragmatically, their 'way of doing business' is to include both suppliers and customers within the value chain and its communications.

The venture/'market-in' business adopts the Japanese perspective by taking a medium- and long-term view of the market and combines it with Western approaches to market analysis and a focus on innovation and product diversity. McHugh and his co-authors contend that 'Their basis of competition is quality, lead time and flexibility and they engage their partners up and down the value chain in discussions regarding these competitive aspects.' They employ system based strategies, which are the essence of strategic operations management:

■ Vertical coordination/virtual integration of a 'logistic network' that 'integrates' the interest and activities of suppliers and customers throughout the value chain

■ The co-makership logic in design and development procurement, production, marketing and service delivery, not only in operations

■ A rationalised supplier base that becomes integrated into the business and provides quality, flexibility, and agility, as well as cost reduction

■ A common information system for planning and controlling the value chain and that identifies change opportunities

■ Consideration of outsourcing support and management processes to specialist partners

Essentially the role of the industry value chain is to identify opportunities to create customer value. This is achieved either by adding value to existing customers or by identifying the value expectations of new customers and coordinating the value chain assets, processes and capabilities to meet these expectations. Figure 8.2 illustrates the principle of the value chain. The basic task of 'adding value to customers' comprises a structured response to customer satisfaction. By identifying the 'customer facing processes' that meet their value drivers, an integrated value chain structure emerges. The structure is created from an understanding of the capabilities and capacities of a number of existing and/or potential partners, the objective being to meet (or possibly exceed) customer expectations at an optimum level of costs.

Within the value management context, partners become integrated into a 'virtual organisation' in which their processes are modified to meet an overall 'input-transformation-output' model. Cooperation in product and service design is a 'norm'; co-destiny pervades procurement, production, marketing and service delivery. Communications are typically electronically managed to ensure that not only are resources uses optimal but also responses to customer changes in expectations are rapid. The logistics function becomes the 'backbone' of the actual day-to-day execution of the value chain organisation. This is illustrated in Figure 8.3, which identifies the generic processes common to all value chain structures at both the industry and the firm level. At the industry level the decisions concern what has to be accomplished to achieve customer satisfaction and partner stakeholder satisfaction. At the level of the firm, the individual partner stakeholder, the decisions are concerned with how the firm can integrate its processes and capabilities with the other members of the value chain.

Using the value chain for strategic analysis

Market opportunity analysis

The review of the industry value drivers is part of a larger review of product-market and process based opportunities. Market opportunity analysis also includes an assessment of the assets, process and core capabilities that are

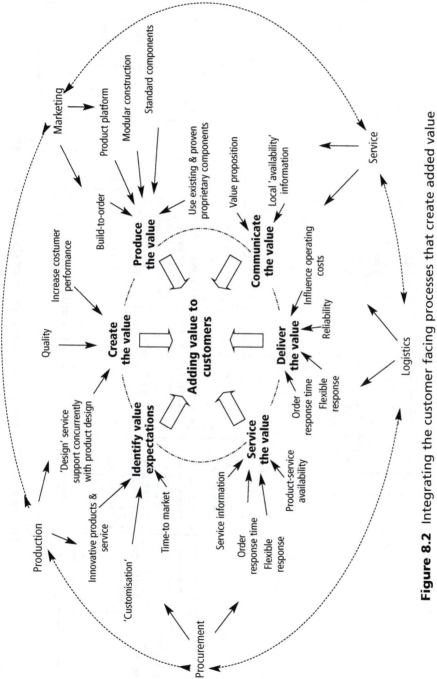

Figure 8.2 Integrating the customer facing processes that create added value

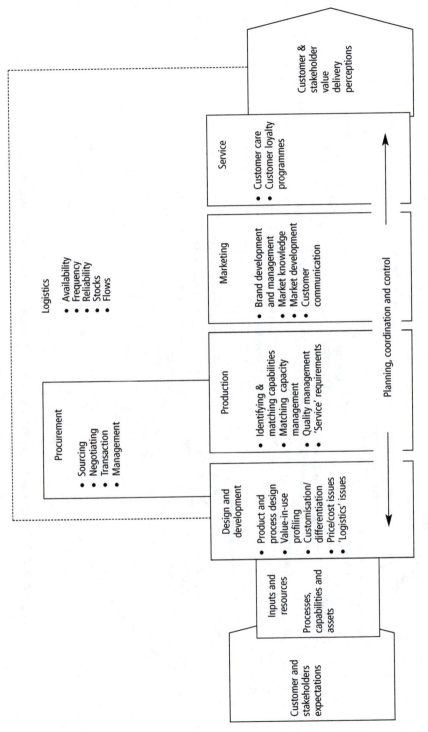

Figure 8.3 A generic industry value chain design: roles and tasks

Customer and stakeholders expectations

Inputs and resources

Processes, capabilities and assets

Design and development
- Product and process design
- Value-in-use profiling
- Customisation/ differentiation
- Price/cost issues
- 'Logistics' issues

Procurement
- Sourcing
- Negotiating
- Transaction
- Management

Production
- Identifying & matching capabilities
- Matching capacity management
- Quality management
- 'Service' requirements

Logistics
- Availability
- Frequency
- Reliability
- Stocks
- Flows

Marketing
- Brand development and management
- Market knowledge
- Market development
- Customer communication

Service
- Customer care
- Customer loyalty programmes

Customer & stakeholder value delivery perceptions

Planning, coordination and control

required if a successful entry is to be made. Each of these topics was discussed in detail in Chapter 5. The analysis discussed above is also an integral part of market opportunity analysis. It is should be clear by now that in value chain management the analysis is more comprehensive, including and aspects of value production and delivery as well as of augmentation. These are the vertical market aspects of added value processes, and the horizontal market considerations of components, products and service augmentation that add value. Included in this analysis is identification of segmentation criteria and the specific value expectations of the segment target customers. In Chapter 7 we considered the relationships that need to be structured and installed – the organisational architecture that determines the nature of relationships among the stakeholder partners, together with their expectations and the contributions they are expected to make. For each there are a number of questions. While the industry value drivers identify the required direction for competitive advantage, they should be considered in context with the required assets, processes and capabilities and their availability. See Figure 8.4.

Current perspectives on the 'evergreen' topic of the product life cycle are of interest. The product life cycle is but one concept that has been debated by marketing theorists for some time. Its value is 'that it provides insights into a product's competitive dynamics. At the same time, the concept can prove misleading if not carefully used' Kotler (1994). Ansoff (1984) offers a different perspective on the product life cycle. His suggestion is to consider not the product but the 'need' that products satisfy. Thus personal communication, from written letters or notes to word processing is an area of need, and the 'changing level of need is the demand life cycle', as shown in Figure 8.5a. Needs are satisfied by technology. Word processing technology has developed over time from quill and vellum, through various mechanical writing applications (pens, pencils, and so on) to typewriters and computer based software processing packages. As each 'technology' is introduced it creates its own demand technology life cycle. Within any given demand technology life cycle a number of product alternatives appear. For example, mechanical writing applications have had numerous variants (refillable fountain pens, ballpoint pens, and so on), and word processing packages are continually updated. Each development is a product for which a product life cycle can be determined. The shape of the product life cycle within its demand technology life cycle is shown in Figure 8.5b.

The issue confronting the firm is which technology life cycle it should invest in. In Figure 8.5c we suggest that in a dynamic industry such as computing, the demand technology changes very rapidly. Added to this feature is the reality of continually increasing costeffectiveness, in which we see not only an accelerating rate of technological development but also decreasing costs. Ansoff (1984) calls the demand technology cycle a strategic business area (SBA), which is 'a distinctive segment of the environment in which the firm does or may want to do business'. The decisions are not easy ones for the individual company. The issues are therefore the cost of entry, the time required to become operational (that is, profitable), and the time period over which the

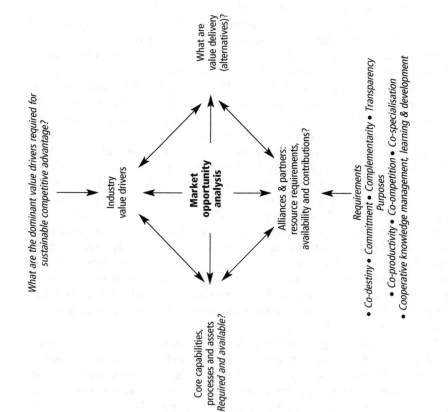

Figure 8.4 Strategic operations planning: the industry perspective

What are the dominant value drivers required for sustainable competitive advantage?

Industry value drivers

What are the segment differentiation criteria? What are the alternative value offers? Where in the value chain will the stakeholders be most effectively 'positioned' to create stakeholder value and competitive advantage?

What are value delivery (alternatives)?

Market opportunity analysis

Alliances & partners: resource requirements, availability and contributions?

Core capabilities, processes and assets
Required and available?

Requirements
• Co-destiny • Commitment • Complementarity • Transparency Purposes
• Co-productivity • Co-ompetition • Co-specialisation
• Cooperative knowledge management, learning & development

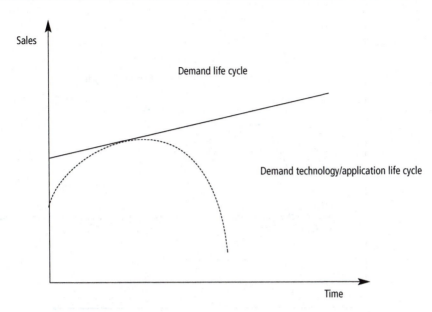

Figure 8.5a A new technology 'managed' PLC

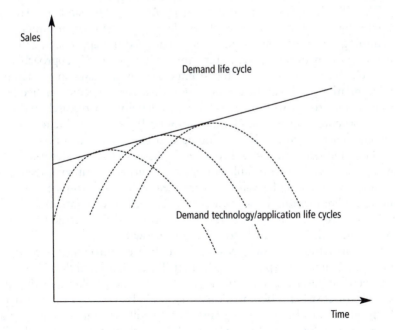

Figure 8.5b Investment decisions in the PLC

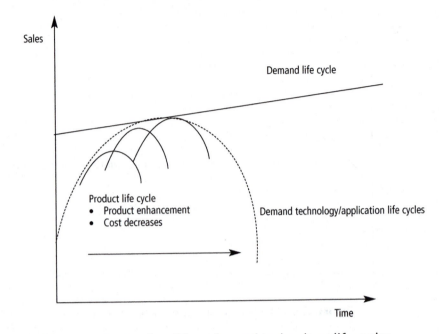

Figure 8.5c Product life cycles and technology life cycles

strategic business area is likely to be effective. The concept of the product life cycle remains interesting and has aroused differing views.

The SBA has also been considered by Abell (1980) and by Day (1999). Abell suggested that markets could be defined in terms of customer function, technology and customer groups. Day broadened this approach by incorporating the notion of added value into the definition. Day's approach used the value chain to identify the relative strengths (or weaknesses) on which to build differentiation. This can be achieved by either using specific, relative performance characteristics within the value chain activities of research and development, procurement, inbound and outbound logistics, production, marketing and customer service, or by developing cost led differentiation..

Day's approach can be said to give emphasis to shareholder value management and may be used to link strategy decisions and strategy implementation through the shareholder value drivers. Clearly, if a company chooses to focus on its differentiation characteristics, the growth of profitability, productivity and cash flow will follow. The task of management is to decide how to deploy the resources it has available to achieve its growth objectives.

Customer functions or needs will be enhanced through differentiation by providing benefits via specific product attributes. The identification of the relevant benefits (and the subsequent response by the producer in the shape of product or cost led differentiation) is typically based upon the uses to which the product is to be put by the customer. It follows that there can be a wide range of uses for a product, which will vary by customer, and all of which should be identified by the supplier.

'Customer groups' (or segments) are identified as those who share similar needs or characteristics which are relevant in a strategic planning context. Segmentation proposes that companies focus on a specific set of needs or customer characteristics.

'Technologies' describe the ways in which customers' needs can be satisfied or functions performed or delivered. Clearly there are often a number of ways in which a need may be satisfied.

'Scope' refers to the extent of the business's involvement in a market. This may exhibit a number of characteristics. For example, a company may decide on geographic scope by which it specifies an area within which it will operate. This decision may be based on either inbound or outbound logistics costs. Day's approach (also using the value chain) considered scope from what is best described as a supply chain perspective. He proposed that management consider scope from an activity perspective by identifying where within the supply chain in the production process – how far forward (toward the end-user/customer) or backward (toward the supplier) – the business should participate. Increasingly scope can become a competitive issue as technology is applied to delivery problems. For example, news media products now use digital formats to 'edit' or customise their products and for transmission over long distances so as not to lose the impact of content currency.

Both Abell and Day describe the concept using a three-vector diagram, reproduced as Figure 8.6. The result is a market cell comprising customer

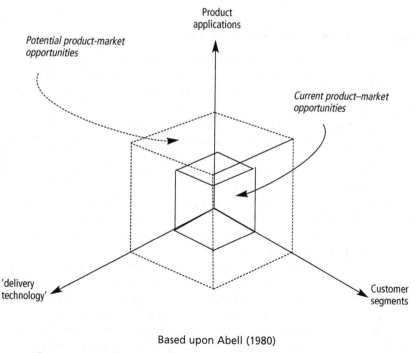

Based upon Abell (1980)

Figure 8.6 Identifying current and potential product-market opportunities

functions (or customer needs) and customer groups (segments) that are satisfied, together with the technology used. The technologies reflect those currently available. Customer functions (needs) represent an extensive range of requirements, some of which are applicable to both segments and technology. It does not follow that each segment will have sufficient demand for each of the customer needs. Clearly the technology applications are equally applicable to each of the segments, but may have greater potential for one or two specifically. The model also offers the facility to explore the impact of partnerships on increasing the business's effectiveness in one or more of the vectors.

The demand life cycle and demand technology life cycle can offer scope for planning the industry value chain. Abell's model identifies a number of product-market directions that become strong options if they can be approached as a structured industry value chain. There are numerous examples. Consider the application of ICT to both supplier and customer relationship management processes. This development has made possible the outsourcing of all or part of the production process because of the facility it offers to exercise close and timely control over production schedules; it has reduced distance and control as operational management problems, thereby opening up access to resource markets offering lower cost alternative for materials, components and labour. In a customer relationship management context there are similar considerations. The internet permits consumer uses in which product information can be accessed; in the B2B market context auctions are being held for the supply of materials and components.

Vertical and horizontal market structures

An extension of Abell's model in a value chain context permits a review of *where* component partner companies may best fit within an industry value chain structure. In Figure 8.7 the growth strategies available to an organisation include horizontal and vertical markets. The inter-organisational, networking structure of the value chain/virtual organisation model offers opportunities for growth that were hitherto difficult to access. Figure 8.7 shows the principle of vertical and horizontal market structures. Examples of vertical markets include design companies, focused service companies and logistics service organisations. The fact that they operate within a value network provides an opportunity to develop specialist skills and resources in the process/activity. Horizontal markets may be focused on particular segments and applications, such as specific product users or resellers. They may also be 'incremental value added' focused.

Vertical markets are based upon the industry value chain. They represent opportunities for organisations within the industry value to move forward or backward within the value chain and expand their activities to include processes for which they identify opportunity to increase the added value captured by the value chain. These opportunities may occur because of value migration, whether due to process management changes (product or service formulation changes), relationship management developments (new entrants), knowledge

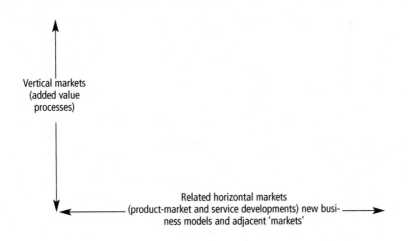

Figure 8.7 Exploring vertical and horizontal 'markets' for competitive activities and partner stakeholder opportunities

management developments (pure or applied research breakthroughs that change the nature of the market), and/or technology management developments (developments in product and/or process innovation resulting in new approaches to the strategy and operational approaches to the value chain structure). Examples are Millennium in the pharmaceuticals industry, and Ford and GM in the automotive industry.

Partnership structures give the ability to access partial markets more readily than can organisations that are not part of a value creation network. As suggested by Figure 8.8, vertical market access can be available in any of a number of value chain processes/activities. Typically, companies involved in these are specialists who offer aspects of product and/or service differentiation that exceed those of competitors.

Horizontal markets exist where substitute products, services, delivery alternatives and alternative product-markets become available. These markets may be based upon product developments, service developments or market (segment) developments. They occur because of the influence of industry value drivers and changing business models. Again the influence of industry value drivers may change product formulation (knowledge and/or technology developments), service applications such as the use of call centres for support (ICT), and possibly product design (the design and development process uses serviceability data to 'design out' problem defects, thereby reducing the need for field service operations). Changing business models also influence horizontal markets. The increasing trend towards asset leverage/low capital-intensity models, in which assets – tangible and intangible – are used across organisations is one such influence. Examples are Dell, Amex (offshore call centres); computer OEMs (partnering with service organisations); KLM and AirUK (international airlines partnering with national airlines); Star Alliance (international airlines' alliance combinations); VW/Audi (automobiles); and the Australian wine industry (virtual business model).

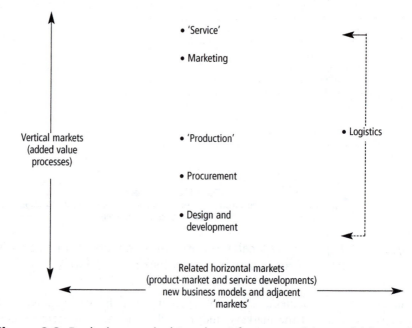

Figure 8.8 Exploring vertical 'markets' for competitive activities and corporate opportunities

Horizontal markets are shown as 'product-market-access' opportunities – specific segments into which modified versions of existing products (or possibly specialist expertise) may be 'inserted'. Often access is made much easier when a 'co-opetition' strategy is adopted. Examples can also be seen in the modified aerospace and military technology products that are adopted by the automotive industry, and in pharmaceutical products moving into FMCG markets.

'Horizontal market opportunities' occur in specific industries. Product-market access opportunities occur in markets where products serve similar functions but the delivery to end-users may take quite different channels. Components, products and service augmentation opportunities occur in flow line production processes and markets such as those of the automotive industry and consumer durables. Examples of incremental added value markets can be found in extraction and continuous process industries. Figure 8.9 provides examples of each of these.

Within value chain structures it is not unusual to find organisations combining their specialist resources to 'exploit' opportunity in both vertical and horizontal dimensions. Figure 8.10 illustrates how this happens in the automotive and industrial equipment markets. The illustration describes the motives for and potential benefits of pursuing an opportunity to combine horizontal and vertical opportunities. Figure 8.11 illustrates the same argument using an example from the extraction/process industries.

Figure 8.12 illustrates an application of the approach to an analysis of the pharmaceutical market. It combines both vertical and horizontal markets with

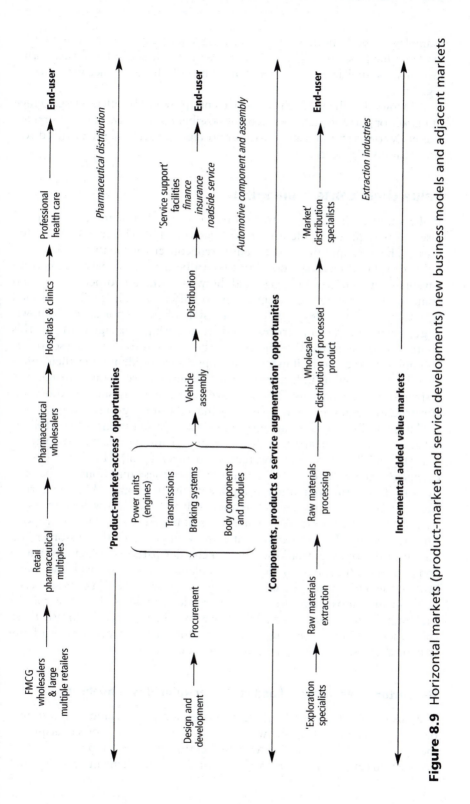

Figure 8.9 Horizontal markets (product-market and service developments) new business models and adjacent markets

FMCG wholesalers & large multiple retailers → Retail pharmaceutical multiples → Pharmaceutical wholesalers → Hospitals & clinics → Professional health care → **End-user**

Pharmaceutical distribution

'Product-market-access' opportunities

Design and development → Procurement

Power units (engines)
Transmissions
Braking systems
Body components and modules

→ Vehicle assembly → Distribution → 'Service support' facilities finance insurance roadside service → **End-user**

Automotive component and assembly

'Components, products & service augmentation' opportunities

'Exploration specialists' → Raw materials extraction → Raw materials processing → Wholesale distribution of processed product → 'Market' distribution specialists → **End-user**

Extraction industries

Incremental added value markets

examples of both horizontal (product-market access) and vertical markets (added value processes). The vertical market example suggests a vertical structure that is similar to that found in some of the pharmaceutical market segments.

It follows that the value chain/virtual enterprise model offers a larger range of market opportunity and involvement possibilities. Partnership structures are also likely to reflect more attractive cost profiles (particularly as far as fixed cost amortisation is concerned).

Value chain context mapping

If the value chain model is to be used as an analytical tool, some initial research is required to identify some 'macro issues'. Figure 8.13 identifies these. The first questions to be answered concern what the fundamental industry value drivers are, how are they to be used to achieve competitive advantage within the industry, and how, if there are other similar and competing value creating systems, they are differentiated. It will be recalled that Chapter 5 was devoted to a discussion of the importance of knowledge, technology, and process and relationship management in this context. It is suggested that the chapter be revisited to review these topics. Examples were given to illustrate the importance of identifying their influence in a number of industry sectors: the automotive manufacturing and distribution industry; distributor network value chains such as those for construction equipment; the fast moving consumer goods industry, and banking and finance. Having answered these first questions, others follow. What are the dominant value drivers required for sustainable competitive advantage? Where are they located? Who owns them? How can they be engaged in the value chain? The importance of these questions can be seen by considering the four other components in the model. What comprises the customers' value model and its value drivers? How can value drivers be analysed in order to establish delivery viability? How can a value proposition be developed that communicates the value offer to the customer and identifies the roles and tasks of the stakeholder partners? What alternative configurations/business models are available? And how will the value production and delivery be coordinated? As Figure 8.13 suggests, for each of these questions there are other, more detailed ones. It is the role of McHugh et al.'s 'integrator', whom we met in Chapter 7, to ask these and other questions. The figure gives a more detailed perspective of the structure and sequence of the analytical process.

The customer value model and customer value driver analysis

The customer value model is a segment-specific interpretation of customer benefits expectations, together with an understanding of the costs of acquiring these benefits. We saw in Chapter 3 that customer value comprises variations on asset management; time management; cost management; performance

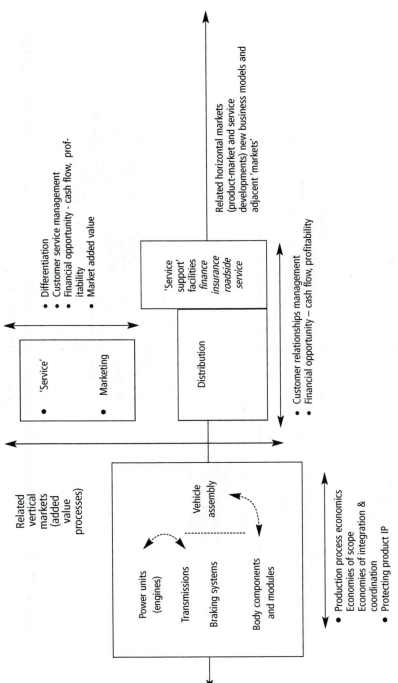

Figure 8.10 Vertical and horizontal markets for competitive activities and corporate opportunities: automotive and industrial equipment

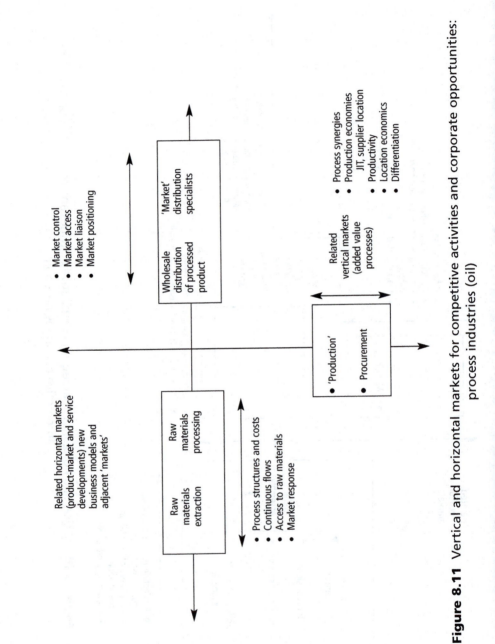

Figure 8.11 Vertical and horizontal markets for competitive activities and corporate opportunities: process industries (oil)

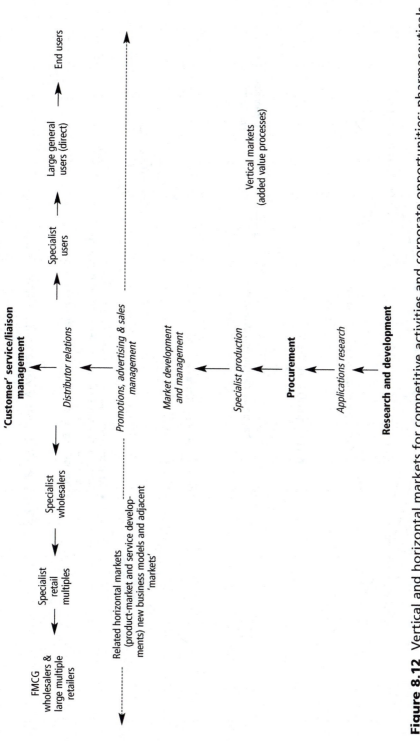

Figure 8.12 Vertical and horizontal markets for competitive activities and corporate opportunities: pharmaceuticals

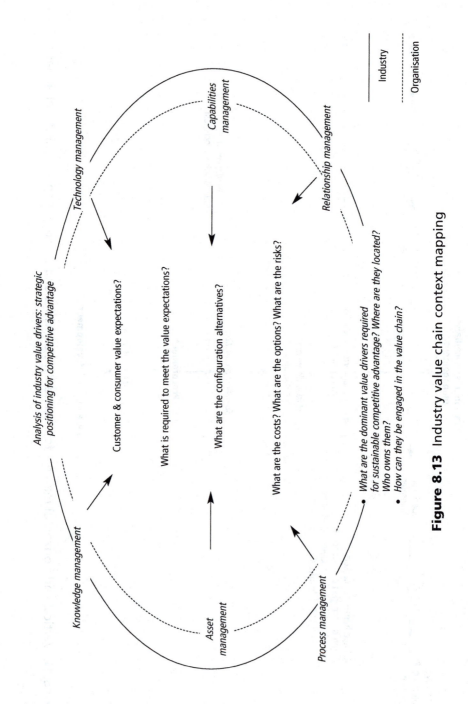

Figure 8.13 Industry value chain context mapping

management (for example, market and financial performance, aspects of customisation, quality, service agility and flexibility, and of product choice and convenience); information management, and risk management.

The analysis of customer value drivers is complex (see Figure 8.14), comprising conclusions from the earlier analysis of industry value drivers, considerations of the expectations of stakeholder partners and implications for strategic and operational resources. An important component is the development of cost profiles and of financial and business risk implications.

While Figure 8.14 is comprehensive and largely self-explanatory, some aspects of it should be explored. The purpose of the analysis is to evaluate the alternatives available for delivering customer value. Given that the value drivers represent customer expectations, the analysis should consider not only the most cost-efficient method of delivery but also a number of other non-cost based considerations. The analysis is therefore seeking an optimal solution. An important consideration is that of the commitment of strategic and operational resources. Apart from the obvious financial implications of short-term and long-term investments, the alternatives available to organisations, and the opportunity costs, can be important. Often an organisation is confronted with choices between pursuing existing or new projects. An Australian FMCG company faced this problem. It had developed a new product and early research suggested very positive consumer acceptance. It also knew that competitors were working with similar products. Given that it had limited production capacity the company decided to outsource the production of a major existing product to a competitor, who had available capacity, and to produce the new product internally. This effectively kept the competitor 'occupied' and contained the information about the new product and process within the company. This protected its confidential information and reduced the commercial risk. As we saw in Chapter 7, the consideration of risk is always of significance in business planning and should never be ignored. It is suggested that, given the organisational structures that are now available and the degree of specialist expertise that is developing, there should be less structural risk involved if the stakeholder partners are experienced organisations.

Developing a value proposition

The term 'value proposition' is widely used, and as a result is equally widely defined and interpreted. Within a value chain context it is described by Figure 8.15. It should identify precisely the organisation's offer to the customer. Furthermore it should also specify in some detail what is expected of the stakeholder partners, identify the organisation's expectations of its customers. Neely et al. (2002) have argued:

> In order to satisfy their own work and needs, organisations have to access contributions from their stakeholders – usually capital and credit from investors, loyalty and profit from customers, ideas and skills from employees, materials and services from suppliers and so on. They also need to have defined what strategies they will pursue to ensure that value is delivered to

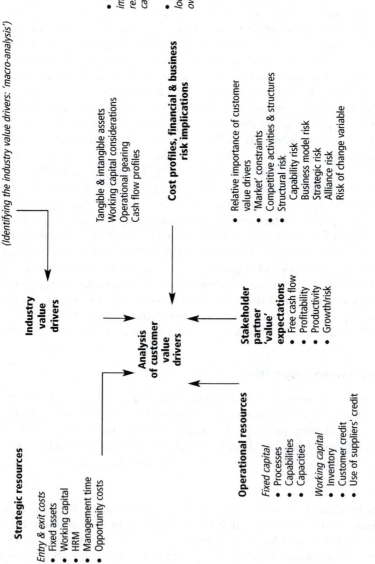

Figure 8.14 Analysing customer value drivers

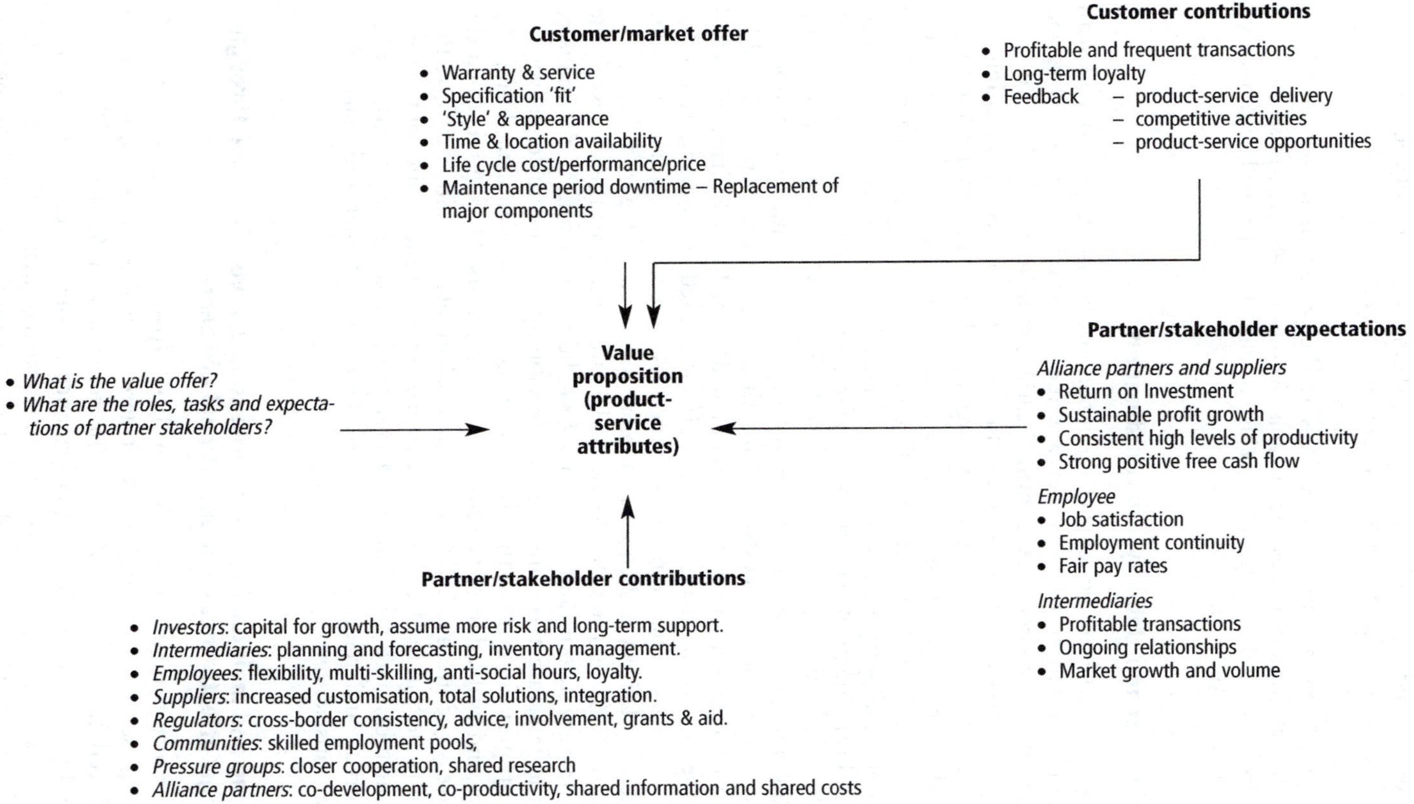

Customer contributions

- Profitable and frequent transactions
- Long-term loyalty
- Feedback – product-service delivery
  – competitive activities
  – product-service opportunities

Customer/market offer

- Warranty & service
- Specification 'fit'
- 'Style' & appearance
- Time & location availability
- Life cycle cost/performance/price
- Maintenance period downtime – Replacement of major components

Value proposition (product-service attributes)

- *What is the value offer?*
- *What are the roles, tasks and expectations of partner stakeholders?*

Partner/stakeholder expectations

Alliance partners and suppliers
- Return on Investment
- Sustainable profit growth
- Consistent high levels of productivity
- Strong positive free cash flow

Employee
- Job satisfaction
- Employment continuity
- Fair pay rates

Intermediaries
- Profitable transactions
- Ongoing relationships
- Market growth and volume

Partner/stakeholder contributions

- *Investors:* capital for growth, assume more risk and long-term support.
- *Intermediaries:* planning and forecasting, inventory management.
- *Employees:* flexibility, multi-skilling, anti-social hours, loyalty.
- *Suppliers:* increased customisation, total solutions, integration.
- *Regulators:* cross-border consistency, advice, involvement, grants & aid.
- *Communities:* skilled employment pools,
- *Pressure groups:* closer cooperation, shared research
- *Alliance partners:* co-development, co-productivity, shared information and shared costs

Figure 8.15 Developing a value proposition

their stakeholders. In order to implement these strategies they have to understand what processes the enterprise requires and must operate both effectively and efficiently. Processes, in themselves, can only be executed if the organisation has the right capabilities in place ... .

Neely and his co-authors are discussing the organisation as a single unit. The value chain approaches the organisation as a multi-enterprise unit, but notwithstanding this, the argument is just as valid. This view will be considered in detail in Chapter 10.

Value production, delivery and coordination

An important role for the value chain 'integrator or visionary' is to work with stakeholder partners to construct a value delivery system. The 'system' includes all of the processes identified earlier, in other words those of identifying the value, creating and producing the value, communicating the value, delivering the value and servicing the value. Value production, delivery and coordination thus assume a critical role in customer satisfaction management. The earlier activities were those of identifying customer value drivers and exploring alternative 'models' necessary to deliver customer satisfaction, both effectively (through a strategic approach that offers exclusivity in either product or process design) and efficiently (by implementing and coordinating an operational system that manages the value specification and production and delivery costs to ensure that both customer and stakeholder partner expectations are met and maintained). The 'model' that evolves will comprise the value chain intermediaries identified during industry value chain mapping. The component processes and considerations of value production, delivery and coordination are described by Figure 8.16.

Figure 8.16 identifies the decisions that are critical for the success of the value delivery system and the viability of the value chain. At the industry level the tasks are those involved in developing a structure to deliver the value proposition around the collective resource base identified during the analysis and evaluation of the customer value drivers. Having identified the effective structure and efficient operational model for value delivery, they must now be 'put in place'. The assets, processes and capabilities of the value chain members are now integrated and checks made to ensure the 'fit' is appropriate and relevant to meet the tasks of customer and stakeholder partner satisfaction.

Creating and maintaining sustainable competitive advantage through strategic effectiveness and operational efficiency

Performance planning and control will be expanded upon in Chapter 10. However, some discussion is relevant here. Earlier discussion in Chapter 3 introduced the concepts of *enterprise value* and *added value*. These are reintroduced here to discuss performance in the context of value chain competitive advantage. It will be remembered that enterprise value is an aggregate NPV return and added value can also be used to measure

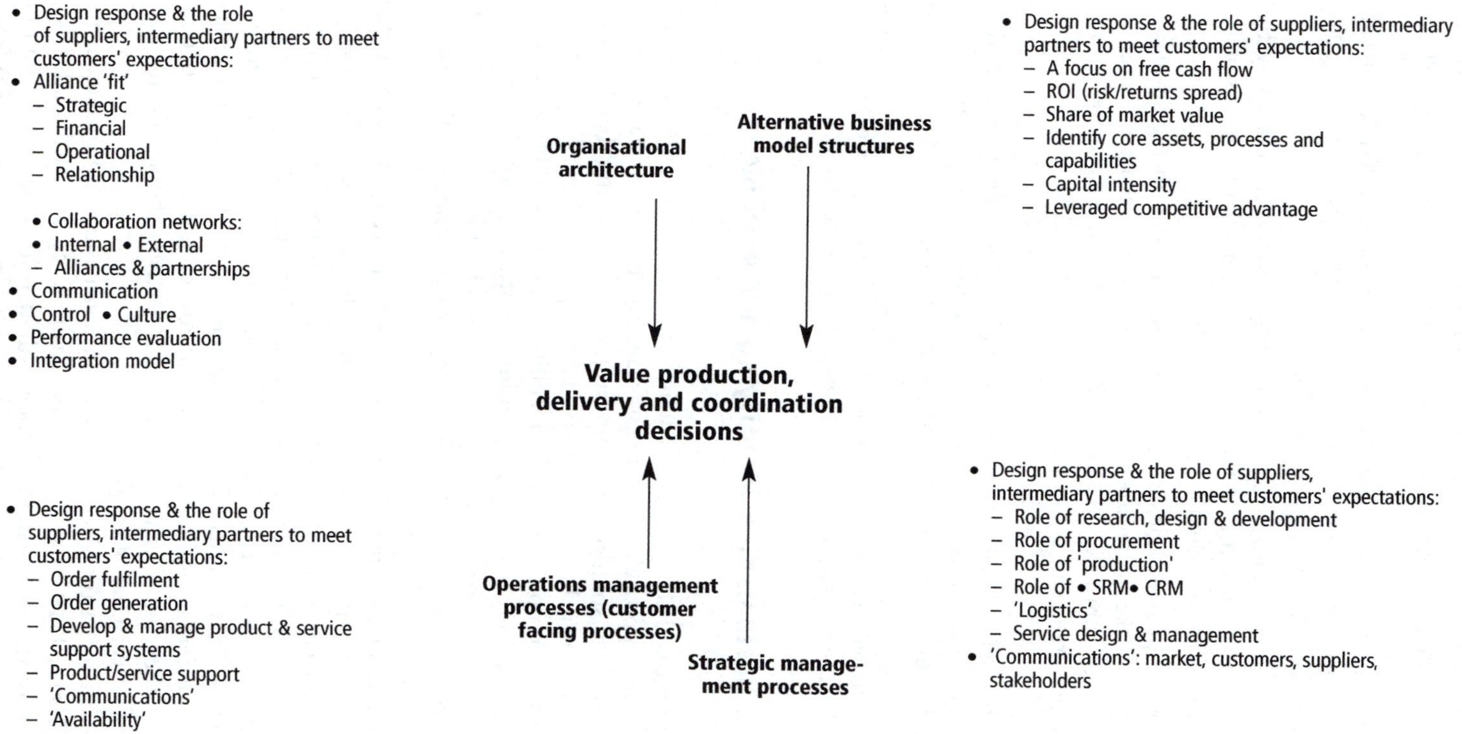

- Design response & the role of suppliers, intermediary partners to meet customers' expectations:
- Alliance 'fit'
  - Strategic
  - Financial
  - Operational
  - Relationship
- Collaboration networks:
  - Internal ● External
  - Alliances & partnerships
- Communication
- Control ● Culture
- Performance evaluation
- Integration model

- Design response & the role of suppliers, intermediary partners to meet customers' expectations:
  - Order fulfilment
  - Order generation
  - Develop & manage product & service support systems
  - Product/service support
  - 'Communications'
  - 'Availability'

Alternative business model structures

Organisational architecture

Value production, delivery and coordination decisions

Operations management processes (customer facing processes)

Strategic management processes

- Design response & the role of suppliers, intermediary partners to meet customers' expectations:
  - A focus on free cash flow
  - ROI (risk/returns spread)
  - Share of market value
  - Identify core assets, processes and capabilities
  - Capital intensity
  - Leveraged competitive advantage

- Design response & the role of suppliers, intermediary partners to meet customers' expectations:
  - Role of research, design & development
  - Role of procurement
  - Role of 'production'
  - Role of ● SRM● CRM
  - 'Logistics'
  - Service design & management
- 'Communications': market, customers, suppliers, stakeholders

Figure 8.16 Industry value production, delivery and coordination

performance at the industry and firm levels. If the value chain is to achieve customer and stakeholder partner satisfaction, four criteria are essential:

- *Effectiveness*: a measure that ensures the strategic decisions are viable and will ensure that growth from new investment in both tangible and intangible assets will produce the desired free cash flow
- *Efficiency*: operating decisions to make existing assets work efficiently by reducing waste and therefore cost, but at the same time ensuring customer vale expectations are delivered
- *Profitability*: adequate margins to cover costs and to offer pricing flexibility are essential. To make the measure relevant it is expressed as a percentage of profit generated from assets that are utilised to generate customer value. Probably more important is to extend the measure to reflect Kay's (1993) measure of competitive advantage.
- *Productivity*: asset management (asset utilisation) indicates how well the assets dedicated to generating customer added value are utilised. Again it is suggested that the approach suggested by Kay be used.

Factors that influence each of the measures are included in Figure 8.17. It can be seen that these are strategic and operational in their context.

Value chain partnerships: identifying and working with partners

It has been suggested that a major benefit to be gained from the adoption of a value chain approach to business planning is that management is encouraged to seek solutions to opportunities by looking beyond the boundaries of its own business and to identify partnership alliances with organisations that complement their capabilities, assets and often processes. Typically this occurs when an organisation identifies an opportunity to differentiate its value proposition or perhaps is able significantly to lower costs in a competitive market by partnering with a company that offers cost-efficient process solutions.

The most successful partnerships are those that have been developed on the basis of clearly identified needs, opportunities for both organisations to enhance their current performance levels and clearly defined roles and tasks. Figure 8.18 suggests how this can be achieved. For each value process the activities that most closely contribute and respond to customer value drivers are determined and the alternatives identified and evaluated. Clearly the result may be that no external solution can be found. However, if an external option appears to be the cost-efficient solution both partners should identify the expectations that each has of the other.

An approach to partnership identification, evaluation and management is shown as Figure 8.19. Initially the value chain 'integrator' will undertake a planning exercise and this strategic focus will identify processes within the value chain that may benefit (in terms of cost-efficient value delivery) from

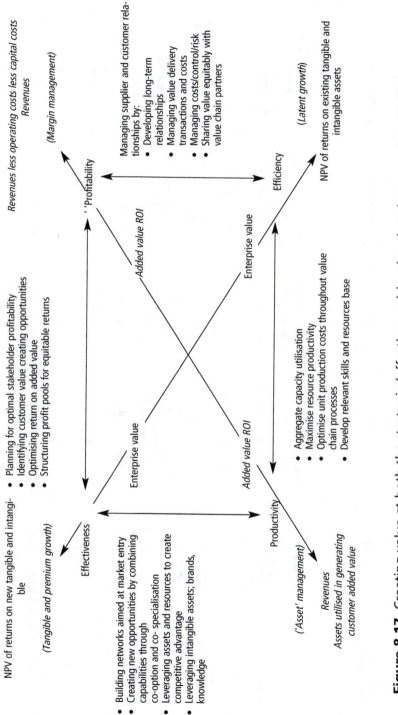

Figure 8.17 Creating value at both the strategic (effectiveness) level and at the operational (efficiency) level

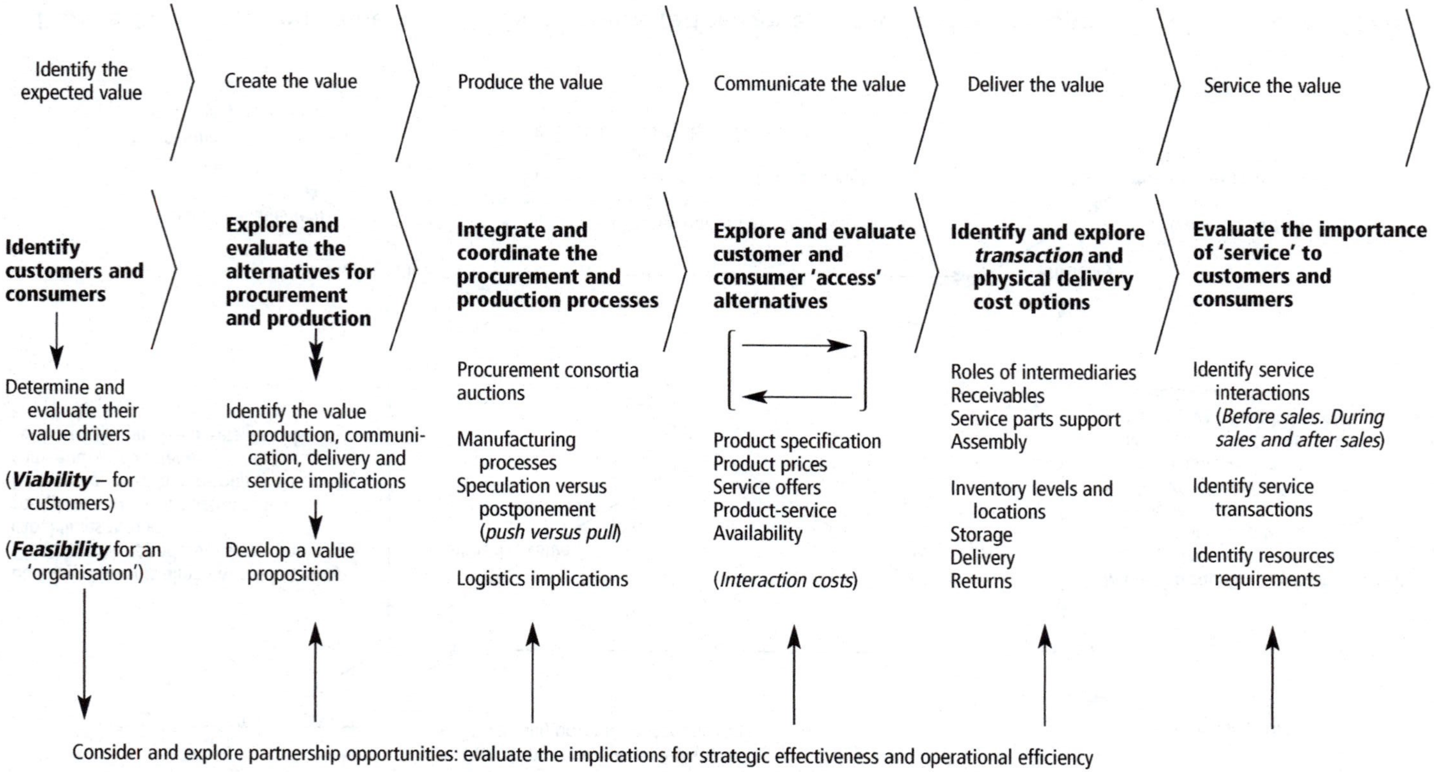

Figure 8.18 Partnership decisions require clearly defined criteria

a partnership arrangement with a specialist organisation. Once the roles, tasks and performance expectations of the partnership are agreed, each partner is responsible for implementing the operational responsibilities that fall to them.

Figure 8.20 illustrates the procedure that is typical of the role of a service organisation in the computer industry. It is not unusual for equipment manufacturers to partner with specialist service organisations in order to offer their end-user customers prompt and efficient after-sales services. This is particularly the case for warranty services and for end-users for whom loss of productivity can be damaging.

Successful partnerships are those based upon mutual gain. In the case of service providers, the provider will enter the partnership if its primary objectives are likely to be met, and will remain with it provided they continue to realise satisfactory growth. For the 'manufacturer' the same obtains. Provided the agreed levels of service are delivered to each category of customer, and are delivered at the agreed level of cost, the partnership will prove to be a satisfactory solution. Partnerships develop and are sustained for as long as each partner's objectives are met. Figure 8.21 suggests a range of qualitative and quantitative motives for membership, together with measures indicating the level of maturity reached by the value chain. The fundamental issues are that any member should be 'better off' working in partnership with other value chain members, and that as value migrates within the value chain, members are is willing and able to adjust the value structure.

Mature and developing value chains

It is suggested that value chains evolve over time. Much like products and markets they exhibit specific characteristics during their development cycle. *Mature* value chains are those in which:

■ The 'value' objectives of both value chain partners (VCPs) and value chain customers (VCCs) are consistently met, suggesting continuity and stability of membership
■ Entry and exit are stable
■ VCPs have well defined roles and tasks that reflect their expertise and that are performed to uniform satisfaction
■ Members are considered to be 'industry specialists'
■ Partnerships have optimal membership numbers
■ Typically, VCPs focus on a limited range of processes

Developing value chains by contrast are those which:

■ Demonstrate instability in the numbers of partners *and* their roles and tasks. Typically, in immature value chains there is evidence of indecision

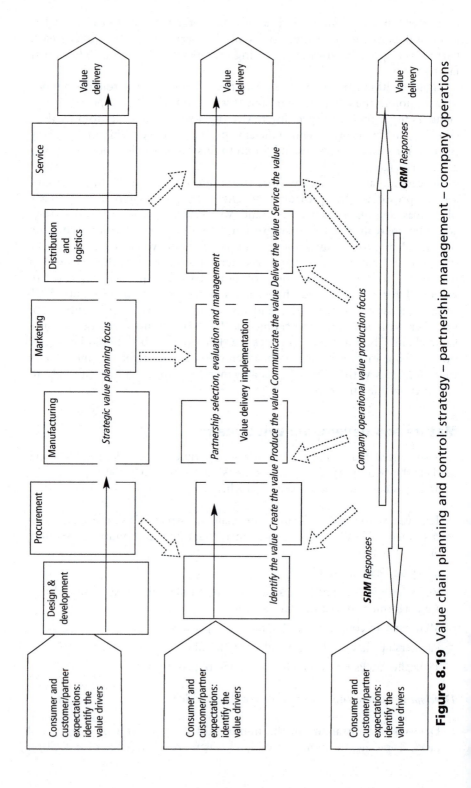

Figure 8.19 Value chain planning and control: strategy – partnership management – company operations

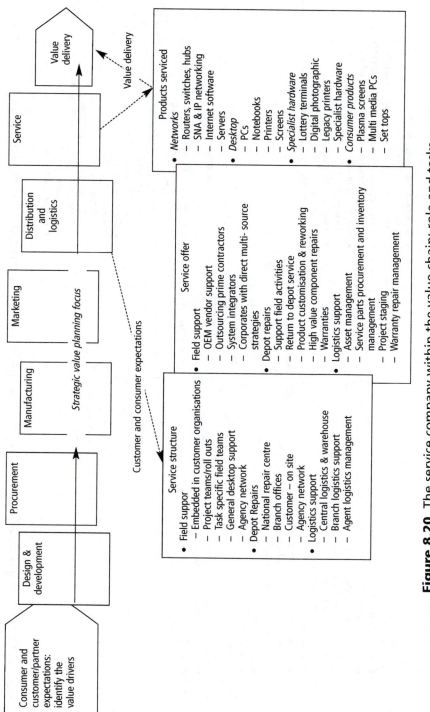

Figure 8.20 The service company within the value chain: role and tasks

Maturity indicators

- Stability of membership numbers
- Defined roles and tasks
- 'Width and scope' of members roles and tasks
- Optimal number of interactions and transactions
- Equitable distribution of market added value
- Growth rate of members exceeds or matches industry growth rate
- Productivity of resources
- Sustainable measure of competitive advantage. *Relative (output - input)/input*

Qualitative issues

- Value chain role & influence
- Market influence & positioning
- Brand profile
- Market response expectations
  - Customer service
  - Inventory availability
- Access gained/given:
  - Integrated RD&D
  - Knowledge/IP
  - Process & product technology
  - Supplier & customer relationships
- Corporate control
- Funding decisions

Quantitative issues

- Investment/Divestment effectiveness of:
  - tangible assets
  - intangible assets
  - working capital
  - processes & capabilities
- Reduce financial and market risks
- Reduce market entry & exit costs
- Improve added value profile
- Increase share of market added value
- Reduce time-to-market profile
- Share/reduce the cost of product development
- Improve current fixed capital effectiveness
- Improve current working capital effectiveness
- Reduce asset intensity
- Increase asset utilisation
- Achieve improved production economies
- Improve financial gearing
- Improve operational gearing
- Increase free cash flow generation
- Reduce risk

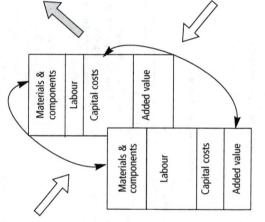

Figure 8.21 Developing value chain relationships: quantitative and qualitative issues and maturity indicators

and difficulty in the acceptance of specific roles within the value chain structure.

■ A number of the partners may assume they can operate across the value chain. The inadequacies of assets, processes and capabilities results in sub-optimal performance and eventual disintegration of the structure.

■ Demonstrate their immaturity with an instability in the number of partners entering and leaving the value chain partnership structure; hence there is a constant turnover of members.

Mature value chains exist in the automobile industry, in construction and in the pharmaceutical industry. *Developing* value chains may be found in the computer services, consumer durables and apparel industries.

It is essential that companies understand the nature of their value chains. Considerable time and effort can be expended attempting to make a value chain operate effectively and efficiently and unless the characteristics of the industry value chain are first determined, not only may some fundamental strategic errors and appointments be made, but the operational tasks are likely to be inefficiently conducted.

Concluding comments

The industry value chain typically needs an entrepreneurial approach if it is to be strategically effective. This chapter referred to the early contribution of Coase and gave a reminder of the network, modular, and 'virtual' origins of the value chain. Of particular importance to the development of value chain thinking were contributions by McHugh and Beech. McHugh and his colleagues identified relevant criteria for virtual and value chain structures, while Beech was an early advocate of the principle of thinking first in terms of the industry demand chain, then when customer expectations were identified and evaluated, in terms of the task of operational delivery through a supply chain structure.

The chapter also considered alternative approaches to evaluating the demand chain – market opportunity analysis – and here contributions by Kotler, Ansoff, Abell and Day were synthesised. The need to consider stake-holders as partners, together with the requirement to meet their expectations and to identify the contributions required of them was attributed to Neely et al. Finally, the chapter addressed the selection and management of partners and the necessity to ensure that the mutual expectations of members are realised.

CASE STUDY 8.1

Adapting to industry change: AustPost accepts electronic messaging

(Based upon Rachel Leblhan, 'AustPost gets the electronic message', *Australian Financial Review*, 18 October 2005)

Email and SMS electronic messaging resulted in a decline in AustPost's profitability from its conventional mail delivery services in 2004/05. Market growth was a minimal 0.4 per cent; rising costs and a freeze on stamp prices were cited as the causes, as well as the significant growth of electronic messaging.

AustPost's response was an aggressive adoption of the 'new technology'. Its annual report suggested that it would 'continue searching for new revenue-generation opportunities by working even more closely with major mailing customers, promoting the effectiveness of mail as a communications medium and looking for new product opportunities'.

Product-market developments have been significant. In 2004 AustPost launched an electronic notification service, Mail2Day, which sends electronic notification to post office box holders advising them that they have received mail. The cost per customer is modestly set at $A7.50 per month. Customer growth is some 25 per cent a month. Another product, Electronic Data Interchange (EDI) Post, a service that targets bulk mail users, has shown record results with revenue increasing by 17.2 per cent and volumes by 30.1 per cent. EDI Post's eLetter system accepts data electronically from clients. It is printed, enveloped and mailed. Development continues to improve the production of tickets and a fully personalised direct mail service.

AustPost has also established an 'innovation and product development' activity to identify and pursue new opportunities in the cost-efficient production of mail. The activity is investigating digital colour printing that incorporates personalised, variable data for short-run marketing campaigns. An attractive aspect of the service will be the ability to personalise both the exterior and the interior content of the mailing piece. Expectations are that this will increase campaign response rates and clearly ROI for both AustPost and its clients.

Other product-market developments include enhanced parcel tracking, aimed at providing the high-volume market segment a service using radio frequency ID (RFID) tags. AustPost has been experimenting for some time with RFID tagging to track international mail and now seeks to expand its application in the domestic and bulk mail areas. While Postbillpay remains a volume business, with some 170 million transactions in 2004/05, an increasing number of transactions are being carried out via the telephone and the internet. In 2004/05 telephone transactions increased by 43 per cent and internet transactions by 19 per cent. The increase in electronic usage has directed AustPost's attention towards working with bill payment partners to offer an internet based payment service that will operate on the partners' own websites, under their brands but using the Postbillpay infrastructure. Customised internet based bill payments services are also offered – 'biller branded internet'. Western QGE Insurance, Energex and AGL are already using the service and the offer is being expanded.

Discussion topics

AustPost is quite unique as a postal service in its adaptive strategy formulation, which embraces not only new technologies but also changes in potential client business models to expand its own business model. For some years it has used the competitive strength that it has in the facility to call on almost all commercial and consumer locations daily or on a regular, frequent basis. Identify potential opportunities, using the expertise to assimilate technology and to create partnerships for AustPost and other similar organisations.

CASE STUDY 8.2

Adapting to industry change: the global automotive industry

(Based upon Michael Gawenda, 'End of the line', *Sydney Morning Herald*, 10/11 December 2005; Hans Werner Sinn, 'Workers are losers in the bazaar economy', *Australian Financial Review*, 18 October 2005; Kae Inoue, 'Toyota finds growth in the sum of its parts', *Australian Financial Review*, 21 October 2005; Doron Levin, 'Toyota culture overpowers rivals', *Australian Financial Review*, 1 November 2005; Yunsuk Lim, 'Hyundai partnership pays off', *Australian Financial Review*, 7 July 2005; Anonymous, 'Destroying boundaries: integration and collaboration in the automotive value chain', *UMTRI Research Review*, January–March 2004; Doug Bartholomew, 'Sleeping with the enemy', *Industry Week.com*, 1 May 2005; Peter Roberts, 'Tricky road ahead for local car makers', *Australian Financial Review*, 12 December 2005. *Note:* references in the case study text are to these articles.)

Introduction

Performance differences among the global automotive manufactures suggest that the currently successful competitors have responded to changing demand and supply characteristics. This further suggests that these manufacturers' success points to changes in business models that perhaps the others may need to consider.

Ford and General Motors would probably look back to the mid-1990s and congratulate themselves on their responses to changing customer expectations at that time. The development of product differentiation around product platforms and the addition of SUVs appeared to be pathways to a successful future. Business model changes at that time typically involved the divestment of component manufacturing subsidiaries and the adoption of process changes such as an increase in modularisation in production. For some there were indications that core processes and capabilities were being viewed somewhat differently, but in general terms there was an intention to focus on design and development, and marketing. This was indicated by Jack Nasser's move when CEO of Ford. Nasser acquired some major brands, Aston Martin, Jaguar, Land Rover and Volvo; together with Lincoln, these brands created a 'premium product offer'. The designers and engineers then created differentiated products around a series of product platforms. The best of both worlds was in reach – a differentiated product range with a set of attractive cost led production economics.

Clearly the change envisaged was long-term, but the developments did not pass unobserved nor uncommented upon. Drucker (2001) noted both Ford and General Motors were abandoning the traditional vertically integrated business model, commenting that, for example, General Motors were creating a business for the ultimate car consumer – their aim being to make available the car and model that most closely fit that consumer's preferences. As Drucker noted, the changes to facilitate this were not just sales and marketing driven, but encompassed design and development, and production. Products and services now have multiple applications and business organisations are redefining their core capabilities and processes. In other words, 'value chains' are competing with 'value chains'. At this macro, industry level, value chains can be seen as business network structures, or confederations, that are developing from traditional corporations.

However, 'that was then and now is now', and in a short space of time the global market situation has changed rapidly and with big implications for these major vehicle suppliers. Both demand and supply markets have changed rapidly in the past few years. Not only have the product expectations of existing consumers changed because of indirect market influences (such as the rising price of oil), but new consumers are entering the market from the developing economies (Asia and to a lesser extent Eastern Europe, where basic requirements are maturing into expectations for a more sophisticated product). As we will discuss below, there have been significantly different responses to the changes that have occurred (and continue to occur).

Cost structures were always going to be a problem

A typical response of most organisations to market pressures has been to reduce costs. Usually there is scope for increasing plant efficiencies in large organisations and this has been the response of the major automobile manufacturers. The pattern of the responses has been similar: a tightening of production processes by eliminating non-added value activities or restructuring processes to achieve a desired output. These are short-term measures and avoid major structural change; furthermore, they are not a response to long-term problems. Gawenda (2005) identifies long-term structural reasons for the demise of both Ford and General Motors in the USA. He points to the fact that their costs include healthcare and pension contributions that have been fought for by the unions and were seen as the basis of the workforce life style. These elements are now responsible for a cost burden of $US1,500 to perhaps $US2,000 per vehicle, a major problem for both organisations. He also identifies the fact that for every active employee there are 2.5 retired employees! He contrasts this with the organisational strategies of Japanese companies manufacturing in the USA: Toyota, Nissan, Honda, and more recently Hyundai, who established their manufacturing facilities in the South where unions were much weaker and cooperation rather than conflict was dominant.

Sinn (2005) takes a more macro view when discussing Germany. He contends that the impact of outsourcing on expanding the volume of its high added value manufacturing to low-wage countries has resulted in Germany shifting from a 'producer economy to a bazaar economy' and has produced major shifts in capital and labour markets. He argues that Germany has specialised in export related production, such as automobiles and electronics, and that capital and labour have been attracted to this industry (and other similar export industries) as growth continues, but that the growth of the export related sectors causes decline in other sectors. This, he contends, is excessive specialisation. The result appears to be contradictory – exports boom but employment declines as other sectors are 'starved' of capital. Another factor exacerbates the problem. As a consequence of its welfare state and the impact of unions on employee benefits, Germany has had the highest labour costs in Europe until recent times. As a result all product costs increase and this, together with fierce competition from overseas, has meant the specialist markets beginning to experience declining margins. This in turn results in an increasing reliance upon overseas component suppliers in order to remain price-competitive. The overpriced local labour has little opportunity to find employment because the labour-intensive service sectors cannot absorb the excessive labour costs, margins are low and the returns on capital cannot be diluted still further.

Sinn concludes by suggesting that as this international division of labour continues, the import content of German products will continue to increase, resulting in fewer domestic jobs and less income despite the growth of exports. The solution is for the German labour force to accept the need for greater flexibility in the face of ever increasing global competition.

A constructive view towards partnerships: alternative models

The approach taken by Toyota is quite different. Kae Inoue (2005) describes the constructive approach the company takes towards working with partners. For example, Toyota has recently announced that 80 per cent of its annual cost savings of 230 billion yen has been achieved by working closely with partners such as Denso and Aisin Seiki. Toyota, together with its suppliers, works on developing cost saving designs for current and future vehicles. Toyota's approach is to share the cost savings realised with the supplier company and to guarantee the supplier a certain level of Toyota business. Furthermore, to enhance the relationship Toyota owns equity stakes in its suppliers. At the time Kae Inoue was writing, Denso (with 23 per cent owned by Toyota) anticipated increased profits in the then current financial year – its shares had recently shown a 16 per cent increase. Koito Manufacturing (makers of headlights), who are part owned by Toyota (20 per cent), anticipated its fourth consecutive year of growth and expansion from its US and Indian operations. Suppliers receive two clear benefits from this partnership approach: they have an assurance of growth and they share in Toyota's 'quality' reputation. Toyota also has twofold benefits: a powerful brand that clearly is useful in negotiations with suppliers, and the sense of mutual trust that its approach to supplier relationship management has developed. Furthermore as it succeeds, its suppliers succeed, but as the company has a large aggregate investment in its suppliers it also shares in their profits.

Toyota's success is not simply due to supplier relationship management. Levin (2005) comments that Womack, Jones and Roos (1991) predicted Toyota's success in their book, *The Machine that Changed the World*, which reviewed the Toyota production model (labelled 'lean manufacturing' by the authors) and suggested that it was destined to revolutionise vehicle manufacturing. Levin reports on research conducted on factory efficiency that in turn reported that the average vehicle built by Toyota in 2004 required some 19.5 hours of labour for assembly, compared with 23 hours for each GM vehicle taking and 24.5 hours for each Ford. Levin adds that Toyota's North American plants built 1.44 million vehicles in 2004. The output represented 107 per cent of Toyota's theoretical capacity as it was achieved by working two daily shifts without overtime. In contrast GM and Ford used only 86 per cent of rated plant capacity.

Toyota's approach contrasts markedly with that of Ford, General Motors and Mitsubishi, who have reduced the number of suppliers, presumably in an attempt at reducing interaction and transaction administration costs and increasing the volume of purchases through a smaller number of suppliers. At the time of writing Delphi, a parts suppliers once owned by GM, was in bankruptcy proceedings. Nissan has reduced its suppliers by 40 per cent and divested itself of stakes in about 1,400 assorted associated companies since 1999. Mitsubishi dissolved its supplier network when a substantial part of the equity was owned by DaimlerChrysler, but in June 2005 a group of suppliers (some 158 in number) formed a new group to supply the company.

Hyundai's success in North America has been reported by Lim (2005). Hyundai Mobis supplies parts for new vehicles and for the service after-market. Lim, in an interview with Chung Hyung Mo, a senior executive of Hyundai Mobis, reports that their supplier was in fact assembling 30 per cent of the Sonata sedan three months before the Hyundai vehicles left the plant in Montgomery, Alabama. The relationship is close in all senses of the word; they are ten minutes apart by road and work with interlocking administration systems. The investment by the company, at $US120 million, is the largest overseas investment. The Hyundai Mobis activity manufactures Sonata components but in addition assembles headlights, radiators and condensers as modules and attaches them to the vehicle chassis. Hyundai Mobis has been more successful than its parent. Its industry ratio 12 months' sales divided by plant and warehouse inventories is $US11.58 compared with $US6.34 at Hyundai. Sales per employee are equally impressive: $US1,720 at Hyundai Mobis compared with $US963.87 at the parent company. While there are clearly operating differences to be considered the performance comparisons suggest that constructive approaches to partnerships have much to offer.

Another aspect of partnerships is illustrated by an anonymous report (2004) on supplier attitudes in the industry. A report entitled 'Destroying boundaries: integration and collaboration in the automotive value chain' by the University of Michigan Transport Research Institute (UMTRI) suggests both willingness on the part of the supplier industry and an expectation of closer relationships with the large vehicle assemblers. They express an expectation of closer collaboration in product design and development and in supply chain processes. Interesting aspects of the report suggest that there is considerable ground to be covered in terms of suppliers' own internal integration as well as in external collaboration with the assemblers. They discuss their anticipation of component manufacturers developing towards being 'system integrators' and that the technology to bring this about is well advanced. However, they are not as advanced as their Asian competitors. Internally they are 'half way' along the path towards internal integration and attempts towards external collaboration with the customers are somewhat more distant, with only 'one quarter' of the preparation complete.

Collaboration in design projects between and among groups of automotive manufacturers is not new, nor is it a small activity. Bartholomew (2005) provides a number of examples of industry collaboration and cooperation. Shared risk, shared development costs (to achieve economies of scale and scope), and shared capabilities as a cost-effective way to obtain market based advantages (time-to-market, market share and share of market added value, and so on) are reasons for collaboration and cooperation to be well established and to be increasing.

One of the oldest examples given by Bartholomew (and one that remains strong) is the collaboration between GM and Toyota. New United Motor Manufacturing Inc (NUMMI) was established in 1984 in Fremont, California as a joint venture so that both companies could build vehicles using the same unionised work force, production line, and the Toyota production system (TPS). Toyota sought to gain a manufacturing beachhead in the US and GM was keen to obtain an insight into Toyota's manufacturing methods. For Toyota it was an attractive way to reduce both the risk and the investment of a new plant and for GM it was a practical and cost-effective way of understanding lean production. Competitors Ford and Chrysler opposed the venture and asked the Federal Trade Commission (FTC) to block it. After a 15-month investigation the FTC gave its approval, stating that the joint venture would offer greater consumer choice and would act as a role model for US companies in cooperative labour–management relations. Interestingly, the former GM plant on the site had been closed because of labour relations problems.

The joint venture succeeded largely because of the commitment of senior executives in both organisations, the very high levels of investment devoted to the venture and the thoroughness of the training of key personnel. The joint venture continues to be successful. In 2004 some 6,000 employees produced 311,000 Toyota vehicles and 69,000 GM vehicles

Other examples are presented by Bartholomew. Ironically, in light of Ford's response to the NUMMI project, is one of collaboration between GM and Ford. A joint project to develop a six-speed automatic transmission for front-wheel drive vehicles is motivated by the ability it offers to share risk, cost and technological capabilities. Another joint development venture is between GM and DaimlerChrysler to develop hybrid gas-electric automobiles. With the competition by Toyota and Honda well established, GM and Ford needed to accelerate their product development activities if a competitive hybrid technology was to be brought to the market rapidly. Bartholomew quotes Peter Savagian, the GM director for hybrid systems: 'The competition between the two companies was less important than the challenge of getting a new product to market quickly.' The projects are typically comprehensive and consider operational as well as strategic advantages. The GM and Ford joint venture to design the six-speed automatic transmission has been designed on the basis of standardising components and servicing schedules. Both competitors will benefit from the economies of scale afforded by incorporating common parts, which in turn introduces the possibility of using common suppliers.

Clear and complementary (not necessarily the same) goals are essential to such collaboration, and furthermore they should be transparent, as should the exchange of all relevant information. James Champy (of Hammer & Champy 'fame' and now the chairman of Perot Systems, an IT and business planning consultancy) asserts that these factors are very basic but essential to the success of successful cooperative and collaborative joint ventures. Without clear understandings and clear agreements in place, risk increases and the probability of success decreases.

Focusing on the local industry: a future for Australia's industry

For General Motors Holden (GMH), its Australian operation is not as gloomy as much of the rest of its global activity. It makes the top-selling vehicle, returning a return on sales (ROS) in excess of 6 per cent over the past ten years. GMH has invested $A1.85 billion in the Australian operation over the past three years. It is arguable that this success will continue since in Australia, as elsewhere in the world, the large six- and eight-cylinder vehicles are beginning to lose market share to imported, fuel-efficient smaller vehicles. The recent high value of the Australian dollar has also added problems: export has been difficult but has made imports attractive. An issue for the Australian industry is whether it has the flexibility to respond to changing market characteristics. One recent response from GMH has been to reduce output; a third shift has been closed at the Adelaide plant with 1,400 redundancies. The company has put pressure on suppliers by forcing them now to bid in open auctions against overseas suppliers. This has resulted in a loss of 2,200 supplier jobs and local contracts are moving overseas. During interviews with interested commentators, Roberts (2005) was told that the Australian industry (particularly the 'commodity' sector – components with low intellectual property and low shipping costs) is vulnerable to overseas competition. Success at present is based upon excellence in R&D and engineering. It is widely accepted that both the fall in import protection and the increase in competition from low-cost countries are having an impact. One respondent, GMH CEO Denny Mooney, suggested, 'We need to be deciding on what we can be competitive on with local manufacturing and not throwing money at where we are not,' suggesting that a review of capabilities is becoming essential. Some markets are maintaining their volume – the Middle East with its penchant for large vehicles is stable, but the domestic market is faltering. Expert opinion was that the large-car segment would stabilise and begin to show growth in 2006. GMH, Ford and Toyota have new vehicles planned but it is not expected that the large-vehicle segment will return to its previously dominant position. Toyota appears to have read the changes in the demand chain; the 2006 Camry was made available only with a four-cylinder engine. Ford responded to falling sales of the Falcon by spending $4 million to develop a sports utility vehicle (SUV). In 2005 Ford was able to offset the loss of 10,000 plus

Falcon sales with 21,000 plus, and as at late2005/early 2006 was operating its Melbourne plant at more than 100 per cent of rated capacity. Ford CEO Tom Gorman stated: 'Our ability to read the market and create an all-new vehicle to react to changing trends has proven very successful for our brand ... We need to be aware of changing dynamics, particularly with large and small cars and react accordingly.'

GMH has a flexible plant capacity but apparently lacked the foresight required to respond to consumer demand changes. Toyota's new Altona plant, costing $400 million, will be capable of producing an additional 30,000 units per year, probably for the Thai market. The facility will boast a single body welding line that will be capable of producing several vehicles of different sizes at the same time.

Mitsubishi's future hangs on the success of the recently introduced 380; sales were lagging the targeted 2,500 per month as at March 2006. It also hopes for clearance to manufacture a second vehicle at its Adelaide plant, which has benefited from a $250 million upgrade with new robotics and stamping presses.

The Australian Government is pressuring US and Japanese manufacturers to use more local (Australian) suppliers. A $A4.2 billion programme to support investment and innovation up to 2015 may now need revisiting as it was put in place before China became a major player in the component supply sector of the industry. The industry approves the thrust of the programme. Most see innovation as the direction for the future, particularly as import protection falls from 15 per cent to 10 per cent. Roberts reports that as protection falls, the industry increasingly looks to reduce costs by replacing local suppliers with low-cost offshore suppliers. They consider Australia's high-value skills and technology to be the pathway to future success. Evidence of how successful this can be is provided by Permo-Drive, a NSW based company. Permo-Drive recently licensed its innovative hybrid engine technology to a large US components company, Dana Corporation. Permo-Drive offers a very different concept. The conventional approach for hybrids is to store power in large batteries; Permo-Drive stores power in large commercial vehicles by compressing hydraulic fluids during braking. The company's CEO states that with frequent stopping and starting the system could offer up to 37 per cent in fuel savings. Meanwhile Ford has doubled the size of its engineering staff and has led the development of a new small vehicle (the Fiesta) for India. Toyota has opened a technical facility to develop new projects; a new Corolla for Turkey is a current project. GMH has announced an almost twofold increase in design staff at its Melbourne operation, making it the third largest facility in GMH.

The GMH CEO summarises the issues for the Australian industry: 'Every economy looks for their competitive advantage. One of the things we have in Australia are good technical resources in both design and engineering ... I see us being a strong part of the General Motors product development operation.' This could also be a pathway for other organisations. But is this sufficient without an ability to analyse the industry demand chain?

Discussion topics

Comment on the common approach taken to reduce costs by companies generally. In the twenty-first century, are there alternative methods by which organisations can preempt downsizing decisions?

It could be argued that costing difficulties may be ameliorated by revenue growth. However, healthy revenue increases can only be assured if the value proposition to the end-user customer matches their expectations. Both Ford and General Motors have been wrong-footed by changes in customer value drivers. Perhaps 'changes' is too strong a term; more relevant is the shift in emphasis that has occurred in the value drivers, and possibly their 'rank order' for end-users. Both organisations missed the move towards smaller, environmentally friendly vehicles. There is a suggestion here that neither understand the importance of demand chain analysis and the implications of changes for supply chain structures and management.

To what extent is outsourcing all or part of an organisation's operations (manufacturing and distribution) a short-term, limited response? What alternatives exist?

Partnerships and alliances appear to be becoming a viable solution for a number of organisations in the automobile industry. What issues should an organisation consider when contemplating a cooperative or collaborative strategy with another company?

Undertake a project to identify, in another industry, the kinds of problems and solutions identified in this case study.

CASE STUDY 8.3

Changes in traditional industry relationships when a global company enters

(Based upon Gary Younge, 'Until the pips squeak', *Guardian* and *Australian Financial Review*, 19 April 2005)

McDonald's efforts to reposition itself as 'healthy eating alternative' in the fiercely competitive fast-food market segment were discussed in case study 7.1, Chapter 7. This case considers another aspect of the company's decision.

One particular product, Apple Dippers, may result in major changes in the agricultural industry. Younge contends: 'The chain's influence could alter for ever the method and scale of production, the varieties of apples produced, and the rights of the thousands of workers who pick them, and not necessarily for the better.' Younge quotes Eric Schlosser, author of *Fast-food Nation*, who states: 'McDonald's makes a huge impact, not because they are deliberately out to screw the food system, but because they demand a uniform product.'

McDonald's has a very clear input specification for the Apple Dippers. A supplier identified this: 'It has to be crisp … It should be bi-coloured. Red striped with a yellow background or yellow with a bit of pink. It has to be juicy. I want it sweet, and just under three inches.' The Cameo apple comes close to this specification, and the area director of a large grower in the Oregon region is not surprised at McDonald's choice. McDonald's entry into the apple supply sector has made a difference to the industry but to date has not resulted in 'a revolution'. This is because there is a three-year lead time required between preparation (grafting and the rootstock processes) and then another three years before the apples appeared and further five before harvesting the alternative apple type. Desmond O'Rourke, an economist and the publisher of *World Apple Report*, adds: 'It would be very risky for any apple producer to change their crop now on the basis of what McDonald's might be doing in six years' time.' And this presents a problem because if the demand for apples from McDonald's does grow, the growers would happily shift production from Golden Delicious apples that are easy to grow but increasingly difficult to sell. Cameo apples are the opposite, which explains why not many are produced. They are prone to blight and require intensive care. Furthermore, production is very capital-intensive; pesticides, storage, equipment and the long time-to-market tie up capital in conditions often influenced by constraints over which growers have no control, such as the weather and interest rates. O'Rourke suggests that large growers may be able to respond to the demand but smaller growers will have difficulties. He says that in the North Western states of the US the number of growers has halved from 4,000 to 2,000.

O'Rourke also says that the trend towards closely specified apples was started by Wal-Mart and Safeway; they specify apple size at three inches, as this is an optimal size for display within an area closely controlled on a square-foot basis. McDonald's will require a standard size and consistent taste because of its global value proposition – its meals taste the same wherever you are in the world. He further suggests that it will be only the large suppliers who will be able to meet these expectations consistently.

Another important issue is identified in Younge's article. Erik Nicholson, a union organiser in the Oregon region, suggests this has happened previously with potatoes and beef, and considers it will be the same for apples. He forecasts that the industry will become vertically integrated, and that 'unless as a grower you are "tied" to a supplier, you will not get the business'. He also forecasts that packers will become growers, and comments on the extent of their industry power as being greater than that of either the state or the federal government. Size is essential, with small growers having considerable difficulty in competing. Some distance away in Boardman, Oregon there is an example of what Nicholson calls 'industrialised agriculture': a supplier of milk to McDonald's operates a dairy farm of 30,000 cattle, being part of a 376 square kilometre agricultural complex that also provides potatoes to McDonald's. The labour force comprises immigrant workers, living in trailer parks and chipboard housing, often below the poverty line. Constant pressure on costs results in long hours, and they were denied breaks until bad publicity forced the issue. Pay is $US7.75 an hour.

Nicholson says: 'The story of industrialised agriculture is that the big consumer starts to squeeze the producer on price, and after a while there's only one place where they can make savings: the workforce.'

Discussion topics

This case raises a number of issues. Clearly that of social responsibility is a major concern and should be considered.

Another topic concerns product development and the role of the supplier in developing a product specification. Given the extent of power that large multiple retailers and fast-food operators can exercise, is there a model in which cooperation and collaboration can be developed rather than conflict?

REFERENCES

Abell D F (1980) *Defining the Business: The Starting Point of Strategic Planning*, Prentice-Hall, Englewood Cliffs, NJ
Ansoff H I (1984) *Implanting Strategic Management*, Prentice-Hall, New York
Baldwin C Y and K B Clark (1997) 'Managing in an age of modularity', *Harvard Business Review*, September/October
Beech J (1998) 'The supply-demand nexus: from integration to synchronisation', in Gattorna J (ed.) *Strategic Supply Chain Alignment*, Gower, Aldershot
Coase H R (1937) 'The nature of the firm', *Economica*, 4
Day G (1999) *The Market Driven Organisation*, Free Press, New York
Dell M with C Fredman (1999) *Direct from Dell: Strategies that Revolutionized an Industry*, HarperCollins, London
Drucker P (2001) 'Will the corporation survive?', *The Economist*, 1 November
Kay, J (1993) *Foundation of Corporate Success*, Oxford University Press, Oxford
Kotler P (1994) *Marketing Management*, 8th edition, Prentice-Hall, New York
McHugh P, G Merli and W Wheeler III (1995) *Beyond Business Process Reengineering*, Wiley, Chichester
Neely A, C Adams and M Kennerley (2002) *The Performance Prism: The Scorecard for Measuring and Managing Business Success*, Financial Times/Prentice-Hall, London
Tedeschi, R (2000) 'Comment', *Australian Financial Review*, October
Womack J P, D T Jones and D Roos (1991) *The Machine that Changed the World: The Story of Lean Production*, HarperPerennial, New York

CHAPTER 9

The Value Chain: the Firm's Perspective

LEARNING TOPICS

On completing your study of this chapter you will have been introduced to and considered the following topics:

- Reviewing the value chain as a management concept
- Corporate positioning in the value chain; deploying core assets, capabilities and processes
- Value production, communication and delivery; the firm's perspective
- Revisiting the partnership decision; selecting and working with partners
- Managing for equity in the value chain

Introduction

Previous chapters have explored the development of value as a strategic concept. There has been an emphasis on the emerging difference in supply chain management and demand chain management that has in turn offered a different view of the value chain concept. It has been argued that value chain strategy and management has the expansion of customer satisfaction as its primary objective, as opposed to the optimisation of supply chain costs while meeting specified customer objectives. Value chain management is a proactive approach to customer satisfaction, using the demand chain to identify specific task characteristics for the design of the supply chain.

Reviewing the value chain as a management concept

There are other examples of value chain strategy and management. Brown (1996), using the newspaper, video entertainment and banking industries as examples, suggests:

> The emerging value chains [in these examples] promise to restructure [these industries] and redistribute value among different components and players in the value chain.

Brown also suggests, using Porter's views on competitive advantage, that 'The way in which [a business] manages its value chain will affect its cost structure and the differential benefits offered to its customers, and thereby its competitive advantage.' This latter comment is of less interest than the first. The restructuring and redistribution of value issues are central to value chain analysis, strategy and management.

Still more examples are available. Lai (2000) presented Hewlett-Packard's (HP) view of the shift or transition from the traditional product focused business design towards a customer focused design. Figure 9.1 illustrates the HP philosophy, which is clearly based upon the concept of value chain management in which customer needs rather than corporate core competencies are given primary focus. In this example the realisation that flexibility is essential is very clear. It suggests that the paths trodden by Dell, Nike and others are applicable to both products and services.

It will be recalled from previous chapters that Hagel and Singer (1999) suggested that this move is also becoming evident in companies such as Ford and Volkswagen (VW). For some types of vehicle this has already occurred. BMW SUVs and Mercedes-Benz estate cars (station wagons) are manufactured in Austria by Magna International, a Toronto based automobile parts maker ($US13 billion in 2002) (Forbes Global 2003). In 2003, Magna Steyr was the only parts company offering its automobile manufacturer customers a fully outsourced engineering and production facility. The manufacturers provide Magna with the styling for a new model and the chassis on which to build it, and Magna executes the engineering, builds the assembly line and produces the vehicles. This is not new in European automobile manufacturing; Fiat and VW used outsourced design facilities to produce specialty vehicles. Outsourcing the manufacturing of engineering as well as design and production frees production capacity for mainstream vehicles. The investment and cost profiles are both interesting and attractive. Labour costs in 2003 were estimated to be 30 per cent lower in Austria than in Germany, with the start-up investment estimated at $100 million rather than the $500 million that would have been required to expand BMW's capacity. Saab too are benefiting from the lower labour costs and have outsourced the 9-3 convertible to Magna. The North American volume automobile ranges are unlikely to follow this trend. One reason is that the production processes of the large Detroit manufacturers are designed for high volume/low cost production; and another reason is that excess capacity has dogged the industry for some time, and with soaring oil prices likely to be the rule – not the exception – plant and labour utilisation in 'home based' facilities will have priority.

Hagel and Singer's process model of the firm suggests it can be worthwhile for organisations to review their individual value chain processes and assess where they can add most value for customers and shareholders. Porter's (1985) initial value chain model had this in mind with:

> ... a firm's value chain is embedded in a larger stream of activities that I term the value system ... Suppliers have value chains (upstream value) that create and deliver the purchased inputs used in a firm's value chain. Suppliers not

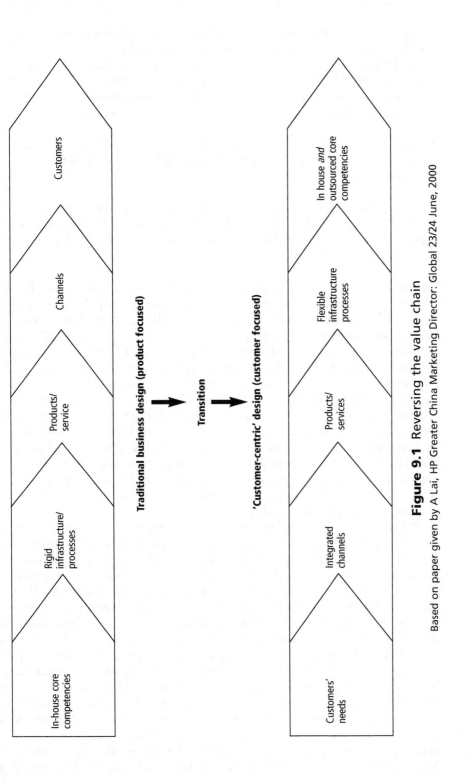

Figure 9.1 Reversing the value chain

Based on paper given by A Lai, HP Greater China Marketing Director: Global 23/24 June, 2000

only deliver a product but also can influence a firm's performance in many other ways ... Channels (intermediaries) perform additional activities that affect the buyer, as well as influence the firm's own activities. A firm's product eventually becomes part of its buyer's value chain ... Gaining and sustaining competitive advantage depends upon understanding not only a firm's value chain but how the firm fits into the overall value system.

But this is argued to be a somewhat constrained view of the value chain/virtual model that is emerging. Parolini (1999) is critical of the Porter model, arguing that it:

> ... attempts to broaden the strategic perspective and to consider links with both upstream and downstream value chains, but it clearly takes the viewpoint of the company making the analysis, without ever fully considering the end-user's point of view ... .

Another perspective of the firm's value chain is offered by Hines and Rich (2000), who suggest there to be a difference between the supply chain/value chain and what they describe as a *value stream* (Womack and Jones 1996). They are suggesting that the supply chain/value chain (they do not differentiate between them) includes all activities of *all the companies involved*, whereas the value stream refers only to the specific parts of the firms that actually add value to the product or service being considered. They suggest it to be a more focused and valid view of the value adding process. There is a problem with this view. The authors admit to there being no 'real' methodologies for understanding the value stream concept. It follows therefore that there is no reliable methodology for evaluating the impact of any activities that may be addressing value builders (the future value drivers) and not currently adding full value. In addition to this the value stream concept (with its cost led focus) really offers nothing more than the supply chain disciplines followed unsuccessfully by the companies discussed in earlier chapters.

This view raises an interesting perspective concerning the direction taken by this text. We have argued that unless customer expectations are considered together with those of the value chain owners/stakeholders, the value system cannot survive. It follows that the value chain component firms should conduct an analysis of their positioning and roles within the value chain. Their objectives should be concerned with value optimisation rather than maximisation for either the customer or the stakeholder. Thus the analysis should consider value production feasibility and value delivery viability. It will be recalled that value production feasibility occurs when customer value perceptions equal or exceed expectations (customer value drivers) and customer satisfaction perception occurs. Value delivery viability exists when one or more of the value delivery options are acceptable to a group of partners/stakeholders.

The corporate or organisational value chain shown as Figure 9.2 shares the process structure of the industry value chain but reflects the decision making issues typical at an organisation level. Figure 9.2 indicates the range of process decisions likely to be made; clearly within the context of virtual structures typical

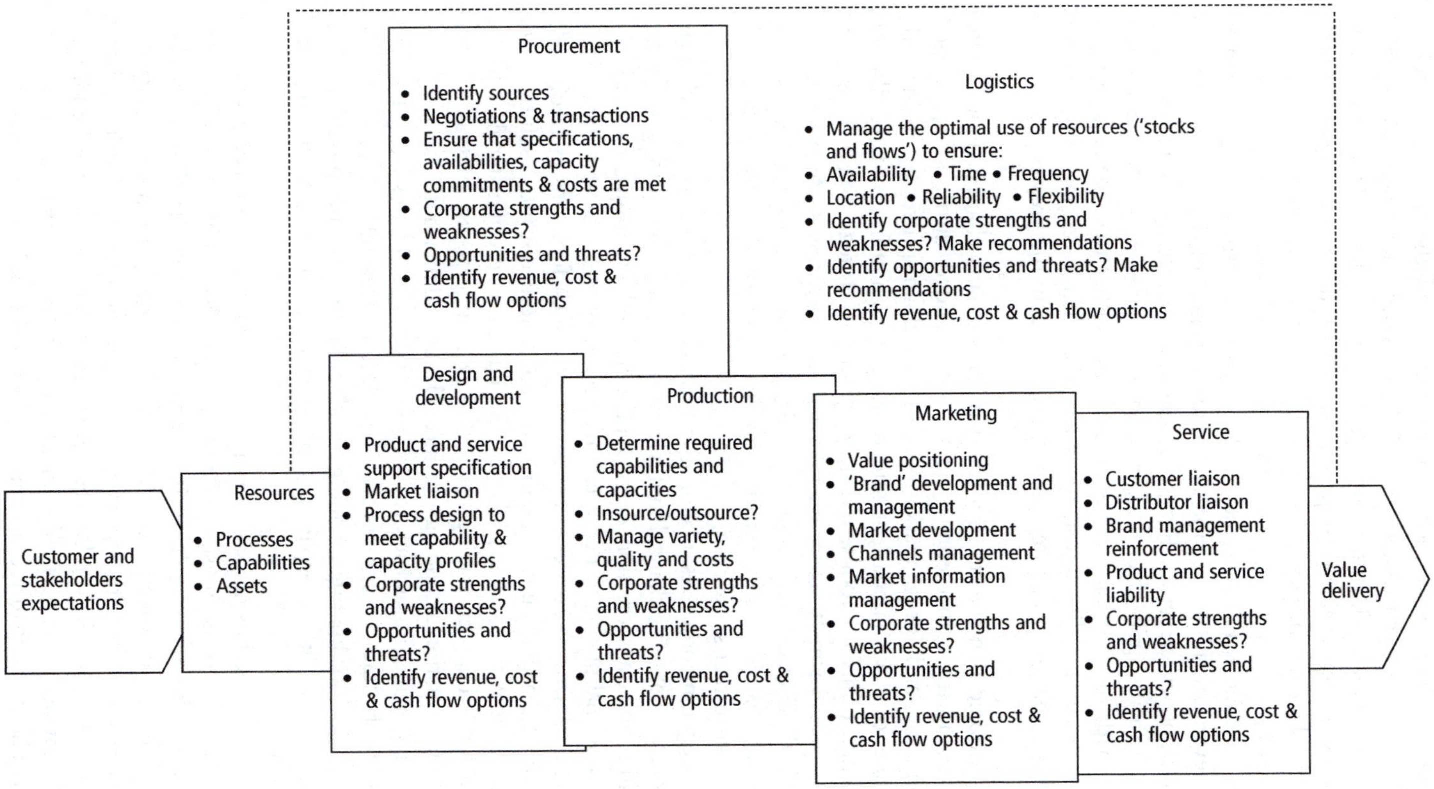

Figure 9.2 A view of 'corporate' value chain processes

Customer and stakeholders expectations

Resources
- Processes
- Capabilities
- Assets

Design and development
- Product and service support specification
- Market liaison
- Process design to meet capability & capacity profiles
- Corporate strengths and weaknesses?
- Opportunities and threats?
- Identify revenue, cost & cash flow options

Production
- Determine required capabilities and capacities
- Insource/outsource?
- Manage variety, quality and costs
- Corporate strengths and weaknesses?
- Opportunities and threats?
- Identify revenue, cost & cash flow options

Procurement
- Identify sources
- Negotiations & transactions
- Ensure that specifications, availabilities, capacity commitments & costs are met
- Corporate strengths and weaknesses?
- Opportunities and threats?
- Identify revenue, cost & cash flow options

Logistics
- Manage the optimal use of resources ('stocks and flows') to ensure:
  - Availability • Time • Frequency
  - Location • Reliability • Flexibility
- Identify corporate strengths and weaknesses? Make recommendations
- Identify opportunities and threats? Make recommendations
- Identify revenue, cost & cash flow options

Marketing
- Value positioning
- 'Brand' development and management
- Market development
- Channels management
- Market information management
- Corporate strengths and weaknesses?
- Opportunities and threats?
- Identify revenue, cost & cash flow options

Service
- Customer liaison
- Distributor liaison
- Brand management reinforcement
- Product and service liability
- Corporate strengths and weaknesses?
- Opportunities and threats?
- Identify revenue, cost & cash flow options

Value delivery

of the value chain it is unlikely that any one organisation will assume a role across each process. The issue for each of them is to identify the assets, processes and capabilities that add customer value *and* competitive advantage and focus on them *within* the value chain structure. Beech (1998) considered the topic of business processes from a value chain perspective. He argued for an integration of the supply and demand chains:

> The challenge can only be met by developing a holistic strategic framework that leverages the generation and understanding of demand effectiveness with supply efficiency ... First, organisations must bring a multi-enterprise view to their supply chains. They need to be capable of working cooperatively with other organisations in the chain rather than seeking to outdo them. Secondly they must recognise the distinct supply and demand processes that must be integrated in order to gain the greatest value.

Beech proposed that the core processes of the demand chain include product development, trade marketing, selling, value added distributors, category management, and store marketing. Supply chain processes include the purchasing of raw materials, manufacturing, warehousing and distribution, purchasing of finished goods, and store operations. Integrating processes that synchronise the supply and demand chain core processes are planning and servicing; these ensure that supply and demand do in fact integrate and offer benefits such as reduced inventory investment, improved return on assets and enhanced customer satisfaction.

The integrating processes (planning and servicing) are detailed by Beech. Planning processes comprise channel strategies; planning of manufacturing; inventory; distribution and transportation; demand planning and forecasting, and marketing and promotional planning. Beech emphasises the need for these to be an inter-organisational activity. Service processes include such functions as credit order management; load planning; billing and collection; dispute resolution, and promotional activities. Service processes coordinate the flow of materials, information and funds between trading partners. Beech suggests an integrated model including information technology, finance, HR and administration.

The supporting infrastructure is being driven by IT systems. They are required to handle routine transactions, but increasingly IT plays a more critical role in coordinating planning, production, purchasing, production and distribution data at an expanding number of levels and with expanding complexity.

Thinking of the business as a number of integrated core processes enables management to focus on streamlining the processes and identifying inter-organisational linkages which result in creating more value for less effort. This is very different to current activities aimed at reducing functions simply to reduce costs, often with no tangible impact on value outputs. Beech comments: 'It is the linking between enterprises that can lead to the ultimate goal of moving beyond supply chain efficiency to integrating supply with demand. The performance outcome is synchronisation.'

A strategic perspective is taken by Armistead et al. (1999). The authors identify themes 'associated' with business process management. Strategic choice and direction imply that because an organisation cannot pursue every opportunity it makes choices or trade-offs which determine the resource patterns of organisations and eventually the development of core competencies. These, in turn, lead to competencies that influence subsequent strategy. Strategic business process management forces companies to; 'examine their form and structure', having an influence on boundaries, structure and power within organisational design. An important component of the authors' model is the market value chain which 'links the stages which add value along a supply chain'. They suggest that *within* an organisation the market value chain is taken to be the conceptualisation of the core processes and activities which represent the organisation in process terms: 'They capture the activities which start and end in the organisation and link with other organisations in the chain.' They further suggest that the market value chain reinforces the resource based view of the organisation because it forces the identification of core processes from which core competencies and competitive advantage emerge.

Performance management is another perspective on strategic business process management which 'relies on the management of resources and on a series of measurement systems', without which progress towards goals and any necessary corrective action are not possible. Organisational coordination occurs internally and externally (that is, with suppliers and customers). This is particularly 'pertinent as the boundaries of internal processes become more ill-defined'; it could be argued that it is even more important than the boundaries between value chain organisations (such as the prosumer relationship between customer and supplier). This perspective adds emphasis to the importance of relationship management. The authors also identify knowledge management as a component of their model. Organisational learning and knowledge management are enhanced by business process management; it 'provides a framework for organisational learning and can incorporate the management of knowledge'.

Heikkila (2002) reports on Nokia's 'Handshake' programme – 'a demand chain efficiency improvement project' with several of their customers. The emphasis of their research was based upon the notion that (Vollmann and Cordon 1998):

Demand chain management puts emphasis on the needs of the marketplace and designing the (supply) chain to satisfy these needs, instead of starting with the supplier/manufacturer and working forward.

Heikkila's conclusions from an extensive literature search suggest overwhelming agreement on a number of key concerns relating to stakeholder expectations:

- *Performance management:* time management, relating to time-to-market (NPD), production cycle time, order cycle time, 'customisation', quality, reliability, unit cost of output, warranties and service support, flexibility, choice options and aesthetics (Stalk 1988; Womack and Jones 1996; Womack et al. 1991)

■ *Cost management*: purchase price plus; fixed costs concerns (supply sourcing and evaluation, transaction and negotiation, installation), and *variable costs concerns* (operating costs, maintenance, and product disposal)

■ *Risk management*: financial risk ('market'/investor response, shareholder 'value' management, inventory obsolescence and excesses); marketing risk (reading market signals and customer and 'stakeholder' response, demand patterns and forecasting errors); personal and social risk (B2B and B2C customers) (prestige, commitment and other relationship based problem outcomes) (Fisher 1997; Metters: 1997)

■ *Information management*: an effective infrastructure that avoids delays, is focused and accurate, credible and comprehensive, and accessible (transparent); 'cooperative' relationships between and among suppliers and distributors to share end-user information increases the success of interdependence

■ *Operations configuration*: an integrated production and logistics structure that optimises performance by crossing functional and organisational boundaries (Feitzinger and Lee 1997; Pine 1993)

■ *Customer and supplier relationships*: Heikkila recalls work by economists Williamson (1985) and Perry (1989) which suggests that 'resource owners increase productivity through cooperative specialisation' (Dyer 1997); Heikkila adds that 'Productivity gains in the supply chains are possible when firms are willing to make transaction or relation-specific investments.' He concludes (from the literature) that success is the result of commitment, continuity, communication, and trust

An overriding issue is the increasing appeal of 'an integrated or holistic process-based approach seen as an *effective* way to drive companies towards a competitive advantage' (Hines and Rich 2000). Hines and Rich, investigating the efficacy of an integrative approach to demand chain management, identify the importance of customers' value profiles as the basis for creating competitive advantage. They present an argument that suggests marketing philosophy is becoming focused on matching customer needs, with the solution being based upon delivering 'needs based value' rather than arbitrarily expanding the product range and number of product variations as a means of increasing market share. The emphasis becomes one of capturing the share of market added value, and to do so requires an integrated approach that is both intra-organisational and inter-organisational, 'developing marketing, cost, and operations approaches ... able to speak to one another'. The authors used a technique that focuses the operations of a whole company, requiring it to codify its strategic direction and establish a set of key performance indicators to ensure that all processes and activities are designed to produce optimum results. 'Policy deployment' is an approach that is used to focus the operations of a company to achieve a set of expected results. Given the increasing application of the holistic approach to business structures, the model has appeal.

Figure 9.3 suggest a model for undertaking the task of integrating demand chain processes with those of the supply chain. Central to the model is the acceptance that satisfying stakeholder interests is essential if the business model is to be a success. Two very important influences are the policies that determine

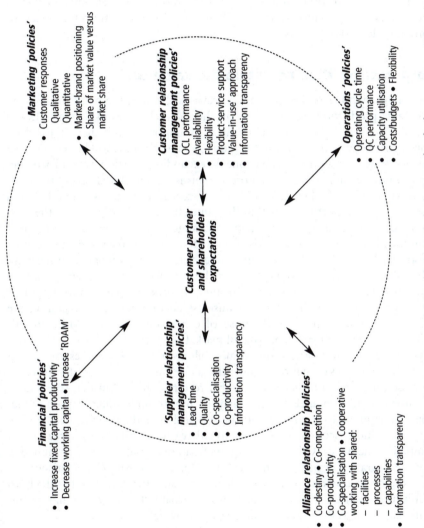

Figure 9.3 Policy deployment model for demand chain/supply chain process management

The following text appears within the figure:

Marketing 'policies'
- Customer responses
  - Qualitative
  - Quantitative
- Market-brand positioning
- Share of market value versus market share

'Customer relationship management policies'
- OCL performance
- Availability
- Flexibility
- Product-service support
- 'Value-in-use' approach
- Information transparency

Operations 'policies'
- Operating cycle time
- QC performance
- Capacity utilisation
- Costs/budgets • Flexibility

Customer partner and shareholder expectations

Financial 'policies'
- Increase fixed capital productivity
- Decrease working capital • Increase 'ROAM'

'Supplier relationship management policies'
- Lead time
- Quality
- Co-specialisation
- Co-productivity
- Information transparency

Alliance relationship 'policies'
- Co-destiny • Co-ompetition
- Co-productivity
- Co-specialisation • Cooperative working with shared:
  - facilities
  - processes
  - capabilities
- Information transparency

supplier and customer relationships. However, unless there is a balanced view taken concerning the financial, marketing, operations and alliance relationship policies of an organisation, it is unlikely that a successful integration of the demand chain and the supply chain will occur. While the outcome will be an optimal solution (given that the interests and expectations of customers, alliance partners and shareholders will inevitably differ), the model, by using a principle of 'desired outcome KPIs', offers an opportunity to establish performance expectations based upon other components of the business model. And, further, it encourages an exploration of the possibilities of virtual structures that meet the corporate desired outcomes.

Corporate positioning within the value chain

Value migration has been discussed in previous chapters, the point made being that value production can move within the value chain. Mark Levin, CEO of Millennium, was reported as seeing this as an important influence on the decision as to where to locate within the industry value chain. It will be recalled that Levin's strategic response has been one of 'expanding into downstream activities across several major product categories'. This is matter of identifying the decisions confronting the firm. Not only is it necessary to match specific skills and resources with opportunities within the value chain, but it follows that the their attraction is very likely to shift and to change as the business environment changes. Given this, the role of the firm within the industry value chain can be illustrated by Figure 9.4. Successful value chain partners work together with other partners, each of whom offers complimentary expertise – assets, processes and capabilities. In the example of Millennium, Levin has pursued the opportunities offered in a rapidly changing business environment by integrating the expertise of the company with those of other organisations. Millennium's approach requires constant appraisal of market opportunities and a clear knowledge of the current 'worth' of the firm's abilities. Figure 9.5 suggests a starting point. If the organisation is to identify with a role within the range of value chain processes, it is sound business sense for it to establish itself in that role and to monitor potential competition that may attempt to undermine its positioning. This will require it to conduct a rigorous self-analysis and take a prospective view of product and process developments, together with a similar long-term view of competitive activities. Often this suggests to an organisation that, possibly due to value migration or perhaps an external shift in the industry characteristics due to changing technology or maybe relationship structures, it may be timely to shift its positioning within the value chain. Internal factors may also suggest this to management as the organisation develops new skills.

Value production, communication and delivery

Overview

The industry view of value production, communication and delivery takes an overall, macro approach. It is concerned with the architecture issues of the

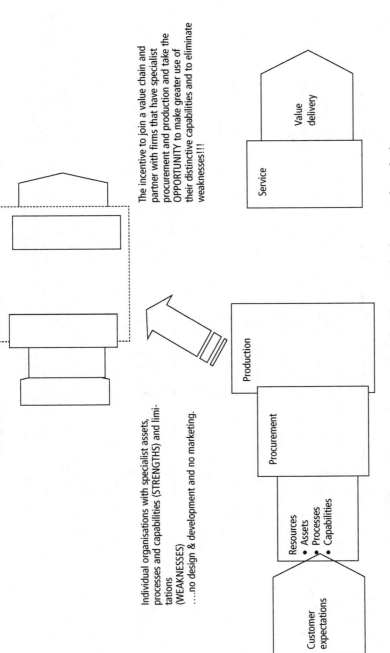

Individual organisations with specialist assets, processes and capabilities (STRENGTHS) and limitations (WEAKNESSES) ....no design & development and no marketing.

The incentive to join a value chain and partner with firms that have specialist procurement and production and take the OPPORTUNITY to make greater use of their distinctive capabilities and to eliminate weaknesses!!!

Customer expectations

Resources
- Assets
- Processes
- Capabilities

Procurement

Production

Service

Value delivery

Figure 9.4 Integrating into an industry value chain

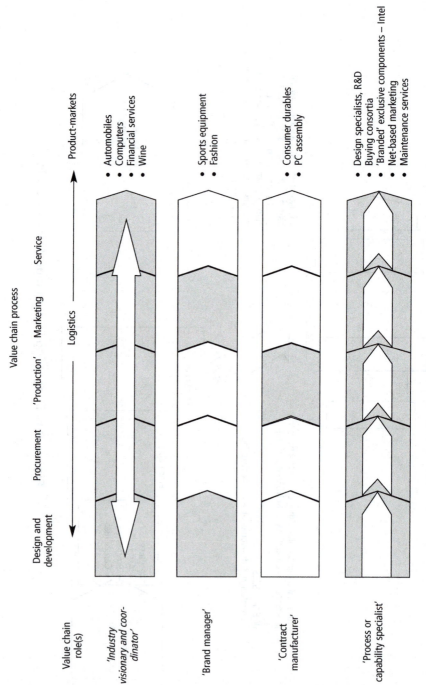

Figure 9.5 Strategic alternatives in the value chain

overall production, communication and delivery process. At the level of the firm, however, the focus is upon process management (the integration of its suppliers of materials, components and modular units into its 'production processes'), and process coordination (the integration of its process output(s) into those of the other value chain members).

The firm's perspective is shown as Figure 9.6. While the topics are the same as in the industry view, their emphasis is quite different. *Organisational architecture* decisions at the level of the firm concern integration and coordination with the architecture of the value chain. These involve strategic and operational considerations. The strategic considerations are for the firm to attempt to adopt or at least to recognise and work with the control, culture and management style that is accepted by the majority of the value chain partners/stakeholders. Similarly it should acknowledge the decision making, and the reward, motivation and incentive systems operating within the industry value creation system. There are obvious reasons for so doing. For example, quality control, production methods and incentive systems are closely linked. A component supplier in a high-technology industry is unlikely to maintain the quality specifications its downstream customers require if it adopts an output based payment system. Similarly, the firm's performance measurement and management evaluation should be integrated with those of other value chain partners.

Operations management processes should be aligned with customer facing processes, as can be seen in Figure 9.7. A number of sub-processes, or activities, are shown as components of the primary value chain processes. Within the firm it is essential that the roles of these processes in creating added value for the customer are identified and managed efficiently. Overall the success of one value chain over another is dependent upon the integration and coordination of the individual firm processes which differentiate the value delivered to customers and which are responsible for developing and maintaining customer satisfaction during the order generation and fulfilment processes. Clearly integration of the firm into the communications systems of the value chain is essential. Recent moves by the largest FMCG retailers in Australia appeared to be coercive towards their smaller suppliers, but in effect they were aimed at increasing efficiencies within the supply chain component of the value chain. Increasing the flow of inventory movement results in lower levels of inventory in the overall system, thereby increasing cash flows.

The choice of production process is an important decision. Chapter 4 demonstrated how quite different operations approaches are required when responding to market segment opportunities. Hayes and Wheelwright (1979) proposed linking product decisions with process decisions. Since then a number of authors have used variations on the original model to demonstrate strategic aspects of operations decisions. Both Brown (1996) and Hill (2000) offer variations of the model. It will be recalled that Chapter 5 discussed changing patterns in response to customer differentiation expectations. Figure 9.8 relates differentiation and volume choices. The diagram suggests how operations processes may be selected with the knowledge of choice and volume characteristics. Case study 9.3 towards the end of this chapter demonstrates the

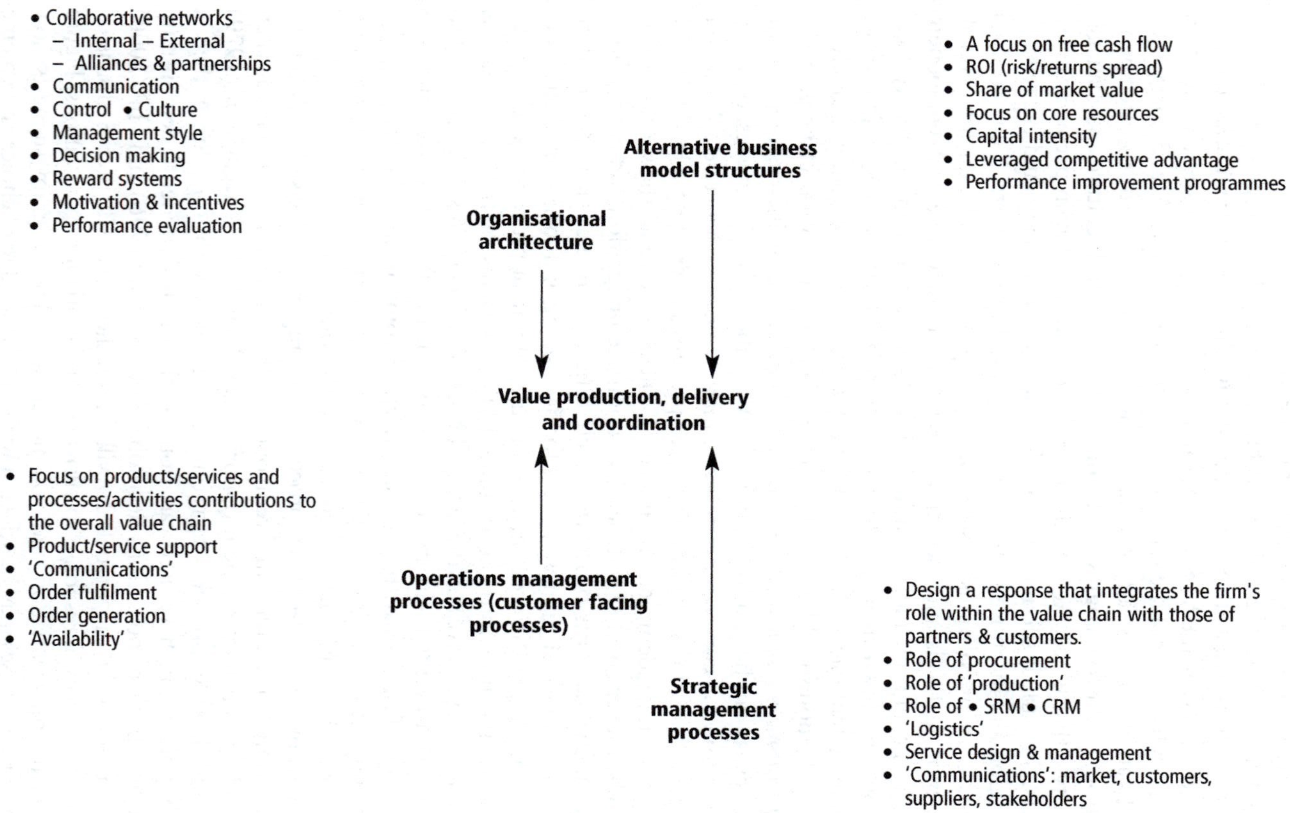

- A focus on free cash flow
- ROI (risk/returns spread)
- Share of market value
- Focus on core resources
- Capital intensity
- Leveraged competitive advantage
- Performance improvement programmes

**Alternative business
model structures**

**Organisational
architecture**

→ **Value production, delivery
and coordination** ←

**Operations management
processes (customer facing
processes)**

**Strategic
management
processes**

- Design a response that integrates the firm's
  role within the value chain with those of
  partners & customers.
- Role of procurement
- Role of 'production'
- Role of • SRM • CRM
- 'Logistics'
- Service design & management
- 'Communications': market, customers,
  suppliers, stakeholders

- Collaborative networks
  – Internal – External
  – Alliances & partnerships
- Communication
- Control • Culture
- Management style
- Decision making
- Reward systems
- Motivation & incentives
- Performance evaluation

- Focus on products/services and
  processes/activities contributions to
  the overall value chain
- Product/service support
- 'Communications'
- Order fulfilment
- Order generation
- 'Availability'

Figure 9.6 Value production, communication and delivery

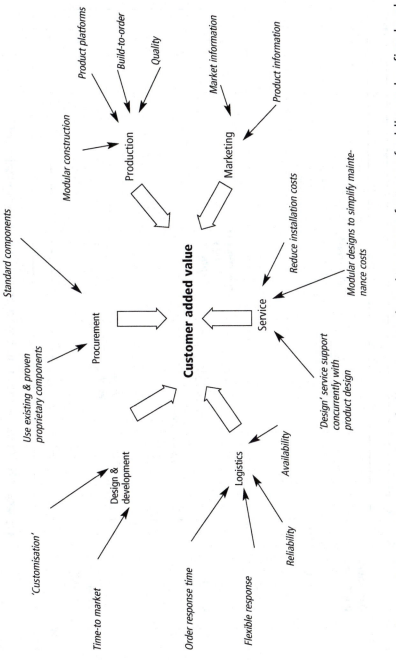

Figure 9.7 Identifying customer facing processes is an important feature of adding value firm level

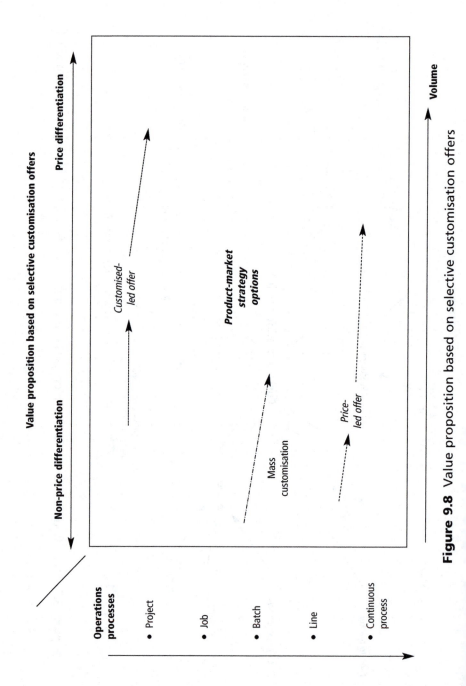

Figure 9.8 Value proposition based on selective customisation offers

effective use of the model when competing against offshore, low-cost labour competition in apparel supply markets.

The *alternative business model structure* that is selected for the value chain is assumed to be that which optimises overall value chain performance. Ideally the value chain coordinator should plan both the aggregate operating and cash cycles to ensure a coordinated and cohesive flow of products and materials, information and cash. This can prove to present difficulties for the smaller partners in the value chain if payment cycles and inventory management processes are not agreed or perhaps ignored. This aspect of value chain design and discipline was discussed in the previous chapter. Equitable share of the market added value can also be a contentious issue, particularly between large and small partners. To this end focusing on core assets, processes and capabilities by the members with ongoing performance improvement programmes becomes essential.

The firm's perspective of *strategic management processes* should be one of meeting the expectations for cooperation with other value chain partners. As the 'virtual model' evolves, processes that were once the province of the firm are becoming industry or value chain processes. The growth of aggregate procurement within the automobile and pharmaceutical industries is an example of how buying efficiencies can be improved. The application of ICT to these processes can further enhance their efficiencies. However, emerging research is beginning to identify issues with internet auctioning; a number of problems are reported in which suppliers are unable to meet the volumes (and therefore presumably the prices) agreed with customers.

Individual supplier relationship management and customer relationship management decisions are also the responsibility of the firm. The concerns of risk, return and overall performance are part of the decision-performance management set of the individual component firms in the value chain.

It follows that for both the value chain and its partners to be successful, value production, delivery and coordination should be considered both at the 'macro' industry level and at the 'micro' level of the firm. For the firm, this implies that it knows and accepts its role within the value chain. This has to be based upon an understanding of how its assets, processes and capabilities integrate into the overall industry value chain structure. For this to work at the firm level, each partner member should understand the processes of the value chain, their own contributions, and how these 'fit' into the overall structure. To do this requires detailed knowledge of the value chain processes.

In what follows, for each of the primary value chain processes we shall explore how, at the level of the firm, they can be integrated and coordinated to ensure both cost-effective and cost-efficient contributions to the overall success of the industry value chain.

Design and development

Design and development has a key role in the value chain. To be successful it requires not only an understanding of the characteristics of the market but an underlying understanding of the customer value drivers and their importance in delivering customer value. Knowledge of competitive activities and, possibly more importantly, their processes and capabilities is essential if design and development is to 'build' competitive advantage into product and service designs.

Much of the work conducted by design and development teams is now directed towards shared architecture or shared technology. The objective is to develop products that share parts and components that do not contribute to a brand identity but, because they are not visible, can be common across a range of products. Shared architecture increases the company's engineering, purchasing and manufacturing efficiencies.

For many organisations the platform concept extends well beyond corporate boundaries; partnerships and joint venture design and development programmes are established with other companies in the industry.

Design and development is also responsible for understanding how, where and by whom the product will be 'manufactured', who will 'deliver' the product and how, who will be using the product and how it will be used, how the value will be serviced and reinforced and what the cost profile alternatives are. See Figure 9.9.

Procurement

Procurement as a process has become strategically important. As Figure 9.10 suggests, procurement management's role is becoming integrated with those of finance and production. There are new tasks for procurement in the 'new economy' environment, with sourcing tasks extending beyond the identification of suppliers who can meet specification, volume and price requirements. The internet has introduced the concept of buying auctions, and pressures on cost have introduced co-opetition in procurement, with firms collaborating with their competitors to purchase components that do not add differentiation to the product but are basic items. The buying exchange established by the major Detroit based vehicle manufacturers COVISNET proposes significant reductions in costs. Management also has the task of working with competitors in an increasing number of buying exchange groups. Procurement managers work increasingly with supplier R&D staff to customise required inputs. Procurement management should work closely with the rest of production management to ensure that operating and cash cycles are coordinated in an attempt at optimising cash flows throughout the value chain. This shift of emphasis does not suggest that establishing, agreeing and monitoring budgets are any less important. Nor does it suggest that the traditional tasks of negotiating and transacting are any less important; they remain but have changed as the industry drivers have created new a trading environment with different approaches.

Production

Production's role has changed in much the same way as has that of procurement. By working closely with design and development, production decisions

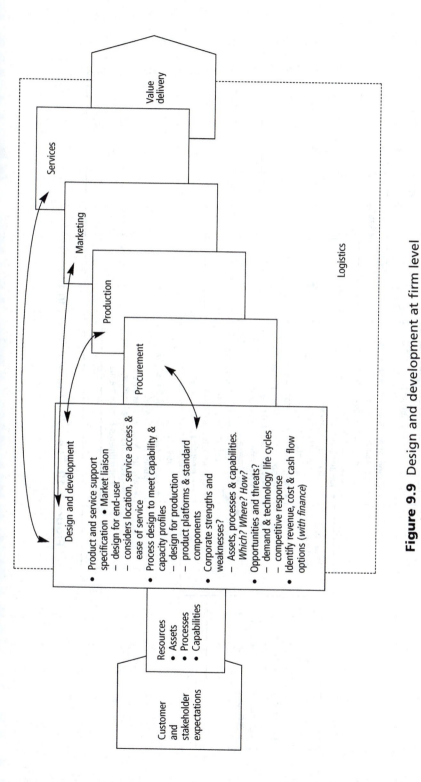

Figure 9.9 Design and development at firm level

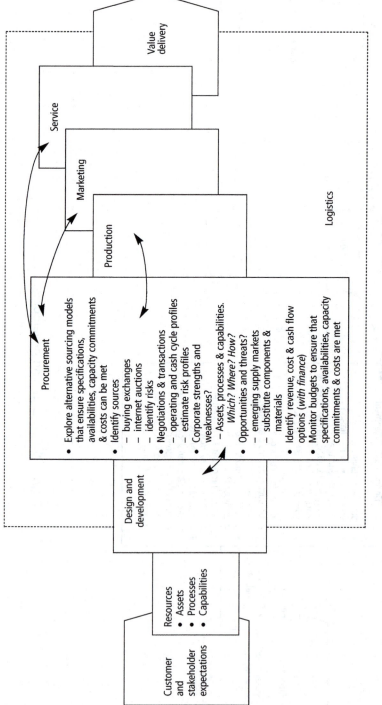

Figure 9.10 The role of procurement in the firm

The figure contains the following labelled elements:

- Customer and stakeholder expectations
- Resources
  - Assets
  - Processes
  - Capabilities
- Design and development
- Procurement
- Production
- Marketing
- Service
- Value delivery
- Logistics

Procurement box contents:

- Explore alternative sourcing models that ensure specifications, availabilities, capacity commitments & costs can be met
- Identify sources
  - buying exchanges
  - internet auctions
  - identify risks
- Negotiations & transactions
  - operating and cash cycle profiles
  - estimate risk profiles
- Corporate strengths and weaknesses?
  - Assets, processes & capabilities. *Which? Where? How?*
- Opportunities and threats?
  - emerging supply markets
  - substitute components & materials
- Identify revenue, cost & cash flow options (*with finance*)
- Monitor budgets to ensure that specifications, availabilities, capacity commitments & costs are met

may now extend well beyond the traditional boundaries of the firm. The application of technology to the field of operations management has induced operations management to extend its tasks into the integration and coordination of
corporate *and* partners' operations facilities. See Figure 9.11.

The introduction of product platform design and of modular manufacturing has led to the need to develop relationship management skills. The
economics of production have been replaced by the economics of added value;
consequently production managers are becoming aware of economies of scope,
integration, coordination, differentiation and competition, and of relationship
management.

Increasingly production coordination is more important than the traditional
role of production management, as the focus on differentiation assumes
importance and decisions are made that involve identifying excellence by working with partners who are the acknowledged 'owners' of specialist assets,
processes and capabilities. Another new role for the production manager is the
expectation that they will monitor emerging product and process technologies
and be competent in appraising their impact on the organisation.

Marketing

Marketing has additional roles and tasks. See Figure 9.12. The growing importance of share of market added value rather than (as well as) market share has
introduced changes to marketing. Figure 9.13 illustrates the importance of this
change in emphasis. Figure 9.13a demonstrates the usual result that occurs
when a firm attempts to increase market share. Typically, at the early stages of
this growth its 'return on investment' is high, particularly in a growth market
with fragmented competition. However, when the market reaches some stability and/or competition becomes organised, the previous returns on growth
are less. If the firm continues its expansion of market share the 'incremental
returns' decrease (due to decreased rate of market growth) but the costs can
continue to increase. Figure 9.13b suggests that a strategy of increasing share
of market added value is likely to offer better returns, particularly if the firm
monitors value migration and adjusts its value chain position to take advantage
of opportunities arising from value shifts. There is also the possibility that by
changing the value chain positioning and its partnership structures the total
costs can be reduced. It is arguable that the costs involved in Figure 9.13a
could also be reduced; the likelihood is that the fixed cost component will
increase as the firm 'invests' in the brand.

Marketing also acts a conduit between the market (end-users and distributors) and design and development through the demand chain. We described
the current view of design and development and the 'market' earlier. Precise
product use characteristics are required by designers if an efficient design is to
result. By using marketing in this context, end-user behaviour can be understood and possibly accommodated in product design at its early stages. The
traditional role of market channel development has also changed for some
organisations. Marketing as a value chain process can become involved in

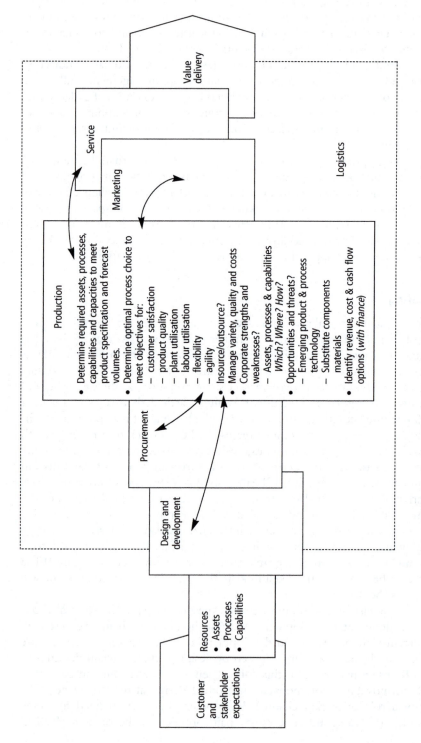

Figure 9.11 The role of production in the firm

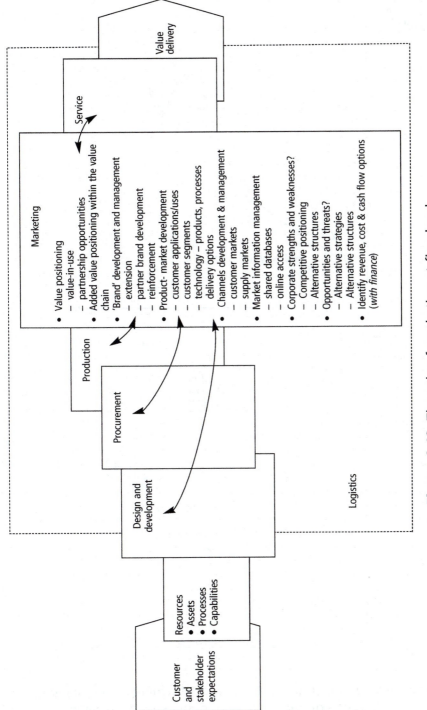

Figure 9.12 The role of marketing at firm level

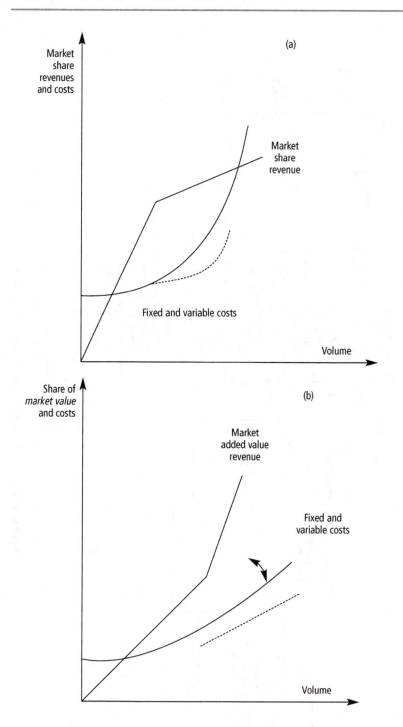

Figure 9.13 Comparison of the costs of obtaining market share versus the costs of obtaining share of market added value

identifying derived demand opportunities. A close understanding of customer expectations and perceptions can be used to adjust suppliers' outputs to meet some downstream customer preferences.

Service

Service has become a major feature in the moves by value chain partners to differentiate product-service offers. See Figure 9.14. For some time service was primarily used to reinforce customer continuity by closely managing aspects of distribution performance such as delivery frequency and reliability, and product availability. The application of ICT to customer service management roles and tasks has had significant impact. The application of the internet to company–customer communications has broadened the 'meaning' of customer service. It is now understood to include customer involvement in product design and development as well as applications such as online order progress management.

In the value chain, service innovations are appearing which enhance the benefits received by vendor and customer organisations. The introduction of collaborative planning, forecasting and replenishment (CFPR) by Metcash, an Australian fast moving consumer goods distributor with turnover of $A7.6 billion, is an example. Initially introduced with 20 suppliers, the mutual benefits became readily apparent. Suppliers are given a 'better picture of product flows through the warehouses and stores'; this benefits both Metcash and its suppliers; their forecasting gains accuracy while for Metcash information on logistics efficiencies became apparent very quickly. A downstream supply partnership innovation involving Metcash and 7-Eleven offers the latter an opportunity to optimise its delivery programme Crowe (2004).

Service organisations have also appeared in the value chain. In the mid-1990s the market context changed again with the advent of large-scale outsourcing and the market entry of specialist outsourcing organisations such as EDS and CSC. These organisations offered to take over the entire scope of their customers' IT activities, in effect vertically integrating again along the whole of the IT services value chain. An alternative model was offered by AWA, which did not attempt to compete in offering 'end to end' solutions, but instead made its service offering more focused, forming a new partnership dynamic so that it sat as a quite distinct element in the overall value chain and was able to team with these larger organisations to fulfil specialist roles, essentially as a sub-contractor. The large outsourcer in effect became the value chain coordinator, with complex process innovation being key to successfully coordinating the various partner inputs. From the service providers' perspective this evolution has required constant reinvention. The nature of their relationship with their customers has changed from a set piece maintenance contract at fixed rates that were rarely negotiated riding on the back of hardware sales, to a dynamic relationship with a series of partners.

Apart from product innovation this has required significant process innovation. In AWA's case the centerpiece is its 'AWAre' proprietary information

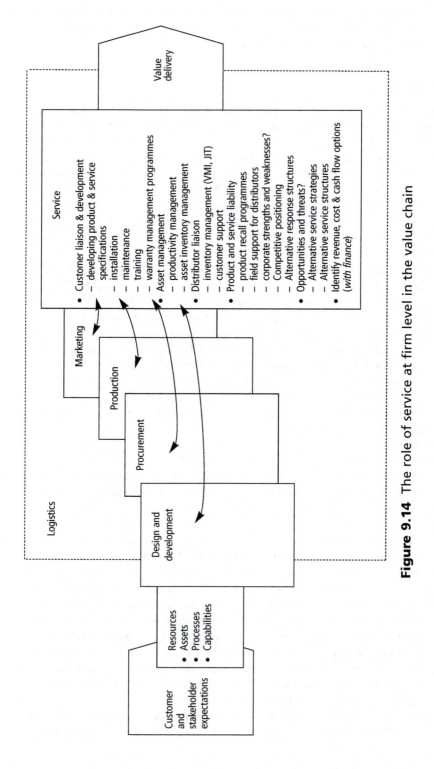

Figure 9.14 The role of service at firm level in the value chain

management system. This is the primary tool for interacting with partners and tailoring the company's services (supply) to meet partner/customer demands (managing service calls). Not owned but accessed and used by major customers, it is a major element in AWA's 'access' to the value chain and in effectively operating in it. While AWAre's principal function is call management, it is in fact the base for all AWA service activities from interfacing with customers, its own technicians, and agents; it encompasses not just field activities, but those of the workshop, logistics asset management and billing. AWAre's historical origins means that it is essentially a relational database. This gives inherent flexibility in managing information and makes it very well suited to this type of application compared to the hierarchical architecture more common in similar generic systems.

Logistics

The role of logistics as a materials and information flows manager remains strong at both levels of the value chain. It could be argued that the growth of very large retailing organisations such as Wal-Mart has increased the importance of logistics management. The introduction of just-in-time (JIT) and vendor managed inventory (VMI) programmes has made the management of time and information an imperative; the lack of inventory at a customer's distribution centre or at the point-of-sale will not only result in lost sales but is likely to have major repercussions on customer relationships.

Accurate, reliable, timely deliveries meet the objectives set for operating and cash cycle objectives. Accurate and timely invoicing will enhance the cash management processes of all value chain members. See Figure 9.15.

Summary

The firm within the value chain is one of a number of partner stakeholders. It offers some specialist skills or expertise that the value chain structure needs; this is the sole reason it is there. We have identified above the activities in each of the primary value chain processes that should be present within the value chain. The concept of the value chain (and indeed of all virtual models) is that it is an aggregate of relevant, but individual, expertise. It follows that at the firm level we expect to see focused contributions by the stakeholder partners. The task of the 'visionary' is to identify a combination of the necessary skills, expertise and resources (assets, processes and capabilities) that will make the value chain successful, and having done so then to integrate this combination into a value creation system. The ongoing task then becomes one of ensuring that this combination is both strategically effective and operationally efficient. The tasks for each firm then become twofold: process management and process coordination, key requirements if the value chain is to succeed. The remainder of the main part of this chapter discusses some of the issues that need to be considered.

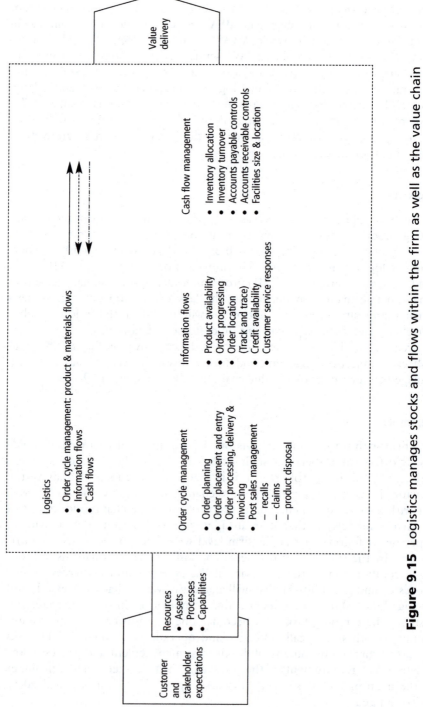

Figure 9.15 Logistics manages stocks and flows within the firm as well as the value chain

Assessing, selecting and working with partners

Two considerations are important to the final decision about whom to work with. The first of these is the availability of specific resource inputs (assets, processes, materials, labour, and so on) and the sensitivity of the value chain to these. If the final output is reliant upon a resource input for differentiating the end product (quality, performance or perhaps cost characteristics), a view must be taken concerning the relationships to be developed by the firm with suppliers. If the input is widely available, a commitment such as leasing or a guaranteed off-take of the input is probably necessary. Conversely, if the input requires specific characteristics resulting in 'customisation', then joint venture/vertical integration options would appear preferable.

Widely available inputs having a low impact on the final output do not usually require such strong supplier relationships. Clearly supply markets should be monitored to ensure continuity of availability but beyond this no close partnerships are required. For low sensitivity but 'specific' inputs, tighter supplier arrangements are preferable. Leasing contracts or some form of vertical coordination (a low-level equity investment) are often a solution.

Another important consideration is that of weighing business risk (fluctuations in planned market volume and market share) against the capability profile of the organisation. Distinctive capabilities that have a strong impact in situations where business risk is high should be owned, or integrated into the value chain if ownership is difficult (due to patents or other exclusivity situations). If business risk is low then a partnership with a market specialist would appear to be the solution. For capabilities that have low impact and are reproducible, outsourcing arrangements should be satisfactory across the range of likely business risk conditions.

Managing for equity in the value chain

A major problem that occurs in value chain structures is the imbalance of 'power' and the implications this has for individual members' performance. The growth of large retailers with dominant market positions is a common global phenomenon. The reports of use (and abuse) of channel power are numerous, as we saw in Chapter 7.

Each member of the value chain will seek to minimise inventory holding (for cost, storage and obsolescence motives); at the same time they will attempt to maximise cash flow. Clearly such individual (and selfish) actions can only result in problems. Not only will there be financial difficulties for many members, but it is very unlikely that inventory will be in appropriate places at appropriate times, with the end result being failure because intermittent and erratic supply can only result in customer dissatisfaction and defection.

Matching payables and receivables 'adds balance' to supplier/customer relationships, facilitating cash flow management throughout the value chain. and preventing the situation identified in Chapter 7 whereby very large organisations are being subsidised by their smaller competitors.

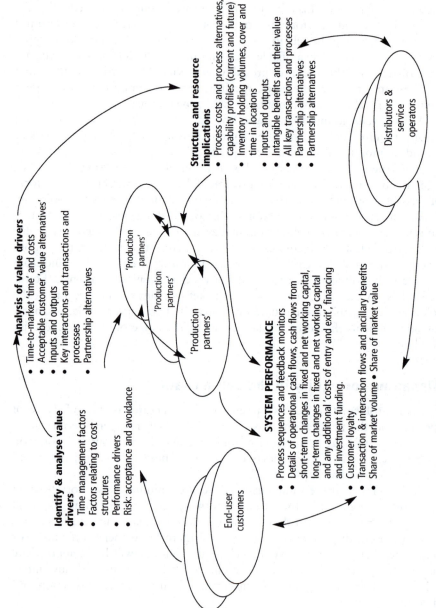

Identify & analyse value drivers
- Time management factors
- Factors relating to cost structures
- Performance drivers
- Risk: acceptance and avoidance

Analysis of value drivers
- Time-to-market 'time' and costs
- Acceptable customer 'value alternatives'
- Inputs and outputs
- Key interactions and transactions and processes
- Partnership alternatives

Structure and resource implications
- Process costs and process alternatives, capability profiles (current and future)
- Inventory holding volumes, cover and time in locations
- Inputs and outputs
- Intangible benefits and their value
- All key transactions and processes
- Partnership alternatives
- Partnership alternatives

'Production partners'

'Production partners'

'Production partners'

Distributors & service operators

End-user customers

SYSTEM PERFORMANCE
- Process sequences and feedback monitors
- Details of operational cash flows, cash flows from short-term changes in fixed and net working capital, long-term changes in fixed and net working capital and any additional 'costs of entry and exit', financing and investment funding.
- Customer loyalty
- Transaction & interaction flows and ancillary benefits
- Share of market volume • Share of market value

Figure 9.16 Structuring and managing the value chain

Concluding comments

Figure 9.16 suggests an approach to value chain design using an approach described by Gottfredson et al. (2005), which we met in Chapter 5. Commencing with customer value drivers identifies the ultimate performance criteria. Evaluating the operational and financial feasibility of the value drivers indicates the performance expectations of partner organisations, and at the same time compares these with partners' market and financial expectations.

The creative component of value chain design is the way in which resources are marshalled and deployed. For example, Dell Computers have structured an innovative value chain based upon process innovation that manages to coordinate customer order and payment processes with component ordering on suppliers, and with assembly processes that meet a delivery offer acceptable to customers and meeting the operating and cash flow efficiency objectives of Dell's suppliers, many of whom are themselves major companies. An ongoing review of partner abilities as well as expectations is necessary. Hewlett-Packard found that their Singapore distributor developed assembly skills; following a review of costs and customer delivery performance expectations, HP restructured this particular component of the value chain by shipping components rather than assemblies into the distributor, thereby lowering inventory management costs.

System performance expectations therefore become a central feature of the value chain performance planning and control process. Monitoring customer responses and changes to partner capabilities and expectations enables a competitive advantage position to be established and maintained.

CASE STUDY 9.1

Using a partner to develop mutual advantage

(Based upon 'Tesco eyes film download service', BBC News, 6 May 2005; 'Sony wants an iTunes for movies', BBC News, 7 May 2005)

At the time the above articles were published, UK multiple FMCG retailer, Tesco, was planning to launch a movie downloading service to build on the success it has had in the online music sector. Tesco has a 10 per cent share of internet music sales and considers films as the next digital opportunity for expansion. The company launched an online DVD rental service in March 2004, and soon had 30,000 customers registered with the service.

Concurrently, Sony announced at a US Digital Hollywood conference that it was seeking to create an 'iTunes for movies', planning to make its top 500 films available digitally in the next year. Sony Pictures Entertainment, MGM Studios, Paramount Pictures, Universal Studios, and Warner Brothers have formed a partnership, Movielink, which now provides access to a limited catalogue of 'legal' films. The Sony objective is to set business models, pricing models and distribution models in a similar way to that established by Apple.

There is some nervousness within the industry concerning the distribution of the downloaded content, particularly to portable devices. The growing popularity of portable entertainment devices such as Sony's PlayStation Portable (PSP), capable of playing a range of multimedia content, is beginning to dispel this concern. Other film makers such as Lions Gate Entertainment and Disney have announced forthcoming film titles that will be available in this format.

Discussion topics

How should the major players in this venture evaluate their partnership policies?

CASE STUDY 9.2

Using specialist partners to explore opportunities

(Based upon Mathew McAdam, 'Brand new products becoming reality', *Australian Financial Review*, 12 April 2005)

Lateral thinking is often not a capability that focused management can claim. Quite often the opportunities that may be available from brand extension are not 'seen' as they may well be out of the mainstream of the business. Real Brand Holdings, a Sydney based brand and business development agency, recently won a commission from Kellogg's. The company has been tasked with exploring Kellogg's archives to identify new ways of capitalising on its century-old brand name and to 'extend' the brand beyond its core cereals business.

Real Brand claims that it has accessed over one million items of archived data material that will be used to develop breakfast ware, cups, plates and cutlery, all bearing the Kellogg's logo. The first batch of 'Vintage Kellogg's' was due appear in US stores by the end of June 2005. According to ACNielsen nearly three quarters of new products and brands fail within their first two years, suggesting that a strategy to extend already developed (and in this instance clearly successful) brands into new markets has merit.

Discussion topics

Three issues arise here. One concerns the efficacy of brand extension and the grounds on which it could be successful. Another concerns the use of a specialist partner to explore the opportunities that are available. The third issue raises the question of implementation: who should be responsible for 'making it work in the marketplace' – the specialist partner or the brand owner?

CASE STUDY 9.3

Using the product/process matrix for creating competitive advantage as a sourcing option

(Based upon G Newman, 'Flexible Bonds stretched, but working to sew up niche markets', *Australian*, 22 October 2005; P Roberts, 'How textile survivors fashion a profit', *Australian Financial Review*, 6 December 2005)

To compete against the low-cost labour advantage of Asian manufacturers, Bonds, owner of Pacific Brands (an Australian based manufacturer of branded apparel) has identified a market segment whose expectations could be met competitively. Newman reports comments by Richard Abela, head of manufacturing and supply for the Bonds group, suggesting that provided a manufacturer is selective in the market segment they choose there is scope for an organisation that avoids commodity products that require significant labour input. The Bonds factory focuses on products 'where the margins are not so critical and customers are prepared to pay a premium'. Bonds' manufacturing process focuses on monitoring costs and speed of production, through a vertically integrated production process and long-term agreements with its suppliers. Inventory holding is maintained at three days' supply. Bonds is able to produce a finished garment 'from yarn to a finished product in just four weeks, compared with the Chinese who require 12 weeks'. Chinese manufacturers are increasingly unwilling to accept small garment runs as they are now more interested in the volume markets of Europe and the US.

Bonds has invested in equipment specifically for small-batch runs. In Australia, 5,000 items is considered medium-sized, 'so small for Chinese manufacturers that it would be done in the sample room, with the attendant quality problems'. Certainty of supply continuity is also an area where local manufacturers can offer advantage. The recent EU–China WTO and quota problems and those of the Australian Customs computer system demonstrate the drawbacks to relying exclusively upon overseas suppliers. Bonds also sees added value product-markets as an opportunity. Markets such as school uniforms that require specific crests and designs are of interest.

Bonds has benefited from Federal Government funding. They used a grant to help fund a new packaging machine to reduce packaging costs by 50 cents an item. Abela is conscious of the fact that the company needs to monitor and reassess the economics of manufacturing in the industry as innovation is an ongoing process.

Another company that is managing to remain viable is a footwear manufacturer, J Robins and Sons. They operate a multi-skilled workforce of 250 employees who 'move between work stations as part of a small-batch production process that gives Robins the flexibility to design, make and deliver a pair of shoes in only two weeks'. Again it is the inflexibility of China's production systems, requiring long production runs, which means it cannot compete in the fashion segments of the shoe market. Roberts reports a comment from the managing director of Robins: 'If you were looking at getting a new design from China you would be lucky to get the finished product back within 3½ to four months ... We test the market with small production runs and, if they are successful, we can come back and repeat the order.'

Roberts reports some depressing aggregate production figures for the Australian textile, clothing and footwear (TCF) sector. TCF manufacturing production slumped 16 per cent in 2004/05 (Council of Textile and Fashion Industries). Employment declined by 14.4 per cent from 61,500 to 52,600 people, the textiles sector reduced its labour force by 8,300 employees, some 32.3 per cent of the total.

Roberts, like Newman, has found other successful organisations. Melba has managed to expand by innovating in niche markets such as automotive seating and speciality fabrics for use in protective clothing for the police, military and fire services. Melba has avoided the apparel sector because of the volume-price issues posed by China (comment from Melba's CEO). Bruck Textiles remain competitive in mass markets by 'being leaner, keener, more aggressive and more respectful of customers', according to CEO, Alan Williamson.

While Bonds, Robins, Melba and Bruck Textiles have been successful by a strategy of specialist products offering characteristics that attract higher margins or by adopting lean principles, other companies are not so fortunate. Once global leaders, Actil (cotton sheeting) and Sheridan (a dye house) are examples of the not so fortunate companies.

Roberts gives examples of two men's suit manufacturers who have remained successful by pursuing a sourcing strategy to match specific price points. Both Berkeley Apparel and the Stafford Group use imported products to meet product-mix needs at lower-level price points, but their own labels at the high end of the price spectrum.

Discussion topics

Suggest an approach that organisations could adopt to match product-market opportunities with operations processes.

Do the examples identified in this case suggest that such a solution should adopt the notion that vertical and/or horizontal integration is preferable to virtual models?

CASE STUDY 9.4

Value migration and new skills: moving along the value chain

(Based upon K Hille and P Marsh, 'Brand-new future for component makers', *Australian*, 27 November 2005)

Brands are an interesting component of the value equation. They clearly form part of the consumer's evaluation of a product. In the case of commodity products like flour, sugar and tissue paper it is arguable that brands are losing their importance in the purchase decision. For prestige products such as fashion apparel, fine wines and liquors and the higher end of the motor vehicle market, brands still however clearly represent a disproportionate amount of the price and value equations.

Similarly, as noted elsewhere, intangibles, including brands, form a much larger proportion of a firm's overall worth than was the case in the early twentieth century. It might even be suggested that that in commodity markets such as those of fast food and soft drinks, brands like Coca-Cola and McDonald's are key value generators and more important to the firm's success than the underlying physical products.

How then do brands fit into the value chain? Must a successful company have a successful brand? The consumer and IT electronics market is an interesting example. In the 1950s and 1960s Japanese electronics products were largely synonymous with low-cost and perceived lower-quality products. Yet from that emerged powerful brands such as Sony, Panasonic, and Pioneer that are not only considered equal to or better quality than traditional Western brands such as Philips, Thompson or RCA, but command a price premium. In the 1990s Korean brands such as Samsung and LG emerged from similar backgrounds.

Is this a case of lower-cost producers building brands over time and using that investment to drive underlying value? Certainly the importance of brand seems to have spurred the latest wave of emerging electronics giants from China to cut short the process and simply acquire well known Western brands – Lenovo have done this with IBM personal computers and Haier recently failed in its attempt to acquire Maytag.

There is however another perspective. Many Asian companies in the computer components industry build their businesses around providing products to the large, well known 'branded' businesses based on economies of scale and lower-cost production. Many such as BenQ (Taiwan), Foxconn (Taiwan), Suncorp (China) and Humax (Korea) have built expertise in design and development. They go beyond being what was traditionally thought of as an 'original equipment manufacturer' (OEM) to become an 'original design manufacturer' (ODM), or develop product ranges that are then sold to other companies who brand and market them. This is attractive in product-markets that are moving towards 'commoditisation'. The notebook and telephone handset product-markets are examples of such opportunities, with Dell, Hewlett-Packard and others effectively the brand managers of products made by ODMs.

Will these OEM and ODM companies follow in the footsteps of Sony and Samsung and become brand powerhouses in their own right? Acer (Taiwan), which produced its first Acer branded computer in 1981, is now the world's fourth biggest branded computer manufacturer. It too has 'spun off its production to become a pure marketing company'.

Humax (Korea), a manufacturer of electronic devices for adapting television receivers to accept digital signals, is already moving into higher added value products such as digital TV, to be marketed under its own brand. In China both Galanz and Haier have used OEM expertise to move into selling branded products. Haier has met with international success.

Certainly these examples can be seen as exemplifying value chain migration, with firms starting life doing one thing and ending up doing another, moving from physical production as the primary driver of value to management of intangibles – particularly brand. However, is this migration 'natural'? Do firms inevitably migrate 'up' the value chain to segments that are 'higher-value'?

Some interesting issues are highlighted by Michael Marks, CEO of Flextronics (Singapore), the world's second largest contract manufacturer for the global electronics industry. He suggests that Flextronics would never introduce a product to compete with one of its customers. Furthermore, Tim Bajarin, a US based consultant with Creative Strategies, suggests that the huge costs of establishing a brand, in the region of 10 to 20 percent of revenues, together with the requirement for quite different skills such as marketing and distribution, are now critical barriers. Few companies can afford the decades that Sony and Samsung took to build their brands. The favoured business model may become one that identifies customers who are attempting to become 'market leaders' in specialist segments and who are willing to pay a premium for a differentiated product that offers a solution to market success.

Delta Electronics (Taiwan) is an example of this strategy. The company is a leading manufacturer of power supplies for computers, and is attempting to become a leading force in the specialist area of 'cold cathode' devices, fluorescent lights which are used in flat screens for monitors and television receivers. Delta have an advantage because they can 'bundle' this component with their inverters when selling to flat-panel makers.

Another value chain positioning strategy, used by BenQ, is to 'export' the design and manufacturing model in specific product areas into sectors yet to be explored. Taiwanese electronics companies that are primarily involved in consumer products are moving into the automotive industry. Mitac has acquired a large share of the car based global positioning system (GPS) product-market, and Ausustek has indicated an interest in medical electronics.

Discussion topics

How would an organisation evaluate an alternative value chain position? What should be its primary objectives?

An ongoing value chain audit may offer expansive organisations a means by which opportunities can be identified. How could this be established?

Are all industries candidates for value migration and value chain repositioning?

REFERENCES

Armistead C, J-P Pritchard and S Machin (1999) 'Strategic business process management for organisational effectiveness,' *Long Range Planning*, 32(1)

Beech J (1998) 'The supply-demand nexus: from integration to synchronisation', in Gattorna J (ed.) Strategic Supply Chain Alignment, Gower, Aldershot

Brown S (1996) *Strategic Manufacturing for Competitive Advantage*, Prentice-Hall, London

Crowe D (2004) 'Metcash feeds suppliers data', *Australian Financial Review*, 30 November

Dyer J (1997) 'Effective inter-firm collaboration: how firms minimize transaction costs and maximize transaction value', *Strategic Management Journal*, 18(7)

Feitzinger E and H L Lee (1997) 'Mass customisation at Hewlett-Packard: the power of postponement', *Harvard Business Review*, 75(1)

Fisher M L (1997) 'What is right supply chain for your product?', *Harvard Business Review*, 75(2)

Forbes (2003) *Forbes Global 2003*, Forbes, New York

Gottfredson M, R Puryear and S Phillips (2005) 'Strategic sourcing from periphery to the core', *Harvard Business Review*, February

Hagel J III and M Singer (1999) 'Unbundling the corporation,' *Harvard Business Review*, March/April

Hayes R H and S C Wheelwright (1979) 'The dynamics of process-product life cycles', *Harvard Business Review*, 57

Heikkila J (2002) 'From supply to demand chain management: efficiency and customer satisfaction', *Journal of Operations Management*, November

Hill T (2000) *Operations Management: Strategic Context and Management Analysis*, Palgrave Macmillan, Basingstoke

Hines P and N Rich (2000) 'Understanding improvement areas in the value stream', in Hines P, R Lamming, D Jones, P Cousins and N Rich (eds) *Value Stream Management*, Financial Times/Prentice-Hall, London

Lai A (2000) Greater China Marketing Director, Hewlett-Packard, *Global*, 23/24 June

Metters R (1997) 'Quantifying the bullwhip effect in supply chains', *Journal of Operations Management*, 15(2)

Parolini C (1999) *The Value Net*, Wiley, Chichester

Perry M K (1989) 'Vertical integration', in Schmalensee R and R Willig (eds) *Handbook of Industrial Organisation*, North-Holland, Amsterdam

Pine B J III (1993), *Mass Customisation*, Harvard Business School Press, Boston, MA

Porter M (1985) *Competitive Advantage: Creating and Sustaining Superior Performance*, Free Press, New York

Stalk G (1988) 'Time: the next strategic advantage', *Harvard Business Review*, 66

Vollmann T E and C Cordon (1998) 'Building successful customer–supplier alliances', *Long Range Planning*, 31(5)

Williamson O E (1985) *The Economic Institutions of Capitalism: Firms, Markets, Relationship Contracting*, Free Press, New York

Womack J P and D T Jones (1996) *Lean Thinking: Banish Waste and Create Wealth in Your Corporation*, Simon & Schuster, New York

Womack J P, D T Jones and D Roos (1991) *The Machine that Changed the World: The Story of Lean Production*, HarperPerennial, New York

CHAPTER 10

Performance Planning and Control

LEARNING TOPICS

On completing your study of this chapter you will have been introduced to and considered the following topics:

- Planning and performance measurement: a review of current thinking
- Basic issues in planning performance measurement
- Performance measurement in 'new economy' organisations: the 'performance prism'
- Planning and performance: a 'new economy' total organisation perspective
- Value chain planning considerations: evaluating the viability; customer added value; identifying the fixed and variable costs; cash flow analysis
- Performance planning; planning options and performance metrics
- Evaluating alternatives for growth

Introduction

In an environment that is constantly changing and in which competition can often come from the unexpected it is essential that organisations have systematic processes in place with which to modify performance measuring systems and performance measures.

Planning and performance measurement: a review of current thinking

Kennerley and Neely (2003) present evidence to show that few organisations have such responses in place as will ensure their performance measurement systems continue to reflect their environment and strategies. The authors present case study evidence to show that:

... a well designed measurement system will be accompanied by an explicitly designed evolutionary cycle with clear triggers and:

- Process – existence of a process for reviewing, modifying and deploying measures
- People – the availability of the required skills to use, reflect on, modify and deploy measures
- Systems – the availability of flexible systems that enable the collection, analysis and reporting of appropriate data
- Culture – the existence of a measurement culture within the organization ensuring that the value of measurement, and importance of maintaining relevant and appropriate measures, is appreciated

Through the case study the authors demonstrate the factors facilitating the development of measurement systems that are relevant to the changing environment in which this particular company found itself. They contend:

The data collected ... shows that the managers ... now recognize the process, people, and culture and systems capabilities necessary to manage a measurement system over time. They recognize that these capabilities did not exist within the organization during the first phase of their management systems evolution, and action has been taken to ensure that the capabilities are in place to ensure that the evolution is effective in the future.

Perhaps it is the conclusions the authors reach that are the most significant directions for the 'visionaries' or 'integrators' responsible for developing virtual organisations. Without a structured and relevant approach to performance measurement the organisation may not be aware of the extent of the success of the innovative organisational structure, nor will it be aware of the need to make changes if the performance is to be maintained.

An SAS 'White Paper' (2001) proposes a broad approach. While this is an attempt at selling software, the seven topics outlined below introduce a framework that, regardless of whether or not a particular brand of software is used, has some validity.

1. Enterprise performance management is a key factor, comprising:

- A company- (organisation)-wide strategy that is identified, accepted and managed by all 'partners'
- An organisation-wide 'vision' that is used to align processes and capabilities. Where these are not available in-house they are identified and incorporated
- Functional units aligned to meet the strategic direction of the organisation

2. Proactive rather than reactive structures:

■ Business cycle compression creates the need for organisations to identify opportunities and threats ahead of potential competitors.

■ Virtual organisations that are flexible and lean are able to respond more effectively and more quickly than vertically integrated organisations.

3. Abandoning the 'silo' mindset:

■ Extending corporate transactions and interactions beyond the organisation's existing boundaries

■ Embrace value chain and value net concepts to their full extent

4. Understand and leverage relationships:

■ Worthwhile relationships are long-term, they are not managed on a transaction by transaction basis.

■ Processes should be managed on a relationship basis extending across functional, organisational and even international boundaries.

■ 'Value' is a stakeholder issue; value criteria should be determined and monitored for long-term success.

5. Automate 'best practices':

■ Ideally processes should be 'self-learning' and 'self-tuning' and be able to capture and share best practices, performance metrics and experience. In this way knowledge is created and it follows that:

■ Decision making becomes more effective.

6. Communicate 'customised' information:

■ Stakeholders must understand the vision, direction and structure they have agreed to be part of.

7. Create knowledge rather than just capturing data:

■ Understand the messages from 'day-to-day' transactional data.

■ Creating knowledge systems that relate to the business model is essential.

SAS suggests there to be common problem areas. For example, financial management typically lacks vision in creating structures and is more secure with well established performance measures. For many organisations customer relationship management, while recent as a 'collective concept', is viewed from a quantity rather than quality perspective; they prefer to measure its success by market share rather than share of market value. Combining 'knowledge' with structured data processing analysis can result in a powerful method or tool for exploring long-term customer relationship scenarios, identifying how value propositions *might* be met by valued customers. Supplier relationship management, not typically practised in most companies, is another process for which clear performance metrics are necessary, and again these should be qualitative as well as quantitative. For example, organisational spending patterns should be identified, with suppliers' performance 'ranked and rated' against meaningful criteria such as organisational objectives. A knowledge base should be established that enables potential areas for cost rationalisation, consolidation and buying power indices to be identified and put into effect. Such a knowledge base would also permit the exploration of procurement strategies on both intra- and inter-organisational bases. Human resource development and management can also benefit; combining strategic information with workforce performance analytics will facilitate the evaluation of HR alternative strategies against qualitative and quantitative organisational expectations. Not only can the HR strategy be considered but, more importantly, so too can the future organisation structure.

Bryan and Hulme (2003) identify the comprehensive nature of corporate performance management:

> By definition, corporate-performance management involves corporate- and not just business-level managers. Unlike operating performance, which can be driven by 'vertical' line-management processes, corporate performance requires 'horizontal' processes involving company-wide collaboration to generate and share ideas, establish accountability, and help allocate resources effectively. Scarce resources now include not only capital but also discretionary spending as well as the talent and management focus needed to find, nurture, and manage new projects that could boost future performance. Major corporate-wide initiatives, such as programs to improve the management of client relationships and to create new product-development and corporate-purchasing processes, would all be part of the effort.

And:

> A particularly important part of the portfolio mix should be initiatives to communicate with and influence the expectations of major stakeholders—customers, regulators, the media, employees, and, above all, shareholders and directors. The involvement of all parts of the company in this area is essential, since strong corporate performance means results that meet or exceed the stakeholders' expectations.

Basic issues in planning performance measurement

Neely et al. (2002) comment:

> Performance measurement is a topic that is often discussed but rarely defined. Literally it is the process of quantifying past action, where measurement is the process of quantification and past action determines current performance.

The authors continue by making an essential point:

> Organisations achieve their defined objectives – that is, they perform – by satisfying their stakeholders' and their own wants and needs with greater efficiency and effectiveness than their competitors.

This is a valuable contribution. Neely et al. are suggesting, as does Porter (1996), that performance planning and measurement occurs at two levels: a strategic level and an operational level. Strategic success requires *effective* planning and control, while operational success is achieved with *efficient* planning and control systems. The authors suggest that this perspective is helpful in identifying aspects of strategic decisions that are qualitative in their nature and influence, such as product/service reliability – an effectiveness metric. Efficiency measures are typically related to cost performance. And further, the authors identify the role of stakeholders, and the need to consider their roles and expectations, if both strategic and operational objectives are to be realised. They offer the basis for a working definition of a performance measurement system (based upon Neely et al. 2002):

> A performance measurement system enables informed decisions to be made and actions to be taken because it quantifies the effectiveness and the efficiency of past actions throughout the 'organisation' through the acquisition, collation, sorting, analysis and interpretation of appropriate data.

In their work in this area the authors suggest five criteria that any performance measurement approach should address:

- That there be a clear understanding of *who* the stakeholders are and *what* they require
- That the organisation establish and clearly articulate *what* it requires from its stakeholders
- That strategies that reflect the interests of all participants
- That processes are in place to ensure the 'organisation' can implement its strategies
- That capabilities facilitate the operation of the processes

Neely et al. discuss performance from a traditional corporate perspective, which requires to be modified to meet the needs of the organisation structures of the 'new economy'. Stakeholders become partners, and their requirements and their contributions become as central to the success of the 'organisation' as are those of the coordinator and visionary who may initiate the structure.

The notion of interrelated systems is not new. Koch (1994) refers to the role of information technology and its ability to span corporate boundaries, necessitating a review of inter-organisational structures and relationships.

Well before the IT revolution, thought was being given to the *functional* aspects of distribution versus the view that considers distribution as an activity performed by a number of *institutions*. Intermediaries are seen as system functionaries, their designations are incidental: 'what is critical is the system design through which functions can best be performed' (Dommermuth and Andersen 1969). The impact of information systems extends beyond distribution channels (as suggested by Short and Venkatraman 1992) and now has an impact across entire operational processes. Thus their comment concerning the impact of information systems, that '[they can] redefine market boundaries, alter the fundamental rules and basis of competition, redefine business scope, and provide a new set of competitive weapons', is particularly relevant. Add to this the idea that just as importantly, they change the emphasis in inter-organisational relations from *separation* to *unification* (Stern et al. 1996), and the contention that inter-organisational functions and processes are becoming increasingly integrated leads to a significant role for strategic operations management.

The growth of 'virtual organisations' has added emphasis to the need for a strategic perspective. Oates (1998) discusses outsourcing in the context of virtual organisations. He refers to a contribution by Moran (in a *Daily Telegraph* supplement on outsourcing, 28 May 1997) to the effect that outsourcing was no longer seen as 'a way to reduce costs, it is now perceived as a route to improve business performance and competitive strength'. Oates also refers to a survey by Andersen Consulting, aimed at finding out what 350 executives expected their companies to look like in 2010. Comments regarding outsourcing suggest that cost reduction remains as a prime motivating force, but six other reasons were offered:

- To improve overall business performance
- To sharpen business focus
- For accessing external skills
- For improving quality and efficiency of the outsourced process
- To achieve competitive advantage
- To create new revenue sources

These benefits are often more easily realisable through virtual organisation structures (Beech 1998):

> Rather than owning assets, companies look to outsource functions to achieve a high level of flexibility in providing services. There is a shift in focus to communication and linkages between the various outsourced functions and distributed assets.

The organisation extends its interest and influence into developing and managing networks of logically related assets (the virtual organisation). The owners of the processes clearly have their own objectives.

Performance measurement in 'new economy' organisations: the 'performance prism'

Neely et al. (2002) have developed an approach to performance planning and measurement that addresses the expanding spectrum of stakeholders. A review of recent business trends by the authors leads them to conclude:

> The point is that the only way sustainable way of delivering shareholder value in the 21st century is to deliver stakeholder value and this means enhancing, maintaining and defending the company's reputation on a broad range of fronts.

Neely et al. suggest that the 'demands' made on organisations are in fact two-way. While the stakeholders seek to improve their 'lot' through more 'profitable' relationships (looking for closer and longer relationships, not simply increased profitability and productivity), organisations are beginning to programme and structure their expectations of stakeholders. The authors identify typical contributions expected of stakeholders:

- Investors: capital for growth, assume more risk and long-term support
- Customers: profitable and long-term loyalty, feedback
- Intermediaries: planning and forecasting, inventory management
- Employees: flexibility, multi-skilling, anti-social hours, loyalty
- Suppliers: increased customisation, total solutions, integration
- Regulators: cross-border consistency, advice, involvement, grants and aid
- Communities: skilled employment pools
- Pressure groups: closer cooperation, shared research
- Alliance partners: co-development, co-productivity, shared information and shared costs

Clearly the inter-relationships between stakeholder and organisation are becoming structured as corporate boundaries reach beyond their legal entities and become inter-organisational. Neely and his colleagues conclude that:

> Indeed the very concept of stakeholder value itself should perhaps be quantified in terms of the strength of the interrelationship.

Value led management

As we saw in Chapter 1, corporate structures (as well as decision making processes) and corporate behaviour are changing dramatically and rapidly. Davidow and Malone (1992) suggest:

> The complex product-markets of the twenty first century will demand the ability to deliver, quickly and globally a high variety of customised

products. These products will be differentiated not only by form and function, but also by the services provided with the product, including the ability for the customer to be involved in the design of the product ... a manufacturing company will not be an isolated facility in production, but rather a node in the complex network of suppliers, customers, engineering and other 'service' functions.

And:

... profound changes are expected for the company's distribution system and its internal organisation as they evolve to become more customer driven and customer managed. On the upstream side of the firm, supplier networks will have to be integrated with those of customers often to the point where the customer will share its equipment, designs, trade secrets and confidences with those suppliers. Obviously, suppliers will become very dependent upon their downstream customers; but by the same token customers will be equally trapped by their suppliers. In the end, unlike its contemporary predecessors, the virtual corporation will appear less a discrete enterprise and more an ever-varying cluster of common activities in the midst of a vast fabric of relationships.

And again:

The challenge posed by this business revolution argues that corporations that expect to remain competitive must achieve mastery of both information and relationships.

And later, Pebler (2000) comments:

The virtual enterprise of the future will be much more dynamic and sensitive to the need for tuning operational parameters of the enterprise as a whole, including capital spending for both producers and service companies, optimising the whole chain of value creation. The future world will be characterised by knowledge management and collaborative decision-making by way of virtual teams. Virtual enterprises will be empowered by a willingness to do business in more productive ways and by information technologies that eliminate barriers between stakeholders and radically improve work processes.

Clearly the way in which we measure performance needs to be reviewed in light of these changes.

Neely et al. (2002) argue that the 'balanced scorecard' focuses on financials, customers, internal processes, plus innovation and learning. In doing so it downplays the importance of many of the stakeholders. As discussed earlier, it can be modified to do so. They also consider the strengths and weaknesses of other models. The 'business excellence' model takes a broader view of performance and considers a wider set of stakeholders, 'but also contains a host of dimensions that are effectively unmeasurable'. Similar comments are made concerning the Baldrige Award and others yet to be implemented. Neely et al. conclude that 'they are all partial or point solutions, offering insights into some of the dimensions of performance that should be measured and managed, but by no means all of them'. They suggest the 'performance prism' rectifies this shortcoming by integrating the strengths and weaknesses of them all, thereby 'offering a more comprehensive and comprehensible framework'.

It is safe to assume that an inter-organisational approach to strategy will differ from that of a single company working with (and recognising the needs and contributions of) its stakeholders. And here another assumption: given the dynamic nature of value in many industries, the most likely 'common denominator' will be cash flow. Margins are changing as both value and profit migrate (Gadiesh and Gilbert 1998). It follows that the success of the virtual organisation and of its component partners is more readily measured in the overall *free cash flow* generated. To calculate this we need to consider the additional funding required by the business if it is to achieve its objectives. This will consist of equity and/or debt combinations. This introduces not only the cost considerations but also the perceptions of risk that the 'market' may assume, and issues of corporate control. The 'value of the business' then becomes the value of the free cash flow at a discount rate that is judged to be appropriate in reflecting this risk. These levels of cash flow form an important feature of Figure 10.1.

Figure 10.1 links strategies to objectives. Given the assumption that free cash flow is the primary objective of the virtual organisation, the figure first identifies the components of this primary objective. The model uses the principle of the Dupont model, that there are links between profitability management, productivity management and financial management; and further, these links can be used to explore the options available to the organisation to maximise free cash flow. The primary strategies that will drive the organisation towards meeting its free cash flow objective are product-market development, customer retention, customer attraction and improved operational efficiency.

Planning and performance: a 'new economy' total organisation perspective

Given the changes in strategy and structure perspective, it follows that neither the 'balanced scorecard' nor the 'performance prism' offer precisely the approach needed to plan and measure performance in the virtual communities that are beginning to become a feature of many sectors. The 'inter-related approach' of Kaplan and Norton (1992) and the 'stakeholder approach' of Neely et al. (2002) can be combined into a performance planning and measurement mode. Figure 10.2 presents a framework for the model. It extends the Neely et al. model by adding structure and asset base decisions. Both are justified by the composition of the virtual organisation model, which works on the premise that it is *managing* assets rather than *owning* assets that has impact on performance (Normann 2001). The overriding purpose of any business organisation is for it to increase its 'value' to its owners. The ownership may be diversified. This does not detract

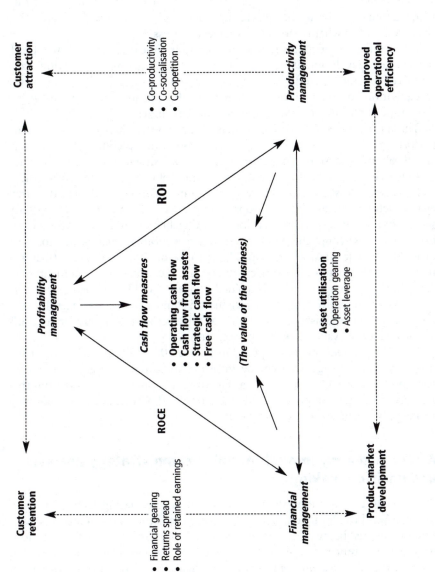

Customer attraction

Customer retention

- Co-producitivity
- Co-socialisation
- Co-opetition

Profitability management

Productivity management

ROI

Cash flow measures
- **Operating cash flow**
- **Cash flow from assets**
- **Strategic cash flow**
- **Free cash flow**

(The value of the business)

ROCE

Asset utilisation
- Operation gearing
- Asset leverage

- Financial gearing
- Returns spread
- Role of retained earnings

Financial management

Improved operational efficiency

Product-market development

Figure 10.1 Integrating the objectives and strategies

from the primary requirement: without ongoing financial success the survival of the organisation is under threat. Accordingly the purpose of the organisation is to increase the NPV of the free cash flow generated. This can only be achieved if the stakeholder expectations are met *and if* the stakeholders make the necessary contributions. These are suggested in Figure 10.2 and include capital for growth, long-term loyalty, feedback, and 'solutions', together with a shared view of success and of what is required to achieve success.

In the selection of appropriate strategies, four basic ones are essential: product-market development; customer retention; customer attraction, and improved operational efficiency. These strategies ensure the growth of the 'organisation' by maintaining growth from the existing business but at the same time exploring and exploiting new opportunities.

The appropriate structure is also essential. The concern here is not simply with performance; it is also focused on qualitative issues such as control, commitment and flexibility. Decisions on performance options should only be made when there is a clear agreement on the terms of value delivery set by the customer.

Processes are essential, too. Processes are 'strategy facilitators'. Unless the 'strategy- structure- process fit' is appropriate, it has been found that the long-term success of the organisation is very doubtful. Capabilities 'underwrite' the success of the processes in implementing strategy. There is another issue: the development of an asset base from which the capabilities can be developed. Kay (2000) argues that the development of a strong capability base is essential if the momentum of competitive advantage is to be maintained. Indeed it could be argued that neglect can lead to competitive rigidities, which in turn eliminate any advantages that may once have been established. It follows that the asset portfolio must be regularly monitored for relevance as well as performance.

Performance metrics are proposed in Figure 10.3. Empirical evidence from ongoing research suggests that the measures indicated are typical. Some are new and some are difficult to obtain. However, a number of organisations that are becoming increasingly involved in alliances and partnerships are beginning to adopt both the structure and the metrics.

A 'new economy' model for value chain strategy analysis and decision making

Earlier chapters have identified a number of differentiating factors between the 'new' and the 'old' economies. One of these is the shift of emphasis away from profit as being the primary financial objective, towards cash flow. Another difference is the point referred to earlier, made by Normann (2001), that it is *managing* assets rather than *owning* them that has impact on performance. And a third factor concerns the increasing role of knowledge management, technology management, relationship management and process management in the creation of competitive advantage within the industry value chain structure. Given these factors (and clearly they are not the only differences), a planning model should include these considerations. Figure 10.4 represents a planning model that incorporates these features and

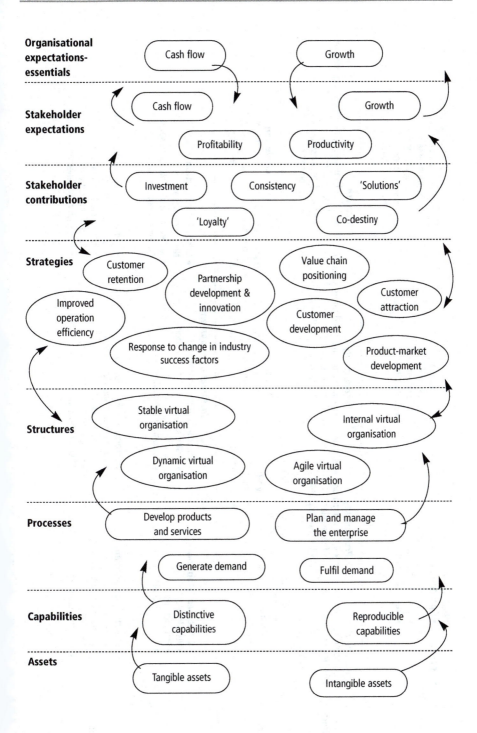

Figure 10.2 Planning and performance: a 'new economy' perspective

The 'enterprise' perspective of performance

Clash flow
- Operative cash flow
- Cash flow from assets
- Strategic cash flow
- Free cash flow

Growth
Comparative:
- Key indicators
- Product-market
- Competitor

Financial involvement
- Share of investment
- Share of assets
- Share of revenues
- Share of profits
- Share of cash flow

Stakeholder expectations

Investment
- Economic cash flow
- Share price appreciation
- Dividend growth

Profitability
- Profit margin on current and future sales
- Long-term profitability

Productivity
- Ratio of current and future sales to total assets
- Long-term productivity

Growth
- Ratio of 'business growth rate to growth rate of the 'market'
- Ratio of 'business' growth rate to growth rate of competitors

---

Stakeholder contributions

Investment
- Capital for growth
- Assume risk

'Loyalty'
- Support
- Commitment

'Solutions'
- Co-productivity
- Co-option

Consistency
- Conformity
- QC

Co-destiny
- Cooperation
- Co-specialisation
- Learning

Customer retention
- Visits/orders
- Transactions
- 'Loyalty'-T/O rate

Customer development

Customer penetration
- Customer purchases/ total customer purchases
- Customer relationship 'quality'

Customer attraction
- New customer accounts
- % New customer sales/total sales
- Customer from competitors

Strategies

Value chain positioning
- Innovator
- Integrator and coordinator
- Specialist
- Infrastructure provider

Partnership innovation
Shared benefits and shared costs
- Product development
- Process development
- Service development

Product-market development
- NPD and patents
- % new product/total sales
- Share of market value
- Free cash flow generated

Improved operational efficiency
- Operations capacity
- Value analysis   Working capital
- Operating cycle

Response to change in industry success factors
- Technology strategy • Knowledge management strategy
- Relationship management strategy
- Process management strategy

Structures

Stable virtual organisations
- No of O/S suppliers
- Length of p'ships
- Cash flows

Dynamic virtual organisations
- No of new partners
- No of new ventures
- **Cash flows**

Agile virtual organisations
- No of new ventures
- No of temporary partnerships

Internal virtual organisations
- Financial
- Time
- Customer loyalty

Processes

Develop products and services
- Sales from new products & services
- Time-to-market
- Budget performance

Generate demand
- Response rates
- No of proposals/enquiries
- Level of investment in new/improved products

Fulfil demand
- On-time deliveries
- OCLT performance
- Inventory performance
- Returns

Plan and manage enterprise
- Product/service fulfilment
- Demand generation
- Time-to market
- Cash flows

Capabilities

Distinctive capabilities
'Value' generated from:
- R & D • Brands
- 'Relationships'
- Knowledge and processes

Reproducible capabilities
'Value' generated from:
- Out sourced components and services

Assets
- NPV of free cash flow
- Return on assets
- Return on equity
- Relevance

Figure 10.3 Setting performance measures for a 'new economy' organisation

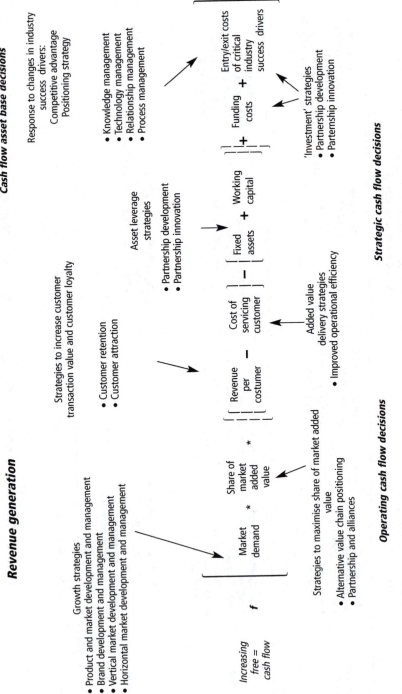

Figure 10.4 A 'new economy' model for value chain strategy analysis and decision making

offers an opportunity for alternative value chain structures to explore structural and relationship options, using free cash flow as an overall performance metric.

It will be observed that in order to evaluate the alternatives, the figure includes the four other components of the cash flow model introduced earlier. To explore the revenue generation options, market demand and share of market added value are explored. As the task concerns future planning, it is necessary to forecast market demand and the alternative values of the share of market added value that alternative strategies and structures offer. The model links these with the strategy options that will influence these outcomes, that is, product-market development and customer attraction (growth strategies) and changes in value chain positioning (strategies to maximise share of market added value). It may be recalled that comments made by the CEO of Millennium (Champion 2001) argued that value migration was directing them to move down the value chain into the production and marketing processes in order to maintain their growth performance level..

Operating cash flow decisions concern customer interactions and transactions. Customers' level of loyalty is another obvious influence, and therefore alternative customer retention and customer attraction strategies, to increase customer transaction values and customer loyalty, together with improvements in operational efficiency (added value delivery strategies), need to be evaluated. The expansion of FMCG multiple retailers into non-food product groups and service products is an example of customer retention and attraction. In Case Study 9.1 in Chapter 9, we met the planned launch of a film (movie) downloading service by the UK retailer Tesco.

Partnership innovation is becoming an important feature in the growth of strategies to develop cash flow from asset base decisions. In Australia, both of the leading supermarket chains have followed the same pattern of partnership innovation to introduce petrol sales into their merchandise mix. Woolworths was first to do so with a European approach in which it sold Woolworths branded petrol from its existing sites, together with a few freestanding locations. Coles entered the market by acquiring a number of Shell locations in New South Wales and Victoria but maintained the Shell brand. Subsequently Woolworths followed a similar pattern by working with Caltex. This is an example of asset leverage strategies in which leverage is exerted on both the tangible and intangible assets of a partner.

Partnership development is an example of an 'investment' strategy. We saw in Chapter 8 that GM and Ford are collaboratively developing a six-speed automatic transmission for front-wheel-drive vehicles. Other projects typically match non-core, but essential processes. Timken and SKF, bearing manufacturers, share logistics and e-business activities. Panasonic and Hitachi are collaborating to develop and expand the worldwide market for plasma TVs.

Reviewing the changes occurring in the relative importance of industry success drivers has implications for strategies based upon strategic cash flow decisions. In previous chapters the views of Mark Levin, CEO of Millennium, were cited. Millennium sees problems with the current structure of its industry, particularly as the profitable areas of the value chain are not in the R&D

process alone. Levin suggests the future instead lies in personalised medicine, involving knowledge and technology based industry drivers: 'One day, everyone will have their own genomes mapped out and stored in memory chips, and doctors will look at the information in those chips and prescribe accordingly.' A strategy to achieve this goal is based on extending the alliance and partnership models that have proven to be successful for Millennium. He suggested that Millennium will emerge with a strong position in the industry value chain based on this networked R&D.

Value chain planning considerations

Achieving 'fit' with relevant partners

We have often made reference to the idea that resources are to be managed, not necessarily owned; this is an important consideration when considering performance planning in the value chain. Figure 10.5 extends the discussion by posing questions concerning the resource requirements for customer value delivery. What are the process, capability and asset requirements? What are the costs? What are the options? And what are the risks?

McKinsey has been researching the advantages and disadvantages of partnership arrangements. There are some interesting findings and these have implications for the topics discussed.

Hagel (2004) identifies a number of advantages that partnerships offer. Hagel focuses on offshore in an overseas context; however, the principles of 'offshoring' are equally applicable to relationships with domestic partners/suppliers. The 'real' issue becomes one of what is required to deliver customer value. Hagel argues that the decision should extend beyond cost advantages to include distinctive skills, capabilities, and high-performance processes. It follows that all three have implications for investment and therefore for assets. Hagel offers an array of examples across product and service fields. Some striking examples of cost and performance advantages are cited. For example, eTelecare, a Philippines based call centre company, has a number of major US organisations as customers. One customer reported that it took eTelecare 25 per cent less time to handle incoming calls than it took its own call centre or others that it had used. Another customer, a leading US electronics firm, found that eTelecare's handling time for technical support to end-users was almost 40 and 16 per cent less than that of its own US and its Indian call centres respectively. Another US electronics organisation found that manufacturing technology tripled, and order cycle times and defect rates were lower, after moving its manufacturing operations into Asia.

Hagel is suggesting that there is evidence that a number of companies (and countries) are extending their 'competitive advantage' beyond the simple cost advantage to offer expertise in process design rather than product design, and are developing world class expertise in specific technologies. Organisation structures are often quite different. Thus eTelecare invests heavily in recruitment and training supervisory staff. Their operational structure suggests

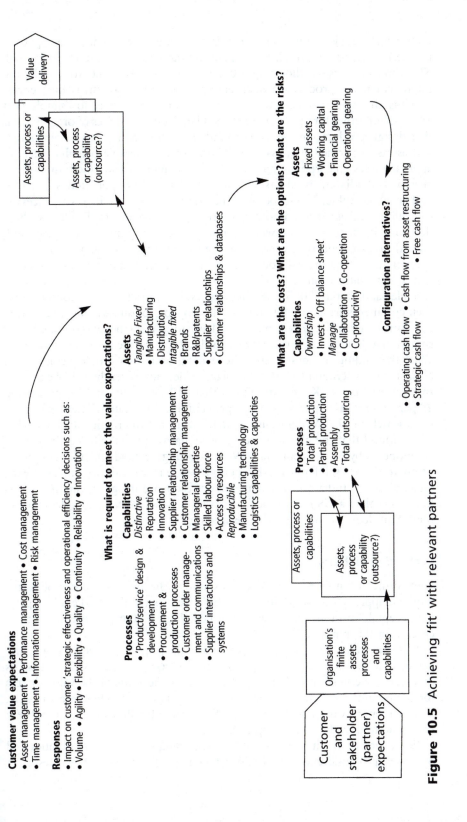

Customer value expectations
- Asset management • Peformance management • Cost management
- Time management • Information management • Risk management

Responses
- Impact on customer 'strategic effectiveness and operational efficiency' decisions such as:
- Volume • Agility • Flexibility • Quality • Continuity • Reliability • Innovation

What is required to meet the value expectations?

Processes
- 'Product/service' design & development
- Procurement & production processes
- Customer order management and communications
- Supplier interactions and systems

Capabilities
Distinctive
- Reputation
- Innovation
- Supplier relationship management
- Customer relationship management
- Managerial expertise
- Skilled labour force
- Access to resources

Reproducibile
- Manufacturing technology
- Logistics capabilities & capacities

Assets
Tangible Fixed
- Manufacturing
- Distribution

Intagible fixed
- Brands
- R&B/patents
- Supplier relationships
- Customer relationships & databases

What are the costs? What are the options? What are the risks?

Processes
- 'Total' production
- Partial production
- Assembly
- 'Total' outsourcing

Capabilities
Ownership
- Invest • 'Off balance sheet'
Manage
- Collabotation • Co-opetition
- Co-producivity

Assets
- Fixed assets
- Working capital
- Financial gearing
- Operational gearing

Configuration alternatives?
- Operating cash flow • Cash flow from asset restructuring
- Strategic cash flow • Free cash flow

Assets, process or capabilities

Assets, process or capability (outsource?)

Value delivery

Assets, process or capabilities

Assets, process or capability (outsource?)

Customer and stakeholder (partner) expectations

Organisation's finite assets processes and capabilities

Figure 10.5 Achieving 'fit' with relevant partners

higher costs; eTelecare has one supervisor for eight staff members as opposed to one for twenty in a similar US operation; however their duties differ, with eTelecare supervisors allocating 10 per cent of their time to developing improvements to processes. Hagel reports significant productivity differences.

Thus the approach becomes one of looking not merely for simple cost savings, but rather for opportunity costs. Hagel gives examples of organisations that design products and services round the identified processes, capabilities and assets of partner organisations. There are considerable benefits. Such an approach frees up corporate resources to focus on developing the business into current and adjacent products and markets that offer opportunities to create higher added value. It also permits the company to apply its own processes, capabilities and assets to reinforcing current product-markets. The key to these decisions is, first, to know what resource mix is required to be successful; second, to ascertain the ownership of the various resources; and third, to be a competent integrator and coordinator in the design and management of a competitive value chain.

Bailey and Farrell (2005) identified issues that impact the US economy (and their comments are applicable to other developed economies), but suggest that the current negative effects may well have long-term benefits because they should enable national organisations to develop new technologies and ideas. What the findings suggest is that the benefits and costs should be appraised against the 'fit' criteria to ensure a balanced decision is reached. For example, they report that a UK bank has found that its Indian call centre is processing 20 per cent more transactions, and 3 per cent more accurately. They also report on research by the Washington based Institute for International Economics, which found that the global sourcing of IT hardware has reduced the cost of components by 30 per cent since 1995, boosting demand and adding considerably to the US GDP during that period. Trade in services has similar effects; a technician in India can read a magnetic-resonance-imaging scan at a much lower cost than a US medical technician. While this creates unemployment in the US, it does expand life saving technologies.

Evaluating viability

Some difficult but far reaching decisions follow. Having identified an opportunity that appears feasible (customer acceptance), its viability (stakeholder partner acceptability) remains to be established. Figure 10.6 proposes a series of criteria for this purpose.

Customer value response expectations and the response expected from partner stakeholders form a starting point. The exercise continues with an analysis of a series of criteria aimed at identifying the implications of the value drivers for the potential structure of the value chain partnership. These are strategic, financial, operational, and relationship 'fit' criteria. It will be recalled that these criteria were introduced in Chapter 8.

'Strategic criteria fit' explores issues concerning core assets, capabilities and processes and considers the implications, for competitive advantage, of investment

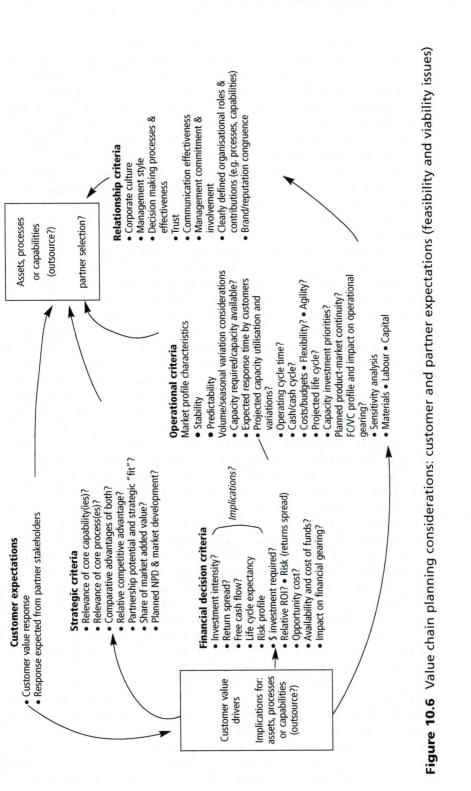

Customer expectations

● Customer value response
● Response expected from partner stakeholders

Assets, processes
or capabilities
(outsource?)

partner selection?

Relationship criteria

● Corporate culture
● Management style
● Decision making processes & effectiveness
● Trust
● Communication effectiveness
● Management commitment & involvement
● Clearly defined organisational roles & contributions (e.g. prcesses, capabilities)
● Brand/reputation congruence

Strategic criteria

● Relevance of core capability(ies)?
● Relevance of core process(es)?
● Comparative advantages of both?
● Relative competitive advantage?
● Partnership potential and strategic "fit"?
● Share of market added value?
● Planned NPD & market development?

Operational criteria

Market profile characteristics
● Stability
● Predictability
Volume/seasonal variation considerations
● Capacity required/capacity available?
● Expected response time by customers
● Projected capacity utilisation and variations?
● Operating cycle time?
● Cash/cash cycle?
● Costs/budgets ● Flexibility? ● Agility?
● Projected life cycle?
● Capacity investment priorities?
Planned product-market continuity?
FC/VC profile and impact on operational gearing?
● Sensitivity analysis
● Materials ● Labour ● Capital

Financial decision criteria

● Investment intensity?
● Return spread?
● Free cash flow?
● Life cycle expectancy
● Risk profile
● $ investment required?
● Relative ROI? ● Risk (returns spread)
● Opportunity cost?
● Availability and cost of funds?
● Impact on financial gearing?

Implications?

Customer value
drivers

Implications for:
assets, processes
or capabilities
(outsource?)

Figure 10.6 Value chain planning considerations: customer and partner expectations (feasibility and viability issues)

and ownership alternatives. The questions asked will include how the options will respond to specific strategic concerns such as time-to-market responses and similar strategically critical requirements. 'Financial criteria fit' seeks to maximise the free cash flow that will be available from the alternative structures. Questions will include considerations of both return and risk profiles – where they occur and the equity of their spread. 'Operational criteria fit' seeks to ensure the viability issues. These, as can be seen from Figure 10.6, are extensive. 'Relationship criteria fit' concerns important qualitative issues such as the willingness of various partners to accept a specific role within the value chain, and the important concerns of matching management cultures and styles into a cohesive decision making set.

The 'viability' concern should involve a close consideration of costs. Very little has been written concerning cost management in value chain/virtual organisation models. However, there are some significant issues that should be addressed. Shank and Govindarajan's (1993) contribution is based upon the Porter value chain framework comparing it with their view of a value added approach. They argue that Porter's value chain approach is external to the firm, 'seeing each firm in the context of the overall chain of value-creating activities of which it is only a part, from basic raw components to end-use consumers'. The value added approach, they argue (which for them commences with purchases and ends with sales), has the 'key theme' of maximising the difference (the value added) between purchases and sales. The difference here is not so much the 'from/to perspective'; rather it is their definition of value and of the parties involved. The current perspective of value concerns the benefits delivered and the costs of acquiring those benefits (the concept of value-in-use), and it considers *all* stakeholder parties involved – customers, suppliers, employees, investors, and so on. Furthermore, if the logic of value chain analysis is accepted (that is, that it optimises both the value delivered and the costs of delivery, and therefore the organisational architecture options), these criticisms are no longer relevant.

Shank and Govindarajan also use Porter's strategy model to identify the importance of strategic alternatives as regards aspects of cost management, citing work by Gupta and Govindarajan (1984) and Govindarajan (1986). They identify significant differences in the approach to costing issues as between differentiation and cost leadership strategies. These are useful but tend to be intuitive and rather limited. What is much more helpful is the attention they draw to the need to look beyond the simple models of microeconomics for input and to consider the broader models provided by the economics of organisation. They suggest that there are structural cost drivers, basing these on the work of Scherer (1988), and executional cost drivers, based on Riley (1987).

Structural cost drivers include scale, scope, experience, technology and complexity. Executional cost drivers include workforce participation, total quality management, capacity utilisation, plant layout efficiency, product configuration, and the 'exploitation' (optimisation) of supplier and customer linkages within the value chain. It is interesting to note that for both the structural and the executional cost drivers, linkages with the industry drivers (knowledge, technology, relationship and process management expertise) can be found). Shank and Govindarajan suggest that changes in volume are of less relevance to strategic cost analysis than consideration of how the cost position is influenced by the firm's comparative position on the various drivers that are relevant in its competitive situation.

Clearly there are other important considerations and Figure 10.7 identifies an approach to analysing these. It is important to begin by identifying the customer and stakeholder partners' value drivers. In Figure 10.7 these are taken from the previous discussions on both topics. Two other components for the analysis are important. Investment and risk alternatives consider the impact of the value delivery options on working capital and tangible and intangible fixed assets. Working capital considerations identify the efficiencies of inventory management (amounts, locations, ownership costs). Tangible fixed asset concerns are based upon the ownership and utilisation of operations facilities. Issues that impact on costs are capability relevance (that is, whether the value can be delivered at an acceptable level of costs), risk of obsolescence due to technology dynamics, and financial performance. Intangible fixed asset concerns are focused on market acceptability of the value offer, time-to-market, the implications of intellectual property (IP) ownership rights, and again, financial performance.

Cost driver analysis is based upon a modified view of the Shank and Govindarajan approach. As Figure 10.7 suggests, structural cost drivers are based upon a more recent view of the economics of production, relevant to the asset leverage approach favoured by current value chain thinking. Economies of scale and scope, while remaining important, are complemented (and in some installations may be supplemented) by economies of differentiation, integration, design, and process. Explanations of these are given in the diagram. Operational cost driver analysis is based upon the economics of coordination (interactions and transactions); the application of total quality management (TQM) techniques to manage output at an acceptable level of quality that in turn responds to customer value expectations; infrastructure economies of scale; procurement economies (the use of buying exchanges and e-auctions), and partnership economies (the cost-efficient management of partners in order to meet customer value expectations at optimal costs and with an acceptable level of market added value).

The argument throughout this text has been that value delivery is a process that results from an understanding of the demand chain that is relevant to the target customer segment and from a structured response through a customised or dedicated supply chain. This approach is extended into the consideration of added value in the value chain, the identification and location of fixed and variable costs, and cash flow analysis and management.

Customer added value in the value chain

Figure 10.8 identifies the potential opportunities to add value in the value chain by meeting identified customer value drivers. The example given is hypothetical but suggests a process in which opportunities are sought to meet the

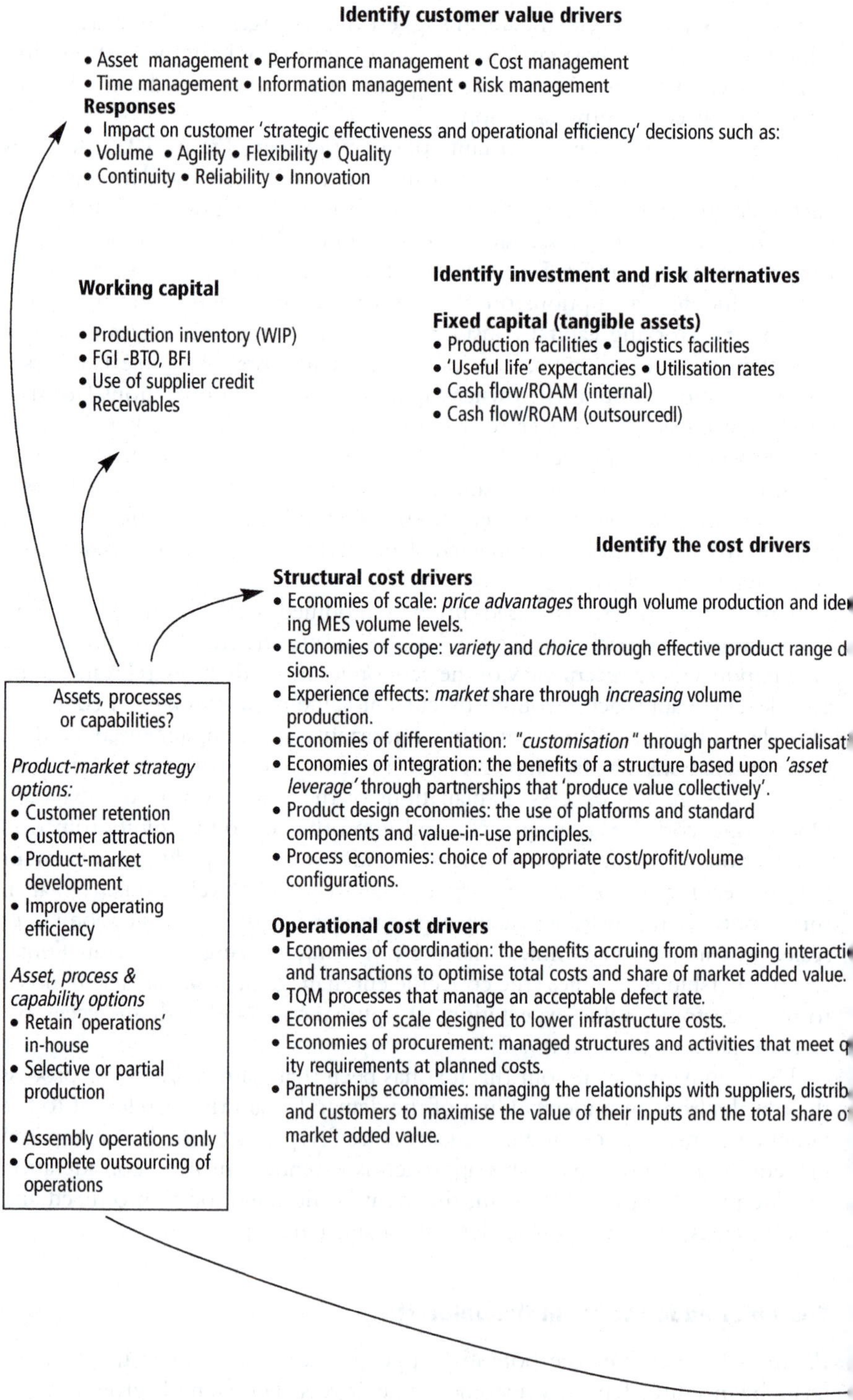

Identify customer value drivers

• Asset management • Performance management • Cost management
• Time management • Information management • Risk management
Responses
  • Impact on customer 'strategic effectiveness and operational efficiency' decisions such as:
  • Volume • Agility • Flexibility • Quality
  • Continuity • Reliability • Innovation

Working capital

• Production inventory (WIP)
• FGI -BTO, BFI
• Use of supplier credit
• Receivables

Identify investment and risk alternatives

Fixed capital (tangible assets)
• Production facilities • Logistics facilities
• 'Useful life' expectancies • Utilisation rates
• Cash flow/ROAM (internal)
• Cash flow/ROAM (outsourcedl)

Identify the cost drivers

Structural cost drivers
• Economies of scale: *price advantages* through volume production and ide∎ing MES volume levels.
• Economies of scope: *variety* and *choice* through effective product range d∎sions.
• Experience effects: *market* share through *increasing* volume production.
• Economies of differentiation: *"customisation"* through partner specialisat▪
• Economies of integration: the benefits of a structure based upon *'asset leverage'* through partnerships that 'produce value collectively'.
• Product design economies: the use of platforms and standard components and value-in-use principles.
• Process economies: choice of appropriate cost/profit/volume configurations.

Assets, processes
or capabilities?

Product-market strategy options:
• Customer retention
• Customer attraction
• Product-market development
• Improve operating efficiency

Asset, process & capability options
• Retain 'operations' in-house
• Selective or partial production

• Assembly operations only
• Complete outsourcing of operations

Operational cost drivers
• Economies of coordination: the benefits accruing from managing interacti▪ and transactions to optimise total costs and share of market added value.
• TQM processes that manage an acceptable defect rate.
• Economies of scale designed to lower infrastructure costs.
• Economies of procurement: managed structures and activities that meet q∎ity requirements at planned costs.
• Partnerships economies: managing the relationships with suppliers, distrib▪ and customers to maximise the value of their inputs and the total share o▪ market added value.

Figure 10.7 Match the 'drivers' with investment and cost issues

Fixed capital (intangible assets)
- R & D/patents • Brands
- Supplier relationships
- Customer relationships
- Knowledge based systems/IP
- Process R & D • Life expectancies
- Leverage opportunities
- Cash flow/ROAM (internal)
- Cash flow/ROAM (outsourcedl)

Assets, processes
or capabilities?

(Outsource?)

Identify stakeholder partner value drivers
Investment
- Economic cash flow • Share price appreciation
- Dividend growth
Profitability
- Continuity of margin growth • ST & LT profitability
Productivity
- Balanced ratio of current & future sales to total assets
- LT productivity
Growth
- Balanced ratio of 'business' growth rate/market growth rate
- Comparative 'business' growth rate/competitors' growth rate

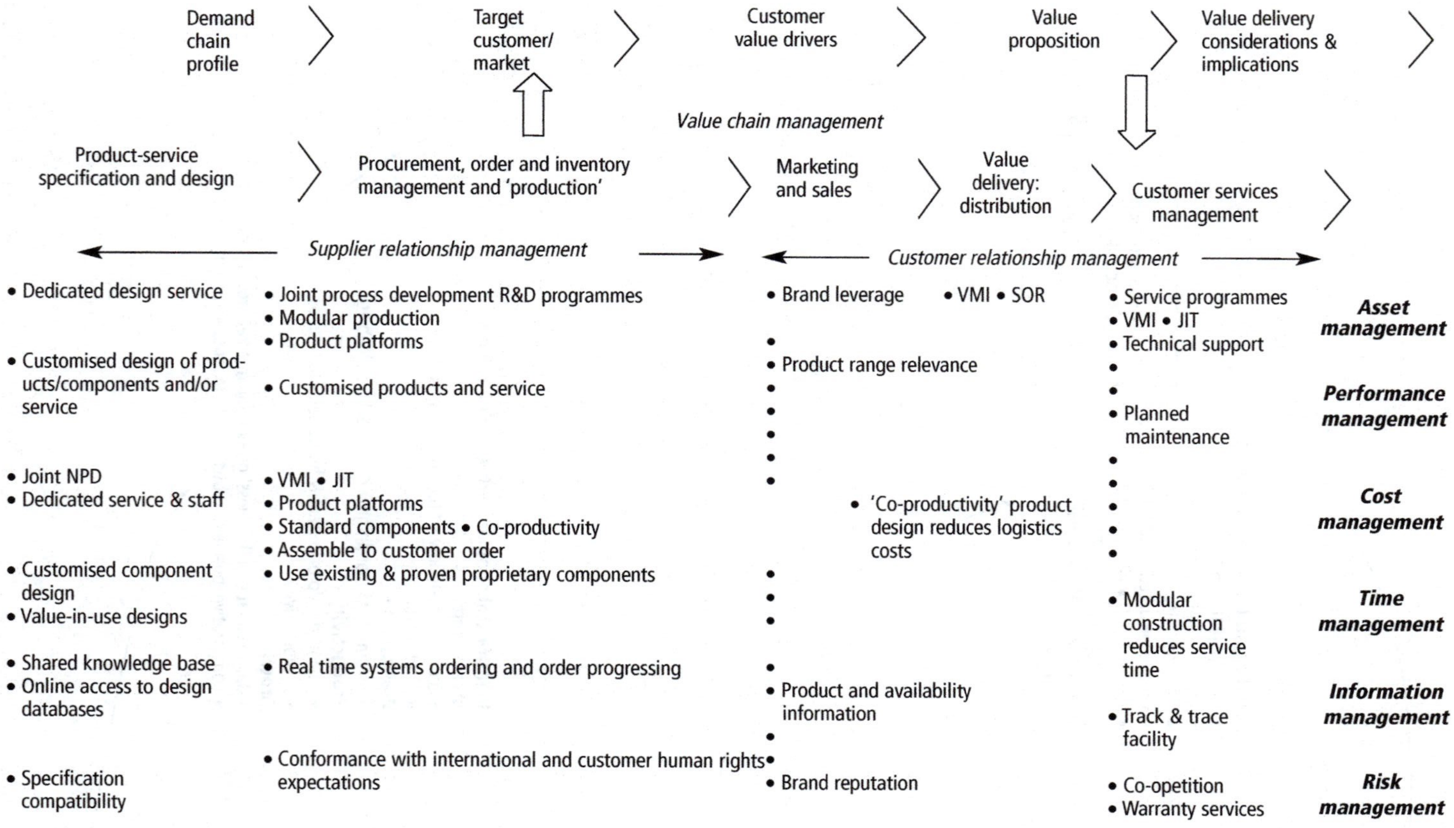

Value chain management

Value chain stages (top flow):
Demand chain profile → Target customer/market → Customer value drivers → Value proposition → Value delivery considerations & implications

Process stages:
Product-service specification and design → Procurement, order and inventory management and 'production' → Marketing and sales → Value delivery: distribution → Customer services management

Supplier relationship management → → *Customer relationship management*

Product-service specification and design
- Dedicated design service
- Customised design of products/components and/or service
- Joint NPD
- Dedicated service & staff
- Customised component design
- Value-in-use designs
- Shared knowledge base
- Online access to design databases
- Specification compatibility

Procurement, order and inventory management and 'production'
- Joint process development R&D programmes
- Modular production
- Product platforms
- Customised products and service
- VMI • JIT
- Product platforms
- Standard components • Co-productivity
- Assemble to customer order
- Use existing & proven proprietary components
- Real time systems ordering and order progressing
- Conformance with international and customer human rights expectations

Marketing and sales
- Brand leverage
- Product range relevance
- Product and availability information
- Brand reputation

Value delivery: distribution
- VMI • SOR
- 'Co-productivity' product design reduces logistics costs

Customer services management
- Service programmes
- VMI • JIT
- Technical support
- Planned maintenance
- Modular construction reduces service time
- Track & trace facility
- Co-opetition
- Warranty services

Management dimensions (right-hand column):
- *Asset management*
- *Performance management*
- *Cost management*
- *Time management*
- *Information management*
- *Risk management*

Figure 10.8 Identifying opportunities to add customer value in the value chain

value drivers. The objective should be to extend the competitive advantage of the value delivery system, not merely to meet levels of competitive necessity. By addressing specific value drivers it becomes possible to target the added value towards specific customer expectations.

Identifying fixed and variable costs

Value delivery activities involve costs. As we have seen, Shank and Govindarajan (1993) suggest that change in output volume is of less relevance to strategic cost analysis than consideration of how the cost position is influenced by the firm's comparative position on the various drivers that are relevant in its competitive situation. It follows that, having identified the customers' value drivers, the alternative organisational structures together with their costs must be identified. Figure 10.9 illustrates a likely structure of fixed and variable costs that will be necessary if the value proposition is to be delivered. Such analysis is useful later when the evaluation of structural options uses activity based management techniques to identify the activities that are responsible for generating costs.

Cash flow analysis

Cash flow analysis is an essential activity in value chain planning. It is helpful in identifying both effective structures and efficient ways and means of managing the value chain. Figure 10.10 uses the cash flow model introduced earlier to identify the assets, processes and activities involved in value identification, creation, production, communication, delivery and service maintenance. The model permits an evaluation of alternative structures, given customer and stakeholder partner expectations, together with the implications for cash flow performance. The analysis performed earlier (identifying cost structures) becomes a necessary input.

Performance planning: planning options and performance metrics

Planning and control should be integrated processes, rather than being sequential. This ensures that what is seen as a necessary objective will be measured appropriately; the metrics will match management's performance priorities. This approach also ensures that operational and strategic performance criteria are closely related.

The approach taken here is based upon the cash flow model developed earlier but repeated here for convenience. In Figure 10.11 the planning process is based upon achieving optimal free cash flow. It follows a model first advocated by Ansoff (1968). It will be recalled that Ansoff's planning matrix was based upon closing a planning gap, and the model was based upon minimising the risks by ensuring that opportunities to increase market penetration were first pursued, followed by product development, market development and then diversification.

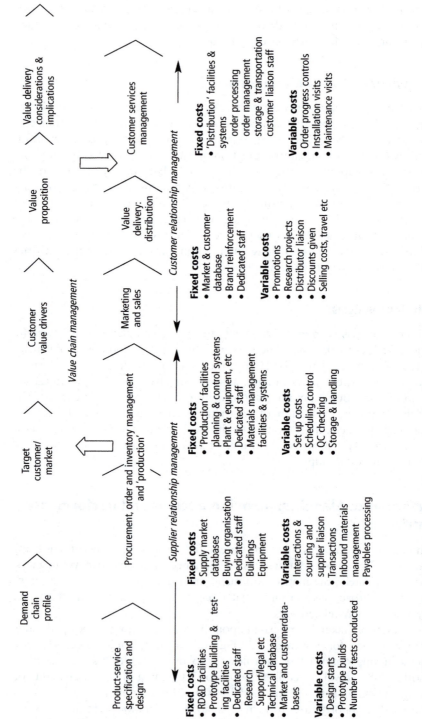

Figure 10.9 Identifying fixed and variable costs and their planning and performance implications

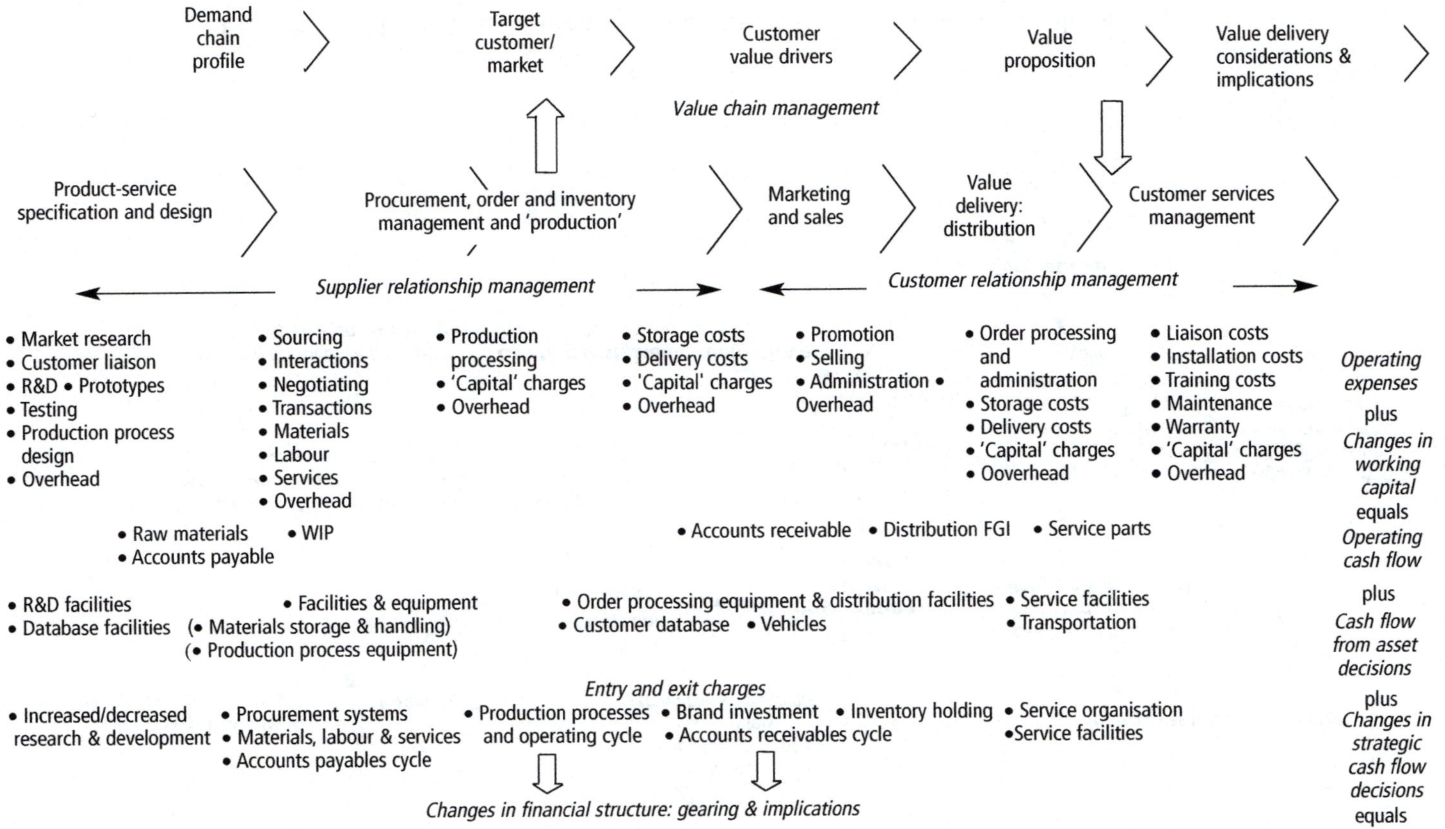

Figure 10.10 Value chain cash flow analysis: an operational perspective

Demand chain profile

Target customer/ market

Value proposition

Value delivery considerations & implications

Value chain management

Product-service specification and design

Procurement, order and inventory management and 'production'

Customer value drivers

Customer services management

Supplier relationship management

Customer relationship management

Marketing and sales

Value delivery: distribution

• Market research
• Customer liaison
• R&D • Prototypes
• Testing
• Production process design
• Overhead

• Sourcing
• Interactions
• Negotiating
• Transactions
• Materials
• Labour
• Services
• Overhead

• Production processing
• 'Capital' charges
• Overhead

• Storage costs
• Delivery costs
• 'Capital' charges
• Overhead

• Promotion
• Selling
• Administration
• Overhead

• Order processing and administration
• Storage costs
• Delivery costs
• 'Capital' charges
• Ooverhead

• Liaison costs
• Installation costs
• Training costs
• Maintenance
• Warranty
• 'Capital' charges
• Overhead

Operating expenses

plus

Changes in working capital

equals

Operating cash flow

• Raw materials • WIP
• Accounts payable

• Accounts receivable • Distribution FGI • Service parts

• R&D facilities
• Database facilities

• Facilities & equipment
(• Materials storage & handling)
(• Production process equipment)

• Order processing equipment & distribution facilities
• Customer database

• Service facilities
• Transportation

plus

Cash flow from asset decisions

Entry and exit charges

• Increased/decreased research & development

• Procurement systems
• Materials, labour & services
• Accounts payables cycle

• Production processes
• Production and operating cycle

• Brand investment
• Accounts receivables cycle

• Inventory holding
• Service organisation
• Service facilities

plus

Changes in strategic cash flow decisions

equals

Free cash flow

Changes in financial structure: gearing & implications

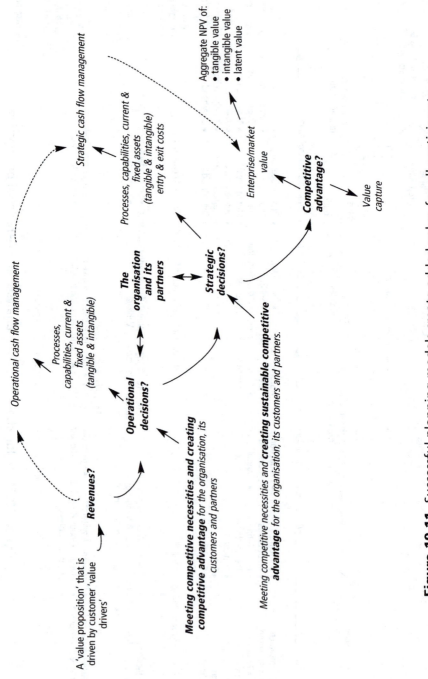

Figure 10.11 Successful planning models create added value for all participants

The argument offered by Ansoff was based on the logic that any planning for growth should focus first on products and/or markets that the organisation was familiar with, as these were likely to offer lower risk than growth strategies that required resources to expand into lesser known product-markets, or perhaps into completely unknown areas.

Figure 10.11 follows this approach but does so using cash flow as the primary business objective. Ansoff's original model was a single-organisation model, whereas the virtual approach is multi-organisational. The planning and control model developed here considers how performance can be improved by considering three horizons:

■ Operational alternatives and decisions
■ Restructuring assets to enhance cash flow and remain competitive
■ Alternatives for growth

Operational alternatives and decisions

An operational focus suggests that we are considering an option which requires a consolidation and productivity approach, or in the context of the Knight and Pretty (2000) risk management model, identifying growth opportunities from latent value. Essentially we are managing operational cash flow and the components that influence it and are influenced by it.

Figure 10.12a suggests the considerations that should comprise the decision making. An increase in operational cash flow is likely to be realised by making changes to the design of the existing product range, using value engineering techniques or perhaps standardising components. A review of the procurement activity may suggest advantages that are available if structural changes can be made, such as joint venture procurement with competitors to reduce the costs of inputs that have no appreciable impact on end product differentiation. A review of component input format may suggest ways and means of reducing the operating cycle (and the cash cycle). The location of work-in-progress (WIP) and finished inventories within supply and distribution processes in the supply chain may also offer additional opportunities. Decisions to improve working capital productivity are to be considered. Modifications to the use of inventory, and to management of supplier payables and customer receivables should be sought in order to improve the cash/cash cycle.

There are a number of control issues that have an influence on operational cash flow decisions. The impact on operational gearing (the fixed cost/variable cost structure) that results has implications for risk, particularly if major changes are made (such as a decision to outsource a larger proportion of the organisation's production outputs to a larger number of partners). Also to be considered are changes in supplier, distributor and customer relationships that may result from these operational changes.

The necessary performance measures for monitoring operating cash flow are suggested in Figure 10.12b. From the customer and the distributor perspectives we are attempting to maintain competitive necessity aspects of

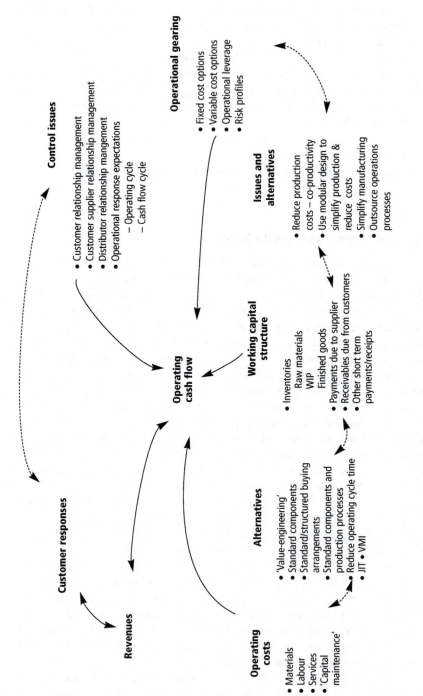

Figure 10.12a Operational alternative and decisions

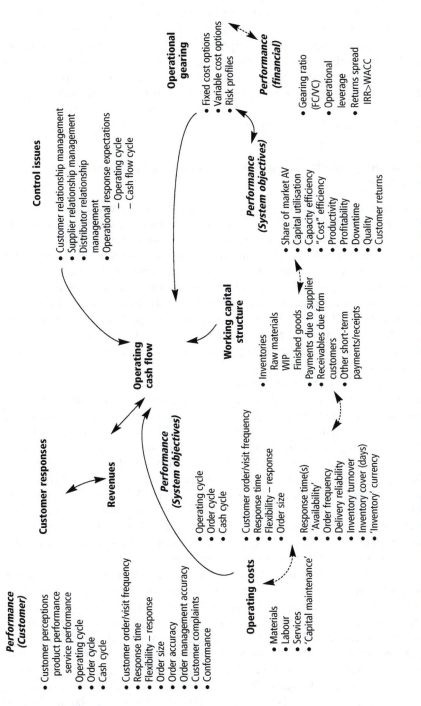

Figure 10.12b Operational alternatives: decisions and performance measures

Performance (Customer)

- Customer perceptions
  product performance
  service performance
- Operating cycle
- Order cycle
- Cash cycle
- Customer order/visit frequency
- Response time
- Flexibility – response
- Order size
- Order accuracy
- Order management accuracy
- Customer complaints
- Conformance

Customer responses

Revenues

Control issues

- Customer relationship management
- Supplier relationship management
- Distributor relationship management
- Operational response expectations
  – Operating cycle
  – Cash flow cycle

Operational gearing

- Fixed cost options
- Variable cost options
- Risk profiles

Performance (financial)

- Gearing ratio (FC/VC)
- Operational leverage
- Returns spread IRR>WACC

Operating cash flow

Working capital structure

Performance (System objectives)

- Share of market AV
- Capital utilisation
- Capacity efficiency
- "Cost" efficiency
- Productivity
- Profitability
- Downtime
- Quality
- Customer returns

- Inventories
  Raw materials
  WIP
  Finished goods
- Payments due to supplier
- Receivables due from customers
- Other short-term payments/receipts

Performance (System objectives)

- Operating cycle
- Order cycle
- Cash cycle

- Customer order/visit frequency
- Response time
- Flexibility – response
- Order size
- Response time(s)
- 'Availability'
- Order frequency
- Delivery reliability
- Inventory turnover
- Inventory cover (days)
- 'Inventory' currency

Operating costs

- Materials
- Labour
- Services
- 'Capital maintenance'

the value offer and perhaps develop some competitive advantage(s). The success of this will be demonstrated by the responses tracked in customer performance and system performance. But for the organisation the system performance outcomes that are important are the working capital measures and the financial performance measures. In other words, operational cash flow performance concerns meeting (or improving upon) customer product and service expectations, but, at the same time ensuring that share of market added value, capital and capacity efficiency metrics, and associated performance objectives are all met.

Restructuring assets to enhance cash flow while remaining competitive

Changing the asset structure of the business can have significant impact on its cash flow performance. Such changes require a longer time perspective on the individual organisation and its relationships with customers and stakeholder partners. Changes to both tangible and intangible fixed assets are likely to be far reaching. For example, there is a major shift towards producing all or large proportions of manufactured and service support outputs on a global basis. An increasing number of organisations are working with offshore partners in research and development. General Electric has established a 10,000-strong research facility in Bangalore, where 20 per cent of the activity is long-term conceptual research. India is also attracting large commitments for pharmaceutical research (Aldrick 2004).

These decisions have far reaching effects. They clearly have a major impact on short-term cash flow situations, particularly if the tangible assets are sold; but the long-term impact on costs and the delegation of control of the business to partner organisations must be explored. Figure 10.13a addresses these issues by identifying the important control issues that require decisions and the changes that may occur in the way in which the business operates with its partner organisations. A number of current and topical strategies have been identified in Figure 10.13a, but the essential issues to be addressed concern the distinctive and reproducible process and capabilities possessed by individual organisations, and the sensitivity to possible changes, both on the part of the customers' responses and on the part of the overall organisation's cost structure.

A number of performance measures are used to monitor changes in these strategies. The response of customers is best measured by considering customer retention and customer attraction performance, as can be seen in Figure 10.13b, together with customer responses to products and services support. Organisational performance measurement (system performance) is largely financial: cash flow produced, 'returns', efficiencies of fixed and working capital, changes to brand (reliability image), and an added value perspective of competitive advantage. The control issues, or as they have become, control objectives, should be constantly reviewed against the planned system performance objectives.

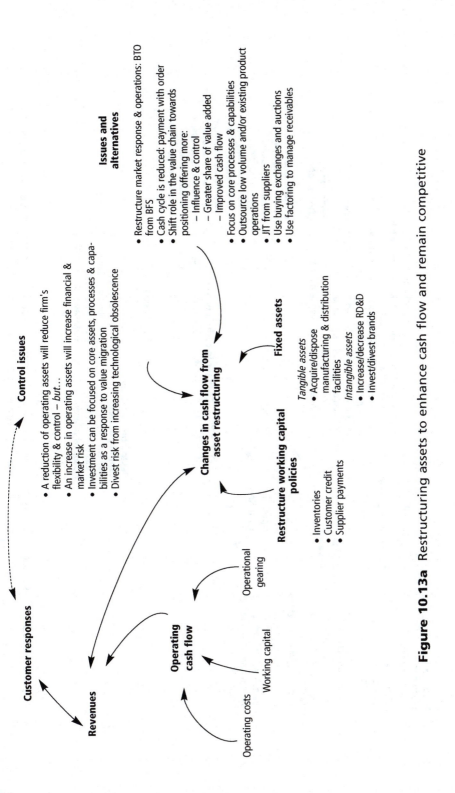

Control issues

- A reduction of operating assets will reduce firm's flexibility & control – *but…*
- An increase in operating assets will increase financial & market risk
- Investment can be focused on core assets, processes & capabilities as a response to value migration
- Divest risk from increasing technological obsolescence

Issues and alternatives

- Restructure market response & operations: BTO from BFS
- Cash cycle is reduced: payment with order
- Shift role in the value chain towards positioning offering more:
  - Influence & control
  - Greater share of value added
  - Improved cash flow
- Focus on core processes & capabilities
- Outsource low volume and/or existing product operations
- JIT from suppliers
- Use buying exchanges and auctions
- Use factoring to manage receivables

Fixed assets

Tangible assets
- Acquire/dispose manufacturing & distribution facilities

Intangible assets
- Increase/decrease RD&D
- Invest/divest brands

Changes in cash flow from asset restructuring

Restructure working capital policies

- Inventories
- Customer credit
- Supplier payments

Customer responses

Revenues

Operating cash flow

Operational gearing

Working capital

Operating costs

Figure 10.13a Restructuring assets to enhance cash flow and remain competitive

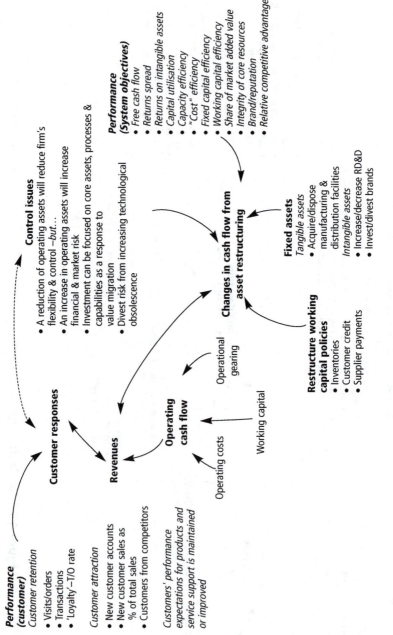

Performance (customer)

Customer retention
- Visits/orders
- Transactions
- 'Loyalty'—T/O rate

Customer attraction
- New customer accounts
- New customer sales as % of total sales
- Customers from competitors

Customers' performance expectations for products and service support is maintained or improved

Customer responses

Revenues

Operating cash flow

Operating costs

Working capital

Operational gearing

Restructure working capital policies
- Inventories
- Customer credit
- Supplier payments

Changes in cash flow from asset restructuring

Fixed assets
Tangible assets
- Acquire/dispose manufacturing & distribution facilities
Intangible assets
- Increase/decrease RD&D
- Invest/divest brands

Control issues
- A reduction of operating assets will reduce firm's flexibility & control –but...
- An increase in operating assets will increase financial & market risk
- Investment can be focused on core assets, processes & capabilities as a response to value migration
- Divest risk from increasing technological obsolescence

Performance (System objectives)
- Free cash flow
- Returns spread
- Returns on intangible assets
- Capital utilisation
- Capacity efficiency
- "Cost" efficiency
- Fixed capital efficiency
- Working capital efficiency
- Share of market added value
- Integrity of core resources
- Brand/reputation
- Relative competitive advantage

Figure 10.13b Restructuring assets to enhance cash flow and remain competitive: decisions and performance measures

Alternatives for growth

Growth of strategic cash flow will require a view that is prepared to become involved in new product-markets and (very likely) with new value chain structures if the opportunity appears from outwith the industry. The decisions involved are identified in Figure 10.14a. As well as the asset profile changes that the previous model focused upon, there are issues here concerning market entry and exit costs and with them levels of risk and their acceptability. Typically the investment required is similar to that decided upon earlier, but there is one significant difference and this concerns the lack of familiarity that exists. It follows that there are likely to be potential partners who can play a significant role in the growth programme but who will also influence the structure, and therefore the control issues, in the value chain that emerges. The issues and alternatives that confront the organisation concern the role that each member is required to assume and the eventual structure adopted to pursue the opportunity.

A range of strategic performance metrics are proposed by Figure 10.14b. They are all either market or financial performance related and follow from the discussion and themes developed throughout this text. However, one or two may need more explanation. For example, the beta profile is an interesting metric. Usually beta values are used to measure relative risk as between specific industry returns and the current average return from the 'market'. It follows that a beta>1 score suggests that there is more risk in the average associated with an industry or product-market than there exists in the 'market' overall. The very point about value chain/virtual organisation structures is that the organisation structure should not only reflect the most effective (strategic) structural option, and the most efficient (operational) option, but should also be designed with the purpose of reducing overall risk; the lower the weighted beta value, the lower the risk perceptions of the 'market' and the lower the cost of borrowing finance.

Evaluating alternatives for growth

Finally, we need to consider how we can evaluate the alternative value chain structures that appear as attractive candidates. As the model is based upon free cash flow, the results form the basis for implementation of the value chain strategies. However, it should be noted that the cash flow model has be modified to accommodate the strategic approach that would be expected. From the market opportunity analysis, reliable revenue forecasts would be developed. Using these, value delivery alternatives would explore the implications for alternative strategic cash flow decisions, asset based cash flow decisions and operating cash flow. Figure 10.15 proposes a model based upon the value return on investment (VROI) model that was proposed by Rappaport (1983). The VROI model compares a proposed strategy (or possibly strategies) with existing strategy options. It uses the resource requirement difference to calculate an ROI. Here our interests are to compare the NPV of the competing cash flows; we are not using the resource cost differences because the purpose of the

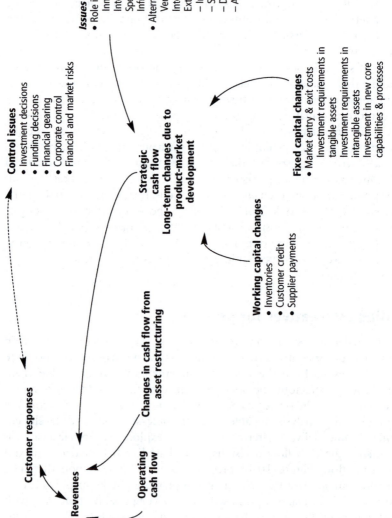

Figure 10.14a Alternatives for growth

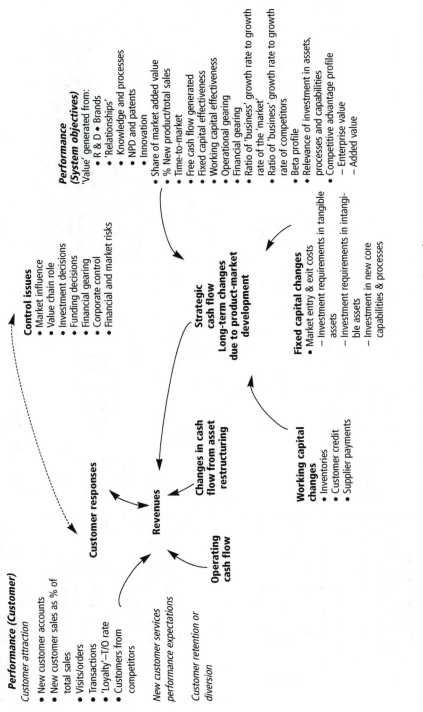

Performance (Customer)

Customer attraction

- New customer accounts
- New customer sales as % of total sales
- Visits/orders
- Transactions
- 'Loyalty'–T/O rate
- Customers from competitors

New customer services performance expectations

Customer retention or diversion

Customer responses

Control issues

- Market influence
- Value chain role
- Investment decisions
- Funding decisions
- Financial gearing
- Corporate control
- Financial and market risks

Performance (System objectives)

'Value' generated from:
- R & D • Brands
- 'Relationships'
- Knowledge and processes
- NPD and patents
- Innovation

- Share of market added value
- % New product/total sales
- Time-to-market
- Free cash flow generated
- Fixed capital effectiveness
- Working capital effectiveness
- Operational gearing
- Financial gearing
- Ratio of 'business' growth rate to growth rate of the 'market'
- Ratio of 'business' growth rate to growth rate of competitors
- Beta profile
- Relevance of investment in assets, processes and capabilities
- Competitive advantage profile
  – Enterprise value
  – Added value

Revenues

Strategic cash flow

Long-term changes due to product-market development

Changes in cash flow from asset restructuring

Operating cash flow

Working capital changes

- Inventories
- Customer credit
- Supplier payments

Fixed capital changes

- Market entry & exit costs
  – Investment requirements in tangible assets
  – Investment requirements in intangible assets
  – Investment in new core capabilities & processes

Figure 10.14b Alternative for growth: decisions and performance measures

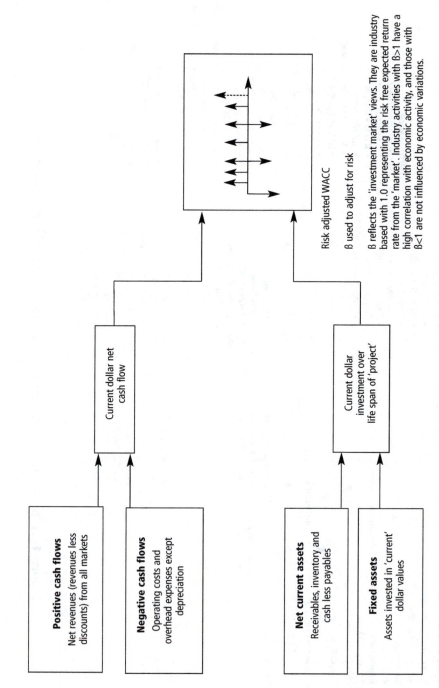

Figure 10.15 Using CFROI to evaluate alternative business models

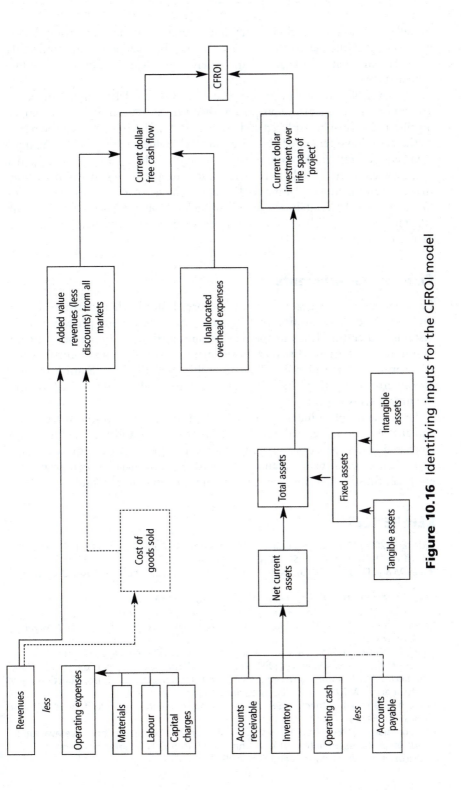

Figure 10.16 Identifying inputs for the CFROI model

overall evaluation is to include structural differences in the comparison. Hence it follows that the relative resource costs will be included in the individual appraisals and that joint costs (as and where they occur) will be accounted for at that stage.

The cash flow return on investment (CFROI) model extended in Figure 10.16 is similar to that of Rappaport in that it offers a means by which competing alternatives can be explored and evaluated. It differs in that given the nature of the cash flows generated (based upon Kay's value added model), the input data required reflects Kay's argument concerning the measurement of added value, which is created when 'revenues' exceed input values. It will be recalled that these are materials, labour and a capital charge that includes depreciation *and* a cost for the capital used in creating added value. Figure 10.16 is readily adaptable to a spreadsheet application that then facilitates evaluating a number of alternative scenarios.

Concluding comments

Performance planning and control is more difficult when partnerships are involved. Neely's suggestion that the essential 'variables' are process, people, systems and culture leads to the realisation that the multi-enterprise organisation presents quite different performance planning and control issues. Enterprise resource planning for the multi-enterprise organisation requires an understanding that the need for the continued viability of *all* partner organisations is a given.

Performance planning and control systems in partnership structures should aim at being proactive, with an effort made to understand the relationships of leveraged assets, processes and capabilities and the obvious requirements of coordinated performance planning. Coordinated knowledge management is essential; thus the development of a learning organisation helpful.

REFERENCES

Aldrick P (2004) 'Outsourcing going to hit professions', *Daily Telegraph*, 11 November

Ansoff H I (1968) *Corporate Strategy*, McGraw-Hill, New York

Bailey M and D Farrell (2005) 'Exploding the myths of offshoring', *McKinsey Quarterly*, 30 June

Beech J (1998) 'The supply-demand nexus: from integration to synchronisation', in Gattorna J (ed.) *Strategic Supply Chain Alignment*, Gower, Aldershot

Bryan L L and R Hulme (2003) 'Managing for improved corporate performance', *McKinsey Quarterly*, 3

Champion D (2001) 'Mastering the value chain', *Harvard Business Review*, June

Davidow W H and M S Malone (1992) *The Virtual Corporation*, HarperCollins, New York

Dommermuth W and R Andersen (1969) 'Distribution systems: firms, functions, and efficiencies', *MSU Business Topics*, Spring

Gadiesh O and J L Gilbert (1998) 'How to map your industry's profit pool', *Harvard Business Review*, May/June

Govindarajan V (1986) 'Appropriateness of accounting data in performance evaluation: An empirical examination of environmental uncertainty as an intervening variable', *Accounting, Organizations and Society*, 9(2)

Gupta A and V Govindarajan (1984) 'Business unit strategy, managerial characteristics, and business unit effectiveness at strategy implementation', *Academy of Management Journal*, 27

Hagel J (III) (2004) 'Offshoring goes on the offensive', *McKinsey Quarterly*, 30 June

Kaplan R S and D P Norton (1992) 'The balanced scorecard – measures that drive performance', *Harvard Business Review*, January/February

Kay J (2000) 'Strategy and the delusion of grand designs', in *Mastering Strategy*, Financial Times/Prentice-Hall, London

Kennerley M and A Neely (2003) 'Measuring performance in a changing business environment', *International Journal of Operations & Production Management*, 23(2)

Knight R and D Pretty (2000) 'Philosophies of risk, shareholder value and the CEO', *Financial Times*, 27 June

Koch C (ed.) (1994) 'The power of interorganisational systems', *Indications*, 11(1)

Neely A, C Adams and M Kennerley (2002) *The Performance Prism: The Scorecard for Measuring and Managing Business Success*, Financial Times/Prentice-Hall, London

Normann R (2001) *Reframing Business*, Wiley, Chichester

Oates D (1998) *Outsourcing and the Virtual Organisation*, Century, London

Pebler R P (2000) 'The virtual oil company: capstone of integration,' *Oil & Gas Journal*, March

Porter M (1996) 'What is strategy?', *Harvard Business Review*, December

Rappaport A (1983) 'Corporate performance standards and shareholder value', *Journal of Business Strategy*, Spring

Riley D (1987), 'Competitive cost based investment strategies for industrial companies', in *Manufacturing Issues*, Booz, Allen and Hamilton, New York

SAS Institute (2001) *Enterprise Performance Management: Strategies for Surviving in the Web-Speed Economy* (White Paper), SAS, Cary, NC

Scherer F M (1988) *Industrial Market Structure and Economic Performance*, 2nd edition, Rand McNally, New York

Shank J K and V Govindarajan (1993) *Strategic Cost Management*, Free Press, New York

Short J E and N Venkatraman (1992) 'beyond business process redesign: redefining Baxter's business network', *Sloan Management Review*, Fall

Stern L W, A I El-Ansery and A T Coughlan (1996) *Marketing Channels*, Prentice-Hall, Upper Saddle River, NJ

CHAPTER 11

Value Chain Applications

LEARNING TOPICS

On completing your study of this chapter you will have been introduced to and considered the following topics:

- Design of value chain models based upon managing; revenues, working capital and fixed assets, investment funding, and free cash flow
- Applications of the model from a range of industries
- More detailed case study applications

Introduction

In earlier chapters it was argued that successful organisations in the 'new economy' are those which first identify customer value drivers and value builders by researching the demand chain characteristics which profile the industry product-market(s) that operate. It was also argued that this affords an opportunity for the organisation to design a customised supply chain that will meet customers' product and service expectations. Figure 11.1 suggests how they first identify the customer value drivers and value builders and use these as a basis for developing an effective value delivery strategy.

Clearly it is more difficult to implement strategies from which a number of participants benefit, but the growth of such structures is evidence of the fact that such strategies can be implemented and be successful. Normann's (2001) argument concerning the *management* rather than the *ownership* of assets is fundamental to the value chain. The attraction for all partners is the release from the burden of owning fixed assets and therefore being required to make decisions that are often volume oriented (a production orientation) rather than market based (customer-centric). There is a strong incentive to reduce the burden of fixed costs and improve corporate performance through partnerships and alliances. In the Australian wine industry this has proved to be a popular model, albeit one with problems.

318

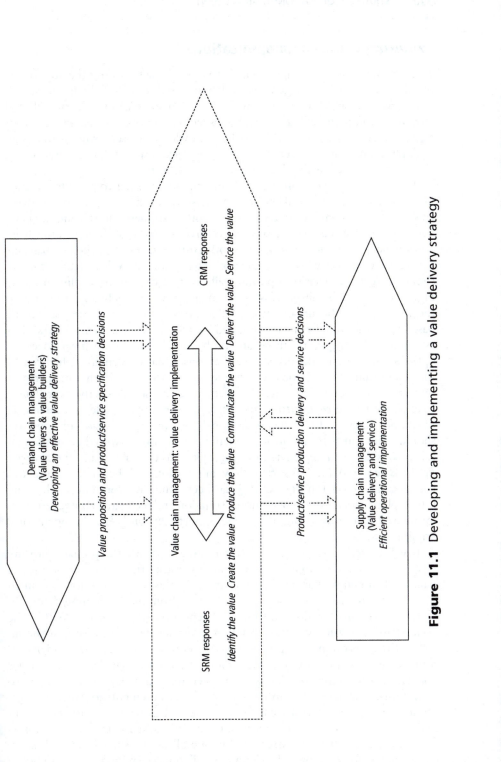

Figure 11.1 Developing and implementing a value delivery strategy

Exploring value chain applications

This chapter provides an approach that is useful for exploring the application of the value chain. Three generic models are used to do so; the first is shown in Figure 11.2, which uses an analysis of the demand chain to identify selected customers and their value drivers. A prospective approach would also consider aspects of customer value builders. This knowledge is used as input to design a supply chain that considers the product-service response and its production alternatives, as well as the 'logistics' of value delivery.

The basic objective of any value chain structure, then, is to provide value for both its customers and stakeholder partners. Value chain innovations provide an opportunity to create added value for both customers and stakeholder partners, the innovations may be product or process based, and often result from a partnership approach. Given that both customers and stakeholder partners have clear views on what this approach comprises, the value chain structure should reflect the decision options available that can optimise this outcome. Figure 11.3 models this process by identifying revenues as being a response to the relevance of the organisation's value proposition. This response will be based upon the added value content and 'worth' to the target customer(s). But as Figure 11.3 suggests, there are both *operational* and *strategic* decision options, involving marketing strategy responses that in turn are influenced by the added value expectations of customers and partners. Clearly time perspectives are important and the model reflects these. It also reflects the overall need to establish strong *competitive advantage*, measured by considering the impact of the potential (and feasible) operational and strategic decision options. We should point out here that in some planning situations it would be more logical to consider the *competitive advantage* likely to be realised and the *strategic decisions* required (and the cash flow implications of them) to ensure this happens. The model in Figure 11.3 has been found to work effectively using it to explore expanding an operational situation and its related strategic scenarios as well first considering a strategic opportunity *and then* the operational implications.

It will be recalled that earlier chapters suggested that the primary measure of corporate success should be free cash flow rather than a notion of 'profit', which is by definition an artificial construct. In this sense, cash flow is defined more from a managerial perspective and differs from the accounting definition which answers to taxation and financial reporting requirements. Within the context and structure of a value chain the components of free cash flow should follow the decision making processes of the value chain. Figure 11.3 identifies four decision points: revenue generation, the operational decisions that are concerned with inventory levels, and receivables and payables. Changes to operational strategies result in changes to cash requirements for working capital and fixed assets, thereby changing the asset base and the cash flow from assets. Strategic decisions concerning the investment in tangible assets (processes, capabilities and assets) and intangible assets (such as R&D, brands, management and employee development) will impact on long-term cash flows. Free cash flow is influenced by funding structure decisions while *value capture*

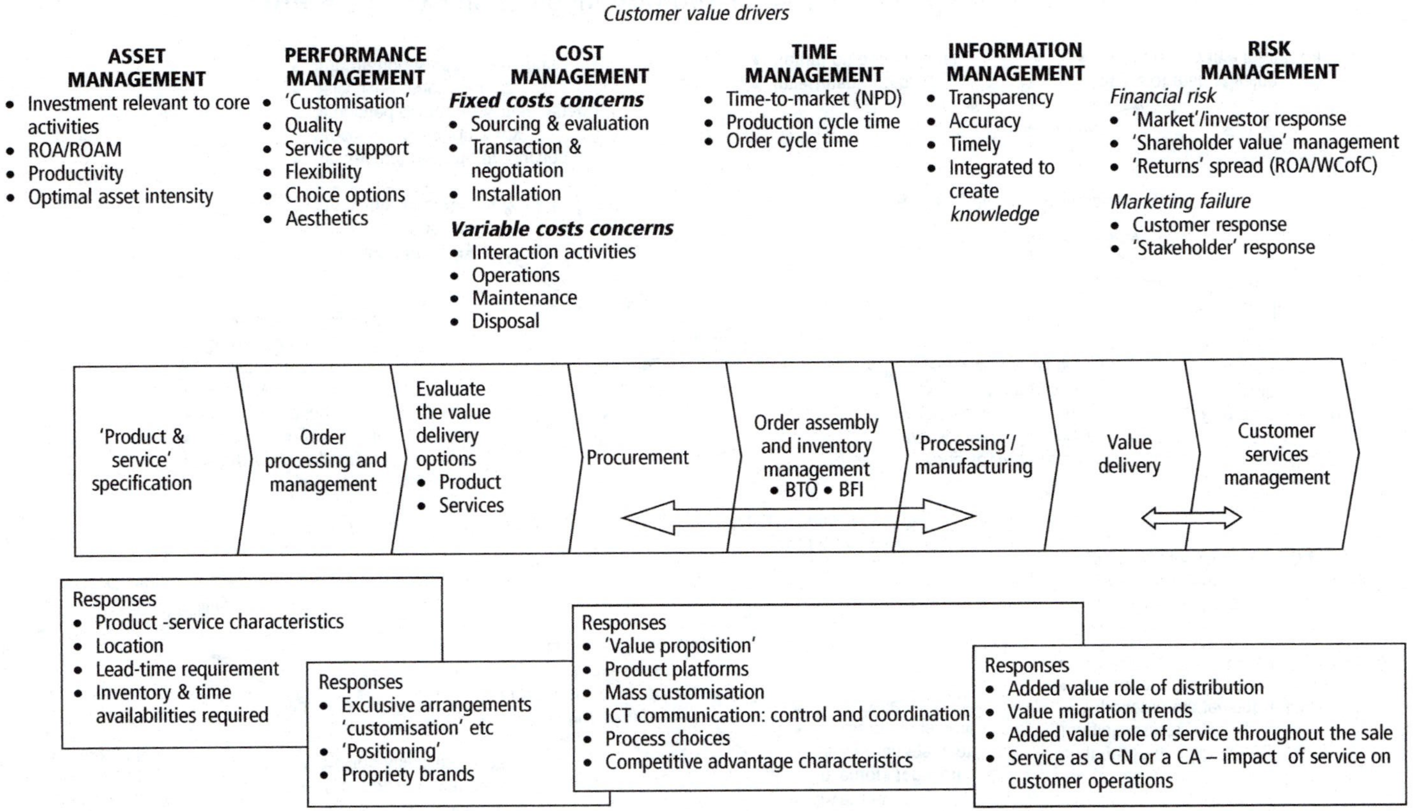

Customer value drivers

ASSET MANAGEMENT	PERFORMANCE MANAGEMENT	COST MANAGEMENT	TIME MANAGEMENT	INFORMATION MANAGEMENT	RISK MANAGEMENT
• Investment relevant to core activities • ROA/ROAM • Productivity • Optimal asset intensity	• 'Customisation' • Quality • Service support • Flexibility • Choice options • Aesthetics	*Fixed costs concerns* • Sourcing & evaluation • Transaction & negotiation • Installation *Variable costs concerns* • Interaction activities • Operations • Maintenance • Disposal	• Time-to-market (NPD) • Production cycle time • Order cycle time	• Transparency • Accuracy • Timely • Integrated to create *knowledge*	*Financial risk* • 'Market'/investor response • 'Shareholder value' management • 'Returns' spread (ROA/WCofC) *Marketing failure* • Customer response • 'Stakeholder' response

Supply chain stages:

'Product & service' specification → Order processing and management → Evaluate the value delivery options • Product • Services → Procurement → Order assembly and inventory management • BTO • BFI → 'Processing/ manufacturing → Value delivery → Customer services management

Responses (under 'Product & service' specification)
- Product -service characteristics
- Location
- Lead-time requirement
- Inventory & time availabilities required

Responses (under Order processing and management)
- Exclusive arrangements
- 'customisation' etc
- 'Positioning'
- Propriety brands

Responses (under Procurement / Processing)
- 'Value proposition'
- Product platforms
- Mass customisation
- ICT communication: control and coordination
- Process choices
- Competitive advantage characteristics

Responses (under Value delivery / Customer services management)
- Added value role of distribution
- Value migration trends
- Added value role of service throughout the sale
- Service as a CN or a CA – impact of service on customer operations

Figure 11.2 Using the demand chain profile to focus the supply chain

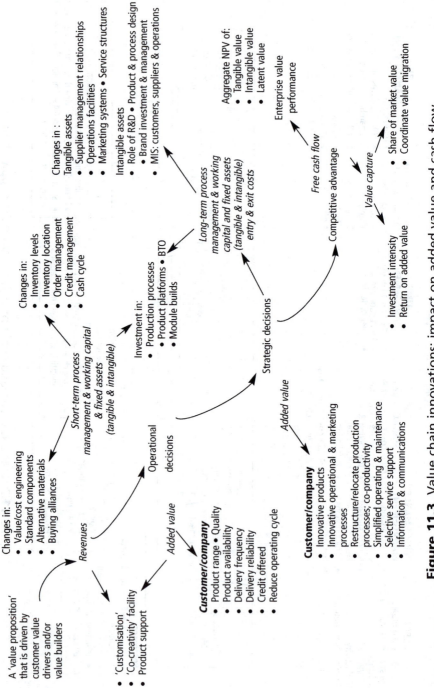

Figure 11.3 Value chain innovations: impact on added value and cash flow

reflects the ability of the value chain to participate successfully throughout the value chain and for each participant to meet their financial and marketing objectives.

The model offers management an opportunity to evaluate alternative value chain structures. For example, operating cash flow profiles can be changed by modifying operational activities; a greater use of assemblies and modules, and a focus on assembly rather than on component manufacturing, can result in lower levels of inventories and decreased cash cycles. The introduction of JIT systems also changes inventory and payables profiles. Supplier rationalisation can result in improved operating profit and credit terms. Decisions to outsource all or some of the manufacturing process will have similar effects.

In the long term, changes in strategic direction are likely to have implications for cash flow management. For example, a decision to pursue an opportunity in an adjacent market segment can have significant implications for both working capital and fixed assets. A specialist cheese manufacturer found this, at considerable cost. The mature cheddar segment appeared to have attractions. Competition was relatively low, and the market for specialist cheeses was being expanded by large multiple retailers. The costs of entry were an increase in both storage costs and inventory – the mature cheese market involved a maturing process period of nine months, a period of time in which the added value could not be realised and in which the product required storage space. The cash flow problems were exacerbated by large volume customers who used their size to protract accounts payment.

Changing cash flow from assets and strategic cash flow profiles can have significant impact on free cash flow. As Figure 11.3 suggests, free cash flow is influenced not only by the amount or size of the funding requirements but also by the type of funds. Debt funding incurs interest charges (an increase in operating cash flow) while equity funding attracts fund raising costs *and* may dilute managerial control of the business. Clearly the value chain concept is attractive as it offers a means by which financial performance can be planed and managed.

The resultant value chain is represented in Figure 11.4 and is an integration or fusion of the demand chain analysis processes and those of the supply chain. The value chain represents the processes that are required to identify, create, deliver and ensure the continuity of the value offer for both customers and stakeholder partners.

Managing revenues, working capital, fixed assets and cash flow

Within the value chain the deployment of both working capital and fixed assets is important. There are the cash flow implications that have been identified in the preceding paragraphs, but there also issues concerning customer service. A significant aspect of customer value perceptions concerns service delivery, which has two characteristics. One is the traditional role of inventory in the supply chain, but the other has implications for 'value-in-use' and the

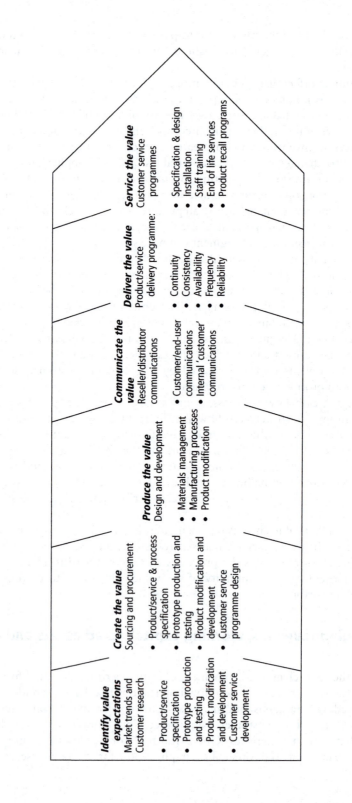

Figure 11.4 Demand chain + supply chain = value chain

Identify value expectations
Market trends and
Customer research

- Product/service
  specification
- Prototype production
  and testing
- Product modification
  and development
- Customer service
  development

Create the value
Sourcing and procurement

- Product/service & process
  specification
- Prototype production and
  testing
- Product modification and
  development
- Customer service
  programme design

Produce the value
Design and development

- Materials management
- Manufacturing processes
- Product modification

*Communicate the
value*
Reseller/distributor
communications

- Customer/end-user
  communications
- Internal 'customer'
  communications

Deliver the value
Product/service
delivery programme:

- Continuity
- Consistency
- Availability
- Frequency
- Reliability

Service the value
Customer service
programmes

- Specification & design
- Installation
- Staff training
- End of life services
- Product recall programs

customer's view of life cycle costs. Often the purchase decision is influenced by service packages (including installation, maintenance, staff training and so on) that can reduce the total costs of purchasing and operations. Figure 11.5 explores these as short- and long-term decisions. Given a clearly defined demand chain profile resulting in specific value drivers and value builders that can be explored, not only for their ability to deliver added value to customers but also for cost-efficient delivery alternatives, it follows that alternative formats for revenue generation, working capital, fixed assets and the implications for funding can be evaluated. However, before a final decision can be made, the impact on the operational gearing of the value chain must be considered. If the resulting structure is one with a high fixed-cost element, there is inherent risk in the organisation, together with a lack of flexibility. Not only could this result in excess capacity, but it is likely to influence investors' funding decisions. This in turn can have implications for borrowing rates and the returns spread of the organisation. Typically, this is influenced by the relationship between debt and equity funding; however, if investors (such as the banks) were to be concerned at the organisation's ability to respond to short-term market fluctuations, then the operational gearing could also influence their decision. Clearly one of the major benefits of the value chain is the ability to choose a structure that optimises return and risk.

Two examples

The Boeing Aircraft Service Organisation

Boeing introduced an added value aspect to its product range with its integrated materials management (IMM) programme, which it claims reduces the operating costs of its commercial airline customers. McClenahen (2004) reports Boeing's estimate that it will save customers some 10 to 20 per cent of maintenance materials costs. He remarks that 'Boeing is adapting a supply-chain management approach from the automotive and electronics industries and introducing it to the aviation industry, where the supply chain historically been fragmented.' The objective are to aggregate and integrate the supply chain in such a way that the information produced will reduce inventories and operating costs for customers, Boeing and the suppliers.

The additional benefit for Boeing is that the information on parts usage will be fed back into design and to customer service engineers, thereby offering an opportunity for creating competitive advantage.

Boeing will be responsible for the purchasing, inventory management, storage and distribution of 'single use' parts such as bushings, clamps, brackets, hoses, seals and so on. Boeing and the other suppliers will *own* the parts, which are stored near the airline's maintenance bases until required, and collect payment from the airlines as and when they are used.

Figure 11.6 identifies the demand chain inputs into the Boeing planning process. The value drivers of improved fixed asset (aircraft) productivity, working capital productivity, the delegation of responsibility for inventory management and the ability to free up capital for the core business are clear. The

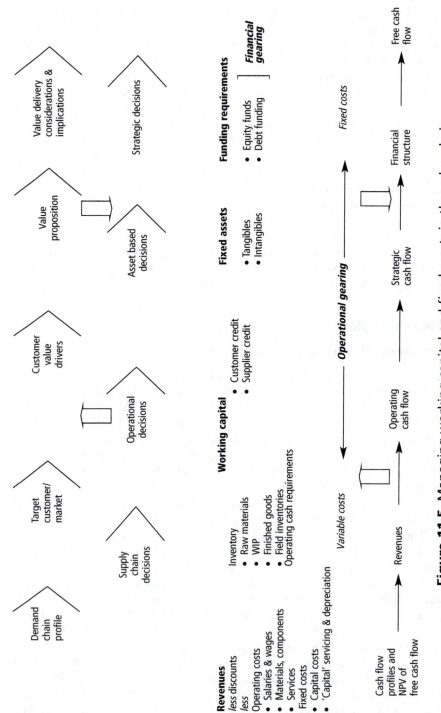

Figure 11.5 Managing working capital and fixed assets in the value chain

resulting value proposition, a customised service parts procurement service implemented by vendor managed inventory (VMI) and just-in-time (JIT) processes, is priced such that the service results in a significant overall cost reduction for the users. Among the responses required from Boeing were customised service parts programmes; online communications with suppliers as well as with customers using electronic data interchange (EDI) linkages; and a knowledge management programme which creates, from parts use data, knowledge that can be input into aircraft design and customer service processes.

Customer and company added value benefits are shown in Figure 11.7, together with the operational and strategic decisions required to implement them. The added value for the airlines is the facility to focus on the revenue generating aspects of airline operations while Boeing takes on the logistics and materials management (and the costs) of aircraft servicing. The strategic implications have yet to materialise. The airlines may be in the initial stages of a global service strategy, as a result of which the engine manufacturers offer timely service. The other long-term benefits are helpful to the airlines and to Boeing: the data captured during service transactions and operations can be converted into a source of knowledge for design and service planning.

The resultant value chain is shown as Figure 11.8. As with the other examples in this chapter, the primary value management processes are identified and the component processes are detailed within each of them. The customer value expectations can be expressed as capital and equipment productivity, reduction of non-core activity costs, and the risks involved in maintaining inventories containing technological equipment. To *create* the value, Boeing is responding with high availability of service parts with an online communication service with their airline customers and Boeing's suppliers. The result is an improved operating cycle as well as an improved cash cycle. To *produce* the value Boeing has a customised service process design for each major customer that not only reflects aircraft type but incorporates flight schedules and frequencies, and global locations of hub operations. The online systems act as a two-way conduit and also as the basis for improved forecasting and planning. Value *delivery* comprises the continuous availability of service parts at specified locations to meet service schedules at zero cost. To maintain, or to *service the value*, Boeing must maintain customers' low service operations costs. This has the twofold benefits of enhanced productivity and cash flow.

Budget airlines

The growth of 'budget'/'no frills' airlines has taken some time to solidify. The successful model introduced and operated by Southwest in the USA has been attempted by a number of market entrants on a global basis. It is not an easy business to manage. Southwest's executive chairman, Herb Kelleher (2004), identified some of the issues and problems with this kind of business.

Kelleher explained that it is a 'hugely capital intensive business with enormous fixed costs'. It is very sensitive to changes in oil costs as these are a significant component of its variable costs. It is also sensitive to the service response

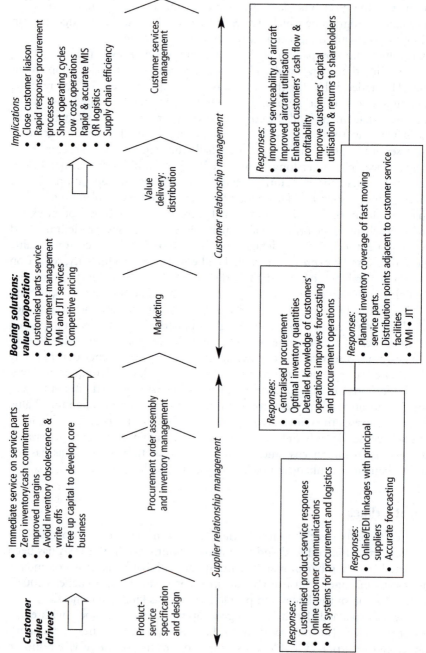

Figure 11.6 Boeing Service Organisation: demand chain management leads to supply chain efficiency

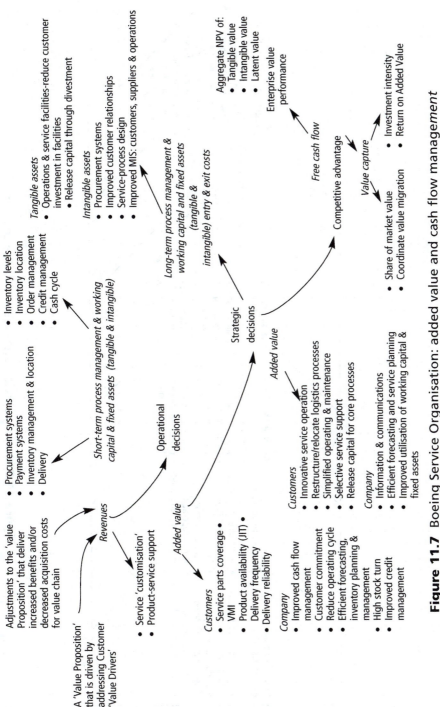

Adjustments to the 'value Proposition' that deliver increased benefits and/or decreased acquisition costs for value chain

A 'Value Proposition' that is driven by addressing Customer 'Value Drivers'

Tangible assets
- Operations & service facilities-reduce customer investment in facilities
  - Release capital through divestment

Intangible assets
- Procurement systems
- Improved customer relationships
- Service-process design
- Improved MIS: customers, suppliers & operations

- Inventory levels
- Inventory location
- Order management
- Credit management
- Cash cycle

- Procurement systems
- Payment systems
- Inventory management & location
- Delivery

Short-term process management & working capital & fixed assets (tangible & intangible)

Long-term process management & working capital and fixed assets (tangible & intangible) entry & exit costs

Operational decisions

Strategic decisions

Aggregate NPV of:
- Tangible value
- Intangible value
- Latent value

Enterprise value performance

Free cash flow

Competitive advantage

Value capture

- Investment intensity
- Return on Added Value

- Share of market value
- Coordinate value migration

Added value

Customers
- Innovative service operation
- Restructure/relocate logistics processes
- Simplified operating & maintenance
- Selective service support
- Release capital for core processes

Company
- Information & communications
- Efficient forecasting and service planning
- Improved utilisation of working capital & fixed assets

Revenues

- Service 'customisation'
- Product-service support

Added value

Customers
- Service parts coverage • VMI
- Product availability (JIT)
- Delivery frequency
- Delivery reliability

Company
- Improved cash flow management
- Customer commitment
- Reduce operating cycle
- Efficient forecasting, inventory planning & management
- High stock turn
- Improved credit management

Figure 11.7 Boeing Service Organisation: added value and cash flow management

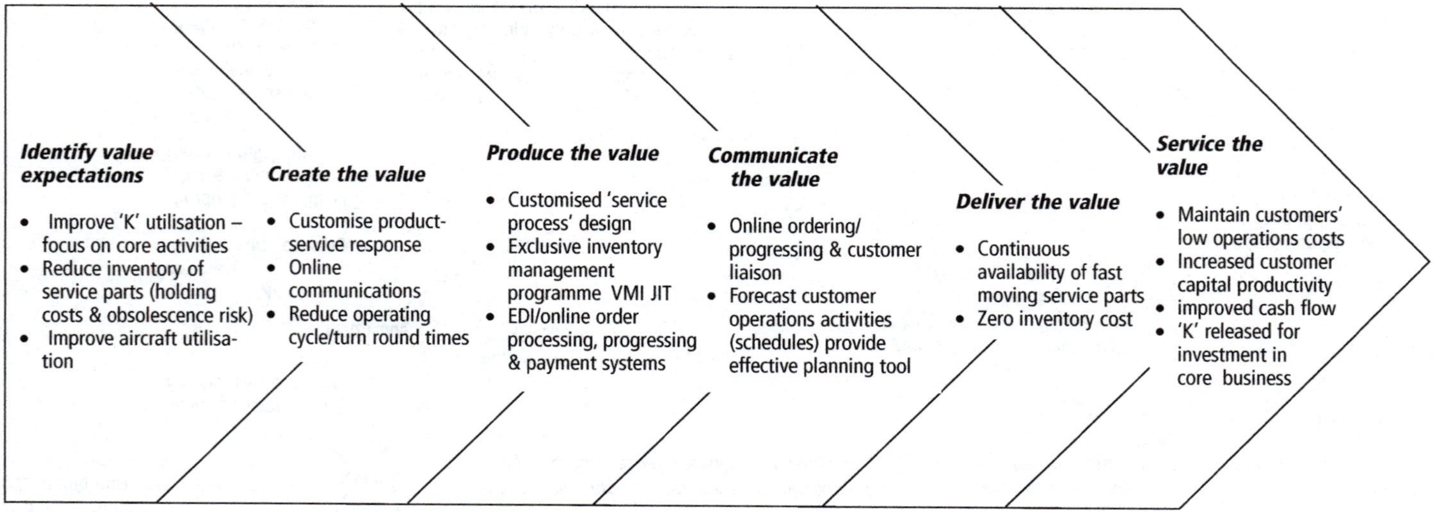

Identify value expectations

- Improve 'K' utilisation – focus on core activities
- Reduce inventory of service parts (holding costs & obsolescence risk)
- Improve aircraft utilisation

Create the value

- Customise product-service response
- Online communications
- Reduce operating cycle/turn round times

Produce the value

- Customised 'service process' design
- Exclusive inventory management programme VMI JIT
- EDI/online order processing, progressing & payment systems

Communicate the value

- Online ordering/ progressing & customer liaison
- Forecast customer operations activities (schedules) provide effective planning tool

Deliver the value

- Continuous availability of fast moving service parts
- Zero inventory cost

Service the value

- Maintain customers' low operations costs
- Increased customer capital productivity improved cash flow
- 'K' released for investment in core business

Figure 11.8 Boeing Service Organisation: value chain model

of customers as employees are required to meet customer expectations. At that time (February 2004) Southwest operated 2,800 daily flights with 387 aircraft to 60 airports in 59 cities in the USA. Safety, and meeting schedules on time, are influenced by 'uncontrollables' such as weather, air traffic control (ATC) delays and airport congestion; even the 'controllables', such as mechanical problems, can present difficulties that have to be overcome. As with all forms of travel there is no product shelf life; an empty seat is 'lost for ever', consequently employees and employee relationships are integral to success. Southwest's business is largely discretionary and consequently can be considered as cyclical. The entire industry is intensely regulated and taxes amount to some 30 per cent of fare revenues. It is a fiercely competitive industry; there is little scope for discretion concerning airports. And as with all airlines, Southwest is vulnerable to 'event risks' such as the September 11 tragedy and outbreaks of global illnesses such as SARS.

Kelleher identified four capabilities that are essential for ongoing success: costs that are lower than those of competitors; a 'strong' balance sheet (debt/equity optimal and the risk perceived as acceptable by lending institutions); debt per aircraft, a specific key performance indicator (KPIs) less than that of competitors, and customer service perceived as superior to that of competitors. Other important criteria include an awareness of threats from the business environment; being quick and responsive; avoiding bureaucratic organisation structures that reflect the 'sense of humour, mutual and self-respect staff at all levels have for each other, and respect for their mutual, joint enterprise'.

Other budget airlines have adopted this model. In Europe, easyJet and Ryanair are the most significant and successful. The formula appears simple but appears difficult to implement for some carriers; both BA and KLM failed to make it work:

- Identify short-haul, point-to-point sectors between secondary, but important, cities
- Use the secondary airports of major cities
- Target business travellers and budget-conscious family travellers looking for speed and low-cost travel with minimum services
- Develop a business model value proposition based upon cost-efficiency – no meals, luggage transfers, seating preferences, and based upon direct selling
- Achieve rapid check-in and aircraft turnaround times to maximise aircraft utilisation
- Develop employee flexibility based upon multi-skilling

The demand chain management analysis is shown as Figure 11.9, and the business model profiling the added value delivered to customers and stakeholder partners appears as Figure 11.10. In both these diagrams the essence of the budget airline offer comes across. Frequency, reliability, safety and product-service consistency constitute a strong theme. At the same time the control of

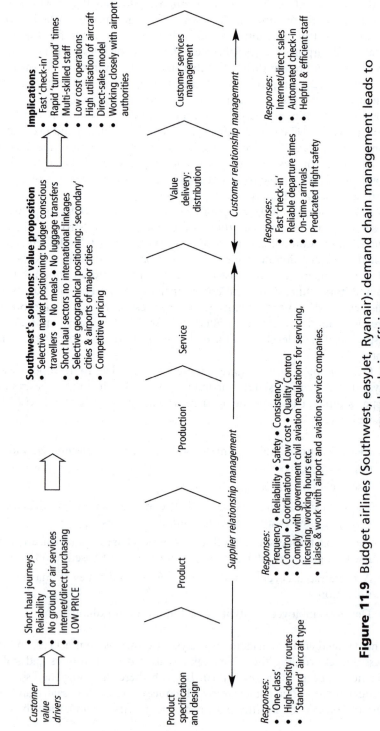

Figure 11.9 Budget airlines (Southwest, easyJet, Ryanair): demand chain management leads to supply chain efficiency

Customer value drivers
- Short haul journeys
- Reliability
- No ground or air services
- Internet/direct purchasing
- LOW PRICE

Southwest's solutions: value proposition
- Selective market positioning: budget conscious travellers • No meals • No luggage transfers
- Short haul sectors no international linkages
- Selective geographical positioning: 'secondary' cities & airports of major cities
- Competitive pricing

Implications
- Fast 'check-in'
- Rapid 'turn-round' times
- Multi-skilled staff
- Low cost operations
- High utilisation of aircraft
- Direct-sales model
- Working closely with airport authorities

Product specification and design

Product

'Production'

Service

Value delivery: distribution

Customer services management

Supplier relationship management

Customer relationship management

Responses:
- 'One class'
- High-density routes
- 'Standard' aircraft type

Responses:
- Frequency • Reliability • Safety • Consistency
- Control • Coordination • Low cost • Quality Control
- Comply with government civil aviation regulations for servicing, licensing, working hours etc.
- Liaise & work with airport and aviation service companies.

Responses:
- Fast 'check-in'
- Reliable departure times
- On-time arrivals
- Predicated flight safety

Responses:
- Internet/direct sales
- Automated check-in
- Helpful & efficient staff

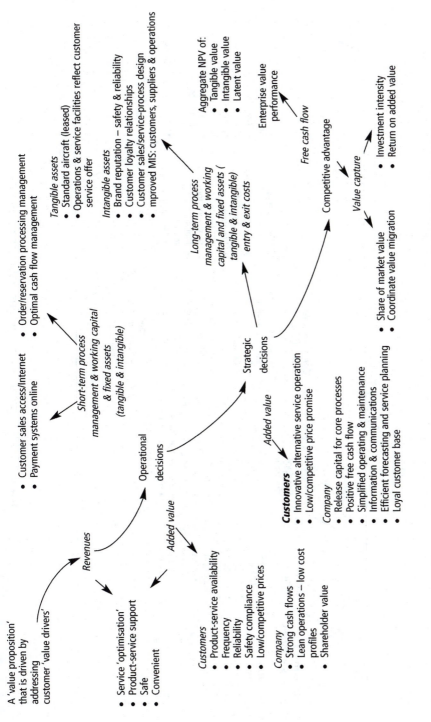

Figure 11.10 Budget airline added value and cash flow management

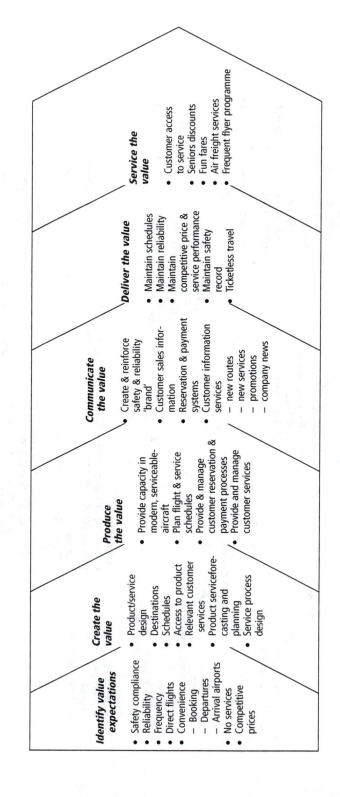

Identify value expectations

- Safety compliance
- Reliability
- Frequency
- Direct flights
- Convenience
  - Booking
  - Departures
  - Arrival airports
- No services
- Competitive prices

Create the value

- Product/service design
- Destinations
- Schedules
- Access to product
- Relevant customer services
- Product service forecasting and planning
- Service process design

Produce the value

- Provide capacity in modern, serviceable aircraft
- Plan flight & service schedules
- Provide & manage customer reservation & payment processes
- Provide and manage customer services

Communicate the value

- Create & reinforce safety & reliability 'brand'
- Customer sales information
- Reservation & payment systems
- Customer information services
  - new routes
  - new services
  - promotions
  - company news

Deliver the value

- Maintain schedules
- Maintain reliability
- Maintain competitive price & service performance
- Maintain safety record
- Ticketless travel

Service the value

- Customer access to service
- Seniors discounts
- Fun fares
- Air freight services
- Frequent flyer programme

Figure 11.11 Typical budget airline value chain model

costs is clearly managed by standardisation of product and service, of equipment and service operations. Clearly, without these controls in place and without the understanding and cooperation of the employees, the business cannot be made to work. The value chain, indicating how these airlines *identify, create, produce, communicate, deliver* and *service* the value is represented by Figure 11.11.

Concluding comments

This chapter has demonstrated the application of the principle pursued throughout this text – that effective (strategic) value chain management is realised by first identifying and understanding the industry and the organisation's demand chain and then designing an efficient (operational) supply chain that delivers customer value. The overall process includes the consideration and evaluation of all delivery alternatives. The approach taken is reflected the following summary statements:

- *Value chain structures* offer customer focused companies a facility to create additional value for their customers by grasping the simple facts that they need to understand customer expectations, purchasing responses and product-service use, *and* that they are unlikely themselves to possess all the resources to service customer needs.

- They first identify customer characteristics, and their 'needs and wants', and then create a multi-enterprise *supply chain* that is cost-efficient and responds to the expectations of customers as identified by the *demand chain*. Together, *demand chain* and *supply chain* process analysis and management comprise the *value chain*.

- *Value chain management* is an approach that synthesises the activities of *all* partner organisations in the value chain: cooperation is essential, not competition and certainly not conflict. In the value chain competitors can become partners.

CASE STUDY 11.1

A value chain approach to healthcare: QE Health, Rotorua, New Zealand

(With thanks to Dr Peter Jones, Faculty of Medicine and Health Science, University of Auckland, New Zealand)

Introduction: the healthcare market

Healthcare is a market. It shares a number of similarities with conventional markets. It has market sectors (segments) for which common characteristics can be identified. It also has customers – patients. It shares similar problems, such as increasingly discerning customers, management structures and performance expectations such as revenue generation, cost management, profit and cash flow generation. It follows that healthcare does not (should not) differ in its concern for customer care.

The ongoing debate within the NHS in the UK is an indication of just how far reaching change may be. A number of medical practitioners, clinicians and administrators were asked for views of the future of healthcare in the UK and their views were published ('Public Agenda' 2004). The application of *technology management* (as well as information communications technology) is seen as likely to bring about other changes that not many years ago would not have been discussed – let alone considered. For example, the use of call centres to handle customer calls (read: patient cries for help) as an initial filter prior to access to general practitioners is envisaged and has already happened in some places. The application of IT for facilitating access to clinical records would already be accepted. *Relationship management* topics include the involvement of independent providers, together with the possibility of the voluntary sector becoming much more involved in healthcare delivery. It follows that industrial management practices may be introduced. The Birkdale Clinic talks in terms of *process management* with a productivity approach: 'high-volume surgery of a repetitive nature such as cataract operations could lead to efficiency gains'. The application of *knowledge management* to healthcare has always been present but the development of learning organisations in the commercial/consulting context is also seen as likely. A comment from the chairman of Birkdale reflects the changing views on developments in the UK:

> It is our vision that the Government will create 'virtual treatment centres' within NHS 'QE Healths' to take advantage of expensive capacity available there during evenings and weekends.

Clearly healthcare management is attracting the attention of commercial interests and it can be expected that many of the recent developments in management theory will be increasingly applied.

'Value' in healthcare is a concept that has been grappled with for a considerable time. It is a term often used indiscriminately and without much thought; numerous interpretations exist. A common theme is that a value strategy is the basis for coordinating the processes that result in 'customer satisfaction'. Choice is an aspect of value that consumer goods vendors use to the advantage of both the customer and themselves – it is widely used to create customer loyalty. It is interesting to note that both political parties in the UK are planning to offer the healthcare customer choice. Revill (2004) comments on the recommendations made in a 'think tank' report, *The New Health Network*, in which choice and empowerment are argued to be essential requirements in a 'new look' health service.

Similarly, value delivery comprises all those activities involved in delivering the product-service attributes that are considered necessary to create customer satisfaction and to maintain ongoing, long-term relationships with customers and in so doing build competitive advantage. Once again we are beginning to witness the application of consumer oriented techniques in healthcare. The importance of customer service performance is beginning to dominate healthcare management vocabulary. Customer responses are important and are increasingly measured. Identifying specific customers and being aware of their value expectations is an important task for healthcare management. It is interesting to note that the structure of healthcare insurance service markets has changed significantly during the past ten years. Waples (2004) reports on research among the insurance companies with major healthcare interests. The number of private medical policies had been static at some 12 per cent of the UK population for the previous 12 years but the proportion paid for by individuals had fallen. The corporate share of expenditure on premiums had increased from 59 per cent to 75 per cent. A view reported by Waples considers that a new product is emerging: 'one that sits alongside the NHS and delivers wellbeing to employees'. Waples' respondents see other changes occurring. One that is pertinent to this discussion concerns the development of service based market segments. The level of service offered, and possibly the service environment, will influence the price paid by the consumer.

Value chain analysis encourages an intra- and inter-organisational review of resource application and identifies alternative methods and structures for meeting objectives. Service suppliers would appear to be in agreement with the view that partnerships and outsourced services are an increasing trend as government seeks to improve the service offer *and* to reduce costs. Waples summarises the views of his respondents:

> There is little doubt, however, that the long-term trend is for huge changes to take place in the health service. The market will become more open and competitive, which will lead to lower costs. It will need strong leadership from the private sector to steer a profitable course through the health revolution.

This case study considers recent developments in the application of value chain analysis, based upon QE Health in Rotorua. Patient care, quality and value in healthcare are becoming increasingly convergent concepts. The importance of patients as customers has increased the focus on quality management and value delivery. QE Health is a specialist in rheumatic disease and rehabilitation, unique in that it is a privately owned and managed entity that services almost exclusively government funded patients. It has a clear mission for the delivery of customer quality and in fulfilling this mission uses a holistic approach (a value chain approach) to customer care. The value chain study of QE Health's product-service delivery has enabled medical practitioners, medical support staff and management to review both value delivery quality and delivery methods. The case study explores the QE Health value chain organisation and process structures and identifies questions concerning healthcare delivery and alternative methods for achieving current results, as well as the future direction of the organisation.

Introduction to QE Health

QE Health is located in Rotorua, New Zealand, specialising in the care and treatment of rheumatic disease and rehabilitation. It is unusual in public healthcare systems in that it is a privately owned and managed entity that services almost exclusively government-funded patients. It has a clearly defined mission:

> ... to provide the highest quality services for rheumatological care and rehabilitation – achieving standards that ensure such services remain the first choice of patients and customers.

To fulfil this mission it adopts an holistic approach to care for patients living with the effects of rheumatism, arthritis and other locomotor disorders resulting in disability. Patients are of all ages and backgrounds and the objective is to help them articulate and achieve their personal goals. These differ between clients, but include effective self-management of pain and disability, and appropriate use of medication and other healthcare resources. The aim is to help people achieve three things: personal value and self-worth; their functional potential, and their potential contribution to social relationships. A 'team approach' to treatment and education makes this possible. Working with QE Health staff, patients achieve maximum physical, psychological and social independence.

A range of specialist doctors, nurses, therapists and counsellors offer the highest care in physiotherapy, spa therapy, occupational therapy, vocational assessment, educational programs, orthopaedic surgery and orthotics. Specialist rheumatology services are provided, mostly on an outpatient basis by doctors working closely with rheumatology specialist nurses. Around 2,000 new-patient diagnostic visits and 4,000 follow-up visits are provided annually at clinics located at QE Health and around the region in outreach clinics. Referrals are also accepted from a wide geographical area for musculoskeletal rehabilitation. QE Health provides residential, day-stay and inpatient services for clients with chronic degenerative and inflammatory arthritis and chronic musculoskeletal pain. These are mostly provided by defined clinical pathways of care (such as a chronic back pain programme), but also by individually customised programmes. Approximately 8,000 patient-days of care are provided annually.

A range of elective orthopaedic surgery is also performed, with around 500 joint replacements annually. The orthopaedic service is regionally funded and provides community services as well as supporting the primary activities of QE Health. As a major tertiary health service provider, QE Health has an active clinical research programme, with government research funding and contracts with the pharmaceutical industry as well as with tertiary education providers. External finance also comes from charitable research funding agencies. Funding for clinical activity comes mainly from government contracts, with a small amount of private health provision for local and overseas clients. Some revenue is derived from the government's workers' compensation scheme and other accident insurance schemes. The market for publicly funded patients is interesting in that neither the patients nor the general practitioners (who are the main source of referrals and also have needs) are involved directly in paying for the services provided. There is, therefore, a third-party payer involved, either a health funding authority or a disability insurance agency, which also has specified needs and expectations. This has allowed QE Health to develop its own service provision according to 'what seemed best'—what it could provide and what it thought it should provide. This poses a danger to the organisation as it attempts to respond to the demands put upon it without a clear definition of what it is being paid to do. This problem is common among publicly funded health providers, but is a real threat to a specialist unit that cannot afford to provide services for which it does not get paid. A value chain study is, therefore, of considerable benefit to the long-term viability of the organisation and the continuity of the services it provides.

A value chain context mapping study at QE Health

Viewing healthcare management in a commercial context

Two views may be taken of value chain context mapping. The first is what might be termed a 'macro' view; an industry value chain that describes how various discrete economic entities interact. This value chain perspective is largely a strategic one. It is a tool to help firms understand how they should be positioning themselves in the market. It is a perspective that is particularly helpful in understanding the movement away from traditional strategies that were historically driven by ever expanding vertical or horizontal integration. In their place are new strategies built around positioning the firm in networks of entities each with their own core competitive advantages, virtually integrated to maximise value creation.

If we take this first perspective of the value chain – the macro or industry driven perspective – the value chain can be seen as all the activities that occur in the industry turning raw inputs into finished product. In a traditional strategic model the imperative would have been for a firm to own and control all of these activities through the process of vertical integration. The oil industry is a good example, with the oil majors aspiring to control everything from exploration, to oil field development, to shipping, to refining and finally retail delivery. In this sense strategic aspiration and industry vertical dominance were almost synonymous.

In the emerging 'new economy' model the onus is changing from ownership of assets, which carries with it the increasingly difficult responsibility of achieving acceptable stakeholder returns on those assets, to participation in virtual industry networks where access to and management of assets assumes more importance. In many senses this poses more difficult questions for management than the older, vertical integration model. Management now has to understand how these networks operate and, more importantly, where best to position the firm in those networks. It is suggested that identification of the key *industry values drivers* is an important part of this analysis. As has been suggested in this text, four such key drivers can be identified, though each of these factors will assume various weighting according to the particular industry: process management, knowledge management, technology management and relationship management.

The industry success drivers required for the healthcare sector managed by QE Health are identified in Figure 11.12. The task for QE Health management has been to assess the contributions it can make to the overall requirements, and identify partners who can provide the remaining contributions.

The second view that may be taken of value chain context mapping is one at a

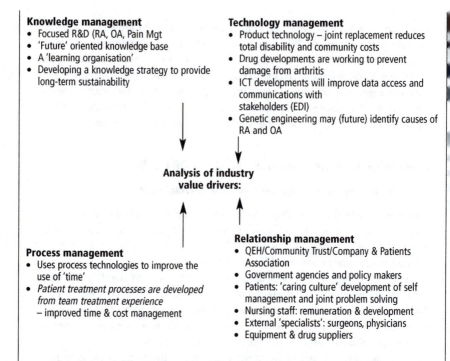

Knowledge management
- Focused R&D (RA, OA, Pain Mgt
- 'Future' oriented knowledge base
- A 'learning organisation'
- Developing a knowledge strategy to provide long-term sustainability

Technology management
- Product technology – joint replacement reduces total disability and community costs
- Drug developments are working to prevent damage from arthritis
- ICT developments will improve data access and communications with stakeholders (EDI)
- Genetic engineering may (future) identify causes of RA and OA

Analysis of industry value drivers:

Process management
- Uses process technologies to improve the use of 'time'
- *Patient treatment processes are developed from team treatment experience* – improved time & cost management

Relationship management
- QEH/Community Trust/Company & Patients Association
- Government agencies and policy makers
- Patients: 'caring culture' development of self management and joint problem solving
- Nursing staff: remuneration & development
- External 'specialists': surgeons, physicians
- Equipment & drug suppliers

Figure 11.12 QE Health: identifying industry value drivers

'micro' level, in other words, by way of a description of how the individual firm operates. This is a business model or operational perspective. It is fundamentally a process driven model, looking at how a particular firm or organisation actually operates and what its core competencies are, or to use the value chain analogy, what its weakest and strongest links are and how these may contribute to meeting customer expectations.

It has been acknowledged that customers consider both the benefits they seek and those they in fact receive from products and services they purchase. Best (2004) deals with the notions of 'value-in-use' and life cycle costing, while, as we saw in Chapter 2, MacMillan and McGrath (1997) argue that the customer life cycle, or the consumption chain, is a means by which '[firms] can uncover opportunities to position their offerings in ways that they, and their competitors, would never have thought possible'. Please review the relevant section in Chapter 2. From these and other contributions there follows the notion that both generic and product-market-specific customer value drivers are important: asset management, performance management, time management, cost management, information management, and risk reduction.

These 'commercial' customer value drivers may be seen in a context of medicine. We discuss the QE Health customer base below, by identifying three distinctive customer groups, each of which can be seen to have expectations that match the generic customer value drivers discussed above. Each of the groups is concerned with the impact that enhanced performance has on business or lifestyle activities. Similarly as regards time management, the ability to provide individual and organisational solutions that improve the use of time is to be welcomed. Cost management also has major implications. The emphasis on the impact of cost management on profitability has permeated all aspects of industrial and government activities. While it could be argued that it has reached excessive (possibly myopic) proportions, it is a fact of life and one of any enterprise must take full cognisance. Healthcare is also very concerned about risk reduction expectations. Many of the preventive healthcare techniques that are current or emergent have risk management in mind.

It follows that unless healthcare managers view their customer base using similar approaches to the more commercial organisations, the task of management will become increasingly difficult. Medicine and healthcare management can no longer claim to be any different from other activities. The introduction to this case study identified some of the changing philosophies, structures and practices that are being considered by UK health policy makers. Many of the concepts and constructs being discussed have their roots in commercial managerial practice. Consequently, rather than avoid them, healthcare management should evaluate them and identify the benefits they can realise.

Customer value/expectations criteria and customer value drivers

During any 'purchase' situation, certain aspects or attributes of a 'product' represent *value* to customers. Attributes enhance a customer's situation, resolve problems, and offer solutions. Customers also have costs. *Customer acquisition costs* are incurred when considering a purchase. Customers maximise value when they select the option for which customer value criteria exceed customer acquisition costs. Both the value criteria and acquisition costs are influenced by external features, such as the 'significance' of the expenditure; the strength of the vendor's brand (reputation); the customer's life cycle/style characteristics, and their purchasing expectations (the benefits to be delivered).

A *customer value model* for QE Health 'customers' is described below and is illustrated as Figure 11.13.

Categories of customer and their value criteria

For healthcare there are four categories of customer: the individual, the general practitioner, the employer and the government. Each has value criteria. Some characteristics and value drivers are shared, others are likely to differ:

- Asset management: employers seek to maximise employee skills and expertise
- Performance management: individuals seek to maximise work and leisure performances
- Time management: individuals and their employers wish to keep treatment time to a minimum

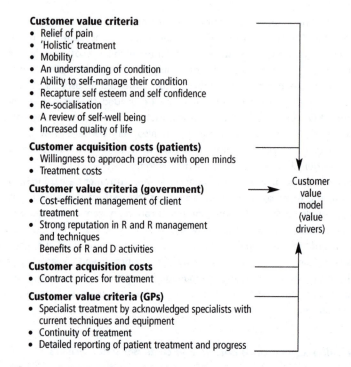

Customer value criteria
- Relief of pain
- 'Holistic' treatment
- Mobility
- An understanding of condition
- Ability to self-manage their condition
- Recapture self esteem and self confidence
- Re-socialisation
- A review of self-well being
- Increased quality of life

Customer acquisition costs (patients)
- Willingness to approach process with open minds
- Treatment costs

Customer value criteria (government)
- Cost-efficient management of client treatment
- Strong reputation in R and R management and techniques
  Benefits of R and D activities

Customer acquisition costs
- Contract prices for treatment

Customer value criteria (GPs)
- Specialist treatment by acknowledged specialists with current techniques and equipment
- Continuity of treatment
- Detailed reporting of patient treatment and progress

Customer value model (value drivers)

Figure 11.13 QE Health: identifying customer value drivers

■ Cost management: cost of treatment and cost of lost output is a concern to both

■ Information management: transparency concerning outcomes of treatment (and not having treatment) is essential to decision making

■ Risk reduction: having/not having treatment has numerous implications

Customer acquisition costs

■ Specification: diagnosis?

■ Search: identifying expertise?

■ Transactions: healthcare insurance?

■ Installation (delivery): skilled treatment?

■ Operation: skilled support staff?

■ Maintenance: post-procedure care?

■ Disposal: return to independence?

QE Health addresses its three customer categories directly. Each has a different perspective concerning both value criteria and acquisition costs. The end-users' value criteria are clear: they seek pain relief, mobility, functionality and training in how they may better manage their lives. A value benefit that is delivered, of which they may not be initially aware, is the re-establishment of self-esteem and the ability to reaffirm control of their lives. Their costs are those for the treatment, and the psychological costs of changing their attitudes towards their condition.

The New Zealand government is an important customer mostly through health funding authorities (at the time of this study organised on a regional basis), but also through the Accident, Compensation and Rehabilitation Corporation (ACRC), New Zealand's workers' compensation scheme. Attempts to deregulate the ACRC have resulted in a number of other insurers entering the market. All these funding streams remain sensitive to policy changes. The funders' value criteria are based not only upon QE Health's delivery costs, but also on its strong reputation for achieving results in the treatment of rheumatic disease and particularly in rehabilitation of the labour force into productive work. Their acquisition costs are controlled by budgets.

General practitioner (GP) 'customers' are concerned to obtain the treatment for patients that will offer effective and long-lasting relief. They also require support in managing chronic and incurable diseases that result in a huge burden of physical and financial disability. Value for them extends beyond the knowledge that QE Health has a reputation for expertise and patient care; it includes the reporting of patient progress and recommendations for treatment. Ability to access such services enhances the value of the GP's own practice. New Zealand has not yet embraced general practitioner fund holding, but in general GPs feel a responsibility to spend public money wisely. It follows that implicitly they are applying cost-effective criteria.

Analysis of customer value drivers

If an organisation is to develop a strong competitive position it clearly needs to identify the value drivers that are important to the end-user customer and to structure a value delivery system that reflects these *and* the objectives of the other value chain participants. It will be recalled from Chapter 2 that Slywotzky and Morrison (1997), in their 'customer-centric' approach to the value chain, suggest that 'Customer priorities are simply the things that are so important to customers that they will pay a premium for them or, when they can't get them, they will switch supplier.' For QE Health it was found that the following describe the important customer value drivers:
Individually prescribed treatment programmes

- Team treatment
- Caring approach towards patients
- Specialist treatment, and;
- Patient follow-up

These value drivers become critical in the value delivery process. They form the basis of performance planning and measurement and as such are examined rigorously. Figure 11.14 indicates the procedure used to do this. *Strategic and operational resources* are clearly essential inputs and a lack of any of these will impact upon both long-term and short-term success. In much the same way it can be argued that

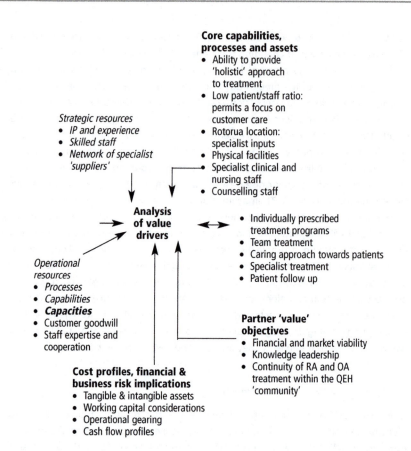

Figure 11.14 QE Health: analysing the customer value drivers: resources, processes, capabilities and costs

without *core capabilities*, *processes* and *assets* in place, not only would QE Health not be the success it has been, but the future would become doubtful as new opportunities appear. For example, its Rotorua location has been an important feature in the past, as it was a national treatment centre. There are also questions concerning developments in care and the relevance the existing capabilities, processes and assets have for the future. Given that they are relevant, questions of ownership patterns should be considered, and similar questions asked concerning future requirements to meet developing treatment methods if these are seen to be important.

Developing a value proposition

Customer value expectations combine with the core competencies of the organisation to produce a *value proposition* that identifies what is to be delivered to the customer and by what means. In other words, the value proposition identifies the benefits and costs for the customer and the internal activities (or processes) necessary to produce the benefits (value). The previous work of analysing the customers' value drivers provides a basis for the eventual value proposition. It has to reflect customer expectations and at the same time be both *feasible* and *viable*; by 'feasible' we imply that the product-service treatment package is deliverable and that it is financially viable. The QE Health value proposition is described by Figure 11.15. It is focused on the holistic treatment of locomotor disorders including rheumatoid and other types of inflammatory arthritis, multiple joint osteoarthritis and chronic musculoskeletal pain. In almost all cases, the physical state of the joints is only one of a number of factors contributing to the overall loss of quality of life.

Just as important is the way in which this proposition is made. The team approach to treatment reinforces the value proposition. Following an initial diagnostic visit, patients are directed towards a team and a specific treatment program. Thus, the customer is receiving a customised response to their condition. The team approach ensures that patients are 'educated' in the issues and the implications of their condition, together with being given an opportunity to understand how best to adapt to their environment. The final aspect of the value proposition is an appraisal of the patient's potential social and economic roles. More often than not, the patient has a negative approach to the possibility of contributing to and enjoying such roles; however, education, support, counselling, physiotherapy and occupational therapy (including vocational rehabilitation) result in a positive outcome, defined as:

Recovery or relief of specific symptoms within a specified time period. A level of

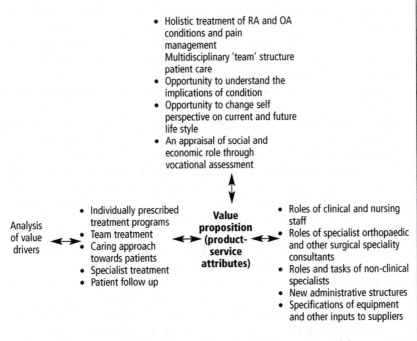

Figure 11.15 QE Health: developing a value proposition

knowledge, self-belief and motivation that maintains the health benefits gained from after procedure care in specified surroundings. QE Health would therefore identify staff, equipment and infrastructure requirements to meet the customer's value expectations.

Value production and coordination

A major skill in the management of virtual enterprises is establishing the most effective position for a partner within the virtual community. As we have seen, no partner will agree to become involved unless the outcome will be to their benefit – that is, they must be convinced that they will become 'better off'. Having identified the required 'success drivers' the next task is to identify where they are located – who owns them and how they can be 'recruited'. Accordingly, organisation structure presents a number of issues for value chain management. Figure 11.16 identifies the considerations that influence value delivery.

There are two overall factors to be taken into account: *organisational architecture* and *market management*. Organisational architecture is particularly important within value chain structures and as a consequence the coordination aspects of what is essentially a virtual structure can have significant impact on performance. Not only is the nature of the structure an important issue to resolve but so too are issues such as the mix of corporate cultures and management styles. Typically individual businesses and organisations work well within the structures they develop around, but this does not guarantee they will work on an inter-organisational basis – often they do not. It follows that this component of the context mapping exercise can be time consuming and will involve consideration of the other factors such as communication, control, decision making processes, reward systems, motivation and incentives, and performance evaluation. Possibly the most difficult task is to deal with the integration of what can be quite a disparate group of interests, methods and expectations.

The organisational architecture for QE Health to cope with market management includes important 'stakeholder' groups. These are customers (patients); referral organisations (GPs); suppliers (equipment and drug companies); an internal market (nursing staff and administrators); 'influencers' (patient groups such as the Arthritis Foundation and Patient's Association, local and national Maori (indigenous) health groups, health service agencies); 'recruiters' (medical and nursing recruitment agencies), and 'investors' (government and other funds providers). Each requires a strategy for managing the interface between QE Health and the market component.

QE Health also has a complex market structure. Its primary market is its patients. A number of patients are loyal customers, who return regularly because of the benefits the facilities offer. Consequently the 'repeat business customer' is important to QE Health. For similar reasons its position with GPs is an important market consideration; they are important sources of revenue continuity. Government sources of business are clearly also important, not only because of the contribution towards revenues and the revenue continuity, but also because of the 'referral influence' government exercises. The very fact that government is a customer acts

Organisational structure:
Organisational
architecture
- Collaboration networks
  - Internal
  - External
  - Alliances & partnerships
- Integration model
- Communication
- Control
- Culture
- Management style
- Decision making
- Reward systems
- Motivation & incentives
- Performance evaluation

Organisational structure:
Market management
- Patents and the patient association: liaison and education
- GPs and community health: maintain awareness of QEH developments
- Suppliers of surgical and clinical services: provision of specialist nursing staff and facilities
- Referral markets: Government agencies (ACC) and GPs are kept aware of QEH services facilities and R and D. Maintain confidence in QEH
- QEH are involved in R and D activities with suppliers of drugs & equipment
- Health professionals and students are encouraged to spend elective periods with QEH R and D
- QEH stakeholders are made aware of R and D developments and market potential
- Competitors are appraised as both competitors and partners

Value proposition (product – service attributes) → **Value production and coordination**

Organisation structure: operations management

'Production'
- Introduction of team treatment management
- Workload planning based upon acuity scales to optimise capacities and capabilities (surgery)
- R and R treatment planned around initial needs diagnosis for clinical, therapy and social inputs

'Logistics'
Planned patient throughput and aftercare needs
- Inventory cover to meet planned surgical activities
- Clear supplier qualifications criteria

'Service'
- Preadmission clinics assess emotional, physical and social condition
- Planned individual treatment programs
- Support equipment rentals
- Follow up treatment
- Accommodation
- Education programs

Figure 11.16 QE Health: producing and delivering the value

to reinforce the overall market position of QE Health, but also makes it vulnerable should government's purchasing policy change. Supply markets are important sources of 'knowledge' and can be helpful in promoting the strengths of QE Health patient care and R&D activities. Recent government research grants and an expansion of drug-trial activity suggest that the important role of QE Health in R&D is being increasingly recognised.

QE Health actively encourages healthcare professionals and students to spend elective periods with the organisation. QE Health considers this activity to be an important aspect of market management as it fosters interest in rheumatoid arthritis and osteoarthritis research and treatment, resulting in increased recognition of the importance of QE Health's activities. Competition exists in healthcare just as it does in other commercial markets; QE Health has local competitors in both the public and private sectors. Competition is keen for patients and funding, with some decisions concerning market positioning (based upon core competencies) and capacity utilisation being necessary. It is not unrealistic to expect a value chain solution to emerge in which both capabilities and capacities are focused on achieving an increase in customer satisfaction.

QE Health's internal structure implements operational tasks and concerns the management of procurement, 'production', logistics and service. Procurement management is an important aspect of QE Health's operations, particularly as it involves expensive prosthetic equipment. By working closely with suppliers, inventory levels are maintained on a 'just-in-time' basis. 'Production' management is the process by which value is 'manufactured'. It is a process during which decisions concerning what, where, how, when and by whom production processes are made to occur; it identifies options for in-house activities and for outsourcing. 'Production' processes are focused on patient care. Team treatment is a means by which the management of clinical treatment is made more individual and effective. It is a form of matrix organisation structure. Patients' treatment programs are partly based upon a physician's diagnosis prior to the program commencing (for instance, newly diagnosed rheumatoid arthritis), but mostly upon the patient defined goals of rehabilitation as determined by team assessment on entry to the program. Surgery 'production' is based upon workload planning, in which the available capacity is allocated on the basis of the complexity of the operation and therefore the theatre time required. Nursing capacity requirements are planned on the same basis, together with a planned patient/staff ratio that will ensure adequate time for patient care. Pre-admission clinics are held to ensure that before an admission date is confirmed the patient is emotionally, physically and socially prepared for surgery. Once a date is agreed and the patient enters, QE Health staff begin to plan the patient's discharge by identifying tasks that will be required, support and facility needs, such as GP involvement, and administrative requirements. The awareness of related technology developments has resulted in nursing staff assuming more responsibility for patient care. This, together with the fact that QE Health is a specialist unit, has resulted in benefits of economies of specialisation *and* cost benefits from an 'experience effect'. These factors contribute to a strong and positive relationship with surgeons, who exhibit a preference to work with QE Health.

Logistics management considers both material and non-material (service and information) flows throughout an organisation. The 'value added' concept here refers to enhancing the perceived value of the 'product-service' to both the customer (patient) and the referral customer (the GP). Economists consider value in terms of utilities created; these are form, possession, time and place. The logistics function is concerned with time and place utilities. Time and place utilities add value in a QE Health context by allowing medical and nursing staff to provide healthcare and customer care in a cost-effective way and one in which confidence is built.

Logistics in medicine is an interesting management concern because it comprises a combination of patient care process, patient logistics (moving patients through QE Health) and materials logistics (the flow of equipment, drugs and information). Logistics is increasingly becoming an area of specialist outsourcing in a number of sectors.

Logistics systems relate to progressing patients through QE Health facilities, after-care needs and administrative procedures. QE Health's holistic approach comprises a complete range of procedures, as outlined earlier. It follows that if high utilisation is to be achieved, then capacity management procedures are important. It must be remembered that QE Health's assets are not only in 'plant' but also in specialist staff; it is essential that patient flows be managed smoothly throughout. There is also an inventory management concern for QE Health, as prosthetic and orthotic equipment are both expensive. Strict inventory management control is exercised to ensure that optimum levels of items are matched with the rate of use and the inventory budget. Supplies are appraised against quantitative and qualitative criteria such as product availability, service response, and staff training, as well as the essential product quality. QE Health has developed a 'just-in-time' approach with its prosthesis suppliers.

There are a number of important service aspects to the operational structure and management of QE Health activities. Pre-admission clinics were mentioned above in the context of productivity planning. However, they are an important characteristic of the QE Health service offer and this is recognised by patients who comment upon the role of the clinics in the overall customer care program.

Possibly the most visible aspect of QE Health's service is the individual care for patients undergoing treatment. Patients are full of praise for staff and for the benefits received. The focus on self-awareness and self-help are the most commented-upon aspects of the treatment, possibly because pain relief was an expected outcome; the ability to be prospective about the future is, for many, a surprise. This feature is extended into follow-up treatment. An additional service feature is the availability of orthotic equipment through purchase or rental services. QE Health's rehabilitation programs do not necessarily require patients to be 'in QE Health', and the service extends to arranging external accommodation. One final aspect of service is the increasing number of educational programs provided within and outwith QE Health by its staff.

Concluding comments

This case study demonstrates the application of the value chain concept in a healthcare situation. The concept offers benefits to healthcare managers because it asks them to disaggregate their healthcare function, to question its efficacy, identify

Customer value criteria
- Relief of pain
- 'Holistic' treatment
- Mobility
- An understanding of condition
- Ability to self-manage their condition
- Recapture self esteem and self confidence
- Re socialisation
- A review of self-well being
- Increased quality of life

Customer acquisition costs (patients)
- Willingness to approach process with open minds
- Treatment costs

Strategic resources
- *IP and experience*
- *Skilled staff*
- *Network of specialist 'suppliers'*

Core capabilities, processes and assets
- Ability to provide 'holistic' approach to treatment
- Low patient/staff ratio: permits a focus on customer care
- Rotorua location: specialist inputs
- Physical facilities
- Specialist clinical and nursing staff
- Counselling staff

- Holistic treatment of RA and OA conditions and pain management
- Multidisciplinary 'team' structure patient care
- Opportunity to understand the implications of condition
- Opportunity to change self perspective on current and future life style
- An appraisal of social and economic role through vocational assessment

Organisational structure: market management
- Patents and the patient association: liaison and education
- GPs and community health: maintain awareness of QEH developments
- Suppliers of surgical and clinical services: provision of specialist nursing staff and facilities
- Referral markets: Government agencies (ACC) and GPs are kept aware of QEH services facilities and R and D.
- Maintain confidence in QEH QEH are involved in R and D activities with suppliers of drugs & equipment
- Health professionals and students are encouraged to spend elective periods with QEH R and D
- QEH stakeholders are made aware of R and D developments and market potential
- Competitors are appraised as both competitors and partners

Knowledge management
- Focused R&D (RA, OA, Pain Mgt)
- 'Future' oriented knowledge base
- A 'learning organisation'
- Developing a knowledge strategy to provide long-term sustainability

Technology management
- Product' technology - joint replacement reduces total disability and community costs
- Drug developments are working to prevent damage from arthritis
- ICT developments will improve data access and communications with stakeholders (EDI)
- Genetic engineering may (future) identify causes of RA and OA

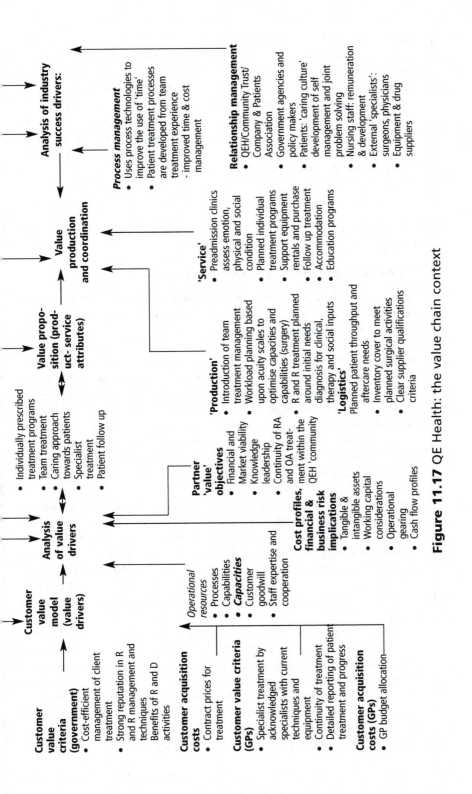

Figure 11.17 QE Health: the value chain context

alternative methods of achieving current results and explore future opportunities. Value chain analysis permits an intra- and inter-organisational review of the cost-efficiency of resource application and thus encourages medical staff as well as management to explore alternative methods and structures for meeting objectives. A complete view of the QE Health value chain map appears as Figure 11.17.

A number of alternatives and opportunities emerged from this study, which there is not space to discuss here, such as the prospect of extending partnership arrangements, and the notion of using staff skills to present preventative options to industry and the wider community.

CASE STUDY 11.2

Repositioning in the value chain: IBM and Dell

(Based upon Simon London, 'IBM needs to press right buttons', *FT International* in *Australian*, 10 May 2005; Louise Lee, 'Hard-driving Dell pushes into services', *Australian Financial Review*, 27 May 2005)

The 1990s were problem years for IBM. Its core business, mainframe computers, which was responsible for its 1970s and 1980s growth, collapsed as the market demanded a different direction. Its current financial position is strong, with a business model that produces a cash flow of $US10–15 billion. This success has been due, primarily, to the success of IBM Global Services, which sells information technology outsourcing and computer maintenance to companies. In 1993 the business was almost non-existent; in 2004 it produced revenues of $US46 billion. Estimates suggest little or no growth from computer hardware or software since 1993.

However, the services division has not maintained the initial growth momentum. Business declined in 2004 compared with 2003 by some $US10 billion ($US53 to 43 billion). Probably more significant has been the change in the service market. The emerging trend towards shorter, less valuable services contracts is making the market easier to access by small competitors. Margins are lower and offshore low-cost service providers are offering lower prices and a wider range of services. IBM's immediate response was to restructure with the loss of 13,000 jobs (May 2005).

A path for the future was described in 2002 by CEO Sam Palmisano, who envisioned an easier world, one in which 'computing power would be little more than a utility, like electricity or the telephone, provided by huge grids of connected machines'. The strategic implications of this, and specifically as regards a strategic direction for IBM, remained unclear until 2003 when the company announced a coherent strategy: 'In addition to selling hardware, software and IT services, IBM would help its customers reengineer their business processes and, for good measure, offer to run everything from customer call centres to logistics to financial administration.' IBM would become a purveyor of 'business process transformation services' (BPTS). These would offer an outsourcing service for customers, giving them access to engineering services and 'even' the intellectual brain power formerly 'locked away' in IBM's laboratories. The potential worldwide market was estimated at $US500 billion, over and above the $US1.2 trillion that companies worldwide spend on IT products and services each year. IBM has said that a 10 per cent market share would be acceptable.

Analysts suggest there to be problems. One problem is that the market itself lacks clarity, being as yet an undefined range of services and one clearly needing some structure. Another problem concerns the nature and the strength of IBM's potential competitors. These include Accenture, Hewitt Associates (HR consultants), and Wipro, the Indian based outsourcer. Simon London argues that while IBM has some sources of competitive advantage, namely its customer relationships and enormous resources. It is arguable that it has the skills to change from an 'IT stalwart into a trusted business partner that chief executives will call upon to re-engineer and run large chunks of their organisations'. The acquisition of PwC Consulting may close this gap. But nevertheless the doubt remains: 'In order to help its customers transform themselves, IBM will need to transform itself.'

Dell has moved well 'beyond the PC' with market entries into related hardware products. In May 2005 the company reported a year-on-year growth of 30 per cent in its computer services initiative. Whereas IBM has taken a 'solutions/consulting' pathway, Dell has focused on expanding basic phone support and repair services, helping businesses load software, recycle and replace old equipment. Dell is focusing on 'corporate customers', particularly those who do not ask for support from Dell's competitors. An interesting point made by Louise Lee is that this is an exceptional move for a company that has designed its business model around direct interactions and transactions with its customers. Dell's service initiative relies upon 'subcontractors willing to take on near profitless assignments'. Lee suggests that if Dell is to succeed it must ensure its partners maintain a very high level of service while expanding its service offer range. Furthermore, as Lee goes on to suggest, selling what is becoming a commodity product is based on efficient management of service operations, and therefore of costs; computer services are very different, requiring investment in knowledgeable people and service parts. In addition, it is a very diverse product-market, ranging from 'coffee spilled on a keyboard [to dealing with] a massive hacker attack'.

Dell has a strategy. It is focusing mostly on jobs that will help boost hardware sales. At the same time it is keeping tight control of costs by using its strong market position to force deals from subcontractors to handle everyday common tasks. This raises questions concerning future strategy. Lee reports on comments from the industry and potential customers suggesting that sooner or later Dell must confront some difficult decisions. For example, it has yet to tackle the operation of customers' technology shops or to provide help to them in finding new ways to use ICT to develop and improve their businesses. Currently the vice president, marketing of Hewlett-Packard's technology services unit sees Dell as no major threat, but infers that with a broader product-service this could change as they (Dell) are forced to accept service contracts involving non-Dell equipment –

contracts such as one reported by Lee for Austin Peay State University (Clarksville, Tennessee) that is valued at $US100,000, requiring the successful company to support existing Sun Microsystems equipment. And again, the point is made that many potential clients prefer a supplier who will provide help in applying technology not simply in managing the equipment Finally, the relationships with contractors remain an issue. Dell's competitors provide low-cost service (using company staff) as an incentive to promote further sales of high-margin products. As Lee suggests, would Dell's subcontractor network be willing to participate in this strategy?

Discussion topics

IBM has suggested by its actions that it has the willingness to retreat from businesses that have become non-core. The sale of its unprofitable PC business to China's largest manufacturer of personal computers is an indication of this. But if, as CEO Palmisano suggests, the remainder of the industry (or a large part of it) also becomes a commodity product, how will this impact on IBM, and will the proposed strategy remain viable?

Use the models presented earlier in this chapter to describe the changes that have been made to the IBM model.

Dell's approach in the context of its value proposition and value delivery is quite different. Consider the value chain positioning strategy implications of both the IBM and the Dell businesses.

Undertake a project that will provide data to show the operational and strategic changes that have been made and their financial implications for IBM.

CASE STUDY 11.3

Value chain analysis and management in the Australian construction industry

(This case study has been developed from an MBA assignment completed by students at the Sydney Graduate School of Management in August 2005. The permission of the students, Steven Tull, Craig Wilkins, Lyn Dewick, Kerry Gould and Claire Breakwell, to use their work has been obtained. Their contribution is acknowledged and appreciated.)

Introduction

Traditionally, competition in the construction industry has largely been 'the bigger, the better'. Physical size and political muscle ensured success. Companies built on a large asset base were the norm. However, competition, along with both product and process innovation, has led to a new focus: the customer. With this focus comes the question of value, and how these major enterprises are constructed to be more cost-effective and more aligned to customer requirements.

The information age has brought along a whole new way of getting the message to the customer, but moreover of getting the message *from* the customer – what does the customer 'really' want and need? Like most industries this century, the construction industry has changed significantly. Largely dominated by inefficient entrepreneurial developers pushing their skyscrapers on the developing capital cities around the world, these conglomerates were driven by inefficient labour practices supported by strong trade unions that had no regard for the customer.

This case study identifies the changes made by one of the world's largest construction companies, Bovis Lend Lease, to become much more customer focused by using the value chain methodology.

Industry and business needs to compete, but not always to survive. Much of this competition is consumer driven. With information technology finding a new 'peak' every second week, consumers are 'information-rich' when it comes to ensuring value for money and wide choice. An educated and informed society should, almost in itself, guarantee that suppliers will work hard to gain and keep your custom. But does it? The risk for consumers is that they have reached a point where technology is seen as an adornment, an enhancement of their life/work experiences. The mobile phone industry is one that appears to be almost self-replicating, with mobile phones taking over from the PC as our most sought-after new 'toy'. Innovation in technology is also now highly relevant in the construction industry, with environmental trends, energy efficiency and architectural considerations influencing customer choice.

The construction industry was historically one of the most inefficient industries in the world in terms of the way in which it went about its processes of constructing major capital projects. Inefficient labour practices and an almost total focus on supply chain requirements such as procurement, largely predicated on rigorous 'tendering' processes and project management, created an environment of major waste and mismanagement. So much so that in 1998 the Deputy Prime Minister in the UK ordered a special task force to investigate possible opportunities to improve the quality and efficiency of the UK construction industry. This task force and the subsequent report detailed major changes that were needed in the supply chain, but more importantly, with a major focus on the demand chain.

Sir John Egan, Chairman of the UK Construction Industry Task Force (1998), stated in his executive summary:

> There is a deep concern that the industry as a whole is underachieving, it has low profitability and invests too little in capital, research and development and training. Too many of the industry's clients are dissatisfied with its overall performance.

One of the companies to embrace the value chain concept early on was Bovis Lend Lease, which formed valuable partnerships and restructured its organisation to position itself better than its competitors to be a more efficient, customer focused organisation.

Nature and scope of the construction industry value chain

Historically, the construction industry focused very heavily on the supply chain and in particular on procurement and project management processes. Competitive tendering was used to create a 'cheapest price wins' mentality, with no understanding of the value component that could be offered by more efficient suppliers. This mentality had no regard at all for the end product delivered to the customer. Project management processes were driven by a 'just get it done' ethic, combined with poor coordination between trades, and poor labour practices.

When the UK government appointed its task force to review the construction industry, it found that major improvements could be made not only to the supply chain processes, but also that significant gains could be realised by understanding the demand chain. Furthermore, a steering group brought together by Bovis Lend Lease, believed that value chain processes used in the automotive industry could be used in the construction industry, and actually brought in senior people from automotive manufacturers and component suppliers in Detroit to prove their point. (Bovis Lend Lease 2001).

This proved to be a significant step, with Bovis Lend Lease leading the industry in change. They undertook some innovative practices and test cases to prove that the changes would work, which are detailed below.

In moving away from a basic supply chain process to a value chain process, the construction industry has four 'generic' key value chain processes, as shown in Figure 11.18.

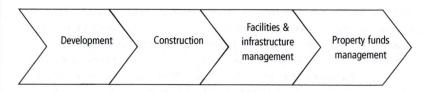

Figure 11.18 Generic construction industry the value chain

Development

In simple terms, the development stage of the value chain encompasses all of the activities that take place prior to any construction work. These activities are those of identifying opportunities, developing concepts, joint ventures or partnering where necessary, and giving due consideration to financing issues and regulatory requirements. This process is one that is not generally well executed within the construction industry. Many companies place their focus on developing a concept for a certain property and securing financial support without really understanding the customer requirements and how they could build in more value.

Construction

The construction section of the value chain covers each of the activities primarily involved and linked with the direct construction work. It will cover processes such as final design and construction management, procurement, project management and materials management. This area of the value chain was identified by many as one that exhibited a significant amount of inefficiency. Poor coordination of trades on-site leads to major wastage of resources and higher costs. The impact of this was major mismanagement of material flows, which created cost 'blow-outs' on materials targets. This process will be discussed further later; however, the Bovis Lend Lease study identified savings of up to 55 per cent to be gained by significant improvement in this area.

Facilities and infrastructure management

Facilities and infrastructure management is a relatively new field, largely created through major construction companies beginning to better understand their customers' needs. It primarily covers all the management and maintenance functions of a capital project that the builder manages on behalf of the customer. A process such as this has many benefits to the customer in that if the builder has built a poor-quality building, then the builder will need to live with the problems associated with it.

Property funds management

This value chain process provides for funds management and ownership of properties by the company in order to build a portfolio of property investments, but also provides cost-effective financing and equity arrangements for future projects. In essence, traditional construction companies 'designed and built'. Now they design, build, manage and maintain, offering a complete value added service from development to management and all the way through. Certainly, not all construction companies undertake all four processes of the generic value chain. It is clear from the research undertaken that many of the main players concentrate only on the two or three areas of the value chain which they consider core to their business.

The construction industry continues to go through change as it endeavours to meet the needs of an ever more demanding consumer. Many major corporations are now seeking buildings and infrastructure projects that clearly meet their business strategies and objectives. Customer organisations now demand buildings that reflect their corporate image. They also demand buildings that reflect environmental values in order to be seen as good corporate citizens. No longer can the industry continue to rely on simple supply chain focused strategies of operation, because they risk being left behind as their customers move forward. The construction industry must focus on analysing and understanding the demand chain while improving supply chain integration. For example, many residential apartment builders are now spending considerable time and resources to clearly understand the needs of their target market, by including such facilities as community areas, swimming pools, gymnasiums and the like.

There are many competitors in the construction industry, all with different business models and value chain strategies. For example, while Bovis Lend Lease openly proclaims its matching of skills, resources, markets and geographics to customers through strategic client teams, Multiplex, one of Bovis Lend Lease's major competitors, focuses on delivering shareholder returns and investment grade assets. It is therefore of little surprise that in recent years the Multiplex organisation is suffering negative press due its archaic management principles and 'family business' culture. Table 11.1 outlines the major competitors in the construction industry and their value chain strategy in comparison with the generic industry value chain.

Table 11.1 clearly highlights that the organisations researched have different strategies in terms of their business model and the focus that they place on the entire industry value chain. However, whilst they differ, it is apparent that these organisations have learnt that not only are *technology*, *knowledge* and *processes* important in being successful in the construction industry, but *relationships* are equally important if not essential. In fact, as Bovis Lend Lease has done, many organisations now spend more time understanding customer needs and in some cases even reward employees and workers for achieving customer goals ahead of time and ahead of budget, thereby driving a 'win-win' culture.

Value chain processes and value chain relationships

Bovis Lend Lease was established in 1999 after a successful association in which Bovis had completed Bluewater, Europe's largest retail and leisure development, for its client Lend Lease Corporation. At that time Lend Lease itself had over 50 years' experience in project and construction management in the Asia Pacific region. It had developed under its original name of Civil and Civic, a company formed from two Dutch companies whose executives had visited Australia to assess opportunities in 1951.

After the completion of the Bluewater development, Lend Lease expanded its global presence and position in the real estate business by acquiring Bovis from P&O

Table 11.1 Value chain strategies of major construction industry competitors

Organisation	Development	Construction	Facilities and infrastructure management	Funds management
John Holland	Yes	Yes	Yes†	No
Baulderstone Hornibrook	No	Yes	Yes	Yes
Mirvac	Yes	No	Yes	Yes
Multiplex	Yes	Yes	Yes	Yes
Leightons	No	Yes	Yes	No
Bovis Lend Lease	Yes	Yes	No	No

† Formal joint venture arrangement

(Peninsular & Orient Steamship Company). Bovis merged with Lend Lease to form Bovis Lend Lease, Lend Lease's new project management and construction services division thus opening further opportunities to provide an extended framework for Lend Lease, its stakeholders and customers, particularly in the areas of technology, information and relationship management.

As identified in the generic industry value chain (Figure 11.18), Bovis Lend Lease today provides to its customers a wide range of skills which encompass construction, design/engineering, design management and procurement management. These skills are applied over various sectors such as commercial, retail, infrastructure and government, with projects undertaken regionally and globally.

An example of Lend Lease's effective management of inter-enterprise relationships is the Minerva PLC retail development in the UK, in which Minerva reached agreement with Lend Lease to develop a 900,000 square foot retail development in Croydon town centre. Lend Lease took responsibility for the development and Bovis Lend Lease undertook the construction. Minerva has set up a Jersey based trust that will own the development; Lend Lease will have the right to subscribe for 50 per cent of the units in the trust one year after completion of the development.

Industry value drivers

Industry value drivers vary between industries and are dependent upon where the industry decides to strategically position itself for a competitive advantage. The construction industry strategy works on relationship management as a key driver for competitive advantage, with technology management, knowledge management and process management playing an important but smaller part in its strategy, as indicated below. Bovis Lend Lease is an especially good example of this positioning.

Knowledge management

The construction industry is organisationally very complex in that it possesses an extraordinary high number of small to medium-sized businesses which contract to the larger organisations such as Bovis Lend Lease. This high number of separate businesses created a fragmented communication and knowledge sharing environment. This fragmentation in turn meant that many separate companies, each with its own cultures, work practices and personalities, managed the ownership and control of many communication and knowledge sharing practices.

Bovis Lend Lease recognises that knowledge and communication are key ingredients in the integration of their construction activities. This is evidenced by their website statement that 'Our ability to apply the best available knowledge is a key point of difference for us in the marketplace. We are achieving this by investing in services like ikonnect, sponsoring Communities of Practice, providing technical skilling and maintaining systems.' The knowledge sharing system called 'ikonnect' was developed by Bovis Lend Lease and is available to nearly 10,000 Lend Lease employees and the employees of clients located across six continents. More importantly though, Bovis Lend Lease also developed ProjectWeb, an internet based project management system. It is mandatory for every supplier and contractor to enter their own build plans and activity schedules into this system, providing Bovis Lend Lease with the ability to ensure all contractor and supplier schedules are integrated with each other. Importantly, though, every supplier and contractor is able to have sight of the schedules of those trades that effectively impact their schedule. This knowledge management system allows Bovis Lend Lease to give themselves, and all stakeholders in the project, information sharing that enables them to be proactive as regards efficiency.

Technology management

From beginning to end, technology is an integral part of Bovis Lend Lease's value chain strategy. With state-of-the-art technology, Bovis Lend Lease is able to visualise to the customer the projected end design. Additionally, technology assists in the coordination and control of projects, schedules, subcontractors and more. Without technology, Bovis Lend Lease would be unable to efficiently plan and execute projects. 'The best way for Bovis to communicate its strategy is through visuals – specifically 3D animation,' said Denis Leff of Bovis Lend Lease (Building Talk 2004).

Bovis Lend Lease was responsible for the design and construction of Lend Lease's Sydney head office in Millers Point, and the local project team was able to gain an understanding of the latest technology from their European colleagues' leveraging of Lend Lease's global capabilities.

Relationship management

Bovis Lend Lease has taken an approach of superior customer relationship management. It has adapted its skills by trade and matched them to markets and then to geographic regions to create strong customer-centric client management teams. These teams work with customers to identify opportunities and to manage communication processes throughout construction processes. In fact, Bovis Lend Lease has discovered through this approach that improved management of the construction processes and application of responsibilities very early on in projects have avoided nasty and costly surprises to the customer at the end of the project.

Leveraging the customer relationship throughout the project has increased the ability to build customer satisfaction at the end of the project rather than engaging in lengthy and often costly disputes over project variations. The cost of these disputes may not only be monetary; they may also impact on relationships. For example, Bovis Lend Lease was awarded a A$57m contract in July 2005 with the Department of Education and the Arts to upgrade and refurbish 250 schools in South East Queensland. Peter Bates, general manager of Bovis Lend Lease, stated that he believed Bovis Lend Lease's ability to manage tight deadlines and deliver projects in an operating environment helped the company win the logistically complex project; the tight schedule meant establishing a strong relationship with the Department of Public Works and the Department of Education and the Arts.

Process management

To ensure the delivery of customer value to all stakeholders, Lend Lease continually works on strategies to deliver value efficiently and effectively by analysing critical success drivers and by identifying business opportunities in markets suited to their capabilities. Scale is leveraged to gain regional and global synergies, particularly in drawing on the experience of other parts of the Lend Lease group business. Greg Clarke, managing director and CEO of Bovis Lend Lease Australia, wrote (Interlink 2005a):

> For Lend Lease, creating sustainable outcomes means improving the social, economic and environmental outcomes in our work, while continuing to deliver the commercial performance expected of us. Creating sustainable outcomes is now an essential part of the way we do business for two main reasons. Firstly, building a better world through more sustainable operating practices is the right thing to do. Secondly, growing our capabilities in this area will minimise risk, build competitive advantage and create value for our shareholders.

Value chain strategies

Typically, the construction industry is capital-intensive and extremely competitive. An organisation's value chain strategy is becoming more and more important, especially considering the improvements in technology which can be accessed by all organisations, and of course considering globalisation.

Day (1999) argues that customer value is delivered more effectively by assuming that the value delivery processes are 'more like loops of interacting processes ... Instead of viewing the process as a chain that delivers value to customers, the market driven firm views the process as an interaction with customers.' This forms the basis of Bovis Lend Lease's value chain strategies – working with the customer to create and design a project and then constructing and managing all elements of that construction, utilising and collaborating with a diverse group of specialist organisations to create an end product.

Bovis Lend Lease initiated change within the construction industry through the way it looked at the total value chain on the Mid City Place project in the UK during 2000 and 2001. In this instance, they compared the application of automotive industry value chain principles and applied them to the construction industry in a 'live' project environment to prove that the fundamentals were the same and hence that significant value could be achieved. Bovis Lend Lease specifically identified the following four key strategies that have shaped the value chain strategy of today.

Design/engineering

Bovis Lend Lease utilises the skills and experience of its employees in the design and engineering of any project. From feasibility analysis to design, Bovis Lend Lease skills include economic analysis, facilities planning, site master planning and site selection, technology evaluations and analysis of financial options (company website, 'How we do it/Design/Engineering'). Bovis Lend Lease is creating a solution for the customer – it is bringing the expertise of its organisation together with the requirements of the customer, government regulators and planners to 'add further value by identifying and eliminating issues early in the design process, offering clients efficiency and superior results' (ibid.).

Design management

Good design management incorporates efficiency, cost management and time scheduling in order to provide the customer with a design that fits their needs, budget and schedule. At all stages of construction, cost allocation and cost accuracy are important, so all costs must be identified in the design management process. Not only does this ensure that the customer remains satisfied but also that all parties involved within the chain remain profitable. Cost management is important from beginning to end, from tender to completion; however, without the right partners, a thorough understanding of the costs involved in all aspects of the project will not be possible. Successful, long-term partnerships will ensure competitive advantage is achieved.

Procurement management

Bringing together the materials, labour and skills of a wide range of subcontractors in any project is an integral part of any construction job. With cost and time constraints it is imperative that all parties within the chain understand the importance of their contribution. Bovis Lend Lease brings together all of these elements with the aim to 'identify appropriate actions to address issues such as bulk and advance purchasing, long lead-time equipment, workload of local suppliers and contractors, site access constraints and all required insurances' (company website, ibid.).

Construction

Bovis Lend Lease 'provides project and construction management skills as part of an integrated offering to clients throughout the world' (company website, ibid.). It is here, at the construction stage, that Bovis Lend Lease brings together all of their value chain processes – process management, technology management, knowledge management and relationship management – to add value to all the other parts of its business. By bringing together its information systems, expertise, experience, skills and relationships with suppliers and customers, Bovis Lend Lease is able to construct the buildings, sports arenas, hospitals and more that they have designed and engineered, and for which they have procured the necessary materials.

Bovis Lend Lease strategies reviewed

Normann and Ramirez (1994) describe *value chain strategy* as the 'art of creating value'. They further suggest that strategy is 'primarily the art of positioning a company in the right place on the value chain – the right business, right products and market segments, the right value-adding activities'.

As identified earlier, Bovis Lend Lease has customised the generic value chain to ensure the skills and capabilities of the organisation more closely match the needs of their clients. In essence their strategies are aimed at addressing the appropriate allocation of risk to manage project cost and time for the client as well as for contractors and suppliers.

To that end they have incorporated several key elements in their business model to enhance and ensure continued growth and sustainable performance: organisation and skills; 3D animation and design ; procurement management, and web based project management.

Organisation and skills

On 8 July 2005, Australia CEO Greg Clarke announced a reorganisation of the organisation's management structure and executive management following the resignation of the head of European operations. In addition, Clarke detailed his plans for a realignment of the executive team in a way that more closely reflected the team's ongoing support for the organisation's growth strategy. The new structure included the appointment of global heads for its retail and community development, construction, and investment management businesses (Lend Lease 2005). The strategy is clearly centred on customer inspired value. The first step is to ensure that they have the right people in the right place. These people apply dedicated skills to a project that are designed to minimise risk and add value early on in the development phase. During the designing and planning, they aim to add value by identifying and eliminating issues in the design process, geared at providing clients with efficiency and superior results. The Bovis Lend Lease team can provide vital assistance to potential clients by offering services such as economic analysis, facilities planning, site master planning, technology evaluations and analysis of financial options.

3D animation and design

The introduction of the 3D animation system allows Bovis Lend Lease to know its business inside and out and to share its knowledge with others who have a stake in the project. The company is now able to assist clients to adapt its real estate requirements in order to respond to ever changing environments, ultimately providing vital support to making the strategy a reality. The 3D system is a computer based multi-dimensional software system that allows designers and clients to view conceptually how the structure will be transformed, allowing a detailed look into all the facilities, attributes and features before and during construction. Bovis Lend Lease has gained so much from 3D modelling that project director Paul Sims stated:

> The 3D modelling is the most sexy thing we're doing here … it helps us plan logically by allowing the team to construct the building on the computer before we

even get to site. This got the contractors thinking about project programming and manning levels in depth at a very early stage in the project.

Procurement management

'Bovis lend Lease relies on good management, a thorough understanding of the market sector and the ability to procure the best subcontractors and suppliers whilst managing the cost objectives' (company website). Through the application of automotive industry principles, Bovis Lend Lease learnt very early the impact of poor process management and the associated impacts of poor resource coordination and material flows. Significant cost savings and productivity improvements were gained through identifying key responsibilities and managing these right throughout a project.

Web based project management

As detailed on its website, Bovis Lend Lease has established a web based project management system that offers a variety of integrated features, providing an overall solution. This versatile system is able to issue all purchase order for materials and equipment; track actual against scheduled delivery of materials; create a catalogue of commonly purchased items, and provide purchasing reports across projects. The organisation strives to ensure that contracts and purchase agreements are negotiated and set with the client's interest as the highest priority.

Construction

The organisation identified the fact that savings in productivity could be as high as 55 per cent by managing the construction processes better. By managing all elements of construction, Bovis Lend Lease brings together the expertise, asset capital and experience of a broad range of organisations. By working together these organisations create a product that will meet the needs of the customer. To illustrate, Bovis Lend Lease took one feature of the automotive industry and applied it: just-in-time planning. This method of build planning involves a weekly project meeting format that rolled over week by week to identify, action and rearrange schedules to ensure project management and suppliers could be managed to maximum efficiency and value. This process maximised the integration of contractors and material flows to the site. 'Build planning will determine the activity and output of every trade on every construction project every day of its duration' (Bovis Lend Lease 2001).

Recently Lend Lease has secured a strategic exclusive alliance with UK based MedicX to design and program-manage a £100m roll out of its GP surgeries across the UK. The aim is to roll out ten surgeries per year with a view to increasing this within three years. The managing director of MedicX asserted: 'I chose Lend Lease Projects because it forms a part of a global project and construction company with significant healthcare experience ... .' This further emphasises Bovis Lend Lease's ability to provide continuous value by extending the services it provides.

Environment

Bovis Lend Lease boasts a community-orientated mandate that has clear and defined objectives with regard to the environment: 'Our environmental sustainable development (ESD) process is predicated on total stakeholder involvement. This ensures that we capture innovation, manage costs, and deliver ongoing benefits for all' (Interlink 2005b). ESD is delivered by establishing performance targets for projects in consultation with the community, authorities and experts; providing management strategy and performance criteria; implementing technical modelling and life cycle assessments; providing document design solutions; and either handing over or staying involved in the long term to assist owners and stakeholders to maintain performance.

Concluding comments

The construction industry is a mature market that has undergone extensive change in the last five to ten years. Previously, inefficient processes that focused solely on the supply chain efficiencies, but with poor client relationships, meant that construction projects often took longer than expected and left customers frustrated and unhappy.

It was clear that with the onset of widespread deregulation, local competition policy and globalisation, with the global stage continuing to get smaller, major change was necessary. The research identifies Bovis Lend Lease as instrumental in making those changes and as a result in strengthening the value chain concept within the construction industry, which now gives focus to both the supply and demand chains.

It has also become apparent that for a construction company to be successful in a global sense, it does not necessarily have to operate in all areas of the industry generic value chain. Bovis Lend Lease, for example, operates only in the development and construction processes (see Table 11.1). It had previously participated actively in the other components of the value chain; however, it soon realised that the development and construction areas are the ones in which they excel. In order to compete in all components of the value chain, they foster strategic partnering arrangements and outsource non-core activities to maximise the benefit or value being offered to the customer.

Today, successful construction companies such as Bovis Lend Lease have recognised that they must have a customer-centric philosophy which not only satisfies their core customer but also the wider community in which they are constructing. They must have strong core values that are both customer- and community-centric. Changes in environmental awareness, along with regulatory changes, have provided a gateway for companies like Bovis lend Lease to enhance their corporate citizenship. They must also have efficient technology and knowledge systems.

According to the UK Construction Industry Task Force (1998):

> We have identified five key drivers of change which need to set the agenda for the construction industry at large: committed leadership, a focus on the customer, integrated processes and teams, a quality driven agenda and a commitment to people.

Bovis Lend Lease has applied these key drivers to all areas of its business. Along with the core values detailing its focus on the needs of the customer and its commitment to the environment through its ESD process, it has developed efficient processes through the use of their ikonnect, ProjectWeb and 3D project management systems. It is this comprehensive mix that allows Bovis Lend Lease to compete on a global level and expose other competitors such as Multiplex who appear to be more focused on shareholder value than customer inspired value.

In summary, Bovis Lend Lease's growth strategy is largely focused on customer satisfaction and is best illustrated in their bottom line compared to that of others in the construction industry. Lend Lease as a complete group had overall revenue of nearly $5 million more than other global Australian owned competitors. It continues to win and complete new projects where some of their competitors have failed, and has made it its business to continue to be at the forefront of change in this mature but constantly evolving industry.

CASE STUDY 11.4

Value chain management through integration and coordination: Li & Fung

Li & Fung describe their organisation as:

A one-stop-shop service; small, dedicated teams of product specialists focus on the needs of particular customers and organize them for them. We provide the convenience of a 'one-stop shop' from product development, through production management, to customs clearance and delivery when required.

A coordinated global network with sourcing offices in 40 countries work[s] together to find the best source for different components or processes. Our policy of not owning any production facilities keeps us flexible and adaptable, encouraging the constant search for quality-conscious, cost-effective producers who can deliver to a deadline.

Offering quick response manufacturing out of Asia since the 1970s. In order to move even closer to our customers, we are currently emphasizing the extension of our sourcing network in markets like the Mediterranean, Eastern Europe and Central and South America.

With a strong sense of [s]ocial [r]esponsibility. We understand that our customers today face an increasingly discerning group of consumers who are not only looking for quality and value, but are also concerned about how the goods are made. Compliance is a key element along all the steps of our supply chain. Through systematic inspection, audit and vendor education we help customers enforce their high standards throughout the factory base. We are a member of Business for Social Responsibility ... and we also support the principles of the Global Compact ... We adopt a Code of Conduct for all our vendors.

From their Hong Kong base, Li & Fung act for major brand owners, providing a range of service processes for their global principals in an increasing number of partnerships. They work with European and American retailers, sourcing clothing and other consumer products ranging from toys and consumer electronics to luggage. In an extensive interview, Magretta (1998) discussed the role of the company with Victor Fung, the chairman who considers the company to be 'part of a new breed of professionally managed, focused enterprises that draw on Hong Kong's expertise in distribution-process technology'; these are described as a host of information-intensive service functions including product-development, sourcing, financing, shipping and logistics. Li & Fung provide an extensive range of processes, from developing product prototypes from their principal's specifications to managing the logistics of delivering specific consignments to designated locations throughout the world. Meanwhile the brand owner continues with what they are particularly good at – managing the marketing of their brand portfolio. But the basic issue is one of understanding the marketplace, of understanding customer expectations and deriving specifications of the product and service that will deliver the customer value specifications. The Li & Fung business is driven by seven principles which become the organisation's core capabilities (Chang 2003):
Being customer-centric and market demand driven

- Focusing on one's core capabilities and outsourcing non-core activities, in order to develop a positioning in the supply chain
- Developing a close, risk- and profit-sharing relationship with business partners
- Design[ing], implement[ing], evaluat[ing] and continuously improv[ing] the work flow, physical flow, information flow and cash flow in the supply chain
- Adopting information technology to optimise the operation of the supply chain
- Shortening production lead time and delivery cycles
- Lowering costs in sourcing, warehousing and transportation

One reason for Li & Fung's rapid global expansion in the 1990s was the pressure on US and European retailers to cut costs by moving to cheaper sourcing locations. This has prompted the company to move into South Asia and Africa. Another influence has been shortening demand (and demand technology) life cycles. Central American and Mediterranean operations help Li & Fung to serve the US and European markets much faster. Li & Fung's global expansion is also a direct outcome of the company's intent to add more value to its trading activities. By identifying an appropriate supplier, managing the product through the manufacturing process, providing samples and feedback control information, exercising quality control and managing the delivery logistics, Li & Fung is an example virtual factory.

Magretta (1998) describes how Li & Fung have developed 'dispersed manufacturing' and a value chain response that allows their customers to delegate many of the essential but lower-value added tasks which Li & Fung manage. The company was founded in 1906, since when it has been taken through a series of developments by Victor Fung and his brother, making the transition from buying agent to

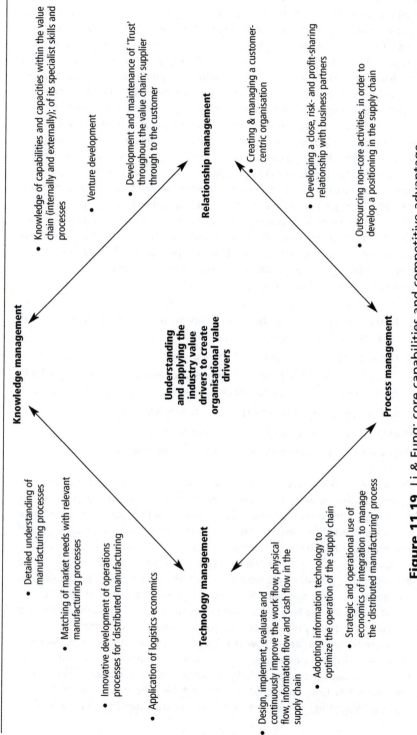

Figure 11.19 Li & Fung: core capabilities and competitive advantage

supply chain manager. Magretta suggests that Li & Fung 'are creating a new kind of multinational, one that remains entrepreneurial despite its growing size and scope'. In the context of a definition of strategic operations management, Li & Fung have extended their business well beyond supply chain management and represent one of the few examples of companies that have combined both supply chain management and demand chain management. They are rapidly building the knowledge technology and relationship based infrastructure to become effective strategic operations management exponents.

Core capabilities, value positioning and competitive advantage strategy

Li & Fung understand the industry value drivers and how the organisation can use these to obtain competitive advantage by creating core processes and capabilities that reinforce this positioning. This is supported by a network of partners who supply non-core processes and capabilities. Figure 11.19 identifies these and suggests the inter-relationships of knowledge, technology and relationship management. Underlying the Li & Fung business is a wealth of knowledge that has been developed over the years. This knowledge is market and 'technology' based and supplemented by the relationships built over time. Furthermore, Li & Fung demonstrate expertise in managing the process interfaces between each management category. Their expertise in the knowledge management/technology management dialogue is clearly demonstrated by their understanding of the production and logistics processes required to meet the quality/cost/time requirements of customers. This has led to a core competence – distributed manufacturing and logistics economics management – basic features of strategic operations management.

Knowledge management/relationship management is driven by the depth of trust developed by the company with both customers and suppliers. This interface has resulted in Li & Fung being able to identify work with and develop entrepreneurial organisations. It has also led to the development of a customer-centric organisation structure. The technology management/relationship management interface is dominated by the management of the economics of integration (Michael Dell's asset leverage concept). Process management includes both manufacturing and logistics and adds a behavioural (relationship management) aspect to distributed manufacturing. It interfaces with both technology management and relationship management. The process/technology management interface reflects Li & Fung's constant search for, and application of, related improvements that can be used to enhance the service offered to customers. The process/relationship interface is important if Li & Fung are to maintain the level of service output to client companies.

Knowledge, technology and relationship management are also important influences on value positioning and strategy decisions. Knowledge management provides a perspective on both supply and customer markets that can be used to 'locate' the value chain for maximum strategic effectiveness. Li & Fung use their accumulated knowledge of both supply and customer markets to offer a customised service to their retailer customers which meets the latter's target market (and market segment) profiles. The efficient transfer of information among suppliers and customers enhances the Li & Fung competitive advantage of being close to both supply and demand markets and, at the same time, facilitates their customers' management of the demand chain. The result is a considered decision concerning *what* value is required, *where* the value should be positioned and *who* the principal partners in the value chain are to be.

Technology management provides another perspective. By understanding the economies of specialisation and integration, Li & Fung can decide upon *how* and *when* value should be produced effectively and reinforce both the *who* and *where* decisions. The use of IT for data transfer makes for effective decisions and efficient management controls.

Relationship management provides additional input into *how* and *who* produces value and, through network trust (and the support infrastructure), ensures effective and efficient implementation of decisions. Value chain management requires transparency across and throughout operations as well as an agreement (and compliance) with an established set of values. Li & Fung assume the responsibility for ensuring the overlap between customer and supplier interest in this regard.

Value production and coordination

Value production and coordination comprise organisation structure, stakeholder management and operations management. Stakeholder management is a matching process. Li & Fung customers are delegating their production and logistics coordination processes to Li & Fung and, as a result, release management time to focus on brand, product and customer satisfaction development. Li & Fung 'match' the interests of their customers with those of their suppliers to ensure that all stakeholder goals may be met. These include commercial issues such as profitability, productivity, cash flow and growth, and the lifestyle based objectives of end-user customers. This can be difficult because the latter are quite different, depending upon the marketing strategies of Li & Fung customers, a fact which has resulted in the customer-centric organisation structure favoured by the company.

By the 1980s, Hong Kong had become a relatively expensive and uncompetitive manufacturing location, compared to other countries in much of Asia. In the transistor radio business, Hong Kong faced intense competition from Taiwan and Korea. The situation prompted Li & Fung to improve efficiency and cut costs by reconfiguring their value chain. The company began to send of component kits to China for the labour-intensive assembly process. The assembled transistors were then brought back to Hong Kong for inspection and testing. Li & Fung replicated the strategy for children's toys (especially dolls). It did the design work and prepared the moulds in Hong Kong. The moulds were shipped to China for plastic injection, painting and tailoring of the dolls' clothing. The dolls came back to Hong Kong for inspection, testing and packing. Hong Kong's well developed banking system facilitated efficient credit based negotiations while its status as a regional shipping centre helped in the distribution of products around the world.

For a typical garment order from a European or US retailer, Li & Fung could decide to buy yarn from say, a Korean producer, but have the weaving and dyeing done in Taiwan. It may source zippers from the Chinese plants of leading Japanese companies. Based on quotas and cost of labour, Li & Fung would then decide where the production of garments would take place. To reduce dependence on a single production point, the order would typically be distributed among different factories within the country. In this way Li & Fung are optimising the value chain by coordinating the value chain processes on a global basis. The company argues that not only do the benefits outweigh the costs of logistics and transportation, but the added value of 'specification fit' (that is, the match between the client customer's product specification and the finished product) enables Li & Fung to charge premium prices. Li & Fung's global value chain integration and coordination have also enabled the organisation to reduce order response time. With customers responding to 'fast fashion' value propositions (see the example of Zara in case study 6.1, Chapter 6), retailers now have eight or more 'seasons' a year. Furthermore, there is the need to replenish successful lines quickly, before the next 'season' begins and potential sales are lost. Li & Fung are clearly aware of this operational aspect and are building excellent relationships with their suppliers to ensure that they respond quickly to any situation.

For a company so heavily dependent on outsourcing, quality control is a major issue. Li & Fung carries out regular inspections at the raw materials, manufacturing and finished goods stages, not hesitating to reject items that fail to meet acceptable quality levels. Li & Fung have attempted to differentiate themselves from their competitors by their ability to locate raw materials and components. Trading staff have detailed information on where the cheapest raw materials and components such as embroidery, electronic components and plastics are available. Their suppliers benefit from this company initiated information network. Table 11.2 illustrates the typical Li & Fung supply chain structure.

It is clear that the operations management aspect of the organisation structure is made up of four distinct, but nevertheless well coordinated component processes. An efficient procurement process is a fundamental feature of value production. Li & Fung's extensive knowledge and expertise in managing some 7,500 suppliers is

Table 11.2 Li & Fung's sourcing strategy

Product/component	Source country
Jackets	
Microfibre fabric	Korea
Nylon taffeta lining	Taiwan
Zippers	Japan
Down filling	China
Stitching	China
Toys	
Mechanical drawings	Hong Kong
Plastic moulds	Hong Kong
Customised chips	Taiwan
Assembly	China

Source: Li & Fung website

crucial to the efficient management of the procurement component. It could be argued that this is a key process, since without supply market management expertise, the quality and cost objectives could not be realised. This expertise has resulted in 'assortment packaging', a process in which sourcing expertise results in multi-sourcing to optimise cost/quality value.

Production management has two important features. Production design is a process by which retail customer product range strategy and design can be implemented and a production plan formulated. Li & Fung start with designer concept sketches and then research supply markets for appropriate materials and production methods to ensure the value proposition may be transformed through a relevant production process. Borderless manufacturing involves Li & Fung in identifying and using the specialist manufacturing skills and resources that reflect the value offer their customers are seeking to deliver. Borderless manufacturing extends throughout Asia; garments may be manufactured in a number of countries. The important concern for Li & Fung is that the finished product meets the value (style, quality and cost) objectives decided by its client customer base.

Logistics has been described as being possibly the most important process of strategic operations management. Logistics is responsible for managing much more than inventory flows. In the Li & Fung business model, it is clearly responsible for inventory management but also manages the flow of information within the value chain (particularly the supply chain component). A primary function of inventory is to manage the economics of logistics through unitisation – the management of customer-specific assortment requirements – which saves time and costs by 'delivering' the exact needs to value chain members and eliminating conventional consolidation activities.

The company's website is expected to help Li & Fung offer customised service to even small customers. According to a *Fortune* report (Kraar et al. 2000), 'Right now, a small retailer that orders merely 1,000 polo shirts via an importer, for instance, can usually get them in just one colour. The lifung.com website is designed to take fairly small orders, consolidate them for mass production and still offer the little guy some choices for customizing products.' A web page provides a three-dimensional picture of the basic product along with the choice of fabric. The website allows a high degree of customisation at little extra cost. Buyers can choose collars, buttons, pockets and logos.

Service for Li & Fung is the core offer to its customers. While service processes pervade their organisation, it is the customisation of value chain operations, from working on design and development issues with customers, the matching processes involved in procurement and production (through distributed/borderless manufacturing), the unitisation of logistics and delivery to customer distribution centres, that is Li & Fung's core competence and distinctive competitive advantage feature.

Li & Fung's processes and decisions

Implementation of the Li & Fung value strategy comprises a number of decisions within a skilfully designed business model. The *design profile* process is usually a customer responsibility because customers know their own markets well; therefore concept decisions, branding, positioning and related specific decisions are made by the customer.

Procurement is made up of two processes. Procurement sourcing is an ongoing knowledge based process which identifies expertise, cost profiles and capacity potential throughout the Li & Fung resource market. This particular process is part of Li & Fung's core competence base, not so much the knowledge base's existence but the use it developed by the company. Procurement contracting is another important process for Li & Fung because it is closely associated with the development process. Given a concept by a customer, the company uses its knowledge of suppliers to develop the concept into a product prototype. Implicit in the prototype development is the knowledge that quality and quantity at budgeted costs can be delivered and that once customer approval is obtained, procurement contracts can be issued.

Production and coordination involves Li & Fung in its assortment packaging and distributed/borderless manufacturing activities. As described in previous paragraphs, Li & Fung coordinate production activities across company and national boundaries. Again the knowledge of resource markets, an understanding of manufacturing product and process technologies, and the trust developed from a long period of operating in these resource markets, is part of the Li & Fung competence base and is a primary reason for their success. The process outputs here are quality, quantity, time and budgeted cost.

The logistics process is used by Li & Fung to drive their business. Victor Fung is on record as saying, 'inventory is the root of all evil' (Magretta 1998); a standardised, fully computerised operating system manages order processing and progressing. The logistics process 'connects' customers' design processes with their marketing process, from a product concept to a delivered finished product according to quantity and quality schedules required by the customer.

The Li & Fung activity provides the company's customers with an extensive part of the value chain. By offering a management service for the development, procurement and production processes, customers are able 'to focus on the product development without worrying about where to source it ... We're able to develop products smarter, faster and with cost efficiencies' (Avon Products, press quote 1999). The acquisition of Inchcape's distribution, retailing and contract manufacturing operations has extended Li & Fung's value chain capability. The company is now using its expertise to offer a pan-Asian distribution facility for international business.

Li & Fung's integrated value chain and business model

Figure 11.20 identifies the demand chain inputs into the planning process. The value drivers of both the end-user customer and of the client customer formulate the Li & Fung value proposition: an ability to meet product currency, quality, quantity and time specifications consistently by coordinating production processes through a network of suppliers with relevant capabilities and capacities. Online communications with suppliers as well as with customers, using EDI linkages, a

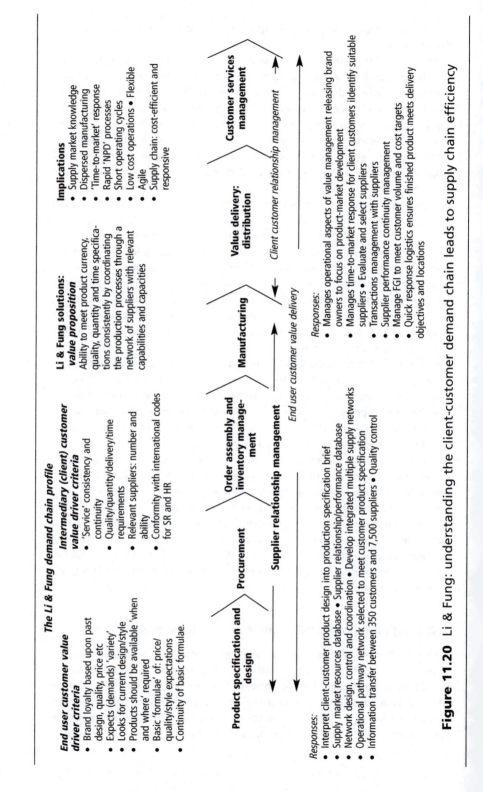

The Li & Fung demand chain profile

End user customer value driver criteria
- Brand loyalty based upon past design, quality, price etc
- Expects (demands) 'variety'
- Looks for current design/style
- Products should be available 'when and where' required
- Basic 'formulae' of: price/quality/style expectations
- Continuity of basic formulae.

Intermediary (client) customer value driver criteria
- 'Service' consistency and continuity
- Quality/quantity/delivery/time requirements
- Relevant suppliers: number and ability
- Conformity with international codes for SR and HR

Li & Fung solutions: value proposition
Ability to meet product currency, quality, quantity and time specifications consistently by coordinating the production processes through a network of suppliers with relevant capabilities and capacities

Implications
- Supply market knowledge
- Dispersed manufacturing
- 'Time-to-market' response
- Rapid 'NPD' processes
- Short operating cycles
- Low cost operations • Flexible
- Agile
- Supply chain: cost-efficient and responsive

Product specification and design → Procurement → Order assembly and inventory management → Manufacturing → Value delivery: distribution → Customer services management

Supplier relationship management

End user customer value delivery

Client customer relationship management

Responses:
- Interpret client-customer product design into production specification brief
- Supply market resources database • Supplier relationship/performance database
- Network design, control and coordination • Develop integrated multiple supply networks
- Operational pathway network selected to meet customer product specification
- Information transfer between 350 customers and 7,500 suppliers • Quality control

Responses:
- Manages operational aspects of value management releasing brand owners to focus on product-market development
- Manages time-to-market response for client customers identify suitable suppliers • Evaluate and select suppliers
- Transactions management with suppliers
- Supplier performance continuity management
- Manage FGI to meet customer volume and cost targets
- Quick response logistics ensures finished product meets delivery objectives and locations

Figure 11.20 Li & Fung: understanding the client-customer demand chain leads to supply chain efficiency

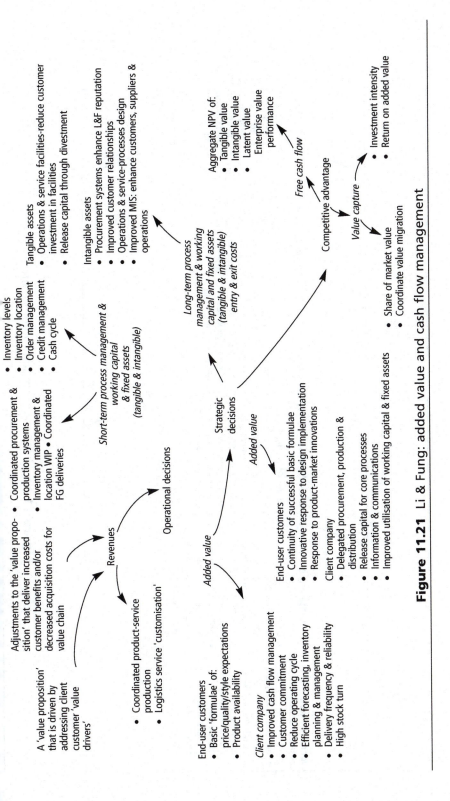

Figure 11.21 Li & Fung: added value and cash flow management

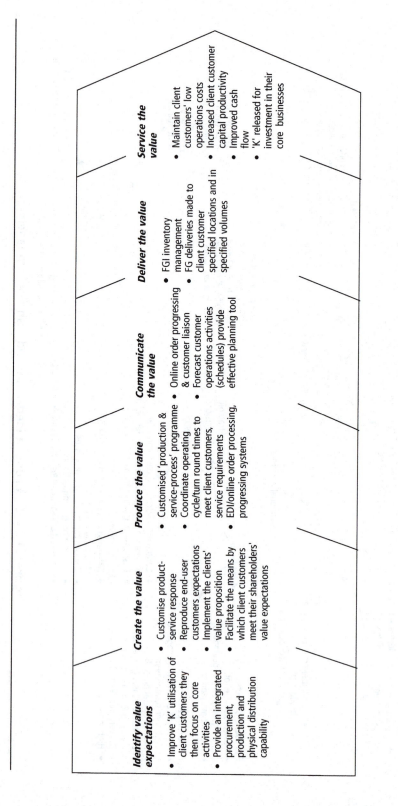

Identify value expectations

- Improve 'K' utilisation of client customers they then focus on core activities
- Provide an integrated procurement, production and physical distribution capability

Create the value

- Customise product-service response
- Reproduce end-user customers expectations
- Implement the clients' value proposition
- Facilitate the means by which client customers meet their shareholders' value expectations

Produce the value

- Customised 'production & service-process' programme
- Coordinate operating cycle/turn round times to meet client customers, service requirements
- EDI/online order processing, progressing systems

Communicate the value

- Online order progressing & customer liaison
- Forecast customer operations activities (schedules) provide effective planning tool

Deliver the value

- FGI inventory management
- FG deliveries made to client customer specified locations and in specified volumes

Service the value

- Maintain client customers' low operations costs
- Increased client customer capital productivity
- Improved cash flow
- 'K' released for investment in their core businesses

Figure 11.22 Li & Fung: company value chain model

knowledge management programme that creates knowledge from supplier relationships and operations data that can be input into customer and company added
value benefits are shown in Figure 11.21, together with the operational and strategic decisions required to implement them. The added value for the client customer
is the facility to focus on the revenue generating aspects of their business while Li
& Fung undertake the procurement, production and logistics operations management. The strategic implication is retailers' ability to focus on brand and product-
market development, in the knowledge that Li & Fung offer a cost-efficient service
for coordinating the operational aspects of the business.

The resultant value chain is shown as Figure 11.22, where the primary value
management processes are identified and the component processes are detailed
within each of them. Customer value expectations can be expressed as capital and
equipment productivity, and reduction of non-core activity costs, while at the same
time knowing that end-user customer expectations are being met cost-efficiently.
To *create* the value, Li & Fung are responding with a highly efficient production
system, the result being an improved operating cycle as well as an improved cash
cycle. To *produce* the value, Li & Fung have a customised production-service process
design for reach major customer that not only reflects the value proposition but
uses online systems to act as a two-way conduit and also as the basis for improving
forecasting and planning. To *deliver* the value, Li & Fung provides finished products
at specified locations to meet promotional and replenishment schedules, avoiding
excess inventories. To *service* the value, Li & Fung must maintain customers' minimum capital input into production-service operations and to maintain their own (Li
& Fung's) costs. This has the twofold benefits of enhanced productivity and cash
flow for the client customer.

Concluding comments

Underlying the Li & Fung business is a wealth of knowledge that has been developed over the years. This knowledge is market and 'technology' based and
supplemented by the relationships built over time. Li & Fung are dependent upon
their client customers' knowledge of their own demand chain characteristics. Li &
Fung's expertise is in managing the supply chain process and the interfaces
between the various value chain processes. Their skill in the knowledge manage-
ment/technology management dialogue is clearly demonstrated by their understanding of the production and logistics processes required to meet
quality/cost/time requirements of customers. Knowledge management/relation-
ship management is driven by the depth of trust developed by the company with
both customers and suppliers. This interface has resulted in Li & Fung being able
to identify work with and develop entrepreneurial organisations. It has also led
to the development of a customer-centric organisation structure.

REFERENCES

Best R J (2004) *Market-Based Management*, Prentice-Hall, Upper Saddle River, NJ
'Public Agenda' (2004) 'My vision for the NHS', *Times*, 22 June
Bovis Lend Lease (2001) *A Radical Step to Take? Improving the Construction Demand Chain*, Bovis Lend Lease Ltd, Harrow
Bovis Lend Lease, www.bovislendlease.com.au
Building Talk, www.buildingtalk.com/news/bov/bov100.html
Chang K M (2003) *Li & Fung – The Orchestrator of Global Supply Chain Management*, Li & Fung Research Centre, Hong Kong
Day G (1999) *The Market Driven Organisation*, Free Press, New York
Interlink (2005a) 'Lend Lease', *Interlink*, 14, March
Interlink (2005b) 'Lend Lease', *Interlink*, 17, June
Kelleher H (2004) www.southwest.com
Kraar L, N Chowdhary and J Rohwer (2000) 'The new net tigers', *Fortune*, 15 May, www.fortune.com
Lend Lease (2005) Media release, 8 July
Li & Fung, www.lifung.com
MacMillan I C and R G McGrath (1997) 'Discovering new points of differentiation', *Harvard Business Review*, July/August
Magretta J (1998) 'Supply chain management, Hong Kong style', interview with Victor Fung, *Harvard Business Review*, September/October
McClenahen J (2004) 'Best practice – piloting materials management', *Industry Week*, www.industryweek.com
Multiplex, www.multiplex.com.au
Normann R (2001) *Reframing Business*, Wiley, Chichester
Normann R and R Ramirez (1994) *Designing Interactive Strategy: From Value Chain to Value Constellation*, Wiley, New York
Revill J (2004) 'Dignity should be the first choice', *Observer*, 27 June
Slywotzky A J and D J Morrison (1997) *The Profit Zone*, Wiley, New York
Southwest Airlines, www.southwest.com
UK Construction Industry Task Force (1998) *Rethinking Construction: The Report of the Construction Industry Task Force*, Stationery Office, London
Waples J (2004) 'Private medicine needs surgery', *Sunday Times*, 21 June

CHAPTER 12

Industry Value Drivers: A Contemporary View of Critical Success Factors

---

LEARNING TOPICS

On completing your study of this chapter you will have been introduced to and considered the following topics:

- A review of traditional perspectives and characteristics
- Competitive necessity or competitive advantage?
- Competitive advantage: a quantitative approach
- Competitive advantage: a qualitative approach
- Different drivers, different outcomes
- A framework for industry value drivers; the role of knowledge management, technology management, process management and relationship management; the implications and impact of time and market changes
- Industry value drivers: strategic positioning for competitive advantage

---

Introduction

The notion of identifying critical success factors as the basis for the strategic positioning of a firm in its marketplace is not a new idea. Identifying these success factors has however seemingly relied more on industry-specific divination rather than some general framework. Indeed Grant (1995) cites Ghemawat (1991) who suggests that attempting to identify key success factors is akin to seeking the Philosopher's Stone, which, it will be remembered, had the power to change anything it touched into gold. It is also often closely tied with understanding and identifying the firm's core competencies, although some debate has occurred over what exactly this tie is. This is not a debate it is intended to pursue here, other than to note that both notions are historically bound up with the concept that core competencies relate to things the firm owns or does, and that critical success factors are similarly things that the firm has, or wishes to have, within the ambit of its control.

A review of traditional perspectives and characteristics

Indeed much of the work on the search for the key success factors has an implied assumption that, once identified, the firm should seek to create or own those success factors, hopefully to the exclusion of its competitors. The strategic framework on which this assumption is made is however shifting rapidly. In particular, in recent years the virtual enterprise model has emerged as a popular approach to strategy. This model is based on a structure of networks between value producers and customers. These networks potentially span what are traditionally thought of as specific 'industries', and therefore require combinations of success factors potentially broader than those traditionally identified.

The model also raises new challenges for management to coordinate the network between and among the virtual enterprise/value chain producers and the customer. Pebler's (2000) comments are significant here, suggesting that 'The virtual enterprise of the future will be much more dynamic and sensitive to the need for tuning operational parameters of the enterprise as a whole, including capital spending for both producers and service companies, optimising the whole chain of value creation.'

How then do you identify critical success factors in a 'new economy' context? It will be recalled from Chapter 1 that Boulton et al. (2000) ask:

> But what assets are most important in the New Economy? How do we leverage these assets to create value for our own organisations in a changing business environment? What new strategies are required for us to create value?

Perhaps the answer at least partially lies in what Normann (2001) called 'a new strategic logic'. This logic requires a more general framework, having at least three elements, to identify and understand a firm's critical success factors. First, it suggests that the concept of critical success factors no longer has to be bound in with notions of control and ownership, but will increasingly be things that a firm simply has access to or can mobilise to its advantage.

Second, a distinction is drawn between necessity and advantage. It is suggested that there are competitive factors that a firm must master simply to be in the race. It is important to identify and understand these as a matter of necessity. Factors which however confer true sustainable competitive advantage are a step further and in all probability rarer beasts.

Third, it is suggested that critical success factors, once identified, have too often been seen as immutable. Instead it is now suggested that they are constantly changing, particularly in a 'new economy' context, as business networks form and re-form. This occurs at a market level as value shifts occur within value chains and networks.

It also does not necessarily follow that the same success factors apply to all the participants in an industry, as different firms may be pursuing different objectives. Success is too often simplistically related to some measure of profitability. It is argued instead that the generation of free cash is a better indicator of corporate success and that accordingly different success factors will relate to each element of that cash flow generation – operating cash flow, cash flow from assets, and strategic cash flow. These elements may vary from firm to firm and over time.

Ohmae (2005) suggests new rules for the 'new economy', adding that there is a problem posed – nobody is yet clear on what the rules are. However, the need for them implies that companies have to rethink everything, from strategy through to structure – and back again – in the dynamic environment of the twenty-first century. Ohmae is suggesting that this approach includes supply and customer markets, together with the business models that made many organisations successful. Ohmae is suggesting a 'prescription' for handling the 'new economy' based upon communications (the introduction of ITC to manage interactions and transactions – technology management); capital (with the notion here that it is now 'borderless' and hence rapidly transferable – aspects of relationship management); corporation (here the concept of the virtual organisation is one reaching across organisational and international borders – and applies aspects of relationship and process management; and consumers (the inference being that online customer contact – aspects of both technology and relationship management – offers a facility to meet customer expectations more closely and more rapidly than ever before.

It is suggested that in a 'new economy' context it is possible to draw up a general framework for exploring factors which are both competitive necessities and which drive competitive advantages, rather than simply relying on industry-specific knowledge. This is built around management of resources and critical characteristics, rather than a fascination with ownership and control. It requires more than a laundry list of short-lived attributes, but recognises that critical success characteristics will change over time as value shifts. These key characteristics include the firm's understanding of the importance and the influence of relationship management, of technology management, the creation and use of knowledge and a strategic view of process operations.

A retrospective view

In the 1980s and 1990s the notion of critical success factors became a well known and widely used concept (or key success factors – KSF. While there are no doubt fine distinctions in the terminology, for the purposes of this chapter the terms are used interchangeably). It was notionally an analytical tool to identify what it was that was required for successful entry into an industry or product-market. Typically, if such success factors were not 'owned', the company would seek to acquire them.

A number of authors have discussed the role of critical success factors. Hofer and Schendel (1978) suggested:

... they [key success factors] are those variables which management can influence through its decisions that can affect significantly the overall competitive positions of the various firms in an industry ... Within any particular industry they are derived from the interaction of two sets of variables, namely, the economic and technological characteristics of the industry ... and the competitive weapons on which the various firms in the industry have built their strategies.

They suggested that these success factors were industry-specific in the sense that they derived from the interaction of the economic and technological characteristics of any particular industry setting. Similarly, Leidecker and Bruno (1984) saw key success factors as:

... those characteristics, conditions or variables that when properly sustained, maintained or managed, can have a significant impact on the success of a firm competing in a particular industry.

They provided examples of key success factors for a number of industries:

- Automobile industry: styling; strong dealer network; manufacturing cost control; ability to meet EPA (Environmental Protection Agency) standards
- Semi-conductor industry: manufacturing process (cost-efficient, innovative, cumulative experience); capital availability; technological competence; product development
- Food processing industry: new product development; good distribution; effective advertising

Hofer and Schendel (1978) had earlier applied the concept to strategic analysis. They suggested that key success factors are important at three levels of analysis: specific to the firm, to the industry and to the business environment. They argued that analysis at each level can identify a source of potential key success factors.

Grant (1995) followed a similar line of argument. He suggested that an analysis of demand (what is it that customers want?), and of competition (how does the firm survive?) would identify the relevant key success factors.

Grant argued that the first question – what is it that customers want? – is best addressed by viewing customers as 'the basic rationale for the existence of the industry and as the underlying source of profit'. The firm must therefore identify who precisely its customers are, ascertain their needs, and then establish how they (the customers) select their supplier(s).

In addressing the second question – competition and how does the firm survive? – the firm examines the industry, its competitive intensity and its key characteristics. Grant suggests that the important characteristics are based upon the dimensions of the aggregate value proposition (that is, the range of customised and price led offers differentiating the market); the intensity of competition; relative cost structures, and the importance of the various economies of production. Figure 12.1 (based upon Grant) offers some examples.

	What do customers want? (analysis of demand)	How does a firm survive? (analysis of competition)	Key success factors

Steel	• Large customers
	• Price sensitive customers
	• Product consistency and reliability of supply are essential
	• Specific technical specifications required for special steels
		• Competition is price based
		• Declining demand is intensifying competition
		• High fixed costs require volume throughput
		• Low cost imports
		• Entry and exit barriers are high
		• Strong unions
		• High transport costs
		• Scale economies are important
			• Cost efficient through scale efficient plants
			• Low cost location
			• Flexibility
			  – adjustment of capacity to output
			  – scope for differentiation of product specification, etc.
			• Low labour costs
			• Minimum of labour stoppages

Fashion retailing	• Demand fragmented by garment, style, quality, colour • Customers willing to pay price premium for style, quality and exclusivity • Retailers seek reliability and speed of supply	• Low entry barriers • Low seller concentration • Few economies • Medium/high retailer concentration • Retail buying power strong • Price and non-price competition strong	• Need to combine mass customisation with low cost operations • Key differentiation variables are rapid response to style and fashion change • Strong customer franchise • Low overhead and labour costs except in less price sensitive segments
Superstore activities: • **food** • **home improvement**	• Low prices • Convenient location • Wide range of products	• Local dense catchments • Customers are price sensitive: price competitiveness a requirement • Uses bargaining power to influence merchandise and other input costs	• Low cost requires operational efficiency, scale efficient stores • Large purchasing volumes to maximise buying power • Wide merchandise ranges • Large sales area • Convenient access (drive time) • Easy parking

Source: adapted from Grant (1995)

Figure 12.1 Identifying key success factors from an analysis of demand and competition

Competitive necessity or competitive advantage?

Grant's (1995) introduction of the notion of 'survival' into critical success factors raises an interesting and important distinction between necessity and advantage. Arguably, a lot of what are often identified as key success factors are essentially *competitive necessities*. Unless they are addressed an organisation will be unable to compete successfully in a selected market or market segment. While they may appear to be sources of advantage to outsiders, in fact they are more akin to a simple market entry status than to true sources of significant advantage over otherwise evenly matched competitors. It could be argued that all of the key success factors identified by Leidecker and Bruno (1984) and many identified by Grant can be seen as competitive necessities.

To create competitive advantage, or perhaps sustainable competitive advantage, something else is required. An organisation such as Wal-Mart has clearly mastered the competitive necessities of retailing, but what has truly set it apart from its competitors? One of its true competitive success factors has been location, with the company historically locating in regional areas away from traditional competitors in city or suburban centres. Initially, developing this key strategic success factor involved skills and thinking that at the time were more akin to those of a real-estate developer, but which are now firmly entrenched in the retail environment. Similarly, though now widely copied, Wal-Mart built a franchise around 'everyday low prices' by enticing established brands to lower costs through technology driven supply chain efficiencies.

This is no doubt to some extent an iterative process, with factors that deliver true competitive advantage mutating over time into simple necessities as they are copied or modified by competitors. Similarly, factors that deliver true competitive advantage do not have to be stunningly novel, and may in fact be improvements on existing ideas, or unique combinations of otherwise mundane factors.

Competitive advantage: a quantitative approach

One striking feature of many of the key success factors identified by Leidecker and Bruno (1984) is their potential transience – they contain few unique or even long-term exclusive items. It may be argued that this lack of permanence potentially reduces the notion of key success factors to almost a shopping list of attributes of competitive necessities that may from time to time generate competitive advantage. There is no doubt however that the generation of competitive positioning is a dynamic process, a process rendered even potentially more dynamic by the drivers underlying the 'new economy'. Harnessing this dynamism in itself becomes a key competitive characteristic.

Key to this is an appreciation that value itself is not necessarily a constant, so that in a real sense the goal posts are shifting as the firm strives to identify and manage key success factors. As we saw in Chapter 3, Kay (1993) defines added value as the difference between the (comprehensively accounted) value of a firm's output and the (comprehensively accounted) cost of the firm's inputs. Please review the relevant material in Chapter 3.

He suggests that added value is a measure of the loss that would result to national income and to the international economy if the organisation ceased to exist:

> Adding value, in this sense, is the central purpose of business activity. A commercial organisation which adds no value – whose output is worth no more than the value of its inputs in alternative uses – has no long-term rationale for its existence.

Competitive advantage: a qualitative approach

Kay's model facilitates an analysis of an entire industry, identifying where added value is the greatest and, importantly, where shifts or migration of value are occurring. As we have seen throughout this text, Millennium Pharmaceuticals is an example of an organisation very aware of the concepts of added value and value migration. Please review the relevant material in Chapter 7. Millennium CEO Mark Levin argues that the value chain (virtual organisation network) for other high-tech products has, after all, tended to break down into a few separate, largely independent markets, each majoring on specific positioning characteristics. The computer industry can be taken as an example: chip manufacturing, computer assembly and delivery, and software and support services are now all quite independently distinguishable but interlinked markets. Where once IBM was dominant across the whole industry, Intel, Dell and Microsoft now coexist as a value chain. Levin says that

> We want to be the leader in personalized drug therapies … our expressed goal is to be the first company to deliver healthcare tailored to the patient's genetic profile. To achieve that goal we need to reach all the way to the doctors and the patients.

A strategy to achieve this goal is based on extending the alliance and partnership models that have proven to be successful for Millennium. Initially these partnerships were based upon Millennium's strong R&D capability, the relationship with the partner being simply one of contract researcher. However, as the company has moved further along the value chain this has changed, the partnerships becoming 50/50 alliances with an increasing ownership stake in the products. This strategy has been based upon identifying and 'acquiring' the capabilities that will be required. Levin identifies a major problem for the industry – the huge investment required in R&D ($2billion to $5 billion) – sums that are encouraging mergers and acquisitions where individual companies are losing their identities. In contrast he suggests that Millennium will emerge with a strong position in the industry value chain based on this networked R&D.

Different drivers, different outcomes

Underlying the notion of key critical success factors is some relationship with outcomes. Grant (1995) proposes the simple accounting relationship of 'profit *equals* revenue *less* costs' as a starting point. In a retail industry context, from this there emerge three important influences: sales per square metre, sales area and gross margin. From these he suggests four key success factors:

■ The role of the store location in determining sales per square foot
■ The importance of retailer buying power
■ The influence of the merchandise mix
■ The role of inventory management systems

However, given the limited nature of profitability as an indication of performance (and its vulnerability to management 'opinion'), it is suggested that cash flow offers a more reliable metric. Furthermore, if a more managerial perspective is taken of cash flow than that taken from an accounting perspective, not only can operational and strategic factors be considered but so too can structural options.

Figure 12.2 identifies how three components make up the generation of free cash – operating cash flow, cash flow from assets and strategic cash flow. Critical success factors do not necessarily relate to all three. For example, key success factors in maximising operating cash flow in a retail environment might include stocking reliable brands at competitive prices. In the supermarket industry this is the battleground of 'everyday low prices' on which most chains compete against each other in some form, whether as a matter of necessity or advantage.

At the asset cash flow level, investment in information technology systems (and forcing suppliers to do the same) to foster supply chain efficiencies is a good example of what was an important competitive advantage to some retailers quickly becoming a competitive necessity.

At the strategic cash flow level, investment in store locations, and in branding and customer loyalty programmes are commonplace examples of factors that would usually be deemed to be competitive necessities and often competitive advantages.

Each of these cash flow components operates on a different timescale and often requires different decision timeframes. In a highly competitive environment like fuel retailing, pump pricing might change daily; oil retail chains develop elaborate systems to maximise pricing advantages. Development of new sites, however, operates on a timescale potentially of years. This has significant implications for the timescales on which key success factors are derived, understood and applied. Different decision making processes and investment profiles apply that will impact the longevity of competitive positions. While it may be an overgeneralisation, success factors related to operating cash flow, such as price, may be quite transient as competitors follow suit often in hours, while those factors relating to strategic cash generation may take years to replicate and will offer sustainable competitive advantage during this period.

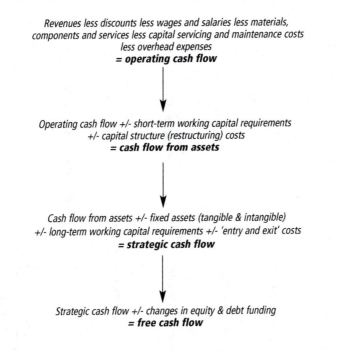

*Revenues less discounts less wages and salaries less materials,
components and services less capital servicing and maintenance costs
less overhead expenses*
= operating cash flow

*Operating cash flow +/- short-term working capital requirements
+/- capital structure (restructuring) costs*
= cash flow from assets

*Cash flow from assets +/- fixed assets (tangible & intangible)
+/- long-term working capital requirements +/- 'entry and exit' costs*
= strategic cash flow

Strategic cash flow +/- changes in equity & debt funding
= free cash flow

Note: Tax payments have been omitted. These may occur at operating, asset management and strategic cash flow management levels depending upon tax regulations. Other charges may also be relevant.

Figure 12.2 The determinants of free cash flow:
the primary business objective

A framework for industry value drivers

As noted above, much of the work in this area has focused on the divination of critical success factors in particular industries. It is suggested; however, that what is required is some broader view of what constitutes a key success factor in a 'new economy' context. Just as Rumelt (1987) suggests that it is underlying competencies rather than their current manifestation in the latest product that are important, it is proposed that a broader framework is becoming necessary for identifying key success factors rather than simply a list of the latest industry or marketplace drivers. It is suggested that such a framework revolves around four generic, but focused value driver frameworks: knowledge management; technology management; process management, and relationship management.

These macro critical success frameworks should be used to help obtain a profile of industry characteristics against which it is then possible to measure 'organisational' performance and consider the influence of what might be called industry value drivers. Having identified these, the next task is to identify where they are located – who owns them and how they can be accessed. A major skill in the management of a virtual enterprise is to establish the most effective position for a partner within the virtual community. Figure 12.3 explores this notion.

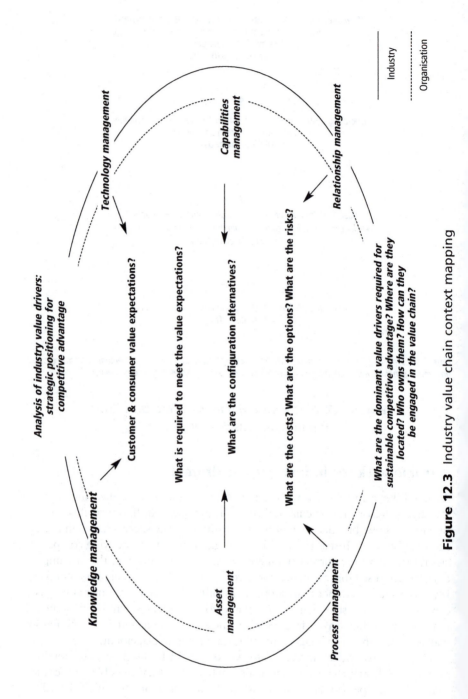

Figure 12.3 Industry value chain context mapping

Knowledge management

Analysis of industry value drivers: strategic positioning for competitive advantage

Customer & consumer value expectations?

Technology management

What is required to meet the value expectations?

Capabilities management

What are the configuration alternatives?

Asset management

What are the costs? What are the options? What are the risks?

Process management

Relationship management

What are the dominant value drivers required for sustainable competitive advantage? Where are they located? Who owns them? How can they be engaged in the value chain?

Industry

Organisation

The diagram identifies knowledge management, technology management, process management and relationship management as industry value drivers. As will be argued subsequently, these will differ not only between industries but also within industries depending upon how the competitors within the industry position themselves when pursuing specific segments or sectors. We can explore this notion by returning to the two examples used in Chapter 5, personal computers and mobile phones. Initially, when both products were perceived as innovative products, it was the function of knowledge management and technology management to provide the leading companies with competitive advantage. The early markets were dominated by price-insensitive customers. Subsequently, as price began to become an important marketing consideration, both supplier and customer and supplier relationship management became more important in addressing the changed value delivery expectations.

From industry competitors' perspective the decision to be made concerns when, where and how to engage in the value chain and to do so in such a way that the individual organisation can benefit. At this point asset management and capability management become important decision issues. Clearly current and likely future market characteristics are important influences on the decision as to where to engage. In developing markets, those in which innovative product responses are essential, capability management dominates the decision. The capabilities to design and develop product solutions and to make them accessible (time-to-market) are essential. Without them, or without access to them, it is unlikely that the organisation will be successful. By comparison, entry into an established market segment, one in which the dominant customer groups are late adopters, even laggards, asset management becomes important. Again we see evidence of this in both the personal computer and mobile phone markets.

Figure 12.3 suggests that once the industry value drivers have been identified it becomes important to identify who owns these and whether they be persuaded to become a partner within a value chain structure. At the level of the firm two other 'drivers' also become important: assets and capabilities. Both assets and capabilities (skills and technology, see Hamel and Prahalad 1994) will require investment unless they are available and their owners can be 'recruited' into partnership. Once again Normann's (2001) observation is valid; the important objective is to access and use both rather than necessarily own them! Assets and capabilities were more fully dealt with in detail in Chapter 5.

There is evidence to suggest that the four generic value driver frameworks are becoming important features in planning in 'new economy' business models. Disparate but linked threads are evident in the literature.

Blumentritt and Johnston (1999), for example, identify the importance of knowledge management for value chain (virtual organisation) managers, suggesting that it is:

… the ability to identify, locate and deliver information and knowledge to a point of valuable application is transforming existing industries and facilitating the emergence of entirely new industries.

Furthermore, they suggest that while knowledge is recognised as a key to competitive advantage and is indeed an asset, there are challenges awaiting managers when attempting to 'manage' this intangible asset. The authors debate the difference between knowledge and information, making a signifi cant point that information cannot be substituted for knowledge and that attempts to do so typically result in disaster. The linkages that are created between customer behaviour information and demand management through customer loyalty programmes are an example of the importance of knowledge management as an aspect of critical industry success factors in retailing.

Zineldin (1997), considers technology management, suggesting that:

> Science is the accumulation of knowledge about human beings and the environment. Technology is the application of such knowledge to practical purposes. This is in the context of rapidly changing developments that have expanded the availability of products and delivery systems to both consumer and organisational end-users, suggesting that change may not necessarily require re-investment but rather a change in philosophy. This may involve a new perspective towards technology management creating networks, alliances and relationships with other high-tech companies provides the means to create competitive advantage.

Irani and Love (2001) consider the management of technology within an organisation and suggest:

> Technology management should be seen as a business process that facilitates the development of a comprehensive and robust techno-centric infrastructure, consequently enhancing the delivery of accurate, timely and appropriate services within an organisation, which in turn increases the economic viability of the business.

They refer to a 'technology management gap' that may result in a competitive advantage being jeopardised. The linking of ICT with automated distribution and manufacturing processes to reduce order response times in the FMCG industry is an example of a technology management based critical industry success factor.

Relationship management is essentially the effective (and efficient) coordination of the different internal and external parts of a business. Jarillo (1993) remarks:

> It is not surprising then that the last few years have seen a plethora of articles and books on topics such as networking, value-added relationships, de-layering, modularisation, the need for companies to nurture long-term relationships in all spheres. All these works point in one direction: companies must look at their boundaries with new eyes – things that have traditionally been 'inside' should perhaps be outside, and outsiders might perhaps deserve the treatment of 'insiders'.

The current business environment is arguably changing in such a way that an organisation can grow effectively only by developing strategic networks with its suppliers, distributors and customers. Zineldin (1997) argues that a total relationship approach requires both strategy and philosophy. Philosophy is necessary because it can be used to *communicate* the idea that a major goal of management is to plan and build appropriate close and flexible long-term relationships with partners who contribute to the organisation's long-term success and growth. It guides overall thinking and decision making in the organisation as well as the execution of decisions. A strategy is required because it *emphasises* maintaining the product and service quality of internal and external relationships in order to maintain long-term stakeholder ones.

The strong bond between Caterpillar and its distributor network is an example of creating a total relationship approach. Using product technology (a remote serviceability diagnostic), ICT networks and a committed dealer network, the 'total' Caterpillar network offers a guarantee of reliable and rapid global serviceability to end-users.

As we have seen in previous chapters, processes have defined business outcomes for which there are recipients who may be either internal or external to the organisation. They also cross organisational boundaries; that is, they normally occur across or between organisational (either intra- or inter-organisational) boundaries and are independent of formal organisational structures. Effective organisations now work together to identify core processes. The interest that process orientation and, therefore, process management has for the virtual organisation is its philosophy. It enables virtuality to become reality. Virtuality defines the ability to create partnerships across companies using value chain structures with component companies that work together to maximise the value delivered to customers. The scope of process management is such that it may be applied to strategic and operational tasks and structures alike.

As we have also seen several times in this text, Hagel and Singer (1999) argue that the traditional organisation comprises three basic types of business process: a customer relationship business, a product innovation business and an infrastructure business. The network model (or virtual organisation model) comprises independently owned enterprises that together are a virtual corporation. The virtual corporation is a synchronised model of distributed processes that work together towards a common goal. The incentive for organisations is to facilitate access to new market value-creation opportunities. Dell is a prominent example of a process network. In its early days Dell decided to avoid the burdens of asset ownership, preferring to create partnerships with component suppliers. The process management skill of the Dell model is the coordination of customer 'designed' products with the just-in-time delivery of the components required to meet the assembly of the computer to meet the order. The model minimises inventory holding but meets two very important, customer expectations – product specification and availability.

An important point to be made concerns the rapidly expanding availability of offshore facilities. Emerging supply markets are appearing in the developing economies of Asia and Eastern Europe. An interesting aspect of this development concerns the specialist nature of the developing countries' expertise; for example India has an efficient labour force in software engineering, skilled linguistics (as deployed into call centre operations) and expanding healthcare facilities Korea offers process (production capacity) management expertise, while the People's Republic of China continues to dominate the supply of low-cost labour

Industry value drivers: strategic positioning for competitive advantage

The business environment of the 'new economy' has then resulted in a number of fundamental changes, providing a useful framework with which to analyse the business environment for indications of contributions to successful business structures. Figure 12.4 proposes the framework against which this may take place. It can be expected that one or two of the value drivers will be dominant in specific industry applications. Figure 12.5 identifies industries for which specific value drivers are important. The purpose of reviewing 'macro value drivers' is to obtain a profile of industry characteristics against which it is possible to measure 'organisational' performance and consider the influence of the value drivers. As we saw earlier in this chapter, having identified the critical value drivers, the next task is to identify where they are located. Clearly no partner will agree to become involved unless the outcome will be to their benefit – that is, they must be convinced that they will become 'better off'.

Resources requirements and their implications for organisational alternatives are an important consideration. To make these decisions effective a review, or an audit, of existing capabilities is necessary. Olve et al. (1997) suggest that 'A kind of "competence balance sheet' may be used as an aid in making this kind of strategic choice.' The authors argue that the traditional way of evaluating a company is to analyse its balance sheet, which after adjustments is one way of representing the value of the company. It also indicates the extent to which the company is dependent upon financial gearing; if this is too high, it follows that the company is vulnerable to the vagaries of the market. Conversely, if the company is self-financing it will be expected to earn above average returns to maintain shareholder acceptance. Therefore, the authors argue, there are very few companies that are self-financing. In the competence balance sheet, the 'assets' are the capabilities/competencies required for success and the 'liabilities' show how they are financed, or who owns and provides them. The argument continues by suggesting that the company determines what capabilities (critical success driver components) are needed to compete and the makes a decision on how they should be 'financed'. Figure 12.6 illustrates the principle involved. A number of factors may influence the resulting decision. Clearly the risk/return consideration is important, as is the expected life span of capability, particularly for technological capabilities. Other concerns likely to be important are the impact/urgency relationship and its influence on strategic positioning and resultant competitive advantage.

The eventual decision that is made is influenced by the relative importance of the industry drivers. Figure 12.7a describes the situation that can be seen in the automobile industry. Not many years ago this 'map' would have illustrated a situation in which all four value driver categories would have been promi-

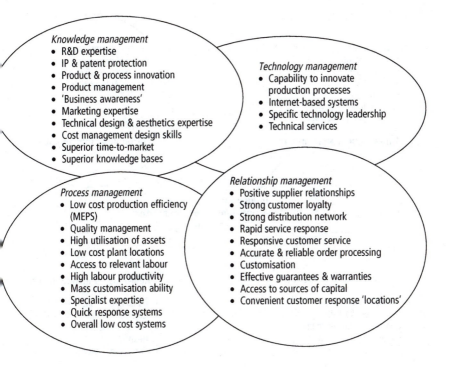

Figure 12.4 Identifying industry value drivers and their components

nent, the emphasis differing little among the major manufacturers. However, attitudes towards the importance of the drivers have changed. Drucker (2001) notes that the traditional response to market pressures was vertical integration on a large scale, citing Ford, General Motors and Standard Oil as leading examples in the early twentieth century. In contrast the new successful corporations are adopting models based on virtual integration, where ownership of the means of production is not the critical factor, but rather it is access to them via networks and partnerships that is important. As we saw in Chapter 1, Drucker comments that the changes required to facilitate this approach are not just sales and marketing driven, but encompass design and development, and production. In other words, as we have several times highlighted, 'virtual organisations' are competing with 'virtual organisations'.

An example: Mitsubishi in Australia

The recent problems of Mitsubishi in Australia (and globally for that matter) illustrate how this approach may be used. The Australian plant has been troubled for some time. Concepts such as 'minimum efficient plant size' become real issues and this is clearly so for the Magna in Australia. The market is unable (or unwilling) to absorb the vehicle in the volumes required to give the company the financial performance it requires. The restructuring announced

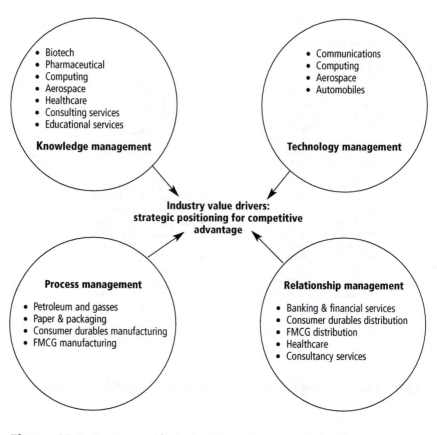

Figure 12.5 Some specific industries where particular framework may predominate

by Mitsubishi in May 2004 suggested that the company had reviewed its problems as a vertically integrated organisation rather than perhaps seeing itself as part of a virtual structure within which it could assume a number of strategic positions depending very much upon market segment opportunities.

Mitsubishi in Australia carries considerable debt and, apart from its four-wheel-drive vehicle range, is not failing to reach volumes of production that are profitable. It could be argued that Mitsubishi has failed to consider the critical value drivers currently influencing industry strategy. If they had done so, they would have concluded that their strategy is no longer viable without partnerships and alliances with other industry members (co-opetition), whereby they would reposition themselves within the volume vehicle segment by offering production capacity to the successful volume brands, or perhaps to partners seeking low-cost entry to the Australian market or to those who, like Mitsubishi, cannot achieve minimum plant size economies. This strategy would enable them to capture a significant share of market added value and maintain a manufacturing presence in a low-volume market.

A decision Mitsubishi made to close its engine plant might have been

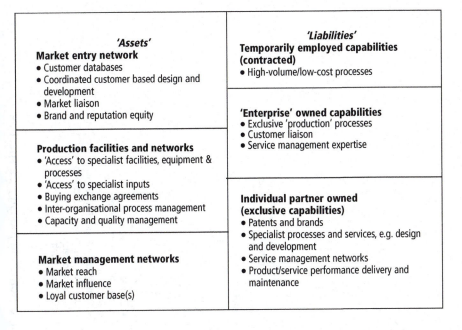

'Assets'	**'Liabilities'**
Market entry network	**Temporarily employed capabilities (contracted)**
• Customer databases	• High-volume/low-cost processes
• Coordinated customer based design and development	
• Market liaison	**'Enterprise' owned capabilities**
• Brand and reputation equity	• Exclusive 'production' processes
	• Customer liaison
Production facilities and networks	• Service management expertise
• 'Access' to specialist facilities, equipment & processes	
• 'Access' to specialist inputs	
• Buying exchange agreements	**Individual partner owned (exclusive capabilities)**
• Inter-organisational process management	• Patents and brands
• Capacity and quality management	• Specialist processes and services, e.g. design and development
	• Service management networks
Market management networks	• Product/service performance delivery and maintenance
• Market reach	
• Market influence	
• Loyal customer base(s)	

Based upon Olve N, J. Roy and M. Wetter (1997), *Performance Drivers*, Wiley, Chichester

Figure 12.6 The virtual enterprise 'balance sheet'

averted with foresight. It could have negotiated an arrangement whereby Mitsubishi used the plant to manufacture a competitor's engine, having combined this with an arrangement that saw the company installing the engine in Mitsubishi vehicles.

It is interesting to note that meanwhile, Ford's export strategy for its Australian operation is considering supplying engineering and product-design services to the company across Asia. The regional vice president, Mark Shulz, commented in an interview reported in *Australian Financial Review* in May 2004:

There are two types of export you can have. There is the physical product, but there is also intellectual capital.

Asia is a key market for Ford but its investment in China, unlike that of General Motors, is modest. Shulz's comments suggest that Ford is aware of strategic alternatives and of the necessity to identify the industry value drivers required to be successful. Other industry examples are illustrated as Figures 12.7b, 12.7c and 12.7d.

In Figure 12.8 these themes are drawn together, illustrating how the four key success frameworks may alter in emphasis and importance in any given instance and over time. However, time has an impact on organisational ability to remain competitive. It is clear from the examples we have considered that the core influences on competitive ability change and are changing continuously. Millennium is but one organisation that continues to assess its ability to remain competitive and to meet both customer and stakeholder expectations. Figure 12.8 suggests

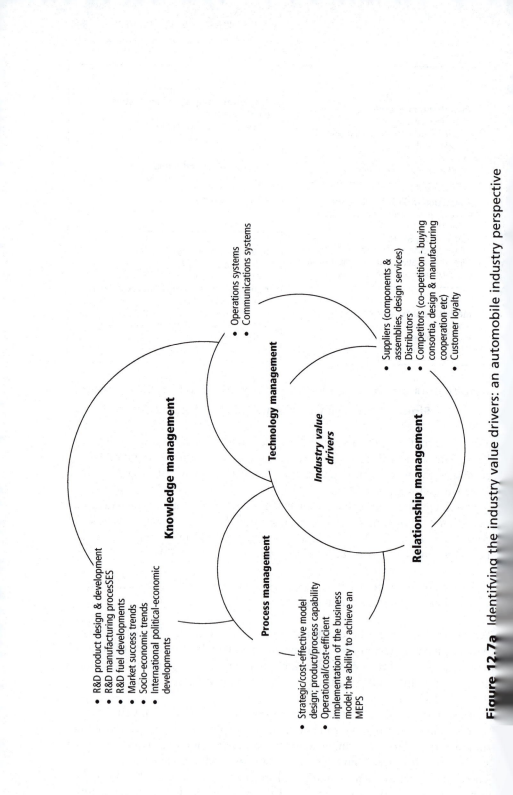

- R&D product design & development
- R&D manufacturing procesSES
- R&D fuel developments
- Market success trends
- Socio-economic trends
- International political-economic developments

Knowledge management

- Operations systems
- Communications systems

Technology management

Industry value drivers

- Suppliers (components & assemblies, design services)
- Distributors
- Competitors (co-opetition - buying consortia, design & manufacturing cooperation etc)
- Customer loyalty

Relationship management

Process management

- Strategic/cost-effective model design; product/process capability
- Operational/cost-efficient implementation of the business model; the ability to achieve an MEPS

Figure 12.7a Identifying the industry value drivers: an automobile industry perspective

hat organisational planning ignores the rate of change of the 'new economy' business drivers at its peril.

Concluding comments

In a simpler world, ownership of the means of production was nearly always a key success factor for a business. This does not now always follow, and indeed may be a relatively inefficient application of capital and generator of cash.

The model proposed in this chapter attempts to cut the umbilical cord of ownership and success. Instead it suggests that the competitive landscape is one that is rapidly changing as market value chains shift. In this context, some framework is even more necessary to identify and harness those things that will contribute to a firm's success. It is suggested that a distinction between those elements that are necessities and those that are true advantages is a basic element of any such framework. It is also suggested that understanding the timeframes for success factors in terms of their contribution to cash generation gives an insight into necessary decision processes. Finally, some general categorisation of success factors into those influenced by knowledge, relationship, technology and process gives a general roadmap.

The proposed model offers both vertical and virtual organisations an opportunity to be more flexible in the approach to strategy and structure decisions. It is likely that as more organisations become virtual and shake off the restrictive constraints of traditional organisation structures, we can expect to see even more innovative organisation structures, like that of Dell, appearing as 'new economy' business models.

CASE STUDY 12.1

Low labour costs and the outsourcing decision

(Based upon Anonymous, 'Outsourcers look nearer to home', *Australian* and *The Economist*, 6 December 2005; 'The rise of nearshoring', *The Economist*, 1 December 2005)

Skype has a reputation for being a leading Voice Over Internet Protocol (VOIP) service. It is the maker of software for free (or low-cost) phone calls from internet connected computers. It is a global business and was recently acquired by eBay for $US2.6 billion. The programming work for Skype was undertaken by a team located in Tallinn, Estonia, not in the global centre of IT outsourcing, India. Skype employs a small, young (average age 28) but very skilled work force. Tallinn also hosts Elcoteq, a Finnish company that manufactures mobile phones for Nokia and other companies. Elcoteq's workforce is large (3,000), middle-aged, semi-skilled, does repetitive tasks and is modestly paid. Whereas 20 per cent of Skype's labour force is foreign, Elcoteq's workforce comprises local employees. Elcoteq is struggling to stay competitive whereas Skype is booming. The region's one-time competitive advantage, low-cost labour, is diminishing, partly because of the even greater price

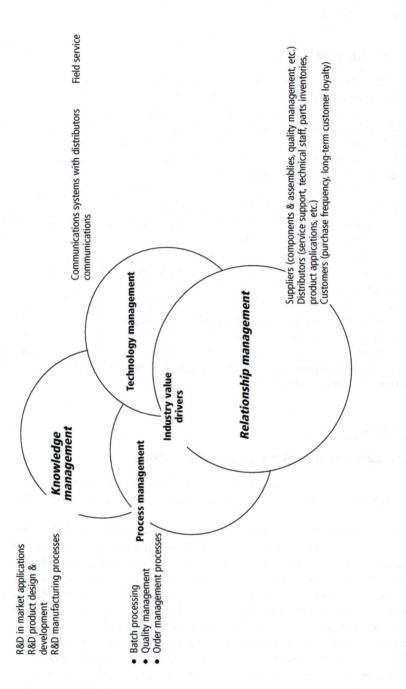

Figure 12.7b Organisations dependent upon value adding retailer (distributor) networks eg: construction equipment

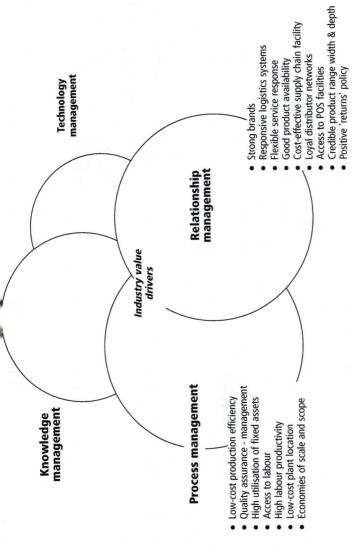

Knowledge management

Technology management

Process management

- Low-cost production efficiency
- Quality assurance - management
- High utilisation of fixed assets
- Access to labour
- High labour productivity
- Low-cost plant location
- Economies of scale and scope

Industry value drivers

Relationship management

- Strong brands
- Responsive logistics systems
- Flexible service response
- Good product availability
- Cost-effective supply chain facility
- Loyal distributor networks
- Access to POS facilities
- Credible product range width & depth
- Positive 'returns' policy

Figure 12.7c FMCG industries

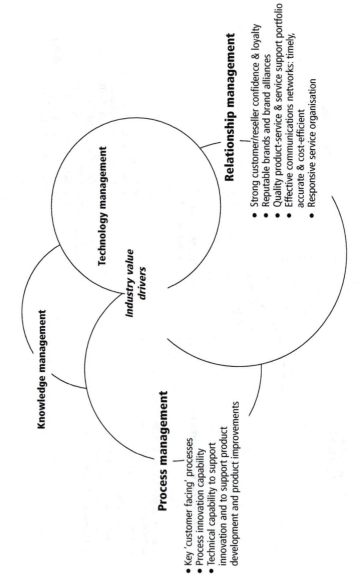

- Financial management expertise
- Knowledge of international financial markets

Knowledge management

Technology management

Industry value drivers

Process management

- Key 'customer facing' processes
- Process innovation capability
- Technical capability to support innovation and to support product development and product improvements

Relationship management

- Strong customer/reseller confidence & loyalty
- Reputable brands and brand alliances
- Quality product-service & service support portfolio
- Effective communications networks: timely, accurate & cost-efficient
- Responsive service organisation

Figure 12.7d Banking and financial services

advantage of China and because of the increase in wage rates that is a feature of increasing prosperity.

The authors of the above articles suggest that the collapse of Communism was replaced by attitudes and values that have fostered new approaches to business. The EU is encouraging new disciplines that are fostering the development of capabilities and processes to fit the new EU countries for the twenty-first century. The result has been the commencement of: 'a hunt for lasting advantages based upon talent and geography, rather than low wages'. Western investment is responding and moving rapidly into Eastern Europe.

Clothing imports from the region have increased, at €22.3 billion ($A35.6 billion) now representing 19 per cent of EU clothing imports. The COO of India's Infosys, Amitabh Chaudhry, admits that 'The quality of the work (IT activities) is world class. It matches and sometimes even surpasses the best we do in India.' Infosys has opened a centre in the Czech Republic, with 100 staff capable of working in 13 languages. Chaudhry adds that the 'friendly time zone', good political and regulatory environment, multilingual workers and cultural affinity are major benefits. In addition to the Czech office, Infosys has an office in Prague supplying about 100 technical support staff to multinational companies.

It is clear that the incentive to consider outsourcing is becoming much more than a matter of seeking low labour costs. According to Stephen Bullas, managing partner of the European Centre for Offshore Development (eCODE): 'If I want a huge English language call centre, or to design an aircraft engine using tens of thousands of staff years, I will go to India ... But if I want a small, controllable team of tele-sales people, or back office workers with a cultural fit to the continental EU or Britain, it is much more appropriate to choose an eastern European country.'

Discussion topics

This case suggests that in future both organisations and national governments will need to consider industry value drivers from a competitive advantage perspective. How might this be achieved?

CASE STUDY 12.2

Manila matches its resources to off-shoring opportunities

(Based upon Mynardo Macaraig, 'Manila grabs slice of outsourcing pie', *Sydney Morning Herald*, 14 December 2005)

'The Philippines government boasts it offers cost-competitive, highly skilled, readily available labour with low overhead and a strategic location easily accessible to major Asian cities', reports Mynardo Macaraig. This was confirmed by the Swiss International Institute for Management Development in 2004, rating the

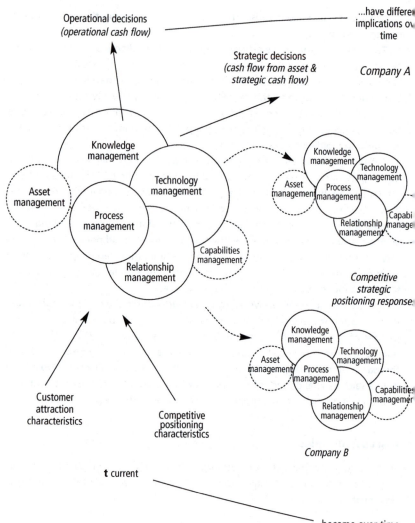

Figure 12.8 Time has four 'dimensions'. Value drivers change over time. Customer expectations and competitive characteristics change; the industry value drivers may therefore change and the operational and strategic decisions that result from these changes can have significant influence for cash flow management at the organisational and industry level

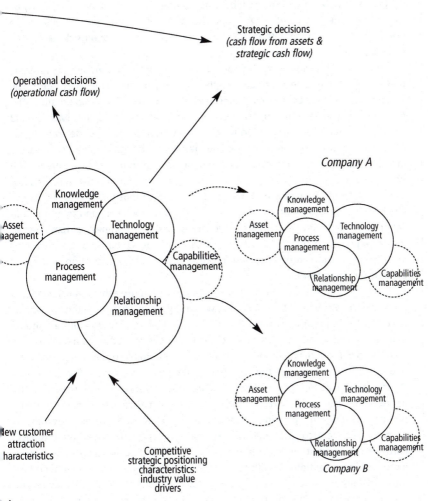

Strategic decisions
*(cash flow from assets &
strategic cash flow)*

Operational decisions
(operational cash flow)

Company A

Knowledge
management

Asset
management

Technology
management

Process
management

Capabilities
management

Relationship
management

Knowledge
management

Asset
management

Technology
management

Process
management

Capabilities
management

Relationship
management

New customer
attraction
characteristics

Competitive
strategic positioning
characteristics:
industry value
drivers

Knowledge
management

Asset
management

Technology
management

Process
management

Capabilities
management

Relationship
management

Company B

future

Philippines' availability of skilled labour as 'number one in Asia'. Another study by the Manila based University of Asia and the Pacific proposed the Philippines as ' a prime competitor to India, thanks to superior skills in English and its closer affinity to western culture'.

An American company, AskMeNow, offers a service to US mobile phone users that enables them to text messages to the company on any topic whatsoever. The answers are researched and communicated back to the US by Filipino staff. The company's managing director, Mark Cohen, said that the Philippines was selected because its employees in the former US colony have a better understanding of American culture and very high language skills. The government's Board of Investments estimates that some 112,000 people are working in call centres in the Philippines, generating $US1.12 billion. In the year 2000, call centres employed just 2,400 people and earned $US24 million. Cohen added that the company sees the Philippines as an excellent source of knowledge based workers and telecommunications engineers. Such advantages have increased the Philippines' competitiveness in the region (particularly in comparison to India and China) and are attracting investment in call centres, business processing, medical transcription and other computer related tasks.

However, concern over the momentum of the recent growth was expressed in a report by the McKinsey Global Institute, which suggested that while the Philippines is currently competitive with India, offering higher quality and more suitable manpower and lower costs, it has problems in areas related to non-labour costs such as power, political and security risks, a less hospitable business environment, and bureaucracy. It warned that the Philippines government must develop a clear strategy to attract foreign investment and develop this essential infrastructure. The Board of Investment is aware of these problems, particularly a decline in the number of English speaking students, and has responded by launching a programme where colleges will offer English courses 'for international business'. Furthermore, in an attempt to reinforce Manila's thrust to expand business processing operations facilities and skills to other major cities, investment is being directed into providing sufficient power supplies, telecommunications infrastructure and fibre optic facilities. The government has also targeted other IT sectors such as software development, engineering design, computer graphics and animation. This expansion will, it is hoped, provide employment for many of the Philippines' accountants and lawyers.

Discussion topics

As the offshore supply market for specialist skills becomes more competitive, the 'customer' companies are becoming more discerning. Factors other than low-cost and skilled labour are becoming important. How might countries such as the Philippines identify emerging needs and respond to them? And having met these needs, how can they ensure that companies attracted to the country are retained in the long term?

CASE STUDY 12.3

India matches its resources to offshoring opportunities in healthcare

(Based upon Saritha Ral, 'India outsourcing a cure-all', *New York Times* and *Australian Financial Review*, 8 April 2005)

The rising costs of healthcare in Western economies have created opportunities for a 'healthcare industry' in India, competing with those of Singapore and Thailand. The Confederation of Indian Industry estimated that some 150,000 'foreigners' visited India for medical treatment in 2003/04. A growth rate of 15 per cent per year is expected. McKinsey estimates this will generate $US2.3 billion by 2012, fuelled by ageing populations and increasing healthcare costs in Western economies. Current comparative costs illustrate reasons for this optimism: cardiac surgery costs are about one fifth of the cost in the US, orthopaedic treatment costs about one quarter as much, and cataract surgery costs as little as ten per cent of those in US hospitals. Ral makes an interesting point when quoting Gautam Kumra, the McKinsey health consultant (and an advisor to the automotive industry), who identified the rising costs of healthcare in large corporations as an opportunity. Kumra comments on the high burden that healthcare represents for large companies such as General Motors (together with pension contributions, amounting to $US1,500/2,000 per vehicle produced and sold), suggesting that GM and other organisations are beginning to seek creative low-cost solutions; offshore healthcare is one such solution.

Diagnostic services are also expanding. Wipro, a software and IT company based in Bangalore, has radiologists analysing X-rays and scans from US hospitals; Ranbaxy, based in New Delhi, tests blood serum and tissue samples from British hospitals.

The Apollo Hospital, located in Hyderabad, has some 200 European and US trained clinical staff, and is equipped with up-to-date medical technology. Gartner healthcare analyst, John Lovelock, suggests that Indian hospitals are well positioned to take advantage of the expanding market for long-term, labour-intensive, in-patient rehabilitation services that are underserviced (as well as expensive) in North America. Some Indian hospitals are finding that well trained staff and modern, well equipped facilities are insufficient. Healthcare decisions are often influenced by perceptions of the surrounding external environment, not only by cost. Local infrastructure, roads, airports and so on are well below international standards, and while internally hospitals can reflect their expertise and efficiency, the external problems are beyond the control of hospital administration.

Discussion topics

Continued growth of offshore healthcare facilities will result in far reaching changes in value chain structures. What might some of these changes be? How can existing healthcare organisations integrate offshore services into their existing value propositions? Identify the information required to make such decisions.

Identify what future trends may occur. What are the implications of these developments?

CASE STUDY 12.4

The Chinese economy and the value chain

(Based upon David Lague, 'China overtakes US as No 1 supplier of IT goods', *International Herald Tribune* and *Australian Financial Review*, 13 December 2005)

The OECD has published data reporting the rapid growth of China's production capacity in the IT sector. China's exports of IT hardware (laptop computers, mobile phones, digital cameras and so on) increased by 46 per cent to $US180 billion in 2004. By comparison the US growth was 12 per cent. The OECD report reveals that China has come close to matching the US in the overall value of its trade in IT products. The purchase by Lenvo, the Chinese computer manufacturer, of IBM's personal computer unit can be seen in retrospect as an indication of China's intention to become a significant supplier in the global IT sector. Lague comments on the view that China's efforts to impose its own technology standards across a range of consumer products, such as mobile phones, digital photography and wireless networks are widely interpreted as a strategy to dominate the global market for IT products. It is suggested that, but for the restrictions based upon 'dual-use technologies' (civilian *and* military uses) applied by many Western countries, this would have occurred earlier.

US concern is that the rapid growth in expertise in developing a strong and powerful IT and consumer electronics sector could have far reaching military consequences. The Chinese military works very closely with the IT industry and the government's research and development sector, supporting the country's rapid military modernisation. The US is also concerned to watch the adoption by the Chinese military of 'practically every information related aspect of military technology that the US is pursuing at this time'. Concern is also expressed at the prospect of the US becoming dependent on China for certain items critical to the US defence industry.

Lague also suggests that China has made progress in its long-term objective of upgrading the capacity of its manufacturing as it strives to become a major economic power. Hong Kong based consultant, Arthur Kobler, suggests: 'It confirms that the Chinese economy is really moving up the value chain from simple manufactured goods like textiles, shoes and plastics to very sophisticated electronics.' What Kobler is suggesting is that as China's manufacturing expertise is increasing, so too, possibly, is its design and development capacity. This, together with the logistics capacity of Hong Kong, would certainly have an impact on global value chain management.

The large and rapid rate of growth in China has been largely driven by overseas investment. Companies such as Intel, Nokia, Motorola, Microsoft and Cisco Systems are largely responsible for the expansion in IT related industries. Lague reports that figures from the Chinese Ministry of Commerce show that companies that had received overseas investment accounted for almost 90 per cent of 2004 exports of high technology products.

Discussion topics

Could it be deduced from this case example that in the very near future the China will dominate global value chains in selected industry sectors? What would be necessary for this to occur? Research the activities of the Chinese consumer durable company Haier before answering this question.

Can Ford's decision to 'supply' design and development expertise to Asia rather than to establish manufacturing facilities be seen as foresighted? What might be the implications of this decision for Ford?

CASE STUDY 12.5

The 'Save Your Factory' campaign

Based upon the 'Save Your Factory' campaign, http://saveyorfactory.com/whitepaper.htm, 12 January 2004; John Terenko, 'New roles for robots', *Industry Week*, www.industryweek.com/PrintArticle.aspx?ArticleID=10443, 2005)

The US government, concerned at the decreasing competitiveness of manufacturing and the escalation of offshoring, has undertaken an initiative to improve the competitive position of US manufacturing. The initiatives are broad; they include a review of potential changes in taxation, healthcare costs, legal issues, energy legislation, and employee training and a focus on innovation and technology. It is this latter issue that is of interest in this case example. The 'Save Your Factory' campaign is aimed at identifying the benefits of innovation and product enhancing technology by encouraging North American manufacturing companies to recognise automation and robotics as more cost-effective and profitable alternatives to offshoring.

The report identifies the many factors to be considered when moving to manufacture overseas. These are suggested to be factory utilisation; inventory requirements; comparative labour force abilities; government support and stability; supply chain strength; quality assurance, and shipping delays. There are also intellectual property issues: the cost of counterfeiting in the automotive industry is estimated at $US12 billion per year, $US3 billion of which is in the US. The report is suggesting that through automation, robotics and other lean manufacturing applications, North America can be cost-competitive with China and other low-cost labour countries.

Automation facilitates quality management, efficiency, control and viability; it also offers the ability to optimise capital and labour usage. The impact on employment numbers is addressed; while it is claimed that typically a robot installation can perform the work of three to five people, thus reducing the cost of labour, the report identifies the fact that over the next 30 years 76 million people will retire from the labour force and only 46 million will be available to replace them.

Some interesting examples are given. Lincoln Electric provided a cost comparison for a customer considering moving production to China. The existing manual production system compared very unfavourably with a similar system in China, costing some 84 cents locally per unit of production compared to 30 cents in China. Robotic welding in the USA was shown to be similar in cost to the manual cost in China. An example based on Mennie's Machine Company (a manufacturer of automotive drive shaft components) makes another comparison. Their manual system was capable of an output of 80 pieces an hour, but the system created difficulties which made it difficult to overcome system delays; an investment in robotics eliminated the delays and enabled the company to reach its full capacity objective of 118 pieces an hour. Weld times were reduced from 1 minute 23 seconds to just 61 seconds, with significantly higher quality and improved process control resulting in reduced scrap rates. The three-shift operation now runs at 95 per cent utilisation, an increase of 15 per cent over the labour system. The robotic system has helped reduce total production costs by approximately 25 per cent. The system is both expansible and flexible, able to accommodate new equipment and new part designs.

Mennie's claims a number of aspects of competitive advantage: accurate and consistent part loading; a reduction in defects; increased productivity; improved control of the entire manufacturing system; lower piece costs, and flexibility to meet future customer demands.

Service applications can also be found. Robobar is an automated drinks dispenser. It is claimed to be faster than manual bar service operations – and more honest! It doesn't drink on the job or 'dip into the till'!! Applications to healthcare are also reported. An Indiana hospital uses a robotic system to manage proton cancer treatment. One robot positions the patient's bed to receive the proton treatment and another signals the first robot to make precise adjustments to ensure the accuracy of the treatment.

Discussion topics

There has been considerable discussion of the application of robotics to manufacturing systems. The adoption is not widespread, due possibly to the investment requirements and/or the fact that insufficient comparative cost evaluation is undertaken. Given the increasing adoption of value chain approaches, how should manufacturers evaluate the offshore vs domestic local capital investment option?

CASE STUDY 12.6

Ford: selecting a capability to create competitive advantage

(Based upon P Roberts and S Aylmer, 'Ford makes designs on Asia', *Australian Financial Review*, 14 May 2004)

The attraction of Asian markets, particularly China, for motor vehicle manufacturers is very obvious. The large potential volume has attracted the largest manufacturers, most of whom have invested in production facilities, typically as joint venture operations with Chinese partners and the encouragement of the Chinese government. At the time of this case (May 2004), Ford was reviewing its Asian operations. Asia is a key market for Ford but to date it had made little impact on the obvious volume target – China. It had two small investments in China, which had resulted in the launch of three models commencing in early 2003. By contrast, GM had been in China since the mid-1990s and in the first quarter of 2004 sold some 122,000 cars, a 10 per cent share of the Chinese market.

Ford's vice president for the region, together with the Ford Australia president, discussed the options for an export strategy for Ford Australia. A possible approach was to leverage Ford Australia's reputation for its high-quality engineering design. by supplying engineering and product-design services to the company's Asian operations. Regional vice president, Mark Shulz, argued, 'There are two types of export you can have. There is the physical product, but there is also intellectual capital.' The decision confronting Ford was whether to join major competitors, GM, Toyota and Mitsubishi, all of whom had committed funds to automotive research, or to compete with others who had opted to establish joint venture manufacturing facilities.

Discussion topics

What are the issues that Ford should consider here?
How should the company evaluate the potential for alternative strategies?

REFERENCES

Blumentritt R and R Johnston (1999) 'Towards a strategy for knowledge management', *Technology Analysis and Strategic Management*, September

Boulton R E S, B D Libert and S M Samek (2000) 'A business model for the new economy', *Journal of Business Strategy*, July/August

Drucker P (2001) 'Will the corporation survive?', *The Economist*, 1 November

Ghemawat P (1991) *Commitment: The Dynamic of Strategy*, Free Press, New York

Grant R (1995) *Contemporary Strategy Analysis*, Blackwell, Oxford

Hagel J III and M Singer (1999) 'Unbundling the corporation', *Harvard Business Review*, 77(2)

Hamel G and C K Prahalad (1994) *The Core Competences of the Corporation*, Harvard Business School Press, Boston, MA

Hofer C H and D Schendel (1978) *Strategy Formulation: Analytical Concepts*, West, St Paul, MN

Irani Z and P Love (2001) 'The propagation of technology management taxonomies for evaluating investments in information systems', *Journal of Management Information Systems*, Winter

Jarillo J C (1993) *Strategic Networks: Creating the Borderless Organisation*, Butterworth-Heinemann, Oxford

Kay J (1993) *Foundation of Corporate Success*, Oxford University Press, Oxford

Leidecker J K and A V Bruno (1984) 'Identifying and using critical success factors', *Long Range Planning*, February

Normann R (2001) *Reframing Business*, Wiley, Chichester

Ohmae K (2005) *The Next Global Stage: Challenges and Opportunities in our Borderless World*, Wharton School, University of Pennsylvania

Olve N, J Roy and M Wetter (1997) *Performance Drivers*, Wiley, Chichester

Pebler R P (2000) 'The virtual oil company: capstone of integration,' *Oil & Gas Journal*, March

Rumelt R P (1987) 'Theory, strategy and entrepreneurship,' in Teece D (ed.) *The Competitive Challenge: Strategies for Industrial Innovation and Renewal*, Ballinger, Cambridge, MA

Zineldin M (1997) *Strategic Relationship Management, a Multi-Dimensional Perspective: Towards a New Co-opetive Framework on Managing, Marketing and Organizing*, Almqvist & Wiksell, Stockholm

Index

CPSIA information can be obtained at www.ICGtesting.com
Printed in the USA
LVOW04s0422050215

425794LV00026B/1138/P